WHISKEY
BUSINESS

WHISKEY
BUSINESS

HOW SMALL-BATCH DISTILLERS ARE TRANSFORMING AMERICAN SPIRITS

TOM ACITELLI

CHICAGO
REVIEW
PRESS

Published by Chicago Review Press Incorporated
814 North Franklin Street
Chicago, Illinois 60610
ISBN 978-1-61373-458-2

Library of Congress Cataloging-in-Publication Data
Names: Acitelli, Tom, author.
Title: Whiskey business: how small-batch distillers are transforming
   American spirits / Tom Acitelli.
Description: First edition. | Chicago, Illinois: Published by Chicago Review
   Press Incorporated, 2017. | Includes bibliographical references and index.
Identifiers: LCCN 2016045148 (print) | LCCN 2016046748 (ebook) | ISBN
   9781613734582 (trade paper) | ISBN 9781613734599 (adobe pdf) | ISBN
   9781613734612 (epub) | ISBN 9781613734605 (kindle)
Subjects: LCSH: Whiskey industry—United States—History. | Distilling
   industries—United States—History.
Classification: LCC TP590.6.U6 A43 2017 (print) | LCC TP590.6.U6
(ebook) |
   DDC 338.4/7663520973—dc23
LC record available at https://lccn.loc.gov/2016045148

Cover design: Jonathan Hahn
Cover image: House Spirits Distillery
Typesetting: Nord Compo

To my in-laws, John and Suzanne Rudy

CONTENTS

PART III

THE CHALLENGE AHEAD

Aperitif

AND THEN THERE WERE CRAFT SPIRITS

2013 | Boston

It was an ungodly hour to be drinking rum. I wanted, however, to see Buffalo Bill Owens, who opened one of America's first brewpubs, and this was my chance. We had spoken by phone and e-mailed several times for my history of American craft beer, yet had never actually met. He had moved on from craft beer to another interest and would be in Boston that weekend in June 2013 to tour a new distillery that his trade group, the American Distilling Institute, helped promote. He knew I lived in nearby Cambridge. Would I like to meet?

The craft beer history had been published, but yes, meeting Bill would be a treat, even if it meant an early Saturday wake-up, as well as a subway ride and a long walk, to a more remote area of South Boston. Two first cousins had started GrandTen Distilling in 2011 in an old iron foundry, one of several long-docile warehouse spaces in Southie, an area that had transitioned from industry and organized crime to biotechnology and food trucks. Matt Nuernberger had an MBA and therefore handled the business side, and his cousin Spencer McMinn was a chemistry PhD who handled the distilling. Matt and Spencer were both there when I arrived, as was Bill, dressed in a black vest over an orange short-sleeved shirt, square brown glasses perched on a perfectly triangular nose just above a thin, white mustache that matched his salty, spiky hair. Bill held court throughout the entire tour, which included a rundown of GrandTen's equipment, such as its gorgeous copper stills, and which ended with samples at the small bar toward the former foundry's front.

I sipped GrandTen's rum . . . and was pleasantly blown away. Fresh and flavorful, clean in mouthfeel and appearance, it tasted like no other spirit I had consumed before—none of that acrid, overly alcoholic taste so common to bigger brands. Instead, the spirit's components were distinct and upfront, particularly the molasses, which provided the rum's sugar. Here was a spirit you could savor, not simply knock back to get drunk quickly.

As novel as their products tasted—I also sampled a whiskey and a gin—GrandTen's operation was thoroughly familiar, from the backstory to the vibe to the physicality. The place looked and felt like a craft brewery: relatively small and, by necessity, cramped; in an area of town that could certainly use the trade; the libations produced in small batches with more traditional methods anathema to bigger, macro-competitors (which, to be honest, probably did not see GrandTen as much of a competitor in 2013); and the cousins Nuernberger and McMinn casual in appearance and tone but unapologetically earnest about what they were doing. Business-wise, too, the distillery was familiar: a start-up in the drinks business crafting its wares for sale locally and not much beyond. The emphasis was on craftsmanship and connectedness, not putting a bottle in everyone's dining (or dorm) room or liquor cabinet. It was much the same ethos that craft brewers had long emphasized, beginning back in the 1960s and really picking up steam in the 1980s, when entrants such as Owens himself decided to start making small batches of beer with traditional methods and ingredients, and selling it locally and not much beyond—in Owens's case, in the same Northern California restaurants where the beer was made.

I easily discovered that I was far from the first to make this spirits-beer connection. The whole thing seemed like a rerun at first glance; only the drink had changed. Connecting what was being called "craft spirits" with craft beer seemed de rigueur in media coverage of the emerging trend. And several craft distilleries seemed to understand that journalists and consumers expected that. The packaging of many craft spirits, and the official backstories provided on websites and in marketing materials, consciously aped and echoed the tradition-heavy, antimacro ethos of craft beer. It worked beautifully to some degree. An industry survey in 2016 found that nearly 60 percent of store owners and 25 percent of bar and restaurant owners thought craft spirits would perform like craft beer sales-wise over time.

Yet I soon discovered that there were more than a few craft distilleries behaving disingenuously when it came to such craft beer–like packaging and marketing. Simply put, there was no tradition, and they were quite macro in a lot of respects. They bought in bulk what the industry called neutral, or rectified, spirits—almost 100 percent pure ethyl alcohol that could then be cut and flavored—and simply rebottled it with craft-like labels complete with bucolic shots of countryside distilleries and talk of local origins. (The only thing local was the bottling.) Or they bought the finished product and did much the same thing—rebottled it with their own misleading labels. There were no government regulations prohibiting these operations from doing either. These faux craft distilleries, I soon realized, accounted for a not insignificant number of what the media often labeled "craft." If they were not a majority, then they were certainly a sizable minority.

Then there was the plain fact that many macro operations produced fine spirits in what for them were relatively small batches. This was particularly true of whiskeys, especially that American original, bourbon. A distillery did not have to be small in size and independently owned to craft a solid whiskey, or even a solid vodka or gin. In fact, it could be advantageous to be large, given that many of the nation's biggest distilleries were also the oldest and therefore awash in the most institutional knowledge about how to make a particular spirit (again, especially whiskey).

These dual realities stood in stark contrast to the craft beer that the media and the industry often compared craft spirits with. There were phantom craft beers, to be sure—macro-brewery products that certainly looked micro. But they rarely, if ever, tasted so. The bigger breweries often used shortcuts, including chemical additives and nontraditional ingredients such as rice, and favored the sort of voluminous output that can be bad for beer, a drink usually best when freshest and therefore closest to its source. Macro-distilleries' smaller-batch spirits, on the other hand, whatever their packaging, often did taste as good as, if not better than, their tinier counterparts' offerings. It was all a muddle.

Try as the media and others might, they could not quite fit craft spirits into the same neat taste rubric as craft beer.

Nor could one fit it into a time line as clean as craft beer's—or American fine wine's, for that matter. Both beverages can trace their post–World War II origins to a handful of events and, at most, to three or four individuals. And both craft beer and fine wine (Merlot, Chardonnay, Cabernet Sauvignon, etc.) can trace their respective chronological ascents in America linearly from Northern California, out into the subsequent decades and the rest of the United States. New arrivals in craft beer and fine wine were usually acutely aware of whose shoulders they were standing on—and that they were standing on them to begin with. Not so craft spirits. Pioneers and producers in this movement developed in different pockets of the country at different times under sometimes profoundly different circumstances and often worked in isolation, usually on a hunch or as a means for that much extra money, unaware of any kindred souls elsewhere in the nation. Accidents of history and America's vast geography were part of the reason for this. The irreconcilable differences in the kaleidoscope of spirits was another. Corn-based bourbon developed in what came to be called Kentucky because that's where the corn and the settlers of Scotch-Irish descent ended up. The hub of starchy vodka production in America in the mid-twentieth century was in Connecticut because of vodka's development in the Old World and then the New during the previous centuries. Sugary rum distillation oozed up from the southernmost reaches of the country because that's where slave-powered sugar cultivation took hold. And on and on. I soon found that trying to sketch the growth of American craft spirits as a multibranch tree from a single clump of roots was impossible and that those who did so were either disingenuous themselves or simply didn't see all the dots still left to connect.

Finally, as many before me, I ran quickly into the ongoing debate over what, exactly, constituted a craft spirit. What were we even talking about here? This was much more contentious than the debate over what defined a craft brewer. The Brewers Association, a powerful trade group with origins in the 1970s, had long offered a definition that at least provided a framework for thinking about craft beer and craft brewing. As for fine wine, France had defined those parameters long ago, as had federal and state regulations about how much of a grape had to be in a certain wine for the winery to call its product by that grape. (Oregon, for instance, required that any Oregon Pinot Noir contain 90 percent Pinot Noir juice from grapes cultivated in the Beaver State.) The debate over a craft spirits definition, on the other hand, spawned multiple lawsuits and pointed recriminations in the media. Some held that the independence of the distillery owner or owners was sacrosanct, the key ingredient to any craft spirits definition. Others thought that traditional ingredients, equipment, and methods mattered more. Still others vehemently argued that operations that were too large, or that grew too large from humbler beginnings, be cast out, whatever the independence of the owners or the ingredients and equipment used. And, of course, many suggested that a combination of these three parameters comprised the perfect definition of craft spirits. It seemed a rabbit hole of nasty nit-picking with no resolution in sight—and no trade group or regulatory body yet authoritative enough to settle matters. The federal government did not define craft spirits and craft distilleries only by output, and did not care to, either. The same went for the states (though some states did account for size, among other standards, when attempting to define a craft distillery). The definitions thrown up by nascent trade groups such as Bill Owens's American Distilling Institute, which dated only from 2002, were largely ignored or just more grist for the rancor mill. Even a gamely thorough attempt from a spinoff of Owens's group—in the form of a fifty-nine-page analysis released in late 2016—failed to settle the matter, though it came closer than anyone or anything before. "There is no universally accepted definition of craft spirits in the industry," the report read, "and the expression 'craft spirit' is not protected in any way."

That was and is true. Yet one feature kept coming up again and again as I waded into the definition debate: volume, or the amount of output. No one and no group, including critics, the federal government, and people within the industry, seemed to dispute that you had to at least make a spirit in small batches to call it craft. A distillery might grow larger over time, producing oceans of a once small-batch offering—but it had to at least start small. Even the largest distilling concerns, conglomerates with myriad holdings at all sorts of price points, made small-batch offerings that looked and tasted different than those made in vastly larger quantities. And even those faux craft distilleries released their offerings in small amounts (and, consequently, ordered relatively small amounts from larger producers). Volume and output mattered; no one disagreed. One could be big, but one had to work small. One could be faux, but not go long. Smallness was the defining characteristic of craft spirits, the ethos that cut through everything.

The term *craft spirits* clouded that characteristic, however, much in the same way that the attempts to fit craft spirits into craft beer's taste template and time line did. Craft spirits and craft beer were complementary, but they were different. The same held for craft spirits and fine wine. The rise of all three beverages after World War II spectacularly altered the American palatal landscape, helping each other find new fans and a prominent place in the nation's commerce and very psyche. America is the biggest wine marketplace on Earth, having wrested that title in 2014 from centuries-long hegemon France. It is also the leader in beer style, the nation that one-time leaders such as Germany and Belgium now look toward for inspiration. American craft spirits has no such international prominence. At least not yet—certain brands and distilling trends are popular overseas, make no mistake, but the industry is light years from enjoying the sort of influence that American winemakers and brewers do. Part of that is age: American fine wine goes back to just after Prohibition in the 1930s and really picked up steam in the 1960s. American craft beer also gained momentum in the 1960s and was stepping onto the world stage by the end of the 1980s. It was not until the 2000s that Americans began talking and writing widely in terms of craft spirits, however.

Much of that writing has focused on trying to define what constituted a craft spirit and, by extension, a craft distillery or distiller. I would argue that the focus should not be on trying to make *craft spirits* stick. It is a term born of the misguided attempt to define the movement in terms of craft beer. Instead, the focus should be on *small batch*, both as an adjective and a noun. Craft spirits made or released in small batches can come from any sized distillery. Yet, these small batches invariably share common characteristics: more traditional ingredients; the precise attentions of an often very skilled distiller; higher price tags; and, most importantly, that more pronounced, multilayered taste I first discovered at GrandTen in South Boston.

Craft spirits, then, should be retired as quickly as possible, perhaps to the same beachfront condo as *table wine*, a once widely used term to describe less-expensive drier wines made from European grape varietals such as Merlot and Chardonnay. I argued in my last book that *fine wine* would suffice for all of it, at whatever price point. To declare otherwise was to ignore the long, slogging history behind the rise of such wines in the United States. They were all part of the same eventual triumph—indeed, the variations in price were a sign of that success. Yet, *fine wine* had long existed as a term to describe at least the pricier plonk. *Small-batch spirits* has not been as widely used as *craft spirits*, but I will use it nonetheless because it describes so much better what distillers are trying to achieve and have achieved. That is because the success of the movement it is supposed to describe renders *craft spirits* largely useless, if not soon obsolete. Curiously, as I type this in the spring of 2016, the same thing is already happening to *craft beer*, with brewers, critics, and consumers increasingly calling for the term to be scotched in favor of simply *beer*—the June 2015 cover of *All About Beer*, the industry's leading trade magazine, declared, CRAFT BEER IS DEAD, LONG LIVE CRAFT BEER. The characteristics and the things to love remain; the term, like with *craft spirits*, just doesn't work anymore. *Small-batch* is not perfect, but it certainly works better.

Should these small-batch distillers and their customers ever settle the definition of their movement, there will be nothing stopping it. Even with the controversy, it is gaining in numbers, in fans, and in institutional heft, the kind of heft able to bend government to its priorities, particularly on taxes, a potential game-changer that this book will explore in-depth, along with other possible shifts poised to help craft spirits thrive. The American craft spirits movement as the twenty-first century chugs along has become one of the most impactful and interesting culinary trends in the nation since World War II. And it's so young, its rise only really kicking into gear in the past ten to fifteen years.

This book is the story of that rise and the conditions that made it possible. The story intersects often with those other two great libationary success stories, fine wine and craft beer. It also runs alongside and then overtakes contemporary trends such as the foodie culture, which has helped change the way Americans eat, and the newfound popularity of cocktails, some made from nearly extinct concoctions that the American craft spirits movement helped resuscitate. Developments in other countries, most profoundly the proliferation of single-malt whiskeys in Scotland as well as lesser-known trends such as the resurrection of micro-distillation of tequila in Mexico, also affected the growth of craft spirits here in ways that cannot be overstated. Also, by necessity, especially in a nation that has long had a rocky relationship with spirits and drinking in general, the book will focus on controversies that almost croaked the whole enterprise. Finally, by necessity as well, I will delve deep into the development of certain macro-spirits, those made in such large quantities from the get-go that they could never be considered small-batch. These spirits, developed and marketed as they were and as successful as they became, set the table for their tinier counterparts later on. Their challenges and triumphs are almost just as important, if not more so, and deserve significant attention. As one noted critic told me early on in my research, Absolut, that mass-produced, exceedingly gimmicky Swedish vodka, popularized the notion of a higher-end spirit in the American marketplace, the sort of superpremium libation consumers asked for by name, price tag be damned. Craft spirits would later feast on that notion.

Finally, what this book is *not* is a tasting guide, nor is it a guide to buying spirits or making them. (That's illegal without the proper licensing—more on that later.) There are plenty of fine examples of those in print and online, including ones that explain such features of distillation as still types and aging processes. I was pleasantly relieved to find that a phalanx of critics had been writing authoritatively for years about the subject of small-batch spirits. I drank deeply from the wells of their analyses and leaned on their research where primary sources could not be found. And, while distilling can be highly technical, I will try to avoid overexplaining those technicalities, which can quickly become a major lesson involving nearly every major scientific field, from botany to physics, with history and anthropology added on. Basically, distillation involves a three-step process: the fermentation of fruit or grains; then the heating of that fermented batch to purify and strengthen it; and then, often, a blending with other spirits or with water to achieve a certain taste and alcoholic strength. Distillers use either a squatter vessel called a pot still or a taller one called a column still for the distillation, or a combination of the two (and a column still is essentially several stacked pot stills). The differences between both will be explained when necessary, as will the differences in various spirits' ingredients, some of which involve additions such as herbs and spices.

Enough with the mechanics. The first of its kind, this book is meant to be a romping tale through the maturation of the American palate when it came to whiskey, vodka, brandy, gin, rum, and other spirits. It jumps around geographically quite a bit—America is a big country and its distillers diffuse, woven into its very fabric from the republic's earliest days—but one theme runs through: the hard-won triumph of small-batch distilling. As the forthcoming tale will tell, victory was far from assured; it seemed to take forever. And just as the moment of greatest glory arrived, the American small-batch spirits movement appeared to sow the seeds of its own destruction.

The story, however, begins decades before all this and fittingly enough: with one man seeking to make a better spirit, one small batch at a time.

PART I

"THAT SHIT WILL BLOW YOUR EARS OFF"
1953–1959 | Loretto, Kentucky

Bill Samuels grew up around bourbon, though he did not particularly like the dark brown, corn-based spirit that had been distilled in Kentucky since before American independence. The Samuels family had been making bourbon commercially since at least the mid-1800s, perhaps even further back to when much of Kentucky was the far western frontier of the Commonwealth of Virginia. Samuels's great-grandfather, T. W. Samuels, started an eponymous distillery in Deatsville, forty miles south of Louisville, in 1844. The ownership structure changed in the twentieth century, including before and after Prohibition in the 1920s and early 1930s, although it always involved the Samuels clan, which lived on Whiskey Road in nearby Bardstown. Neighbors included James Beauregard Beam, whose nickname and surname would grace perhaps the world's most famous bourbon label. The brown-haired, slimly built Bill Samuels, then just twenty-six, took over management of the distillery in 1936, after his father died. Amid this change, one thing held constant: the iffy quality, and therefore taste, of T. W. Samuels's whiskey, which, through its corn-heavy recipe, was technically from the bourbon branch of the stylistic spirit tree.

"That shit will blow your ears off." That was the assessment of Marge Samuels, Bill's wife, of bourbon in general in the 1950s. Distilled primarily from corn, bourbon distillers also typically added rye, a coarse grain that gave it a rougher mouthfeel, and barley, used primarily to spur fermentation. (Its enzymes broke down the grains' starches into sugars, which yeast could then convert into ethanol.) The smell and taste of that alcohol was also front and center for most bourbon, condemning it to be the sort of firewater one knocked back quickly and with a chaser of beer, water, or something else coldly soothing, rather than sipped genteelly for the texture and aroma. Bill

3

Samuels himself had a physical aversion to spiciness. He never ate Mexican food, for one thing, and he found drinking bourbon, even his family's, a chore rather than a delight—something akin to a waking nightmare for a resident of Kentucky, which produced nearly all of the world's bourbon and which very likely gave the spirit its name through its Bourbon County (which was once much bigger than its present-day borders). The state's signature beverage was often described as a back-of-the-mouth drink best swallowed fast for a rollicking buzz, not a front-of-the-mouth one for a tippler to roll around the tongue and savor.

One reason for this perception was the rye-reliant tradition. Another was the larger bourbon industry itself, abetted by the federal government. American bourbon makers staggering out of Prohibition in 1933 faced stiff competition from foreign imports, particularly whiskeys from Ireland, Scotland, and Canada. The former two had never dealt with a widespread alcohol ban, and Canada's experiment with prohibition ended long before that of the United States. To hurry up and compete, bourbon makers released wares that had not been sufficiently aged—bourbon usually spent at least a few years in new oak barrels, which had been charred on the inside first, before bottling. The resultant releases tasted terrible to seasoned bourbon drinkers, and they saddled the brownest of the brown whiskeys in America with a reputation as "swill," according to one observer. Nothing in the rules, though, prevented distilleries from spilling this swill on to the market. Federal benchmarks dictated that a whiskey could call itself bourbon if at least 51 percent of its grain bill was corn, it was aged in previously unused oak barrels that had been charred on the inside, and it entered the aging barrel at a certain alcohol strength (or proof) and was bottled at a certain proof as well. These were not exactly exacting regulations, and some distillers took advantage to produce oceans of so-so product as more and more lighter whiskeys and blends flooded the market.

World War II placed the industry at a further disadvantage. The federal War Production Board took over the distilling industry nationwide and swung it from making ethyl-alcohol-based beverages such as bourbon to industrial alcohol. Materials such as grains and glass became scarcer, too, as the fight against fascism in Germany, Japan, and Italy gobbled up more and more resources. This caused much of the US bourbon industry to stand largely still in the 1940s, when it could have been using the time to ramp up its presence versus the foreign interlopers. Some people in the bourbon industry decided to get out of the game altogether. At the start of the 1940s, Robert Block, a Cincinnati businessman who partnered with the Samuels family during those anxious days after Prohibition, sold control of T. W. Samuels distillery in Loretto to a New York company that then changed the distillery's name to Country Distilleries. Bill Samuels initially fought the sale and then, realizing there was nothing he could do, sold his shares and left the now-former family firm shortly afterward to launch his own distillery. He did not need the money—the sale of the shares ensured a comfortable life, as did some property he already owned. By all accounts, though, Bill Samuels Sr. was a restless sort, especially when it came to bourbon and his family's history with it. He could not just sit around the house in Bardstown. He had to do *something*. The Samuels name in spirits could not be allowed to end with a partner's sale to a third party out of New York City.

Legal wrangling over the new distillery's use of the Samuels name held up Bill Samuels's launch for a decade. An appellate court eventually affirmed a lower bench's ruling that some aspects of the Samuels name could appear on the new distillery's packaging, but it could not use T. W. Samuels as a brand name. That restriction would become a moot point shortly after 1953, the year Samuels purchased a two-hundred-acre farm in Loretto. The farm had been the site of an old distillery, built over ten buildings in the 1880s, that Prohibition forty years later wiped out. Samuels renamed his larger property Star Hill Farm and began restoring the distillery buildings with the aim of producing bourbon. Not just any bourbon, however. To smooth the drink's rough edges, and for his own palatal edification, he developed a recipe that did not include rye and that instead leaned on winter wheat as the secondary ingredient after the style-defining corn, with barley making up the rest of the grain bill. It was not a particularly original pivot. The distillery at Star Hill Farm had made an industrial alcohol using wheat. As for spirits, George Washington's distillery at his Mount Vernon, Virginia, estate had experimented with wheat a century and a half before, as had other distilleries more recently, including Stitzel-Weller in Shively, Kentucky, just southwest of Louisville. Traveling salesman Julian "Pappy" Van Winkle and a friend started Stitzel-Weller in 1935 after buying up a wholesaler and a distillery and then combining the two. Its brands, including Old Fitzgerald and Rebel Yell, used wheat. Samuels was friends with Van Winkle, and he was among those consulted as Samuels built the recipe for his new bourbon around wheat. The secondary ingredient, then, was not new, but the way Samuels intended to wield its effects was positively revolutionary for the early 1950s. Here would be a wheated bourbon deliberately crafted in small batches for drinkers to savor. Perhaps it would change the public's entire perception of bourbon. Such an approach, with wheat at its back, flew in the face of both history and the marketplace.

Star Hill in bucolic Loretto.
MAKER'S MARK

The genesis of bourbon stretched back to at least the Seven Years' War, a conflict between the United Kingdom and France over territories in the New World. The United Kingdom won in the early 1760s and took as part of its booty the area containing the future Commonwealth of Kentucky. Scotch and Scotch-Irish settlers pushed into the new British holding, taking with them their thirst for whiskey. That whiskey had relied upon grains such as barley and rye for its production, grains that were harder to come by in the new land, which the Appalachian Mountains cut off from suppliers on the East Coast and the terrain of which was not as fertile a ground for the sprouts. So the settlers instead grew corn, a crop that Native Americans had long cultivated in the area's rockier, sandier soil. Corn, then, became the ballast for the settlers' whiskey. They also borrowed from French Cognac makers and Caribbean rum distillers the idea of barrel aging, in this case in charred oak, so as to smooth out this harsher whiskey as much as possible (and, as it happened, to turn its color brown). The uniformity of aging for any greater length of time came later. The work involved in producing bourbon was too much for settlers living hand to mouth to have it end in waiting years for a sip. But by the dawn of the nineteenth century, the outline of bourbon as a distinct American spirit was clear—corn, charred barrels, some aging—so much so that the federal government in the following century would use that outline as the parameters for recognizing bourbon as "unlike other types of alcoholic beverages, whether foreign or domestic."

As for the contour of that Bourbon County, it too became much clearer. The domain simply known as Bourbon, after the surname of the French royal family, had once encompassed some thirty-four of present-day Kentucky's counties. It shrank to its current borders just northeast of Lexington in 1785, seven years before Kentucky broke off from Virginia as America's fifteenth state. By that time, this newfangled whiskey style that the county had likely given its name to was spreading throughout the emerging nation via the Kentucky-bordering Mississippi and Ohio Rivers. Many of the industry's first families, too, including the Samuelses and their neighbors, the Beams, were firmly established in the trade around this time. Bourbon and tobacco became the principal exports from Kentucky's interior just after the start of the nineteenth century. Customs officials in Louisville recorded 2.25 million gallons of bourbon passing through just the Ohio River in 1822, a volume nearly ten-fold greater than just twelve years before. Technological improvements in the coming decades, especially the railroads, which shipped vast amounts of corn from newly settled territories such as Nebraska and Iowa, only boosted bourbon's popularity and production numbers. Corn cultivation in the United States leaped from 838 million bushels just before the Civil War to 2.7 billion at the dawn of the twentieth century forty years later. As for that Civil War in the 1860s, it rent Kentucky, a slave state that stayed in the Union, with guerilla warfare, invasions and counterinvasions scarring its landscape. "I hope to have God on my side," President Abraham Lincoln, a native Kentuckian, was reputed to have said at the start of the war, "but I must have Kentucky."

Still, the bourbon flowed. So popular was it that unscrupulous distillers took advantage of its reputation, and of the technological advances, to churn out counterfeit bourbons, usually cheaply made, little-aged whiskey with no more than brown food coloring added. The federal government intervened forcefully, beginning with landmark legislation in 1897 that stipulated the origins and aging times of whiskey in general. The so-called Bottled-in-Bond Act also stipulated when taxes could be collected—generally, after the whiskey comes out of the barrel after years of aging—allowing distillers to better plan their payments. Previously, the federal government could collect at will. The new rules, though, did little to curb the production of inferior bourbons, especially ones that had not been aged sufficiently. Distillers with an eye more on the margins than the mouthfeel continued to churn out the ear-burning firewater that Marge Samuels so disdained.

Still, as Bill Samuels prepared to launch his own distillery on Star Hill Farm, it looked like Americans could not get enough of that corn-infused firewater. From 1951 to 1962, production of Scotch and Canadian whiskey, two of the lighter whiskeys that made their runs at bourbon following Prohibition and through World War II, increased by 12.4 million and 5.3 million gallons respectively. Bourbon production, however, catapulted to 37.5 million gallons during the same period. In 1950 bourbon accounted for nearly a quarter of the bottled whiskey in the United States. In 1961 it would claim just under half. One reason for this was a genuine thirst for the spirit, one born of decades of familiarity. Another reason was a concerted marketing effort on the part of distillers and, in some cases, their corporate parents. Paid advertising in newspapers and magazines painting bourbon as a natural accoutrement to any civilized evening increased several times over during the 1950s—in the case of magazines a stunning thirty-fold. That "shit" might "blow your ears off," but more and more living rooms featured a cabinet stocked with not just one but a few brands of bourbon. Bourbon had entered a statistical golden age of robust demand, with sales on their way to increasing 200 percent for the twenty years after World War II and exports running to more than one hundred nations. The Kentucky-centric bourbon industry had survived Prohibition, the war, intense foreign competition, and its own questionable (and indifferent) quality. And it was thriving. Why mess with a steady success born of centuries of experience? What was T. W. Samuels's great-grandson thinking?

It was not only that his bourbon recipe would substitute milder wheat for chalkier rye; it was also that Bill Samuels planned to produce his whiskey in smaller batches—and charge more for it. The trend as the industry boomed had been toward larger and more modern distilleries, complete with vast warehouse floors studded with stainless-steel vats, tuns for mashing, and tall column stills for large-scale distilling. Samuels's operation would be out of the tinier nineteenth-century distillery in tiny Loretto, with its population of a few hundred souls. And it would lean heavily at first on squatter, more traditional pot stills instead of the long-necked column ones, which, while more efficient, generally did not impart as much complexity and texture to darker spirits such as bourbon (though bourbon makers often employed both, the pot stills were used in a second distillation for those complexities and textures). As for the price, Samuels's bourbon would retail for perhaps as much as three dollars more per bottle than the wares of competitors such as Jim Beam. Not that too many people regarded Samuels's start-up as serious competition. Even relatives saw it as more a hobby than anything. The trend was toward bigger, not smaller, and not just through greater production and grander production facilities. Jim Beam, for instance, conveniently made its bourbon available to bars near the rapidly multiplying number of US military bases worldwide. Besides, rye had worked just fine as the secondary grain in bourbon for as long as anyone could remember. Never mind that Samuels's distillery was not simply out of context for bourbon in the 1950s, it was out of context for American food and drink in general. Americans, a postwar economic boom at their backs, wanted speed and sameness. Swanson introduced the first TV dinners in 1954. They could be zapped to edibility in minutes in microwaves, a newer invention that was on its way to outselling gas-range stovetops. The first McDonald's franchises opened in the early 1950s, and supermarkets arose around the same period—one-stop food shopping for the first time in the histories of many cities and towns.

Nothing illustrated the national craving for sameness and speed in food better than what was happening in drink, specifically in beer and wine. The number of breweries had shrunk precipitously following World War II, as big producers such as Miller and Anheuser-Busch used their superior capital to scale up. Soon five breweries would produce more than half of the nation's beers, and almost everything produced was a bland, watery spin on the classic Czech lager type called pilsner. It was easier to make than more nuanced lager and ale styles and could ship well far and wide on the nation's new interstate highway system, which also grew up in the 1950s. As for wine, a similar consolidation was in order. The E. & J. Gallo Winery out of Modesto, California, was on its way to claiming an incredible one-third of the bottles sold in the United States. And most of those bottles, from Gallo and other competitors, were of sweeter, fortified wines made from nondescript, utilitarian grapes such as Carignan and Alicante Bouschet. Only a handful of wineries worked with the likes of Cabernet Sauvignon and Chardonnay, and their distribution was infinitesimal in comparison, as was the cultivation of grapes they used. Take Merlot grapes. By 1960 the variety covered only fifty acres of California, while Alicante Bouschet, a thick-skinned, pulpy workhorse comfortable with quick fermentations, covered twenty-five thousand. These decades-long trends seemed unlikely to reverse themselves. Analysts, for one thing, were predicting a single American brewery by the start of the twenty-first century.

As for spirits, a consolidation wave loomed for that industry, too, as one-time smaller family-owned operations took on partners to stay financially alive and then grew rapidly, bourbon distilleries especially. The idea of small-batch production in a smaller refurbished rather than brand-new distillery, with a major recipe shift to boot, seemed unnecessarily archaic, a recipe in itself for financial struggle and likely failure. Samuels did it anyway. In decades-long hindsight, it proved a crucial part of a seismic shift for American food and drink.

Nearly a half century after Samuels started distilling in Loretto, a private trade group called the American Distilling Institute attempted the first widely cited definition of what constituted a craft spirit in the United States. The initial part of the American Distilling Institute's definition concerned ownership: "Craft spirits are the products of an independently-owned distillery." Samuels's operation was certainly independently owned as well as operated. The second part of the definition described reach: an American craft distillery should have "maximum annual sales of 52,000 cases" of twelve 750-milliliter bottles. Samuels's output that first year, and for several years after, would number in the hundreds of cases. Finally, the institute declared that to call itself craft, a distillery's product should be "PHYSICALLY distilled and bottled on-site." That is exactly what Samuels did in tiny Loretto. Many would ignore, if not deride, the American Distilling Institute's twenty-first-century attempt at defining a craft spirit. No one could, or would, ignore the contribution Bill Samuels Sr. made. It would take years to recognize it, but his humble toils in a remote area of the American empire—largely notable solely because of bourbon and almost entirely beyond the ken of the coastal elites who dictated America's politics, fashions, and tastes—flew laughably in the face of where the nation's spirits in general were going as the latter half of the twentieth-century got under way. Small-batch production was out; large-scale was ascendant.

This had not been the case two generations earlier. By 1900 there were perhaps eight thousand distilleries in the United States of various sizes making myriad spirits, from whiskeys such as bourbon to vodkas to rums to brandies ballasted by a rainbow of fruits. The industry had deep roots. George Washington's Mount Vernon estate in northern Virginia had been the nation's largest whiskey distillery at the start of the nineteenth century. And spirits, particularly rum and whiskey, including bourbon, were the nation's bestselling alcoholic beverage until the decades after the Civil War, when increasingly well-automated breweries stormed the marketplace with that homogenous bastardization of pilsner and California wineries figured out how to ship farther in bulk more cheaply. The number of distilleries held impressively, however—there may have been around two thousand in 1910—buoyed by vast numbers of bars, especially in larger cities, and the cocktail culture they spawned. Politicians, too, going back to at least the presidential race of 1828, when Andrew Jackson routinely lavished free spirits on rallies of supporters, ensured a steady demand. In Appalachia, including parts of Kentucky, and other more remote areas of the nation's vast interior, home-distilling, often dubbed moonshining, continued into the twentieth century as it had for at least two centuries before, with hand-jiggered equipment and the basest of ingredients.

This steady demand, however, walked hand in hand for decades with a passionate set of critics spurred by religious fervor and genuine concern over the deleterious effects of too much drink. These antialcohol activists had always been able to claim small victories. Most newspapers, and certainly most mass-circulated, family-friendly magazines, did not accept advertisements for spirits. Popular movies and books, huge forms of entertainment in the pretelevision age, often depicted strong drink as the gateway to all sorts of irreversibly hellish behavior. The opposition eventually shifted from the public arena to the political one—and the victories became much more thumping. Beginning with Maine in 1846, several states, as well as local governments such as counties, passed laws banning the sale of alcohol, except in certain circumstances such as for medicinal use. The pace picked up in the early twentieth century as the pace of Americans' drinking picked up. Six states from 1907 through 1909 went dry, bringing the total to eleven. Around the same time, per-person consumption of alcohol, spirits or otherwise, jumped nearly one-third. The echoing brewing boom drove much of this increase. The number of breweries nationwide had peaked at around four thousand in the 1870s and was still counted in the thousands by the second decade of the twentieth century. Moreover, a spike in immigration from southern Europe, particularly from southern Italy, wove wine consumption into the wider daily fabric of American life. These foreign arrivistes and their bibulous ways panicked the mostly native-born antialcohol activists already concerned that the increase in dry territory had had little effect on drinking totals. They then made a historic legislative and media push throughout the 1910s, scoring their ultimate victory, Prohibition, and its enforcing Volstead Act, in 1919. Alcohol was out. Its manufacture, transportation, distribution, and sale, with a handful of strictly enforced exceptions, was illegal throughout America, a nation that George Washington, its Founding Father, had once plied with whiskey.

The number of distilleries in the United States dropped 85 percent during the thirteen years of Prohibition. The ones that survived produced alcohol mostly for industrial use. Nearly all spirits wholesalers, those individuals and firms that distributed the distilleries' products, went out of business. Not surprisingly and despite a now-legendary trade in illegally made spirits, alcohol consumption plunged throughout the 1920s and into the 1930s, to an average of one and a half gallons per person per year, well below the pre-Prohibition average of more than two and a half gallons. Also largely wiped out, or at least forced underground, was the cocktail culture centered on spirits. Certainly gone for good was the use of whiskey, rum, et al., to oil political rallies.

Most pernicious for American spirits was not what Prohibition destroyed but instead what it strengthened. The zealous aversion to alcohol that fueled the push for Prohibition before 1919, and that sustained it through the crime and resistance it spawned in the 1920s, carried on long after its end at the national level in 1933. Alcohol, spirits especially, became exotic to an entire generation of Americans, a feeling that that generation passed down to its progeny and that government at all levels sustained through onerous regulations for opening bars, starting breweries, getting distilling licenses, etc. Wine would eventually cloak itself in an aura of exclusivity and refinement to fully recover. Beer would succeed through sheer volume and massive marketing budgets, not to mention its lower alcohol content. Spirits, on the other hand, carried around the psychological effects of Prohibition like Marley's chains—it became something one should avoid, something associated with overindulgence, with failure even. What one analyst said about wine coming out of Prohibition could be said much more loudly about spirits: a feature of American life going back to before the Revolution, it was now something in "the bastard category of things legally allowed but morally reprehensible."

By 1954 Bill Samuels's new wheat-heavy bourbon was maturing in barrels in Loretto, with a release planned toward the end of the decade. In the meantime, Marge Samuels devised bottle designs and a name for the new distillery and its flagship spirit. She collected pewter, as well as bottles of the famed French brandy called Cognac, and made a point of searching for the physical mark that the individuals behind the finished product often left on the bottle. Moreover, Cognac bottles were sometimes sealed with wax to prevent oxygen from seeping in and ruining the brandy. Marge Samuels devised the name Maker's Mark for the bourbon—the name worked for the distillery, too—and created some prototype bottles, complete with hand-torn beige labels featuring the Star Hill Farm name prominently and its Loretto location. Marge also dipped the bottle tops in hot red wax, which made each one different from the others, depending on how the wax hardened. It was a labor-intensive move that made Bill nervous, but it stuck, as it were, and the red-dipped tip became an international emblem of Maker's Mark.

Or at least it did eventually. In May 1958 Samuels bottled one barrel of Maker's Mark and sent much of it, perhaps fifteen bottles, to a convention of wine and spirits wholesalers in Chicago, in the hopes of landing distributors. He sent some of the remaining few bottles to the Keeneland Racetrack in Lexington for its fall races, and he kept the rest to serve to various civic and business groups with which he was associated, a way to build some buzz for the new brand. The buzz had already started years before. Kentucky's bourbon industry was a clubby affair, and Samuels had called on the expertise of members of some of the other first families, including neighbors in Bardstown such as Jerry Beam, Jim's son, and Ed Shapira, whose family rescued and resurrected the Old Heaven Hill Springs Distillery. He also used his own expertise to divine the best materials for his recipe, including the barrels. For those, Samuels connected with the Independent Stave Company, a Missouri manufacturer that left its oak barrels outside for several months to dry rather than use a faster-acting kiln. The outdoor time reduced the level of the wood's tannins, organic substances that could make spirits astringent and bitter.

It was in these barrels that the first bourbons of Maker's Mark rested for one more summer after that unofficial rollout in 1958. Samuels felt they needed six full seasons to mature. In the fall of 1959, Maker's Mark debuted in restaurants and liquor stores throughout Kentucky, as well as over the Ohio River in southern Indiana and down into parts of Tennessee, which was the nation's second-biggest bourbon-producing state. That was as far as the distillery's reach would extend that first decade. When Bill's son, Bill Jr., entered Vanderbilt Law School in 1964 in Nashville, he realized that he had perhaps the biggest supply of Maker's Mark in Tennessee. The novelty of the packaging, red tip and all, the relative tininess of the distillery itself, the small-batch production of what came out of the specially dried barrels as a smoother bourbon with sweet hints of vanilla on the finish—none of it seemed to stick beyond a coterie of aficionados who recognized the quality when they tasted it but who could only buy so much. There would be advertising, including in august publications such as the *New Yorker*, under the tagline "It tastes expensive . . . and is." But that emphasis on costliness did not help matters, and Bill Samuels's attempt at a better bourbon faded from business plan to hobby as the 1950s bled into the 1960s. He could have pivoted back to rye as the main secondary ingredient and to a shorter aging time to get more product to market faster. Instead, Samuels resolutely stuck to wheat, to the six-year maturations, and to the small-batch approach in the small-sized distillery in Loretto. No one knew it then, but bourbon's day was almost over anyway. The distinctly American spirit style was headed for a sales cliff-dive largely of its own making because of the cheaper, rougher-tasting firewater so many distilleries made.

For Samuels and his family, there was no going back. Not that they had to—the fortunes of the clan were not necessarily tied to their new bourbon; they had plenty to live on. It was more than money that kept Bill Samuels stubbornly on the small and narrow. Bill Samuels Jr., then thirteen, would recount decades later the chilly February day in 1954 that his father kept him and his sisters home from school to attend a little ceremony at Star Hill Farm for the first barreling of Maker's Mark. Bill Sr. told the assembled, which included old friends (and new competitors) from the industry, that his family was leaving tradition behind to invent a bourbon that actually tasted good. It was a deliberately momentous occasion—though no one would realize just how momentous until decades later. He then stuffed a decades-old family recipe for T. W. Samuels into a jug, stuck some other papers in after it, and spread lighter fluid around inside. Finally, he held up a lit match and dropped it in. Just as he did so, one of his daughters put her face over the tapered opening. The resulting burst of flame singed her hair. It was the last time the family hosted a ceremony like that.

CHANGES BREWING

1965–1975 | San Francisco—Napa Valley

"Have you ever been to the brewery?" Fred Kuh asked his regular, a twenty-five-year-old ex-graduate student in Japanese studies from the Midwest by way of Stanford. The young man always ordered the same beer at Kuh's Old Spaghetti Factory bar in San Francisco's trendy North Beach neighborhood: an Anchor Steam.

"No," the young man answered.

"You ought to see it. It's closing in a day or two, and you ought to see it. You'd like it."

The next morning, Kuh's regular took his suggestion and walked the mile and a half from his apartment to the brewery at Eighth and Brannan streets. After about an hour of poking around, he bought a 51 percent stake for "less than the price of a used car." Fritz Maytag now controlled what turned out to be the last independently owned brewery in America making beer in small batches from traditional ingredients—the hallmarks of what came to be called craft brewing.

He could do it. Maytag's great-grandfather and namesake, Frederick Louis Maytag, the eldest of ten children born to German immigrants in central Iowa, had founded the Maytag Washing Machine Company some six decades before. The family firm grew literally into a household name, its machines spreading rapidly, especially with the nation's post–World War II economic boom, which included the development of vast prairies of suburban housing. The revenue allowed Frederick Louis's descendants to expand into other business interests. Frederick Louis II, his grandson and Fritz Maytag's father, used some help from the dairy science department at Iowa State and a herd of Holstein cows his father had acquired for their farm, about thirty-five miles east of Des Moines, to create a blue cheese in the Roquefort style of France. Like the French, Frederick Louis II aged this Maytag blue cheese in caves: two 110-foot-deep ones dug into the Newton farm in 1941. For Fritz Maytag, the cheese business, which he inherited in 1962 when Frederick Louis II died, was a quiet game-changer, something that stuck with him through the years in the Bay Area and right into his ownership of Anchor. "I saw the pride with which my father reacted when people would ask him, 'Have you anything to do with that blue cheese?' I saw that, and I saw that I had a chance of developing a food product that could do the same."

The idea was preposterous in 1965. American beer was trending in the exact opposite direction, away from distinctly made brands and styles to one watery adaptation of the Czech style pilsner made by fewer and fewer well-capitalized operations. Maytag was very aware of the challenge ahead of him. The brewery he bought had been through several owners since its establishment in 1896, during a kind of post–Civil War heyday for American brewing, when the number of breweries swelled to around four thousand and the idea of locally made beer for a local and appreciative audience did not seem so absurd. Anchor had flirted with ruin and disaster a few times in the sixty-nine years before Maytag rescued it. A fire that the Great Earthquake of 1906 spawned destroyed one location, and a fall from one of San Francisco's newly introduced cable cars killed an owner the following year. This difficult history and a dwindling consumer base amid the larger industry's consolidation left "a crude and primitive" brewery for Maytag to find. There weren't any of the flashes of the bigger operations like Anheuser-Busch or Miller—no stainless-steel piping or fermentation vats, not even refrigeration for storing bottled or kegged beers. Instead, Anchor's tiny space in the rumbling shadow of an Interstate 80 overpass contained one pump, some copper kettles straight out of the nineteenth century, and one understandably jaded employee.

The brewery also lacked a serious number of sales accounts. Were it not for eccentric devotees of locally made beer—including Kuh at the Old Spaghetti Factory, who took about ten of the approximately one hundred kegs Anchor produced monthly—Maytag was convinced the brewery would go out of business. He threw himself into salesmanship, distribution, and quality control those first years, schlepping the hilly streets of San Francisco, talking about this so-called steam beer, a caramelly lager made in small quantities with traditional ingredients such as malted barley, hops, and yeast—no adjuncts such as corn to speed fermentation or assorted chemicals to help with head retention or preservation. Just beer as it had been made in the past, before Prohibition set the clock so far back. Try it?

The pitch started to work. The brewery gained more accounts through the late 1960s, and the signature Steam Beer got better and better. Simple tweaks such as a cleaner brewhouse worked wonders for what had been before Maytag a rather iffy beer quality-wise. In April 1971 Anchor also became the first craft brewery since Prohibition to start bottling its beer. A short time later, Maytag was able to hire a distributor, freeing up more of his time for quality control and salesmanship. Finally, the brewery started rattling off an impressive run of stylistic firsts: first new porter since Prohibition, resurrecting the dark, malty style that initially arose in England in the 1800s; first American-made seasonal beer since Prohibition, a spicily sweet Christmas ale; and what came to be recognized as the first American-inflected India pale ale, the citrusy bitter Anchor Liberty Ale in 1975.

Few people noticed, especially not beyond Anchor's growing but still small universe of clients and champions. The vast majority of American beer drinkers wanted their homogenized, watered-down pilsner, ice-cold and in copious quantities, the additives and artificiality be damned. The 1975 debut of Miller Lite, the first widely available light beer in the United States, would only underline this reality. Thin, watery, nearly translucent, and barely bitter (Anchor Liberty Ale was four times as bitter), Miller Lite proved a commercial smash, propelling its maker from the back of the pack of America's top ten breweries to number two behind Anheuser-Busch. That brewery felt compelled to introduce its own light beer offering in 1977 (Busch Light) and again in 1982 (Bud Light). Soon, light beer was the bestselling style in the United States and the most famous American-born style in the world.

This was a sort of success that Fritz Maytag and his small crew simply could not fathom. Anchor Brewing would remain the only craft brewer in America through 1975—and largely a money loser to boot, its well-endowed and tenacious leader all that was standing between it and oblivion (or perhaps a second life as a brand in a much bigger brewery's portfolio). Despite the struggles, Maytag was determined to keep his brewery small. "I want to make all our beer in this building—hands on," he would tell people. That one contemporary described the building as "a dump" was beside the point. Small-batch, traditional, and independently owned—that was the way Maytag wanted things to stay at Anchor, even if it meant its demise. "I mean this," he also said, "we do not want—emphatically do not want—to get too big."

Maytag's intellectual doppelgänger in the wine world would have agreed with everything about his approach and thought process, up to that point about not wanting to get too big. Robert Mondavi wanted his new winery to get big because he thought big, on a grander scale, in fact, than many Americans had ever thought when it came to wine and its potential in the United States. In November 1965, only a few months after Maytag bought control of Anchor down in San Francisco, Mondavi had been unceremoniously booted from day-to-day employment with his family's winery in Napa Valley, called Charles Krug, after the mid-nineteenth-century Prussian who founded it. Though it would be decades, really, before hindsight provided the lens to view them properly, these twin events—Maytag's takeover and Mondavi's termination—marked the respective starts of the stylistic and cultural rebirths of wine and beer in the United States, much as Bill Samuels Sr.'s launch of Maker's Mark a decade before did for the rebirth of spirits. Samuels's Loretto, Kentucky, operation remained an anomaly in spirits, with Maytag and Mondavi more his intellectual cousins than any fellow distillers. The men did not know each other, but they were unwittingly working in concert toward the same seemingly unattainable goal: changing the way Americans drank.

Robert Mondavi faced perhaps the easiest route of the three, though its navigation still looked far from assured. The Mondavis' Charles Krug stood at the intersection of American wine in the mid-twentieth century. On one side were the moneymaking generic wines made from lower-end, more utilitarian grape varieties that were easier and cheaper to grow. They also tended to be pulpier, and therefore produced more juice, and could survive longer train and truck trips to farther-flung vendors. The generic wines these lower-end grapes produced tended to be sweet and strong, and Americans by and large lapped them up, usually from taps attached to bulk containers (hence the term "bulk wines," a twin to "generics") or, more commonly, from glass gallon jugs with screwtops. These generics did not simply outsell but dwarfed drier, more nuanced fine wines, the other, tinier side of the industry at midcentury. By 1960 only a quarter of the wine consumed in the United States was fine wine from higher-end, European-born grape varieties such as Cabernet Sauvignon,

Merlot, or Chardonnay. These were generally simply unavailable outside of major metropolitan areas, which might each have a handful of retailers or restaurants that sold them. Most of the available US-made wine instead flowed from lower-end workhorse grapes such as Alicante Bouschet and Carignan. If Americans ever did buy a bottle of fine wine, it was almost always from a French winery—France had led the world in fine wine production for as long as anyone alive could remember.

Charles Krug was one of the few US producers to craft at least some of its wines from these higher-end grape varieties so long associated with France. Critics particularly toasted its Cabernet Sauvignon, sourced from grapes cultivated in Napa Valley and fermented in open-top tanks made of redwood, a technique introduced in California in the previous century. The Mondavi family, led by parents Cesare and Rosa, purchased the winery in 1943 at the urging of their eldest son, Robert, who saw its potential to add luster to the clan's main business, Sunny St. Helena. That generic-wine producer churned out some five hundred thousand gallons annually of nondescript fare that was nonetheless popular with consumers and distributed beyond California, including to the East Coast. The distribution and the production placed Sunny St. Helena comfortably toward the top of the approximately forty wineries then operating in Napa Valley. Cesare and Rosa, a quiet force behind her husband's public face, saw no reason to tamper with a winning formula that the couple, originally from central Italy, had spent decades devising.

Robert Mondavi was not satisfied. A gregarious, garrulous perfectionist with seemingly bottomless reserves of energy, he had long immersed himself in the tiny world of fine wine in America, which, largely because of Napa, centered on the San Francisco Bay Area. He dined at fine restaurants with decent wine lists; he hung out with the few other fine wine producers in the valley besides Charles Krug; he studied the latest techniques, including in a lab he built in an old water tower behind his St. Helena home; he even spent part of his 1940 honeymoon visiting some of Sunny St. Helena's accounts. Robert Mondavi was very aware that several Americans had tried and failed to turn their countrymen on to fine wine styles such as Cabernet Sauvignon and Chardonnay, that most of the operations that had tried were small by any industry measure: production, distribution, clout in the grape-buying market. A winery owner focused on higher-end grapes might be his business's sole employee, or one of a handful, everyone pitching in on every aspect of the process. Robert, a well-traveled Stanford graduate, was also well aware of the seemingly endless second-class status of the rest of the winemaking world vs. France. And he was convinced that he could change all that.

His chance came in late 1965, after a violent falling-out with his younger brother Peter, who ran the production side of Charles Krug. Simply put, the family and the winery had had it with Mondavi's hard-charging, blue-sky-thinking ways. Even his son, Michael, about to graduate college, was frozen out; and Rosa Mondavi—Cesare had died in 1959—refused to intervene when *her* son pressed her. "If that's the case, Mother," Robert replied, "I'm going to build a winery."

No one had started a significant new commercial winery in Napa Valley, America's premier winemaking region, since Repeal in 1933. That was gutsy enough on Mondavi's part. What really made what he would call the Robert Mondavi Winery monumental was that he would focus exclusively on fine wines from higher-end grapes, the sort most American wineries did not make and the kinds most Americans did not buy. It would be designed from the ground up, as well as conceptually and technically outward, to compete with the top wineries of France, the nation that set the international trends in winemaking. He had high expectations—many at the time would have said impossibly high—that the American wine industry, and the American palate, would follow his lead. It was an audacious approach, ridiculous even, as silly as Fritz Maytag expecting Americans to put down a Miller Lite and pick up something called Anchor Liberty Ale. Some wags called it "Robert's Folly." At the time, Napa Valley was a backwater compared with French regions such as Bordeaux and Bourgogne, a place where business hinged on the sales of generics, and the techniques were rudimentary. No Napa vintners by 1965 regularly used oak barrels to age their wines as they did in France, for one thing. Cleanliness, or a lack of it, often ruined entire batches, too. Andre Tchelistcheff, a Russian-born winemaker who would go on to become one of the most sought-after consultants in the industry, found a rat floating in a vat of Sauvignon Blanc shortly after his arrival in Napa in 1938—and that was at one of the better wineries. Also, while Napa would grow into a kind of Disneyland for oenophiles, in 1965 it was most definitely not a tourist destination. Wineries might convert a spare space for tastings and there was the odd outdoor concert, but there was no collective effort to draw tourists, no fancy restaurants, no tastings with sonorous lectures, nothing from local officials in the city or county of Napa to support tourism. Many of the smaller wineries, in fact, were only by way of gravelly dirt roads off the main route, State Highway 29, which barely ran to two lanes as it passed through much of Napa.

Rejected professionally by his family, the odds stacked against him industrially and karmically, Mondavi, already a couple of years on the north side of fifty, a time when most men are winding down, pressed on with his plans. He lined up investors; he hired architect Cliff May, progenitor of the ranch-style house; and he found a spot just off Highway 29, in the tiny hamlet of Oakville, within some of the region's choicest vineyards. The winery arose throughout the winter, spring, and summer of 1966, designed in the Italianate style, a bell tower and a wide, welcoming archway to be its signatures. That welcoming nature would prove to be one of the most influential aspects of the winery. Mondavi designed it to be a destination point for tourists, perhaps the first vintner in America ever to do so. Mondavi the winery would be a place to not only see the vineyards and the winemaking process but also to enjoy, however briefly, wine-related culture. There would be chairs for languid evenings spent sampling, tour guides speaking with passion and gusto, concerts to pair wine with music. The winery's products would be different and so would its approach to people.

On the morning of September 6, 1966, the Tuesday after Labor Day, a Catholic priest from the nearby Carmelite monastery blessed the newly completed winery, and a mechanical lift hoisted a gondola full of Pinot Noir grapes into a bladed hopper. The Robert Mondavi Winery was on its way.

The debut should have been another culinary event in America, but, like with Fritz Maytag's takeover of the Anchor Brewing Company an hour south in San Francisco the year before, few outside of the operation's orbit noticed. There was no major media coverage, barely any at all, actually, even from the San Francisco newspapers. The audience at the benediction were all people Robert Mondavi knew. The new winery would sell a respectable 2,579 twelve-bottle cases in 1967, from grapes crushed the year before. A 1968 introduction called Fumé Blanc, a silky, light spin on a Sauvignon Blanc style originating in France, helped to first quadruple sales and then to triple them from there in 1969, to more than thirty thousand cases. These numbers still paled against major generic producers—industry leader E. & J. Gallo might sell a hundred million cases in a year—but they were respectable enough to shut up all that talk of "Robert's Folly." Besides, a curious thing was happening in the late 1960s nationwide: fine wines were starting to outsell generics. In 1967 the gap was more than 8.6 million gallons, a gulf that would only grow in the coming years. No one was quite sure of the cause of the change. Some credited baby boomers' rebellion against their parents' preferences for spirits such as bourbon, others the technological improvements, particularly those that helped produce consistently clean-looking wines. Still others noted the rise in wine writing—the *New York Times* debuted its first regular wine column in 1972, as did several smaller publications. Finally, there was the simple arrival of more domestic producers. Robert Mondavi, the first of this new wave, suddenly looked far from ridiculous as the 1970s hustled along. Instead, he looked incredibly prescient, the visionary that American wine, and drink at large, needed.

COFFEE WITH DINNER
1976–1978 | San Francisco Bay Area—Paris

Jörg Rupf had it all when he arrived in the San Francisco Bay Area in mid-1976. He was only thirty-three years old and yet could look back on a successful run as an attorney and as a judge in West Germany's administrative court, which acted as a check on government actions. He could look forward to that career stretching out decades more, ending with a comfortable, pensioned retirement, perhaps in the Black Forest region of southern West Germany, where he had grown up. It was the legal work that brought him to the United States for the first time in 1976, the year the nation was marking the two-hundredth anniversary of its independence from Great Britain. He was on a leave of absence from his government work to study the relationship between government and the arts through a postdoctoral fellowship at the University of California at Berkeley. The time allowed his mind to graze. Rupf, a skillful violinist with glasses and a thick brown beard, settled into the Bay Area easily—a little too easily, it turned out.

Perhaps it was the Bay Area itself, long one of the more temperamentally laid back regions of the United States, one buoyed by equally temperate weather nearly year-round. Or maybe it was Berkeley in particular, the college town that birthed the free speech movement of the early 1960s and became ever-after inextricably linked with the counterculture that emerged later in that decade, particularly in San Francisco's Haight-Ashbury neighborhood. Or perhaps it was Rupf himself, dropped on this canvas and left to paint his own way for nearly two years. Whatever it was, he began to notice something. In Europe, a career defined a person. He or she picked one early, as he had, and stayed in it until retirement, as he planned to do, unless you were particularly unsuccessful. The idea of more than one career in a lifetime was anathema to many European cultures, particularly in West Germany, which was intent on building up its post–World War II economy, as well as its infrastructure and its education system. To stray outside the lines professionally got people to talking and could damage prospects. Rupf, so successful in the law at such an early age, assumed he would be in it forever, the Bay Area leave of absence a mere side trip. Besides, he had a situation many might envy on either side of the Atlantic: a steady job with a guaranteed pension when he retired. Yet he noticed a lot of Americans switching careers midstream, sometimes drastically so. In Rupf's temporary home, things seemed so much more fluid.

Rupf noticed something else about the United States: the drinking habits of Americans. If a restaurant, even in the cosmopolitan Bay Area, had a wine list, it invariably had only three entries: Chablis, Hearty Burgundy, and rosé, the first two more brand names than wine styles. And underneath all three would invariably appear the words "E. & J. Gallo." The brothers Ernest and Julio had scaled Gallo up enormously to the point where its facilities were "the size of oil refineries" and its output so vast it was more cost-effective for the company to manufacture its own bottles than to deal with an outside vendor. The wine they produced, too, had little in common with the European varieties then nearly impossible to find outside of large metropolitan areas such as New York and Los Angeles. No drily refined Chardonnay and Merlot for Gallo. Instead it was branded creations such as treacly sweet Pink Chablis and cheaply strong Thunderbird. This was not the sort of fine wine that Rupf, born in the French region of Alsace and raised just over the German border, had grown up around.

As for beer in America, that horrified Rupf. His mother's family had owned a brewery in the southern German city of Freiburg since the 1870s. Like other German breweries, it specialized in lagers noted for their clean, crisp taste and full flavor. Europe in general had long produced the world's most flavorful, freshest-tasting beers. Belgium, a nation the size of Maryland, boasted nearly two hundred breweries crafting dozens of individual beers and beer styles, many of them ales, the heavier, more complex cousins of lagers. West and East Germany had around five hundred breweries total, most making lagers, but those lagers were often regionally distinct and distinctive tasting. In the United States, aside from the odd import or the small-batch releases from San Francisco's Anchor Brewing Company, all Rupf could seem to find were watered-down, oversweetened versions of those German lagers, what one later American brewer would aptly describe as "alcoholic soda pop." The Miller Brewing Company's Miller Lite epitomized these insipid brews. Introduced the year before Rupf arrived in the States, it quickly became one of the bestselling American beers ever and made the light-beer category the fastest-growing on Earth.

Rupf would have none of it, not the generic wine and certainly not beers such as Miller Lite. So what might he drink with his meals besides water? There was one alternative in particular that he noticed Americans preferred, and it horrified him almost as much as the beer quality: Americans drank coffee *with* their meals, not after. Americans usually reserved that time for a syrupy sweet dessert wine or liqueur, if they drank anything at all.

For Rupf, growing up the son of a forester in Freiburg, where his mother's family ran the brewery, and later in Lake Constance on the Swiss border, the preferred after-meal drink had always been eau-de-vie. Eaux-de-vie were brandies, or distilled fruit juices. But whereas other brandies, such as the vaunted French Cognac, came from certain grapes and only those grapes, eau-de-vie might be born of a number of different fruits: pears, apples, the full kaleidoscope of berries. Eau-de-vie was also clearer than the amber hues of the grape-based brandies, often crystal clear, in fact, due to the distillation process that eschewed skin and went for the fleshy, juicy pulp. And whereas other brandies, Cognac in particular, had long enjoyed a vigorous international trade and the prestige that came with it, eau-de-vie was of humbler stock. It basically emerged because central Europeans, especially those in the Continent's German-speaking regions, needed something to do with the leftover fruit every harvest season in an age before refrigeration. Distilling the juices into a clear, bracing drink that itself required no refrigeration seemed the perfect solution. For centuries Germans, Swiss, Austrians, French, and others got better and better at doing so. By the time Rupf was born in Alsace, the border region that went back and forth twice between warring Germany and France from 1870 to 1919, eau-de-vie was an inescapable culinary accoutrement throughout central Europe, an unpretentious nip usually served in tiny, long-stemmed glasses after a meal. It usually came from a nearby distillery that sourced its fruit locally and that crafted its wares with traditional equipment and methods. As quaint as such an approach would seem in the decades to come, it was all so routine then.

Eaux-de-vie were largely commercially unavailable in the Bay Area when Rupf was there. There might have been fruit brandies for sale, but none made from the fruits traditionally used for eaux-de-vie and none without added sugar. And yet, Northern California positively teemed with fruit, a major physical presence as well as an economic driver. There were the wine grapes, of course, and table grapes, too, but also literally tons of pears, apples, and berries annually. In 1976, the year Rupf arrived in the United States, Napa County produced some 28 tons of apples and 630 tons of pears, never mind nearly 36,000 tons of grapes. In neighboring Sonoma County, the 1976 statistics were even more startling: 141,000 tons of apples, 7,120 tons of pears, and more than 39,000 tons of grapes. Tantalizingly, the vast majority of pears grown in Sonoma were of the Bartlett variety, the same variety popular back in Europe for eau-de-vie (though there they were known as Williams pears). Sonoma's fruit output was worth $24.8 million in 1976 dollars, Napa's $14.4 million. This fruitful bounty, and that of other areas of California and the United States, mostly ended up whole or canned on retailers' shelves. If it ended up in bottles in 1976, it was invariably as wines or fruit juices. It was not meant for distilleries.

What if it was, though? "Such beautiful fruit and quality sunshine," Rupf thought of the Bay Area. "I could to do something with my hands with that."

A revolutionary event half a world away, during the same year that Rupf arrived in America, would inspire him to try. Steve Spurrier, an English wine merchant in Paris, and Pat Gallagher, a Delaware transplant who helped Spurrier run his shop and an attached wine-tasting school, arranged a blind wine tasting at the posh InterContinental Hotel in the French capital in May 1976. It would be old-world French reds and whites from prime winemaking regions Bordeaux and Bourgogne versus upstarts from the burgeoning Northern California fine wine industry, which now stood at the vanguard of a national movement putting more Merlot, Cabernet Sauvignon, etc., in the hands of more Americans than ever before. Robert Mondavi's actions ten years before had helped create an entire ecosystem of critics, distributors, retailers, and associated boosters. Yet American wine remained, along with the rest of the world's, a distant also-ran to France, destined for what seemed like incremental growth, but not the blockbuster status that that European republic enjoyed. Spurrier himself, though several American patrons of his wine shop had enthused about their nation's newest wines, figured the results of his blind tasting would be lopsided. France would win in a walk.

The nine judges, culled from the most rarefied spheres of French food and drink, seemed to think so, too. "Ah, back to France!" declared one judge in French, after tasting a particularly good white. The only trouble was that it was a Chardonnay from Napa Valley, not a white from Bourgogne. Another judge, again in French, dismissed a white from that very region as "definitely California—it has no nose." The bias was so pronounced against American wine and the belief in French superiority so entrenched that the judges simply tasted what they wanted to taste. In the end, the judges ended up awarding the top spots in both the red and white categories to American wines; other American vintages also placed highly. The United States had won, and France had lost—in Paris, with French judges, no less. Luckily for posterity, Spurrier had been able to coax one journalist to the tasting, a correspondent for *Time* magazine, the largest US newsweekly, named George Taber. Doubly lucky, Taber understood French.

As soon as he could, the lanky, thin Taber filed a nearly eight-thousand-word report on the tasting. Editors at *Time*'s headquarters in Midtown Manhattan cut it to 362 words and ran it on page 58 of the magazine's June 7, 1976, edition under the headline THE JUDGMENT OF PARIS. It caused an immediate sensation and became the single most important event in the history of American fine wine, before or since. The storyline was too perfect, especially for an American audience weaned on tales of success through pluck and luck. (One of the top movies of 1976 was just such a tale: the original *Rocky*, starring Sylvester Stallone as the scruffy street-gym boxer who got his shot at the world champ and embarrassed him.) Plus, it did not hurt the triumphalism that quickly surrounded Taber's dispatch that 1976 was America's bicentennial year, brimming already with patriotic fervor. THREE CHEERS FOR THE RED, WHITE AND CRU, crowed a June 13 headline in the *Los Angeles Times*, the last word a spin on the French wine term for growth. CALIFORNIA WINES BEAT FRENCH WINES!, blared the *Times-Picayune* of New Orleans three days later, complete with the exclamation point. The *New York Times*' Frank Prial, perhaps then the nation's most influential wine critic, dedicated two consecutive weekly columns to the tasting and its winning wines. Television news, nationally and locally, picked up the story. It became impossible to miss and soon passed as much into legend as into history, still known by that original *Time* headline, THE JUDGMENT OF PARIS. Overnight, it remade the image of the American wine industry, allowing it, as one Napa winery owner put it, twenty years of growth at a single leap. For Jörg Rupf, the German academic entranced by verdant California, the news from Paris was just the nudge he needed.

A CLEAR FAVORITE
1978 | Manhattan

The three Swedes turned the corner of Manhattan's Forty-Ninth Street, and Sixth Avenue opened up "like a fjord" before them, the concrete canyon packed on either side with the block-long bases of skyscrapers, the peaks of some of which they could not see. It was early 1978, and the government agency in Sweden that had run most of that kingdom's alcohol industry since 1905 had tasked Gunnar Broman, Hans Brindfors, and Peter Ekelund with marketing a new export, the agency's first real push overseas. Vodka was the export. Sweden had a history with the clear, colorless, sometimes flavorless spirit that stretched back at least to the Middle Ages, though the nation was mostly known by the late 1970s for its citizens' binge drinking and its labyrinth of alcohol regulations, including a ban on spirits advertisements except on matchboxes. A Swedish vodka might be a tough sell—brands from the Soviet Union dominated the US market, the Smirnoff label in particular, which could trace its roots to czarist Russia—but that was why the three men were schlepping their way up Sixth Avenue, marketing materials in hand.

Gunnar Broman was their leader. A stoutly compact man with a salt-and-pepper beard, a smoothly bald crown, and warm, jovial eyes, Broman was one of Sweden's top ad men. His Stockholm firm, Carlsson and Broman, was in the process of being acquired, in fact, ensuring a healthy, hefty early retirement for the fifty-year-old Broman. He did not need to be in Manhattan in early 1978. As it was, though, Broman seemed the only one up for the task of selling the American market, and its market arbiters, on a Swedish vodka, at least as far as the Swedish spirits monopoly was concerned. Hans Brindfors was Broman's assistant, a quiet sort behind shaded eyeglasses and with a close-cropped goatee giving him the look of a New York beatnik from a just-past era. The twenty-four-year-old Peter Ekelund, tall and blond, a prototypical Scandinavian, represented the government.

Their destination was the forty-first floor of the fifty-story Burlington House at 1345 Sixth Avenue. That was the headquarters of N. W. Ayer, one of the top advertising firms in the world. Its roster of slam-dunk campaigns came to include "Be all you can be" for the US Army, "Reach out and touch someone" for AT&T, and "A diamond is forever" for jewelry giant De Beers. The walls of the offices that greeted Broman and Co. as they stepped off the elevator were plastered with reminders of these campaigns as well as of famous clients, including celebrities. It was a heady thing for three Swedes. However well-regarded on his home turf of Stockholm, Broman was acutely aware that New York City, and America, was the Big Leagues. For one thing, the city itself, even after its steep population decline during the crime-ridden, fiscally ruinous decade now ending, was about as populous as all of Sweden. For another, the United States was the biggest consumer marketplace on earth, perhaps in history, its households having earned collectively over $1 trillion in 1973, a record for the nation. The baby boomers, those Americans born from World War II to the early 1960s, drove that earning power, another record having buoyed their prospects: four-year college enrollment reached an all-time high in the United States in 1969. The young professionals these schools turned out had money and were looking to burn it. One such fire was firewater. Americans were drinking more spirits in the 1970s than at any time in the twentieth century—this despite the bounce that the Judgment of Paris in 1976 provided fine wine and the ever-decreasing prices of America's ever more homogenous beer. In 1978, the year Gunnar Broman and his associates took the elevator to N. W. Ayer's Manhattan offices to pitch their new Swedish vodka, the average American was putting away well more than one gallon of spirits annually, almost twice the amount of wine consumed, fine or otherwise. And which clear spirit did Americans quaff the most? Vodka.

The spirit originated in northeastern Europe in what is now Poland and Russia. Unlike bourbon, whose genesis can be traced to a handful of decades in a collection of enclaves in Kentucky, the exact location and the birthday of vodka remain unknown and are hotly disputed between Russia and Poland. What is known is that by the Middle Ages the distillation of the clear, always immensely strong spirit was proceeding apace in northeastern Europe, including in Scandinavia, though it was often difficult, if not fatal, to drink. Instead, early vodka was used as ballast for other products, including perfumes, cosmetics, and "vile-tasting panaceas" from quack doctors. It was not until the early-nineteenth-century development of charcoal filtering—literally running the spirit through charcoal to remove impurities—that it took off as a beverage, particularly in the old Russian Empire, which then included much of present-day Poland. By the mid-1800s, the drink was so prevalent and popular that vodka was both the principal source of tax revenue for the czar and the cause of some two hundred thousand alcohol-related deaths annually. Many of these deaths were due not necessarily to too much drinking but rather to shoddy, sometimes downright poisonous vodka that had not been properly or sufficiently filtered. The Russian government would eventually step in by century's end and create a monopoly for vodka sales very similar to the Swedish agency regulating alcohol there.

In the meantime, some Russian distillers took it upon themselves to turn out vodka of consistently good quality. Pyotr Smirnov was one such entrepreneur. Born a serf in 1831 in a rural village near Moscow, Smirnov rose to become one of the empire's wealthiest men, a favorite of Czar Alexander III, who loved his vodka, and a skilled marketer who managed to produce a product that not only looked and tasted the same with every batch but also was festooned with all manner of seals, emblems, and embossing so as to inspire customer loyalty. This customer loyalty was Smirnov's major innovative con-tribution to vodka—the drink itself was little more than grain alcohol filtered through charcoal—an innovation he tried to export to the United States. Smirnov brought his vodka to the Centennial Exhibition in Philadelphia in 1876, where it won medals in tasting competitions, and the Chicago's World Fair seventeen years later. But beyond the odd Slavic-American enclave in a big city such as Chicago or New York, vodka never caught on. Spirits-wise, America was firmly a whiskey nation, the only real challenge to that hegemony coming from lager beer, not some clear, starchy drink from the Near Orient that barely had any flavor and little smell beyond its alcohol. Smirnov died in 1898, shortly before World War I and the Bolshevik Revolution upended the old order in Russia. (A bout of Prohibition, brought on by the start of the war in 1914, did not help matters, either.) Much of Smirnov's personal empire was upended as well, the victorious Communists expropriating his vodka and its production facilities—and nearly hounding his heirs to death.

One of those heirs, a son named Vladimir, escaped a prison camp in Ukraine, where five times he was brought before a firing squad only to be spared, and quickly fled westward. He opened a distillery in Paris under the name Pierre Smirnoff Fils (or Pierre Smirnoff Son, tweaking the family name and using the French spelling for Peter). The distillery flopped. Desperate to salvage any ves-tige of the family fortune, Vladimir cut a deal in a Paris hotel bar to sell the American rights to the Smirnoff name and its product for 54,000 francs, or about $4.1 million in 2015 money. Rudolph Kunett, the Ukrainian-born New York businessman on the other side of the deal, could not believe his luck. It was 1933, and Prohibition had just ended in the United States. Surely he stood to make a killing behind the Smirnoff name with a thirsty American marketplace awaiting. In March 1934, Kunett opened a Smirnoff distillery in Bethel, Con-necticut, about a two-hour drive northeast of New York City. It was the first vodka distillery in the United States since Repeal, producing twelve hundred twelve-bottle cases that first year. Sales would be steady but sclerotic: Americans were just not into vodka. Verging on bankruptcy, Kunnet in 1938 sold the Smirnoff distillery for about $250,000 in today's money to the Heublein food-and-drink conglomerate out of Hartford. Kunnet also got a job with the com-pany, as well as a 5 percent commission on each bottle sold during the next ten years—a not inconsequential sum, as it turned out.

Heublein would go on to buy notable California wineries, as well as distri-bution rights for big beer brands such as Guinness and Bass, not to mention the fast-food chain Kentucky Fried Chicken, but at the time it was a much smaller operation, then best-known for its A-1 steak sauce. It seemed unlikely to lead some sort of revolution for vodka in the United States. Heublein did not even have all the packaging in place when it started rolling out Smirnoff in 1939—the caps said WHISKEY. Yet, the signs were there almost immediately that its newest brand had the trappings of a smash hit. The biggest early sign came from a Columbia, South Carolina, distributor that ordered ten cases initially, then fifty more, and finally some five hundred. John Gilbert Martin, the English-born, Cambridge-educated CEO of Heublein and grandson of its founder, went to see why the Deep South was so thirsty for a Russian drink. What he discovered delighted him. A salesman in South Carolina had put up a giant banner describing the Heublein product as SMIRNOFF WHITE WHISKEY—NO SMELL, NO TASTE.

The marketing, however illegal under federal regulations, craftily tied the otherwise exotic spirit to one that had been familiar, if not phenomenally popular, for centuries. It also apparently gave tipplers an idea, one that germinated elsewhere in the United States around the same time and dramatically changed not only vodka's fortunes but American drinking habits as well. Simply put, people began mixing vodka with things, spawning a whole subspecies of cocktails: the screwdriver (vodka and orange juice), the Bloody Mary (vodka, tomato juice, and selected seasonings), the Moscow mule (vodka, ginger beer, and lime), and more. Vodka even became a prominent alternative to gin as the undergirding for the vaunted martini. The namesake villain in the first James Bond movie, 1962's *Dr. No*, serves actor Sean Connery a "medium dry" martini that's been shaken, not stirred—"Vodka?" an impossibly suave Connery/Bond asks. "Of course," Dr. No replies. (And Smirnoff was clearly the secret agent's vodka of choice as bottles can be seen in his room at a different point in the movie.) Fifteen years before, at a party at her Hollywood estate, Joan Crawford, one of the world's most famous actors, apparently arranged for only Champagne and vodka to be served to her fellow influential A-listers, including for martinis. It was the perfect alcoholic ballast for anything, really: largely flavorless on its own, scentless, and stonking strong at more than 40 percent alcohol by volume. Almost too perfect, as it turned out. Vodka's growth in the decades after Heublein's relaunch hinged in no small part on many consumers' discovery that the spirit left no odor on their breath. One could drink it and, depending on one's tolerance for alcohol, none would be the wiser, the spirit loosed as a secret social lubricant. Heublein played this up in an advertising campaign with the tagline "Smirnoff Leaves You Breathless." One ad showed famously awkward director and actor Woody Allen literally climbing out of a shell. These different uses of vodka paired well with the relative ease of its distillation. It required no aging, unlike whiskey, and Heublein could therefore spill as much Smirnoff on the market as fast as it could make it. Never mind that vodka sometimes *did* have flavors, and often strong peppery, fruity ones at that. The idea of vodka as entirely flavorless was as clingingly incorrect as its being made solely from potatoes. Smirnoff, though, did not have any discernible taste, nor real odor beyond the ethyl alcohol, and for most Americans, the brand came to equal the drink.

And Heublein was making more and more of it as the vodka market bounced and then bounced again—in 1967 vodka, only a generation before unfamiliar to most Americans, surpassed gin, a spirit flavored with juniper and developed in Northern Europe, as the nation's bestselling clear spirit. Fewer than five years after buying the brand from Rudolph Kunett, Heublein was selling more than twenty-two thousand cases of Smirnoff annually in the United States. Competitors soon hopped on the vodka bandwagon, most of them, like Heublein's Smirnoff, domestically produced but with Slavic-sounding names. By the 1970s, only 0.5 percent of the US vodka marketplace was truly imported, compared with some 35 percent for whiskey. Smirnoff dominated that 99.5 percent of domestic production, to the point where "in America," according to one journalist, "vodka *was* Smirnoff."

It was into this import-unfriendly vodka environment that Gunnar Broman and his associates stepped when they exited the elevator at N. W. Ayer's offices forty-one floors above Manhattan that workday in early 1978. Jerry Siano, the advertising agency's well-regarded chief creative executive, introduced the trio to a conference room full of copywriters, art directors, and account managers, all eleven of whom, along with Siano, wore ties. Broman did not. Instead he wore a cardigan sweater over a plaid shirt, chinos, and brown loafers, his reading glasses hanging loosely from a chain around his neck. He surveyed his audience, the first step in winning support for an unprecedented Swedish vodka that the Swedish government hoped would open up a whole realm of export possibilities, not just in spirits. Other export ideas had failed, however. The pressure was on; the words had to be chosen just so.

"I come to you from the land of the thirsty," Broman said solemnly.

After a beat, he laughed. His listeners—luckily—laughed, too. Broman was off, and on to what he had traveled halfway around the world for: a Swedish vodka.

Hold on, one of the Americans said. A Swedish vodka? Wasn't vodka Russian? Even American-made Smirnoff, far and away the most popular brand in the States, was genetically Russian.

Swedish vodka was a real thing, Broman countered, having anticipated the question. It dated from at least 1467, around the time it took hold in nearby Russia and Poland. "It took us five hundred years to bring this Swedish vodka to America," Broman said. "Now the time is right. Now it's here."

Very well. It was time for Broman's slideshow and for the crude plastic mockups of various vodka bottles that Brindfors and Ekelund had schlepped to and around Manhattan. Everyone sat in black leather chairs, while the Swedish adman stood at one end of the conference room, facing his audience facing various movie screens of different sizes at the other end. The lights dimmed.

The initial slide showed the first of six ideas for the Swedish vodka: Country of Sweden. The concept would play off the bucolic splendor that was supposedly Sweden: hills, lakes, fjords, ice-capped mountains, etc. The silk wrapping on the Country of Sweden vodka bottle struck some of the N. W. Ayer people—they were all men in that conference room—as too feminine, like something that should go around a perfume. Besides, as Broman himself noted, the idea might be a little too subdued for a drink as strong as vodka. He moved to the next slide. It showed a blond, well-built, impossibly handsome, assumedly virile Viking of old, an ancestor of the modern-day Swede. "That's what I call a real man," Broman said. "And the Vikings discovered America. Scientifically proven fact." Not sophisticated enough, the Americans quickly concluded. And the Swede in the slide did not match the one depicted on the round little bottle mocked up for the occasion. That awkwardly proportioned Viking—his torso was oddly elongated—looked like something out of an amateurish painting. Broman's next idea was all class: Royal Court Vodka, complete with the name in elegant script below two regal lions flanking an equally regal crest. Was Sweden not technically a kingdom, with a constitutional monarch like Great Britain?

"Here you have a real sense of tradition," one of the copywriters said.

"This could be the angle," another American said. "The king thing."

To Broman, who had slapped crests on other products, including a Swedish beer he helped popularize, the Royal Court Vodka idea seemed a tad too conventional. The next slide was a personal favorite; it depicted a simple pocket flask holding vodka called Damn Swede. Broman imagined drinkers the world over saying "Damn Swede" when they wanted a quick shot of vodka. Still, advertisements in the United States could not carry swear words, so Broman moved quickly onward. He took out several mocked-up bottles painted black and set them all in a row on the conference table. "This is plain vodka in black bottles," Broman explained. (The bottles were, of course empty; he would not have been able to get them past customs at the airport otherwise.) "But it's got something extra. We've added black currant."

The Americans were less than impressed, confused even.

"Gunnar, is this a political thing?" one asked.

"Can a vodka be black?" asked another. "Vodka is supposed to be clear, right?"

Broman reluctantly put away the black bottles—they had been a personal favorite, too. He was down to the final slide and the last idea.

"What the hell is this?" asked an American when the next slide popped up. It showed two squat bottles with no labels, no adornment of any kind, in fact, aside from words written in silver directly on the glass: Absolute Pure Vodka. Three terse lines of gobbledygook filler followed those three simple words.

"Oh, yes," Broman explained. "Pure vodka."

The conference-room table erupted in criticism. The bottles looked like those that hospitals use to store blood or plasma. It was unlikely the federal government would allow "pure vodka" to appear on packaging. It was like calling a Lincoln "the perfect car." Never would happen. Besides, the design, if you could even call it that, was too simple and too sterile, positively "un-American . . . like East Berlin." Seals, crests, and sonorous, sometimes folksy prose printed in elegant font on richly hued paper—that was what you slapped on spirits bottles, especially ones containing vodka. Russian-sounding words didn't hurt, either. Who would notice a bottle without a neck with barely any writing?

Broman started riffling through his slides. The criticism continued.

"You know," one executive said, "on the shelf, even if you put it up front, you'd see a Smirnoff label magnified right through it. And that name, Absolute Pure Vodka. It won't work."

"Smirnoff, yeah," another N. W. Ayer man chimed in. "You can't get around it. That's vodka. With a brand like that . . ."

"Smirnoff leaves you breathless."

"Unforgettable."

"A classic."

"Wrote their own rules."

Finally from the cacophony came a request: "Let's put the crest on it, for god's sake. We've got the lions and the crown, and that crest. Why can't you use the crest and do a real label?"

Broman seemed not to hear. He had, however, found the slide he wanted, and up it went, showing four of the most popular spirits brands in the United States then, including Smirnoff. They were exactly what the crowd had just called for to spruce up Broman's last idea: busy splashes of inviting busyness a consumer could never miss. "Well," he asked, "what do you see?"

No one said a word.

"When all others are screaming," Broman began, "then you must . . . ?"

He waited for them to finish his sentence, but, again, silence. Broman looked to Brindfors for help. Brindfors sighed—he was not as gregarious as his boss—and started the sentence anew. "When all . . . When all the others . . . When they shout . . . scream . . . you whisper."

His last words were drowned out by Jerry Siano, who spun around in his chair to face Broman. "You know what I'm thinking? I'm thinking the absolute Bloody Mary," N. W. Ayer's top creative mind said. "The absolute martini. The absolute Russian."

Broman got out of his intellectual way.

"Absolutely pure," Siano went on. "Absolutely clear. The absolute date. An absolute party. Absolutely . . . absolutely . . . anything!"

The same table that only a few minutes before had erupted in criticism of Broman's final idea—one it appeared he had been leading his audience toward all along—now poured forth their own spin on Siano's eureka moment. Broman stayed out of their ways, too.

"This is explosive stuff," Siano told the room as he stood. "And I love it. We just have to redo the bottle and change the name, and it will be perfect."

There was one more thing that had to happen, though Siano and any of the other Americans could be forgiven for not mentioning it: they needed an Absolute Pure Vodka to fill the bottles.

There was none at that point, only the vague promise from the Swedish government to create one should an export market open up. The N. W. Ayer meeting proved the watershed. Soon the Swedes had their bottle design: the same generally squat vessel with barely any neck, an apothecary bottle from the 1800s Broman saw in Stockholm's Old Town having inspired his original idea. As for the name, the N. W. Ayer people suggested dropping the e: Absolut. That would avoid any regulatory hassles and would also encourage consumers to linger over the bottle as their subconscious invariably tacked an e on the end. "Pure" was out, too, because it seemed to Siano to be redundant. It would just be "Absolut (Country of Sweden) Vodka" in blocky blue or red lettering, followed by "Imported" in similarly sized font and some cursive prose in between explaining the transparent liquid within. As for the transparency, that remained the salient feature of this new product. The lettering was directly on the bottle, as was a single seal near the cap depicting a bearded, bald man who looked not unlike Gunnar Broman. It was L. O. Smith, a nineteenth-century Swedish magnate who had very nearly cornered the kingdom's market on spirits. One of Smith's most popular products had been a cheap potato-based vodka called Absolut Rent Braennvin. Broman's original copy for the bottle mentioned this precursor, though eventually that would disappear as the prose was tightened and the transparency of the Absolut vodka bottle popped all the more starkly. It was like nothing in the American spirits marketplace and certainly different from every heraldry-heavy bottle of vodka out there. The Swedes lined up a small importer, Carillon out of northern New Jersey, and N. W. Ayer under Jerry Siano set about working on what would turn out to be one of the twentieth century's most effective advertising gambits.

That there was no actual Absolut vodka yet seemed immaterial. The marketing alone would pour it down Americans' throats.

FRONT-PAGE NEWS

1980 | Loretto, Kentucky

On August 1, 1980, a Friday, an article headlined MAKER'S MARK GOES AGAINST THE GRAIN TO MAKE ITS MARK appeared in the middle of the *Wall Street Journal*'s densely packed front page. It shared space with articles on the fast pace of inflation and President Jimmy Carter's reelection prospects (CONVENTION COULD BE BLOODY). In newspaper parlance, the article was top-of-the-fold, looming unmistakably out at the *Journal*'s more than two million readers from above the bend that creased the broadsheet for easy placement on newsstands and in newspaper boxes nationwide, not to mention in stacks inside office and hotel lobbies. The article's lead mimicked its headline: "LORETTO, KY—Maker's Mark Distillery has made its mark by going against the grain." From there, though, writer David P. Garino, a St. Louis–based staff reporter at the paper whose beats included the alcohol-beverage trades, wove a tale unlike any other that had appeared in a major American newspaper to date: that of a small, family-owned distillery in a town of perhaps one thousand souls sixty miles south of Louisville, Kentucky's largest city.

> In producing its premium Maker's Mark bourbon, [the distillery] continues to use an intricate six-year aging process and a small

bottling line that are models of inefficiency. It distills only 19 barrels of bourbon daily, compared with hundreds distilled by other
producers. Its ad budget is a meager $1.2 million a year.

But most remarkably, its volume has more than quadrupled, to
about 150,000 cases a year, the past 10 years, while the overall bourbon industry's sales have slipped 26%, to 23.7 million cases.

All the more remarkable, as the article went on to point out, was that
these higher sales came despite a higher price tag: Maker's Mark might retail
for $8.75 for a 750-milliliter bottle versus $5.75 for the much more widely
available Jim Beam bourbon. The higher price tag undoubtedly helped cover
the particular distilling process of Maker's Mark, which was more laborious
than those of its competitors. The distillery simmered the mashed-up grain
that served as the bourbon's base for four hours in cypress tanks. The industry
standard for simmering was a half hour. Maker's Mark bourbon also spent
six years aging before it was bottled, wending its way down the distillery's
six-floor warehouse, from warmer to cooler temperatures. Finally, Maker's
Mark's bottling line might handle forty bottles a minute compared with the
hundreds that competitors lines' filled during the same time, and quality
control was paramount, with inspectors using magnifying glasses to examine
the finished product for any imperfections.

Such smaller batches and production runs, as well as the exacting standards, contributed to an aura of exclusivity around Maker's Mark, one the
distillery was only too happy to cultivate for a growing legion of diehard
devotees, including ones in high places. Tim Lee Carter, a Kentucky con-
gressman, praised the drink as "that incomparable bourbon of bourbons"
during remarks on the US House floor. Even Cuban dictator Fidel Castro
was a fan. When the mayor of Frankfort, Kentucky's capital, visited Cuba
in 1978 on a tour that the National League of Cities arranged, Castro asked
him to send a bottle of Maker's Mark upon the mayor's return. (He never
did.) "For those who ask how good a whisky is. Rather than how much,"
read advertising copy for publications such as *Southern Living*, *Time*, and
Playboy. The approach, particularly the small-batch element of it, stood
out among bourbon producers in the United States in 1980, who generally
sought to scale up production, particularly if a brand proved popular. "If
we had it in our stable," a major distiller told the *Journal*'s Garino, "we'd
promote the hell out of it." Why Maker's Mark was not already doing that
seemed to baffle him. "Maybe they're happy doing what they're doing."

The Samuels clan still behind the bourbon brand born in 1953 was happy, to an extent. Sales were brisk, and Bill Samuels Sr.'s wheat-heavy recipe had proved a favorite among people who wanted to actually taste their bourbon rather than knock it back as quickly as possible. Zoom out, though, and Maker's Mark faced clear, almost existential challenges along with the rest of the bourbon industry. Simply put, fewer Americans were drinking the brownest of whiskeys—most ominously, fewer young people. The baby boomers who came up in the 1960s and 1970s eschewed the drink of their parents and grandparents in favor of other alcoholic options, particularly American fine wine from newer small-scale producers such as the Robert Mondavi Winery in Napa Valley and especially Russian vodka, or at least Russian-sounding vodka in the case of the bestselling Smirnoff brand out of Connecticut. That clear, sometimes flavorless drink very likely born in what was then the Soviet Union became America's bestselling spirit around its bicentennial year of 1976.

The bourbon industry did what it could to appeal to the younger drinkers that it needed to replace older customers. It tried traditional advertising, but that only seemed to accentuate the problem. Jim Beam ran an ad with saccharine songwriter Burt Bacharach and his father, Bert, holding tumblers of the bourbon next to the tagline, "Generation gap? We never heard of it." The man who penned "What's New, Pussycat?" was not going to be enough to reach the fans of Led Zeppelin and the Rolling Stones. The imagery of bourbon in general did not appeal to baby boomers as much as it did their forebears. It was so old-fashioned: the backwoods Kentucky roots, the ornate labels staring out from Mom and Dad's comfortable middle-class liquor cabinets, the advertisements in magazines such as the *New Yorker* that invariably showed a clean-cut man in a conventional suit enjoying his favorite brand just so—none of it gelled well with a looser, longer-haired popular culture. Frank Sinatra and his Vegas Rat Pack drank bourbon and other whiskey, the bourbon-like Jack Daniel's in particular, and they had been huge in the 1950s, an eternity ago. There was also that taste. It had been shadowing bourbon's fortunes since Prohibition, when all that iffy product spilled on to a thirsty market and firewater replaced any sense of finesse. Yet, by the late 1970s, the biggest bourbon brands in the United States, including Jim Beam and Four Roses, still used chalkier, spicier rye as the secondary grain after corn. Major whiskey brands, such as Jack Daniel's, also leaned heavily on rye. While its choice was not quite as exotic as it was three decades before, Maker's Mark remained an outlier because of the wheat.

This loss of consumers could very well have swatted the industry into irrelevance, if not oblivion. Bourbon often needed to age years, which meant that distillers needed to know there was an audience either there or about to come along to buy and consume it. Without that, forget it. Bourbon distillers would have to slash prices and hope for the best, not the soundest business strategy, and the results were predictable. The 1960s turned out to be the late twentieth-century zenith for bourbon. In 1970, according to one historian, the spirits industry sold nearly eighty-five million gallons. By 1983 that number would descend to fifty million, a drop of nearly 40 percent. Distillery warehouses brimmed with stock no distributors needed and fewer consumers wanted. The number of distilleries in Kentucky, which still produced most of the world's bourbon, dwindled from two dozen toward single digits. Not surprisingly, bourbon soon all but disappeared from the national palatal discourse. In 1964 Congress passed a resolution hailing bourbon as "a distinctive product of the United States"—the distinctive spirit of the nation, really—with a promise that "the appropriate agencies of the United States Government . . . will take appropriate action to prohibit the importation into the United States of whiskey designated as 'bourbon whiskey.'" At that high point, where a strong commercial performance intersected with unmistakable cultural cachet, bourbon had been like Champagne, that vaunted sparkling wine that by French law could only be produced in a certain region and made under certain conditions. By the end of the 1970s, bourbon was, according to bourbon historian Dale Huckelbridge, "a mere shadow of what it had once been."

And yet here was Bill Samuels's tiny operation in tiny Loretto in Kentucky's impossibly quiet, rolling bluegrass hills. The distillery had a capacity by the 1980s to produce about one thousand gallons daily. Jim Beam, the largest bourbon brand at the start of that decade, could produce forty thousand gallons in a day. Maker's Mark continued to adhere to strict traditional methods of distilling despite the prospect of greater sales should it wish to ramp up production. Finally, Maker's Mark still traveled more through word of mouth than through conventional marketing methods. Samuels, who conveyed modesty, even a surprised bemusement at the success of his signature bourbon, did advertise. From its earliest releases, Marker's Mark stared from the pages of widely read magazines, reaching eyeballs far beyond isolated Loretto with unabashed prose extolling how expensive and therefore exclusive Maker's Mark was compared with other bourbons. Also, Maker's Mark became one of the first distilleries nationally to place its wares on commercial airlines, beginning with American in 1961. (Samuels knew longtime American CEO

C. R. Smith.) Samuels recognized the potential that the dawn of widespread air travel offered: a trapped audience at thirty thousand feet, willing to perhaps pay a bit more for a tiny bottle of bourbon they might enjoy and then tell their friends, family, or—even better—business colleagues about.

Sales by the 1980s were growing about 8 percent yearly and, while the distillery was by no means some sort of cash cow, it was not struggling, either. Annual sales were on their way to more than $10 million, enough to keep Maker's Mark independent. Contrast this with the fate of Stitzel-Weller, the distillery in Shively that Samuels's friend Julian "Pappy" Van Winkle Sr. cofounded and ran until his death in 1965. The bourbon crash at the end of the 1960s doomed his heirs' control of the company. Norton-Simon, a Los Angeles–based conglomerate formed through a 1968 merger of Hunts Foods, the Canada Dry Corporation, and McCall's Publishing, bought out the Van Winkles in 1972 for an undisclosed sum. Stitzel-Weller was one of the lucky ones: Approximately ten Kentucky bourbon makers disappeared altogether. Others were marginalized beyond recognition. The Four Roses distillery in Lawrenceburg, Kentucky, a half-hour's drive west of Lexington, dated from 1910 and may very well have been the bestselling bourbon in the United States from the 1930s through the 1950s. (The privately held distilleries could be cagey about their sales figures.) Seagram acquired Four Roses in 1943, during that hangover from Prohibition and the restrictions that the necessities of World War II visited upon the industry. The Canadian drinks juggernaut already had a sizable whiskey portfolio, so it gradually relegated Four Roses to the cheaper end of the sales spectrum and then, finally, largely out of the United States altogether. The nation's once-top bourbon became a staple instead of European and Japanese bars and stores.

It was Pappy Van Winkle who served Bill Samuels's son and namesake his first bourbon. It was 1951, and Bill Samuels Jr. was eleven. He was accompanying his father, then in the planning stages of his distillery, to a business lunch with Van Winkle at Stitzel-Weller. There was one thing, though, before the repast could get underway. "We don't go to lunch until after two fingers," Van Winkle said with a smile. He poured his baffled young charge the height equivalent of two male digits. Bill Jr. did not know how to drink bourbon, despite, like his father and other forebears, having grown up around the stuff. Taking the tumbler, he downed the bourbon in one single, searing gulp.

That was the younger Samuels's initiation into bourbon. His initiation into the business of bourbon came much less suddenly. Samuels Jr. worked odd jobs at the Loretto distillery until college at Case Western Reserve and the University of California at Berkeley, where he also earned a master's in engineering. Eschewing the family business, Samuels instead plunged into work for the Aerojet Corporation out of Sacramento, California, on missiles such as the Polaris nuclear ones. His career as an aerospace engineer proved short-lived, however, as a motor prototype Samuels spearheaded failed spectacularly. The motor broke loose from a test rocket, wreaking damage all around it, and soon Samuels was on the phone with his father, looking for work at Maker's Mark. Bill Sr. did not want him, at least not at first. "You need to go to law school or business school and get un-engineered," the elder Samuels told his son. In 1964 the younger Samuels enrolled at Vanderbilt Law School in Nashville, in the heart of Tennessee whiskey country.

Tennessee whiskey is a close cousin of Kentucky-born bourbon, relying as much on corn as the primary grain. Few brands embodied Tennessee whiskey better than Jack Daniel's, which had its main sales office near the law school. Hap Motlow, one of Jack Daniel's grandnephews, worked at the sales office. (The distillery's namesake died in 1911, from a foot infection sustained after kicking an office safe he could not remember the combination to.) Motlow had advised Bill Samuels Sr. as he developed Maker's Mark, both the distillery and the recipe for its signature bourbon. He quickly took the younger Samuels under his wing, teaching the novice about the spirits business as well as executing more mundane godfatherly things such as scoring Samuels and his friends tickets to college football games. In his second year of law school, when it looked like he might finally pivot toward bourbon full-time, Samuels instead found himself an intern in Washington on the recommendation of Kentucky senator John Sherman Cooper and working on patent law at the Commerce Department. After that summer, Samuels finished law school and got a job with a disc brake manufacturer in southern Indiana. He called to give his mentor Hap Motlow the good news.

"Bill, we've got a problem," Motlow responded. "You're going to have to call them and tell them no. I've looked after your ass for the past three years and you are going to go work for your dad for a year and then take the bar, just in case."

The work awaiting the younger Samuels in Loretto was unfamiliar—alien, even, considering his training in both engineering and now patent law. "Your job," his father told him, "is to go out and find customers." All Samuels Jr. could think was that he should have gone to business school in that case. The bourbon industry appeared to be in its death throes, its uneven quality and that big generational shift in drinking habits catching up with it. Perhaps in the late 1950s finding more customers would not have been a difficult task. In the late 1960s, it seemed perfectly Herculean. Bourbon appeared to be irredeemably on the decline, vodka and then fine wine on the ascent. And yet, there was Maker's Mark, its sales always modest but steadily growing, its advertising selective, its initiates still mostly through word of mouth, and its price premium versus other brands. To the elder Samuels, the product was the thing: a better-tasting, smoother drink would draw, and was drawing, new customers. It looked like the younger Samuels, thrust into the unfamiliar role of salesman, did not face that formidable a task after all. His father's emphasis on quality control conjured up memories of one of his first, albeit unpaid jobs outside of the family outfit. When he was sixteen, Samuels Jr. found himself the chauffeur and de facto gopher for Harland Sanders, an honorary Kentucky colonel and an elderly friend of his parents' who was then turning his fried chicken business, started from a roadside gas station stand in 1930, into a fast-food chain. On an early visit to one of the first Kentucky Fried Chicken outposts, Samuels watched Sanders scream at staff and rip a deep fryer out of the wall. The staff's infraction? Screwing up the colonel's fried chicken recipe.

"Was that really necessary?" Samuels asked Sanders when they got back to the car.

"Yes," Sanders replied calmly. "Because now I know that I'll never have to do it again."

Such devotion to quality control and consistency would, of course, make Kentucky Fried Chicken the largest chicken-selling fast-food chain on Earth and Colonel Sanders a national icon. That devotion also appeared to be sustaining Maker's Mark through bourbon's long twilight. Regardless, the writing was clearly on the wall: overall bourbon sales were declining, the industry was losing customers and not adding new ones, and distilleries were closing. Maker's Mark had not made a profit until 1967, and only in the late 1970s would it wipe away debt tied to its launch in the early 1950s. Most of its customers still came from Kentucky, moreover, with the number of retail accounts so small (fifty-four) and close by that Bill Sr. could visit nearly half of them in a single day. Could the distillery sustain itself much longer that way? The answer, as both father and son saw it, was clearly no.

Bill Samuels Jr. became president and CEO of the distillery in 1975 and soon set about extending its reputation beyond the Bluegrass State. To that end, he hired Doe-Anderson, a public relations and advertising firm in Louisville. Together they set about creating a campaign that emphasized what Bill Samuels Sr. had been doing from the beginning: crafting small batches of uniquely made bourbon, packaging them in equally unique bottles, and selling them without too much fuss or fanfare. To get around Samuels's

Bill Samuels Sr. and his son, Bill Jr., in the early 1970s in front of busts of their forebears.
MAKER'S MARK

reticence toward overt marketing, the campaign his son and Doe-Anderson devised centered around material that talked up the craftsmanship aspect, the idea that a consumer would discover Maker's Mark because a friend, a colleague, or a relative had recommended it. The campaign would be not splashy or flashy but rather homespun, almost defiantly so. The approach strayed not all that far from Bill Samuels Sr.'s original conceit built around the "It tastes expensive . . . and is" ads. This was a bourbon made differently and in a different place. A magazine ad from 1975 quoted Winston Churchill in blocky, bold letters: "My tastes are very simple. I only want the very best of everything." A May 1979 article in the *Globe and Mail*, one of Canada's largest newspapers, described Maker's Mark bourbon as "an aristocrat among liquors. The distillery brags that it tastes expensive and that it is expensive." And, as the Toronto-based broadsheet explained, while other bourbon brands started at $4.40 a quart, the same amount of Maker's Mark retailed for about $9.50. One could buy a half pint for around $2.50. Moreover, Maker's Mark was small, the "smallest (legal) U.S. still house, and the only distillery listed in the National Register of Historic Places." The biggest marketing push Bill Samuels Sr. had ever allowed was opening up the Loretto distillery to tours in 1968. Here was his son partnering with an advertising and PR firm to push the brand beyond not only Kentucky's borders but also America's. It seemed only a matter of time before the marketing push scored a particularly big coup.

That arrived in the spring of 1980. Bill Samuels Jr. had a friend named Sam Walker, who had attended journalism school at the University of Missouri in Columbia with the *Wall Street Journal*'s David Garino. Walker also knew Garino's editor, who mentioned that Garino would be in Louisville to report on the annual meeting of insurance giant Humana, which was based in the city. Walker informed Samuels of Garino's imminent arrival, and the CEO of Maker's Mark hatched a plan worthy of an early John le Carré thriller.

The National Park Service had recently named Maker's Mark to the National Register of Historic Places, a first for a distillery. Samuels arranged a party in Loretto to celebrate the designation, and he gave a local news channel exclusive rights to cover it—thereby ensuring coverage of an event that might have been passed over were it not cloaked in the media catnip of exclusivity. He also asked Sam Walker to contact his old classmate Garino and arrange drinks at the Brown Hotel in downtown Louisville, where Garino happened to be staying. Samuels knew the bartender who would be working that evening, and he asked him to turn all of the bar's televisions to the news program carrying coverage of the Maker's Mark celebration. The bartender obliged. There, then, were Garino and Walker, watching an event celebrating the national recognition of this tiny distillery. Garino asked Walker what all the fuss was about. Even though he was a reporter whose beat included Kentucky, he had never heard of Maker's Mark. Walker offered to introduce him to Bill Samuels Jr.

For Samuels, and his marketing agency Doe-Andersen, the ruse to lure Garino and the *Journal* was a risk. Bill Samuels Sr. detested such naked peddling. He wanted consumers to discover his product through word of mouth, and supported his son's approach of talking up the craftsmanship aspect in the current marketing campaign. Simply inviting coverage seemed desperate, if not crass. It could also upend the hard-won exclusivity surrounding Maker's Mark. There was no guarantee the elder Samuels would even meet with Garino, which seemed necessary for any article to work. Still, this was the *Wall Street Journal*, which, along with the *New York Times* and perhaps the *Washington Post*, was one of the nation's agenda-setting newspapers in an era just before twenty-four-hour cable news and more than a decade before the birth of the World Wide Web. Bill Samuels Jr. went for it. As added insurance against his father's reticence, he told him that Garino was an old fraternity brother in town and curious about the distillery. Would Bill Sr. show him around?

He would be happy to. What commenced in Loretto was a meeting of the minds that had a profound effect on the American small-batch spirits movement ever after. Garino seemed to understand exactly what Bill Sr. was going for—the small-batch production, the word-of-mouth marketing, the emphasis on locality and quality—and the pair spent two and half days touring, talking, and tasting. Bill Jr.'s setup appeared to have worked, and his father was not even that upset when he ultimately found out he had shown a reporter around the business rather than the trumped-up fraternity brother. Months passed, and then in the twilight of summer the front-page article dropped like a thunderclap. By 8:15 on that Friday morning, Maker's Mark had added three phone lines to its previous one, and Bill Jr.'s two younger sisters were enlisted to help answer calls of both curiosity and consumption. People wanted to know about and to buy this bourbon they had read about in the earliest edition of the *Wall Street Journal*. The distillery received twenty-five thousand letters in the weeks afterward, and then twenty-five thousand more. It sold out of its available stock and therefore found itself confronting a happy problem: it would take years to age more bourbon to slake this explosion in demand. In the meantime, Maker's Mark under Bill Jr.'s direction set about setting expectations for its new customers. He and his father answered each letter that came in, and the distillery continued to field every phone call it could. There would be thousands before the aftershocks ceased. Maker's Mark also took out advertisements, including a full-page one in the *Journal* soon after the article, explaining that it may be a while before particular areas of the nation beyond Kentucky got their wax-tipped bourbon bottles. Here was the word of mouth that Bill Samuels Sr. always knew could drive his brand. And he and his distillery did what they could to keep the conversation alive. What Maker's Mark did not do was ramp up its production. Instead, it stuck with the same ingredients and processes to produce the same amount as before, roughly 150,000 cases annually. This small-batch approach was "terribly labor intensive," according to Sam K. Cecil, Maker's Mark's vice president of production and one of fifty employees. But it was working.

In the end, the consumers would come to Maker's Mark, money in hand, expectations in mind—not the other way around. It was the fruits of a strategy spawned nearly a generation ago, one that seemed to ensure the speedy demise of America's smallest distiller. Instead it presented subsequent small-batch producers a kind of third way, one palatable even to Bill Samuels Sr., who detested conventional marketing almost as much as he had detested conventional bourbon. As the chairman of a competing distillery would tell

David Garino, "Bill Samuels started from scratch and established a brand of superior quality with a fine image. It's a textbook case of superior marketing."

Whether the magic—and luck—of Maker's Mark came in time to save bourbon as a whole remained to be seen in the new decade. A month and a day after the *Wall Street Journal*'s front-page trumpet blared, the *Los Angeles Times*, then the nation's second-biggest daily, published another article on bourbon, which several other newspapers picked up through the *Times*' formidable wire service and which therefore reached many more readers than the *Journal*'s piece. The lead got right to the grim point, one nobody in America making bourbon, or whiskey in general, could step entirely around:

> The sales line on bourbon whiskey over the last decade or so slopes downward as sharply as a ski run in the Alps. The chart on the slide in high-proof products is almost as steep. Over that period the country has shown such a decided preference for white and light beverages that the old two-fisted drinker has become a curiosity.

THE HITCHHIKER'S GUIDE TO COGNAC

1964–1981 | Cognac, France—Ukiah, California

Ansley Coale had had his doubts about hitchhikers ever since one pulled a gun on him. There was something, though, about the pair on the side of the road now, and he slowed his slate-gray Peugeot 504 to the shoulder of the southbound lanes of Highway 101, just inside California's border with Oregon. It was mid-August 1981.

"I can't believe I'm doing this," Coale thought, as the hitchhikers, a man and a woman, climbed into the car and he rejoined the traffic.

Hubert and Carole Germain-Robin were a married couple from western France. They were picking their way down the West Coast from Canada, toward Mexico and, ultimately, South America. The journey was one of self-discovery for Hubert in particular, as he explained to Coale, a former professor of ancient history at the University of California at Berkeley. The tall, shaggy-haired, bearded Hubert's family had produced Cognac, that great French spirit distilled from grapes, since 1782, making him the ninth generation in the family to learn the trade. The trade was changing, however, as he also explained. Jules Robin & Cie, the family firm, also based in western France, near the city of Cognac itself, had pioneered the bottling of Cognac, rather than the traditional way of selling it in or from casks. This had allowed Jules Robin to not only move its wares farther and wider but also develop special labels, a practice that became ubiquitous among Cognac producers. Then World War II came. The shock of invasion and occupation crippled much of the French distilling and winemaking industries. Although it survived, Jules Robin was never the same following Germany's defeat in 1945. When the firm lost access to the Chinese market later that decade, after the Communists took Beijing, the clock started ticking on its financial viability. Rapid industrial consolidation was the order of the postwar day, whatever the industry: beer, home goods, radio stations, soda pop, even Cognac made for centuries in small batches using traditional methods and grapes grown nearby. In 1964 one of what would come to be called the Big Four of Cognac producers, Martell, bought Jules Robin from an adolescent Germain-Robin's father.

The deal did not dissuade the son from staying in the trade, though at first that life path seemed unlikely. Born and raised near Cognac—and, from age ten onward, in the city itself—Germain-Robin spent his teenage years after the Martell deal toiling on the fringes of Cognac production just to earn some spending money. He painted hoops on the barrels used for aging, for instance, or worked on bottling lines. He had never understood the fuss surrounding the techniques and the culture of the russet-colored, slightly sweet drink that fell within the brandy family of spirits. Besides, he found it too strong to enjoy. This indifference ended shortly after his twentieth birthday, when Germain-Robin enrolled in a distillation course through the Bureau National Interprofessionnel du Cognac, a state school dedicated to just what its name implied. A particularly good teacher there kindled an interest within Germain-Robin—and, even better, landed him a post-school job at a distillery where the distiller had just died.

It was an auspicious time to be getting into Cognac. The consolidation into the Big Four—actually, into the Big Two first, just Martell and Hennessy, and then the others by the mid-1970s—spurred the biggest production boom in nearly a century, as did government support. The late 1960s marked the start of a sort of golden age of Cognac.

Produced in the neighboring Charente and Charente-Maritime regions of France, which include the city that gave the drink its name, Cognac had been popular in France, and with French governments, since at least the Middle

Ages. The regions that would become the hub of the international Cognac trade were also a hub of the international salt trade before that. The export system, via the Atlantic Ocean–connected Charente River, was already in place when more and more people outside the country began to appreciate the quality of the brandies born in the chalky soil of that particular part of France. Like the wines of the Bordeaux region to the south, the grape-based brandies of Charente and Charente-Maritime were by the eighteenth century recognized as the world leader in their libationary niche. (Some brandies, such as grappa, are made from grape by-products such as stems and seeds.) This recognition drove an important development over the next two hundred years, one vital to distilleries' bottom lines: France's Cognacs became protected foodstuffs akin to the sparkling wine from the nation's Champagne region. In order for a brandy to call itself Cognac, it had to originate in Charente and Charente-Maritime; come primarily from the Ugni Blanc grape, known locally as Saint-Emilion des Charentes and better known in the United States as Trebbiano, after the Italian name; be distilled twice in certain ways in pot stills; age for specific amounts of time; and contain no more than 2 percent cane sugar syrup (if any at all) and caramel only for coloring, not flavoring (again, if at all). Such labyrinthine regulations might seem officious, but France did not pick them accidentally.

The mid-nineteenth century had been the previous golden age of Cognac. Relative peace in Europe following the Napoleonic Wars, as well as reductions in British tariffs and the opening of markets such as Russia and much of freshly independent Latin America, meant that Cognac producers "could hardly produce enough Cognac to satisfy the demand." Then, in the 1870s, a vine-munching bug called phylloxera struck Charente, Charente-Maritime, and most of France, devastating a vast amount of vineyards and grinding Cognac production nearly to a halt. Only after American vines were grafted onto French ones to strengthen them did grape-growing levels, around Cognac and elsewhere, start to tick upward. That took years, followed by more years for production and aging. In the interim, unscrupulous distillers, especially in Italy and Germany, started passing off poorly made brandies as Cognacs. Spanish distillers ginned up Coniac and Russian ones Koniak to confuse consumers into thinking they were merely buying some variation of the great French brandy from the great French brandy-making regions. Some of these counterfeit Cognacs were not even made from grapes. Other ingredients might, to say the least, be a little iffy: fake Cognacs produced in South and Central America used shoe leather to darken the drink to make it look like the real deal. The shortcuts were hurting the brand—and the business in

Charente and Charente-Maritime. Producers and traders there had depleted their stocks from that pre-phylloxera golden age, and they needed help.

The French government stepped in forcefully, much as the US government had with bourbon and whiskey around the same time. In 1909 national legislation swept away a bulk of the counterfeits and the imitators by decreeing that to call itself Cognac, a brandy had to come from certain areas of Charente and Charente-Maritime. This added Cognac to France's Appellation d'origine contrôlée, a legendary system created the previous century to rescue the nation's premier winemakers and winemaking regions from their own set of counterfeiters that the phylloxera blight had emboldened. The AOC system basically guaranteed that the label matched the contents: if a bottle said it was Cognac from Charente, then it contained Cognac from Charente. A decade after the original legislation, the government made it a crime to pretend otherwise. Other laws of the period further strengthened Cognac's protected status, including ones requiring producers to register their stills, called alembics, and to declare each year in advance the amount of Ugni Blanc grapes they planned to harvest.

The world wars, beginning with the first in August 1914, offset much of the gains from these hard-won protections, as did Prohibition in the United States from 1920 to 1933. The latter meant the loss of a market that accounted for some 2.5 million bottles of Cognac annually. The wars also meant the loss of thousands of Cognac workers to Europe's grimly efficient armies. Around one-quarter of the farmhands in Charente and Charente-Maritime were killed in the First World War, for instance. By the time the Germans swept into France in May 1940 during the Second World War, the Charente River Valley was still in recovery mode, shaking off the deleterious effects of the first conflict and trying to marshal its production to capitalize on the stronger protections. Most of those efforts, though, ended up satisfying German demands. The occupiers not only skimmed money from any Cognac trading still going on after early 1940 but also simply took millions of bottles for themselves—around twenty million bottles total during the war. At one point, the Germans laid claim to one-third of all Cognac production. It was only through the quiet efforts of a German officer named Gustav Klaebisch that there was a sufficient supply left to kick off that postwar golden age. Klaebisch, who had grown up in the region when his father ran a Cognac trading house before World War I and who later worked as a Cognac importer in pre–World War II Germany, capped how much Cognac various German military units could take. Individual distilleries and wholesalers did their bit by conveniently running out of supplies such as cork and labels when it came to filling German orders.

By the end of the second war, in 1945, the table was set and the Cognac industry was off to the races. The government allowed the planting of thousands more acres of Ugni Blanc and crucially backed the classification of Cognac as an industrial product, rather than an agricultural one, under the rules of what would become the European Union. This allowed Cognac producers to take advantage of looser regulations for industry within much of Europe, opening up more markets and faster. Shipments bounced from 30 million bottles in 1945 to 120 million in the early 1970s. Nearly 120,000 more acres of Charente and Charente-Maritime were turned over to Cognac production during the same period, often with enthusiastic government support. The Middle-East oil embargo of the early 1970s, as well as trade tiffs with the United States through much of the decade, would do little to slow this growth. It truly was the new golden age, indeed the brightest one yet, for the world's premier brandy.

Hubert Germain-Robin was right, then, to plunge in. Yet, what he found upon his immersion bothered him. The consolidation that spawned the Big Four meant that "cognac, already a globally known product, was thus well on its way to becoming a largely internationally owned one as well," according to one analyst. Production might still pivot on Charente and Charente-Maritime—it had to, under French law—but conglomerates for which Cognac was often just another line in the spreadsheet set and managed this production. Size counted. Companies devoured companies. Martell, for instance, bought Jules Robin; Seagram bought Martell; and Pernod Ricard and Diageo eventually split up Seagram. Scaling up to slake demand became the order of the day in the 1970s, and that scaling up meant the near end of Cognac distilling as generations had understood it, including those generations in Germain-Robin's family. For one thing, whereas alembics stills would be hand-operated in the olden days, they were now electrified. For another, those same French laws that ballasted the industry at the start of the twentieth century hamstrung most attempts at innovation toward the century's end, in particular which grapes distillers could use. More than anything, though, it was that frenetic growth, and the focus on more of the same, that bothered Germain-Robin. He saw a way of doing things, an entire way of life, disappearing. So, just past thirty, he set out with Carole for the New World for some soul searching, first across Canada and then down into the United States, by then the world's biggest Cognac market outside of France itself. Only through pure chance did they run into Ansley Coale, himself nearing forty. It was not unusual, however, for Coale to be driving north on Highway 101.

Coale grew up in northern New Jersey the son of his namesake, a giant in the field of demographics. Ansley Sr. directed Princeton University's Office of Population Research for seventeen years, a position that took him around the world as he advised various governments, as well as the United Nations, about population shifts and growth. Coale Jr. followed his father to college at Princeton and then on to the University of Michigan in Ann Arbor, where he studied ancient Greek and Roman history, earning his doctorate and then heading westward in 1971, to the University of California at Berkeley, at the height of its countercultural cacophony. There he taught ancient history but soon tired of the faculty politics. In 1973 he bought an old two-thousand-acre sheep ranch about two hours' drive north of Berkeley in Ukiah, a town of barely ten thousand residents in what was then a largely remote and rugged Mendocino County. The ranch was more than eleven hundred feet above sea level and accessible only via a heavily forested, pothole-riddled, one-lane road. Coale, who wore wire-rimmed glasses, kept his hair closely cropped, and sported a mustache shaped like an inverted V, paid $200,000 for the acreage, although he was not sure what he would do with the place besides use it as a retreat from Berkeley. He left the university in 1975 and moved to Africa with his wife, who was working in public health for the UN aid organization UNESCO. When they returned to the Bay Area, Coale started buying and fixing up old houses in the region. This work clarified his plans for the Mendocino County land. For one thing, he made enough money to move there, which he and his wife did. They also had enough money banked, around $35,000, to perhaps start planting wine grapes. The California wine industry was itself entering a golden age, and the prospects for success, even beyond the storied Napa Valley to the southeast, seemed solid. Coale sold what turned out to be his last renovated house in 1981 and set out on his wine-grape path.

Into that path stepped Germain-Robin. Coale offered to put the tired hitch-hikers up for the night. As they drove to the old ranch in Ukiah, the distiller told the ex-academic of the changes back home in Cognac, of how giant conglomerates were hounding the craft of largely handmade, small-batch brandy distillation out of existence, of how French laws meant to boost the industry were instead now stifling innovation just as more and more people learned of the pleasures and joys of Cognac. Mostly—and this is what Coale heard more than what Germain-Robin actually told him—the younger man spoke of his own desire to perhaps turn back the clock on all of this, stand athwart the change, and save Cognac from its own success. The thought then struck Coale hard: "This will be six times more interesting than planting a vineyard."

FRESH FRUIT IN THE "ROTTENEST CITY"

1981–1982 | Emeryville, California

Luckily for Jörg Rupf, Emeryville was the "rottenest city on the Pacific coast." Those were the words of Earl Warren in 1927, then the exasperated district attorney of Alameda County, which contained Emeryville, and later a governor of California and then chief justice of the United States for sixteen years. The small city between Berkeley and Oakland had for decades liberally adjusted its boundaries to keep out churches and other sobering institutions in order to make the Prohibition-enhanced bordellos, gambling parlors, and saloons that dotted its streetscape feel more comfortable, or at least less guilty. Along the way, Emeryville had developed a reputation as a rather lax place, a reputation that carried into the late twentieth century and into the way the city of barely four thousand residents conducted itself. When Rupf, then, was looking at the turn of the 1970s at where he might start a small distillery, Emeryville cried out to him. He had studied at Berkeley, spent time in San Francisco and Oakland, but they would not do for what he had in mind.

Rupf had reluctantly returned to West Germany in 1978 to present the research he had done through the University of California on the relationship between government and the arts. He knew as he flew home that he would be back. For one thing, he had fallen in love with a concert pianist, whom he would marry. He himself played the violin and nearly followed it as a career path before pivoting toward the law. Another reason was that he simply could not stomach the life he had set up for himself in Europe, however enviable it might seem on paper: barely past thirty, already a judge and a lawyer, a noted scholar now, too. He wanted to try something else and that something else, improbably, was distilling fruit into what had come to be called, quite literally, "water of life"—eau-de-vie. He started doing so in earnest in 1981 and obtained a federal distillery license in January 1982.

Rupf dubbed the new operation St. George, after the patron saint of his hometown of Freiburg in southwestern West Germany, where it was a common after-dinner drink and one with roots in at least the Middle Ages. In

America, it was novel stuff. Rupf knew that—he knew he would very likely be the only person distilling eau-de-vie. With that knowledge naturally came the further realization that there would likely be no market for his wares. Unlike native bourbon, or the brownish scope of other whiskeys, domestic or imported, or mighty vodka in all its crystal-clear sales ascendancy, eau-de-vie was simply not that much of a presence, certainly not a force, in America's spirits marketplace. Beyond this lack of familiarity, Rupf faced other challenges. California did not allow distillers to self-distribute or to sell their products directly to consumers from the distillery. Brewers, including the earliest craft brewers such as the Anchor Brewing Company in San Francisco, were allowed to self-distribute. Anchor's owner, Fritz Maytag, early on simply loaded up a truck with kegs, and later bottles, and drove them around to accounts in the Bay Area. The newer crop of winemakers specializing in fine wines, including Robert Mondavi, were able to tap into a decades-old network of distributors, some of which had continued operating legally right through Prohibition. Some of the smallest wineries even operated on an honor system, leaving bottles in designated spots for consumers to then replace with cash. Distribution, while sometimes a hassle, was never as much of a hurdle for California's tinier winemakers and brewers as it was and would be for the state's craft distillers.

Much of this resistance to self-distribution for distillers, and to new distilleries themselves, was a vestige of Prohibition. The black market that the thirteen-year ban spawned, as well as the dangerous product its underground vendors sometimes traded in, including homemade spirits that caused serious physical harm such as blindness, understandably spooked government officials and elected leaders at all levels. The working conceit for regulation, then, was containment. Distillers could operate, but they had to swim in certain channels, and only in those channels, if they hoped to reach the public. Rupf confronted this early on with, of all government entities, the Alameda Fire Department. It worried that a distillery might explode. Had not backwoods stills blown up during Prohibition? Distillation created tremendous pressure within stills. If not properly released, the pressure could release itself in a tremendous explosion. As it turned out, Rupf got his permit from the City of Emeryville for a fifty-dollar fee, and the building inspector the city sent barely slowed down for an inspection. Fortuitously for Rupf as well was a major legal tweak to that landmark 1897 Bottled-in-Bond Act, which sought to thwart production of dodgy or inferior spirits, particularly faux bourbon. One of its provisions required distillers to provide lodging for a Treasury Department agent, who would monitor who came and went from a distillery warehouse, including owners and employees, and who opened and closed the distillery on workdays. This was to ensure no one tampered with the goods, either to speed production or to avoid taxes based on volume. It was also quite onerous and virtually prohibited a tiny producer such as Jörg Rupf from ever starting up because of the costs of lodging the agent. The federal government removed the agent requirement, effective January 1980, during an era that also saw the legalization of homebrewing at the federal level and several states enacting legislation to allow so-called farm wineries so grape growers could sell wines they made directly to consumers.

Jörg Rupf with St. George's earliest still.
JÖRG RUPF

Had the city inspector slowed down or had Rupf been required to put up a federal agent, there would not have been much to inspect nor to patrol. For around $300 a month, Rupf rented part of a wooden building by some defunct railroad tracks. One of the myriad wineries that had started in the wake of 1976's Judgment of Paris rented the rest of the building. To Rupf, that operation looked like nothing more than a glorified home-wine-making setup. The winemakers might have thought the same about their neighbor. Rupf worked with a four-thousand-gallon fermentation tank left over from another winery that had occupied his leased space before. There he fermented the fruit juice, the first step in making eau-de-vie. He then distilled it in a sixty-six-gallon Holstein still he had acquired secondhand from Europe. He used pears for his first batches, buying a truckload of some twenty tons at a time and using about thirty pounds of fruit for each 500-milliliter bottle. He would eventually switch to 750-milliliter bottles, not unlike the ones many newer wineries started using exclusively, after new federal guidelines in January 1979 designated six metric sizes for wine and spirits. All of this—the twenty tons, the thirty pounds per bottle, the fermentation, and the distillation—translated into roughly thirteen hundred bottles at a time or a little more than one hundred twelve-bottle cases. These bottles Rupf filled in the building's shared basement. He started selling the first ones in the fall of 1982 through a small distributor in San Francisco that specialized in foreign imports—no domestic-heavy distributor would be interested in such small numbers. Rupf produced around 150 cases in 1982 and sold about 40 of them at around twenty dollars a bottle. (Unlike other spirits, especially whiskeys, eau-de-vie does not benefit from aging.) He priced against imports as there were no American-made eaux-de-vie to compare with. His own sales pitch, when he would visit individual restaurant and bar owners, was short and to the point—and positively alien. Delivered in a clipped German accent, his English enunciated better than that of many Americans, the bearded, bespectacled Rupf, looking every bit the cloistered academic he might have become in another life, would reference brandy. Restaurateurs in the Bay Area seemed to know that great spirit based on distilled wine.

"I am from Europe and this is a very common after-dinner drink," he would say. "It's a little different from the brandies that you know and it's not like schnapps." Schnapps was a German-born fruit brandy, usually sweetened with sugar—lots of sugar, when it came to the American market. Eau-de-vie was fruit juice distilled by itself, no sugar added, as Rupf would point out. "It's pure distilled spirits where you can taste and smell the aromatics of the pure fruit."

He tried to sell St. George eau-de-vie on quality and purity, in other words. No gimmicks, no flash—early St. George labels were unadorned beyond the name of the distillery, its location, and a brief description of the contents within. The pitches often did not work, and distribution would remain severely limited in those early years. Thankfully for Rupf, he was not dependent financially on the distillery, nor did he start St. George to make money, necessarily. In its first full year of operation, 1983, the distillery sold perhaps one hundred cases, respectable enough to continue. Though had Rupf known the odds then stacking up against him as he worked alone near the old, unused railroad tracks in perhaps the Bay Area's grittiest locale, he might have reconsidered the law back in West Germany or even the violin in San Francisco.

For one thing, consumption rates for spirits, domestically made or otherwise, were peaking. Simply put, Americans were drinking less eau-de-vie, whiskey, Cognac, etc. Even the rapid ascendancy of vodka could not stem the tide of steady decline—it was the new king of a declining market. Some of this could be traced to the drop in the popularity of bourbon, and of whiskey in general, due to old fans literally dying off and their children and grandchildren unwilling to take their place. A lot of it, too, could be laid at the feet of an American wine industry invigorated by the success of the Judgment of Paris and of the smaller start-ups in California and a handful of other places. Every major American newspaper, and many smaller ones, by the early 1980s had a wine critic, either full- or part-time. No one was filling such a role for spirits, or beer for that matter; or, if they were from time to time, it was usually a moonlighting wine critic. Whatever the reason—and it may have been nothing more exciting than that younger Americans did not like what their immediate forebears liked—post-Prohibition spirits consumption peaked in 1978. Estimates showed that Americans drank an average of between just over one gallon to around three gallons of spirits that year. The number would shrink toward a half gallon in the middle of the next decade.

The very start of that decade would offer a brawny sign of where Americans' drinking habits were headed. Craig Goldwyn was the wine critic for the *Chicago Tribune* and later the *Washington Post*. In the spring of 1980, Goldwyn and the *Tribune* hosted what came to be called the Great Chardonnay Showdown. Twenty-five expert tasters in crisp white jackets at five V-shaped folding tables in an airy, old wine warehouse in downtown Chicago tasted 221 Chardonnay wines blindly as similarly attired volunteers from local culinary schools sluiced about them, refilling and replacing glasses. The competing wines were all selected from Chicago-area shelves, a feat that itself showcased the remarkable growth of fine wine in just the last few years. A consumer would have been hard-pressed to find that many Chardonnays in 1975, even in one of the nation's largest metropolitan regions. In 1980 Chardonnay appeared to be everywhere. Wines from nations as diffuse as Australia, Bulgaria, and France were represented at the Great Chardonnay Showdown. It was one from the United States, however, that took top honors: a Chardonnay from Grgich Hills Cellar, a three-year-old Napa Valley operation cofounded by Mike Grgich, the same winemaker who crafted the winning white in the Judgment of Paris.

The explosive pace of the births of wineries such as Grgich Hills continued unabated in the years following that event, as did the cultivation of acres of Chardonnay grapes. In 1976, the year of the Paris tasting, Chardonnay was not even among the top five most-grown grape varieties in California. After 1976 it was well on its way to being far and away the most planted fine wine grape in America's premier grape-growing state. White wine in all its iterations, Chardonnay being the most prominent, would dominate American drinking habits in the 1980s. This would be the decade of breezy, sweet, lightish-hued wines and wine products. "Everyone's buying white table wine," Joe Columbe told the *New York Times* during the 1980 holiday season. Columbe was the founder and namesake of a Southern California liquor store chain called Trader Joe's that would diversify into other foodstuffs as spirits sales continued to nosedive. "Sales of distilled spirits have been flat for a number of years, but I've never before seen such a dramatic shift out of spirits and into wine as this season." Some analysts were saying that 1980 would be the first year in American history that the number of gallons of wine shipped would exceed that of spirits. This seismic shift was manifested in all sorts of ways no one could have foreseen even ten years before. White Zinfandel, for instance, a juicy, sugary spin on the classic grape that Napa Valley's Sutter Home introduced in 1975, would be the nation's most popular wine style, fine or otherwise, by the mid-1980s, spawning even boxed imitators. Wine coolers, lower-alcohol wine punches first introduced by a Stockton, California, outfit called California Cooler in 1981, would come to account for 10 percent of wine consumption in the United States by mid-decade. This rapid ascent was due in no small part to hegemon E. & J. Gallo introducing its Bartles & Jaymes wine cooler brand in 1985. Jörg Rupf's handmade and hand-bottled fruit spirits could not hope to compete with the white wine boom of the coming decade. He did not know it was coming, of course—had he, Rupf might have reconsidered launching St. George.

The same went for the regulatory environment that was just ascending as he started up in Emeryville. The government, especially at the federal level, had long been hostile to the spirits industry. Memories of the black markets that Prohibition spawned in turn spawned that warren of rules covering everything from labels to bottles to sales to distribution to advertising. The spirits industry voluntarily ceased advertising on radio in 1936 and on television in 1948, moves that media networks and successive federal governments strongly supported. Several states relegated spirits sales to particular stores that the states themselves controlled. Lager and Cabernet Sauvignon might be available at the local supermarket; bourbon and vodka would not be. Self-distribution, including in giant states such as California, was verboten. For many consumers, the only sights of spirits brands came from magazine ads and storefronts. Fine wine continued to penetrate further into the American consciousness in the 1980s—one of the decade's biggest primetime television shows, *Falcon Crest*, which centered around a wine-making dynasty in California, premiered on CBS in December 1981. And cheaper beer brands were everywhere, too, particularly as a part of major sporting events such as the Super Bowl and the Olympics. Budweiser would be the official beer of the 1984 Summer Olympics in Los Angeles, its red-and-white packaging beamed to billions through commercial breaks. Spirits? They were pushed to the perceptional edges of the average consumer. A new president in Washington would work to sideline them even further. Ronald Reagan was no teetotaler. The ex-governor of California was said to love his home state's fine wine—he had it served at state dinners—as well as a vodka-infused version of the orange blossom special, a classic cocktail. As a policymaker, however, Reagan and his White House, with aid from a Congress that the rival Democrats largely controlled, would bring down the full weight of the federal government, as well as the moral authority of the presidency, on the nation's spirits industry.

Jörg Rupf could not have known that, either. He and his St. George were operating largely in a vacuum, much the same way that Bill Samuels Sr.'s Maker's Mark had before it spun the *Wall Street Journal* into taking notice. The stakes were low and the returns minimal. No one spoke of a craft spir-its movement—or, indeed, of craft spirits at all. The term was twenty years from its controversial birth. "Small batch," too, as a commercial concept or product, was unknown. There simply was no such context. If someone were to describe a spirit as "small batch," it would likely conjure up images of illicit stills in some backwoods somewhere, the moonshine of Prohibition lore, throat-searing hooch far from meticulously crafted with the finest ingredients available. Instead, smaller operations such as St. George and Maker's Mark started popping up largely independent of one another, toddling forth in a marketplace that much bigger companies dominated and that was shrinking precipitously amid competition from wine and beer, never mind the hostility of federal regulators. Rupf could have gone into brewing. He had had a chance to acquire for cheap the parts of a beautiful old brewhouse when his maternal relatives shuttered the family brewery in West Germany in 1980. Brewing might have been an easier slog, or at least a less lonely one: Like with the rise of smaller-scale wineries in the wake of Robert Mondavi's launch in 1966, the number of smaller-scale breweries had increased in fits and starts since

Fritz Maytag's takeover of Anchor Brewing in 1965. There were around ten such breweries in the nation by 1982, most of them in Northern California.

As it was, Rupf, in a move both prosaic, in that people had been doing it for centuries, and revolutionary, in that it helped alter the American palate, chose small-batch distillation. It was the road much less traveled at the start of the 1980s, and no one was sure where it would lead.

PART II

PART II

AMERICAN COGNAC

1982–1983 | Mendocino County, California

Hubert Germain-Robin could not have been happier. It was the first week of October 1983, and his wife, Carole, had just given birth to their son. That, and he had recently started making some fantastic brandy.

Germain-Robin and ex-academic Ansley Coale had kept in touch since that chance encounter along Highway 101 north of San Francisco in August 1981. After Hubert and Carole had finished their treks through the Americas, the couple returned home to France, settled affairs there, and relocated to what were then the remote reaches of Ukiah, in California's Mendocino County, about halfway between the Bay Area and the Oregon border. There, in a one-room shed "the size of an icebox" on Coale's two-thousand-acre former sheep ranch, Coale and Hubert Germain-Robin had set about building a distillery to make fruit brandies in the Cognac tradition that was so rapidly dying in France, where it had been born centuries before. It was lonely, isolated work, not only because of the sheep ranch's location, eleven hundred feet above sea level and accessible only via a one-lane road. There was also barely anyone else in the United States doing what Coale and Germain-Robin were doing. They were aware of the novelty and the odds. The so-called Big Four of Cognac—Martell, Hennessy, Rémy Martin, and Courvoisier—produced nearly all of the fifteen to twenty fruit-brandy brands widely available in the United States in the early 1980s. They were French firms with French roots, some planted in the Middle Ages, and their wares were synonymous with fruit brandy, particularly that protected French foodstuff, Cognac.

And the pale yellow Ugni Blanc grape defined so much of that Cognac. It ballasted its taste and helped provide its color. It was even said to contribute to the very mouthfeel and texture of Cognac. Besides, for a brandy to call itself Cognac, the French government required it be made from certain grapes, Ugni Blanc the most common. Take away the grape and you were drastically changing the winning formula. Though that is exactly what Coale and Germain-Robin did. The pair spent $85,000 getting things off the ground, including the purchase from France of an old, swan-necked, hand-operated copper alembic still. It was through that alembic, in that one-room shed on the remote ranch, that Germain-Robin ran fermented juices from various varieties of grapes to try to get the brandy that he wanted. His training in France had centered on the Ugni Blanc, but he was smashing that taboo, dipping into the smorgasbord of grape varieties available to him in Northern California, then exploding with new wineries and wines. Vineyardists were busy tearing up lower-end workhorses such as Carignan, Salvador, and Alicante Bouschet and replacing them with higher-end grape varieties such as Chardonnay, Cabernet Sauvignon, and Merlot. Germain-Robin zeroed in on one variety in particular, a delicate underdog, in fact, when it came to the fine wines pouring out of Northern California then.

Pinot Noir grapes had never been that widely cultivated in California. As late as 1960, the state's biggest block of Pinot Noir was likely the seventy acres on the Louis Martini winery grounds off Highway 29 in Napa Valley. Few wineries made wines primarily from the grape, and those that did produced hit-or-miss results. California Pinot Noirs in the 1960s and 1970s were, according to one historian, "not just disappointing or mediocre; on the contrary, they were plainly flawed and actively unpleasant." A noted critic of the time often described California Pinot Noirs as "dull" and "short." It turned out that this poor quality was due more to improper winemaking techniques than to the grape itself. After all, Pinot Noir was undergirding some fantastic wines out of Oregon by the late 1970s. Whatever its spotty reputation locally, Germain-Robin saw potential in Pinot Noir—or at least it was worth a shot. In the autumn of 1983, he ran a batch of Pinot Noir wine through the hand-cranked alembic twice, as was the custom developed in France. Each distillation took at least eleven hours. The distillations vaporized the wine, with those vapors turning back into higher-alcohol liquid as they cooled. The near-brandy that emerged after the two distillations blew Germain-Robin's mind. He could not really describe it—even decades later—except that it exhibited a sort of finesse reminiscent of, if not better than, the best Cognacs of France. The Pinot Noir also seemed to have provided the perfect lightish color. He pumped his creation into ninety-two-gallon French oak barrels for aging, with plans to blend it before bottling.

Hubert Germain-Robin, left, and Ansley Coale at the launch of Germain-Robin.
ANSLEY COALE

Around the same time as Germain-Robin's Pinot Noir epiphany in Ansley Coale's shed, William Baccala was putting the final touches on a new winery just off Highway 101 nearby. Baccala grew up on a small farm and built a business career in the insurance industry in Southern California before buying fifteen hundred acres of an old Mendocino County cattle ranch in 1978. Capitalizing on the winemaking boom of that era and intrigued by a friend's grape-growing efforts in neighboring Sonoma County, Baccala immediately planted 150 acres of Chardonnay and Sauvignon Blanc grapes, with plans to stay firmly in the grape-growing business and to not transition to making fine wine as well, like so many other vineyardists were doing. But then Baccala befriended Barney Fetzer, an ex–merchant marine who, with his wife, Kathleen, launched a Mendocino winery in the late 1960s specializing in Cabernet Sauvignon and Zinfandel. The Fetzers were seeing solid returns by the late 1970s, and the industry as a whole appeared poised for massive growth in the new decade. Fetzer suggested Baccala give winemaking a try, promising to buy some of the grapes Baccala might grow. In 1981 Baccala created what he called Villa Baccala Winery, using fruit from his own vines and elsewhere. The following year Baccala hired Miles Karakasevic, a Serbian who arrived in the United States in 1962 by way of Canada from what was then Yugoslavia. Though an experienced winemaker with land of his own in the area, Karakasevic also had distillation experience. His family had been involved in the field since perhaps the seventeenth century, the techniques and troubleshooting passed down the generations through the master-apprentice setup. Karakasevic convinced Baccala to acquire a nearly five-hundred-year-old alembic still from France. Within a year, Karakasevic was crafting brandy with it using mostly Colombard grapes, a white variety that French Cognac distillers had long used alongside Ugni Blanc. With a capacity for six hundred gallons annually, Baccala's operation was a sort of distillery within a winery, the first such hybrid of its kind that anyone could remember—though, because of the blending and the aging that would be required, few would notice it until the mid-1980s.

Not so another distillery starting up in 1982 just north of the Bay Area. The media and industry attention mostly had to do with the operation's French backing as well as its literal and figurative Napa Valley roots. Like William Baccala, Jack and Jamie Davies were part of a migration of independently affluent winery owners to that thirty-mile-long valley in the 1960s and 1970s. They ditched their life in Los Angeles, where Jack, a Stanford graduate and a Harvard MBA, was a business executive, and in 1965 bought an abandoned winery near Calistoga that an "itinerant German barber" named Jacob Schram had started in 1862. The couple restored the Victorian mansion on the property, drove out the bats in five caves once used to age wine, and replanted forty acres of vines with Champagne grapes originating in that French region famed for its sparkling wine. With help from other Napa winemakers and vineyardists, including Robert and Peter Mondavi, the Davieses steadily built a reputation for producing fine sparkling wines of their own—due to French trade restrictions, they couldn't call it Champagne—one of the few outfits in the United States since Prohibition to focus on such wares. Their Schramsberg Vineyards scored a particularly big publicity coup when President Richard Nixon had twenty-five cases of a 1969 vintage brought to Beijing for a summit in 1972 between himself and Chinese premier Zhou Enlai. Annual sales soon ascended from one thousand cases to twenty thousand in 1980. It was shortly after the start of that decade that the couple partnered with Rémy Martin, one of the world's four biggest Cognac producers, to make the French brandy in Napa Valley.

Launched in the fall of 1982—the two sides officially announced the joint venture in late September—the Rémy Martin Schramsberg distillery was the first one built in California since Prohibition, besting by a matter of weeks Jörg Rupf's one-man St. George operation in Emeryville. It was also massive by American standards, particularly when it came to brandy distillation.

The distillery imported eight alembic stills and purchased land in the nearby Carneros area of Napa for what would grow to a forty-thousand-square-foot production facility. There were plans to produce as much as thirty thousand cases annually, and the distillery's cellar would be able to hold three thousand ninety-gallon French oak barrels for aging the brandy, made, like Baccala and Karakasevic's early efforts, primarily from Colombard grapes, with Pinot Noir and a couple of others used for blending. (Again, as with verbal acrobatics involved in the Davieses' sparkling-wine effort, this fruit brandy could not call itself Cognac.) Most formidable, though, was the built-in distribution and marketing that Rémy Martin provided the distillery. It could expect its brandy, when it was ready in the mid-1980s, to flow into a network that stretched from East Asia to Europe and all over the United States. This was a global reach unimaginable to Ansley Coale and Hubert Germain-Robin in the shed up on the mountain in Ukiah.

It was not that novel, though. Plenty of distilleries in the United States enjoyed a wide reach thanks to their corporate parentage. Heublein had cleaned up financially on its purchase of a struggling Smirnoff vodka brand. The acquisition had helped that Hartford, Connecticut–based conglomerate grow into the nation's second-biggest spirits company by the 1980s. It paled against the biggest. The Seagram Company's roots stretched to the 1920s, just after prohibition in its native Canada and during that period in the United States. Its founding Bronfman clan grew the firm through both acquisitions and start-ups, including Captain Morgan rum, launched in 1945, and Chivas Regal scotch, launched seven years later, shortly after Seagram acquired a similarly named Scottish liquor and food merchant. By the end of the 1970s, Seagram could record annual sales of more than US$2.5 billion, though some of that had sprung from a remarkable diversification: the company also pro-duced Hollywood movies, made wine through operations in California and New York, and extracted natural gas and petroleum. Such breadth protected the spirits brands of Seagram, Heublein, and a handful of other conglomer-ates against the financial vagaries of a flailing spirits marketplace. Seagram's wine holdings could hoover up the tipplers abandoning its spirits brands, for instance; or maybe they might buy movie tickets. Or, in the case of other Heublein brands, quaff Guinness beer or munch on some Kentucky Fried Chicken. Microscopically tinier, small-batch, independent producers such as Germain-Robin and St. George could not avail themselves of such insurance. It was sink or swim in a shifting marketplace.

At least with fruit brandy and Cognac, the marketplace did not appear so volatile at the start of the 1980s. That golden age that dawned roughly a decade before amid increased production for increased demand, the same age that spurred Hubert Germain-Robin's entry into his family's former field, still glowed very brightly. During the twelve months ended August 31, 1981, 23.5 million bottles were sold in the United States, a nearly 50 percent increase from the same period before. Consumption was also up fourfold in the last several years at a time when overall spirits consumption was down, if not nose-diving. All of this despite the generally higher prices of Cognac bottles. Much of this domestic success could, ironically, be traced to the success of the fine wine that was so unapologetically poaching spirits consumers. "Americans are drinking more wine with dinner," a Cognac trade-group representative told the New York Times. "And that makes it much easier to have a Cognac afterward." The United States was leading the world in Cognac sales growth by the early 1980s, just ahead of British-held Hong Kong, the next fastest-growing market. Such sales leadership was wonderful as a confidence builder in 1982 and 1983, particularly for Germain-Robin, the only one of the three new California entrants dedicated solely to distillation. There appeared to be an audience for handcrafted brandy in the United States. Maker's Mark around the same time proved there was an audience for handcrafted spirits, period. Yet, brandy, like bourbon, needed years of aging to reach its full potential. Would the crowd still be waiting in the middle of the decade?

GLITTER AND GEKKO

1981–1983 | Manhattan—Spring Mountain, California—Loretto, Kentucky

Paul Pacult hated crowds, but his 1982 move to immensely dense Manhattan appeared to be paying off. The mustachioed, bespectacled Pacult grew up in the northern Illinois city of Niles and attended college at the University of California at Berkeley, before dropping out amid the campus's mess of protests and crackdowns. He then moved northward to Sonoma County to pursue Transcendental Meditation, which he studied there as well as in Hawaii and Spain. Returning to the Bay Area in 1973, Pacult got a job in October at what was then called Windsor Vineyards.

A former ballet dancer named Rodney Strong had acquired the winery ten years earlier, after he developed a taste for the stuff while working in

Paris. Strong and his wife, Charlotte, mentored the young Pacult, showing him the ins and outs of a small winery specializing in the likes of Chardonnay, Merlot, and Cabernet Sauvignon years before the Judgment of Paris in 1976 changed everything. The California wine industry would morph into a money-printing juggernaut after that event, but, before, the industry was much smaller and slower. There were perhaps twenty-six wineries in Sonoma in 1973. A generation later there would be nearly four hundred. There were no real job titles at the Strongs' operation, either, certainly no lofty-sounding executive sinecures. Pacult might show up to clean the bathrooms and the tasting room on Sunday morning and find Charlotte right there with him. Another morning he might be enlisted to help pick grapes. It was the perfect all-hands-on-deck ethos for someone like Pacult to soak up as much as he could, which is exactly what he did.

As the 1980s dawned, he saw an opportunity to pivot from the wine industry to writing and educating people about it and its output, a change that would lead to Pacult becoming the nation's most prominent spirits critic. The 1970s, both before and after the Judgment of Paris, had seen a flowering of American media dedicated to both wine itself and to a kind of bucolic wine-infused lifestyle that Robert Mondavi first heavily promoted through his eponymous Napa Valley concern. More American consumers than ever wanted to know not just what wines to buy and why but also what to pair them with food-wise and how to drink and serve them. Publications such as *Wine Spectator*, *Wine Enthusiast*, *Wine Advocate*, and *Food & Wine*, all of which launched in this era, were more than happy to fill the knowledge void, as were any number of less prominent newsletters and guides. Also, by the end of the 1970s, every major newspaper in America had a wine critic, this in an era when most people got their news from broadsheets and tabloids. If a still-young, ambitious would-be writer was going to stake his claim to a slice of the coverage, the early 1980s was the time. Pacult went one better after settling into a loft in Tribeca in downtown Manhattan in its pregentrification days. After working a couple of years at a higher-end wine shop in the borough, he launched a wine-tasting school out of his loft called Wine Courses International. It was one of the first in the United States, though there would be several in New York City alone within a few years. Pacult walked his pupils over four sessions through the different varieties of wine and what made each distinct, how to serve them, and which foods to pair them with. He took no more than twenty students at a time and, within a few years, never had to worry about demand.

A recession had gripped much of the developed world since at least 1980, driving unemployment up and economic growth to a standstill. In the United States specifically, double-digit inflation "seemed a permanent curse," according to the *New York Times,* and the new Reagan administration warned Americans to expect a high rate of joblessness for years to come. And then, on August 12, 1982, the Dow Jones Industrial Average, perhaps the best private-sector measure of America's economic vitality, dropped to what turned out to be recession low of 776.92. A bull market snorted in its pen. Soon the American economy would boom, the financial sector especially, with the stock markets scaling upward. The Dow rocketed toward heights not seen since the early 1970s, and conspicuous consumption became a credo of the new economy. Think of the syndicated television show *Lifestyles of the Rich & Famous,* which debuted in early 1984, or the phrase "greed is good." Screenwriter and director Oliver Stone put those words in the mouth of Gordon Gekko, an atavistic businessman whom Michael Douglas won an Oscar portraying in the 1987 film *Wall Street.* They came to encapsulate almost too perfectly Americans' relationship to spending money throughout much of the decade. And fine wine was one of the things Americans, especially baby boomers now in their forties and fifties, spent more money on than ever during the 1980s.

There were major auctions, including an annual one that spirits-owning conglomerate Heublein organized every year in Chicago, where rare bottles or cases might fetch five figures apiece. There were marathon tastings of equally hard-to-find vintages. A Miami lawyer threw a tasting of sixty-one pricey wines from the famed French region of Bordeaux. An aerospace tycoon in New Orleans organized a three-day jag to sample 115 bottles of Château Lafite Rothschild, one of France's most vaunted winemaking concerns. "Acquisitiveness, or, if you will, greed, is their principal motivation," *New York Times* wine critic Frank Prial wrote in describing such bacchanalia, anticipating Gordon Gekko before the character even existed. For those who could not shell out $20,000 for a single bottle, newer entities such as *Wine Spectator* and individual wineries sponsored weekend-long gatherings for curious tipplers, though they did often charge them in the hundreds of dollars. If a weekend was too long or too expensive, then how about all manner of wine gadgetry and accessories? Sales of corkscrews, racks, and long-stemmed glasses surged, though these were on the cheaper end of the spectrum. Wine refrigerators might run to $1,000, depending on the model and the number of bottles. If racks and corkscrews were too pedestrian—though they would have been odd in most kitchens or living rooms as late as the early 1980s—then a consumer could avail him- or herself of such accoutrements from the *Wine Enthusiast* catalog as a "George Washington 18th-century silver-plated wine coaster, reproduced by the Smithsonian for wine lovers," for $39.50, plus another $1.75 for shipping. Adam Strum, a Gallo salesman in New York who realized fine wine's commercial potential sooner than most, started the *Wine Enthusiast* catalog in 1979 with his wife, as well as the similarly named editorial magazine. More than twenty million shoppers would use the catalog by 1990.

Also at the start of the 1980s, wine menus at restaurants, once truncated to a few selections from E. & J. Gallo and then perhaps a French vintage or two, now vastly expanded. The wine bar as a distinct destination for drinking wine, as opposed to a bar that might serve wine, arose in the early 1980s, too, the concept so novel that a *Washington Post* writer in May 1981 led an article explaining the phenomenon with the question, "What is a wine bar?" Once they did catch on, wine bars became staples of the urban landscape, their arrival often a controversial harbinger of change in a particular neighborhood. And these wine bars and thoroughly wine-stocked restaurants needed experts to advise flush patrons on which bottles to spend their cash. Enter, then, the sommelier or the wine steward (or, occasionally, the master of wine). The ranks of these experts, often trained through an industry group or a restaurant, swelled in the 1980s. Cities at the end of the 1970s might have had one or two restaurants with a sommelier on staff. By the middle of the next decade, every restaurant at a certain price level had to have one.

Finally, expertise in wine in general spiked in the 1980s. Consumers learned more, either deliberately or almost subconsciously. It was hard to miss the expansion of fine wine selections at liquor stores, supermarkets, etc. A phalanx of critics also developed their expertise—and were willing to share it for a price. They were the ones at the auctions, the tastings, the restaurants, and the bars. They even had their own heavily covered tribal gatherings, ones that often set the coverage and the pricing for the entire fine wine industry in the United States. These gatherings included the Napa Valley Wine Auction, launched 1982, and, especially, the Four Seasons California Barrel Tasting. Paul Kovi and Tom Margittai, owners of the Four Seasons, launched the Barrel Tasting in March 1976 to add some shine to the faded luster of their Midtown Manhattan restaurant, which, like the city around it, had declined since the 1950s. The idea was simple: invite a selection of top winemakers to present their latest vintages straight from the barrel—in other words, before they were bottled and available for sale. Kovi and Margittai enlisted Gerald Asher, a member of that phalanx of critics that had arisen since the early 1970s, to curate the selected winemakers and to pick other critics to invite. That particular invite list never grew beyond fifteen or so, and the number of barrel samples never crested eighteen. These limits ensured an exclusivity about the barrel tasting that made it by the start of the 1980s "the wine trade's most glittering social event," a kind of fine wine Oscars. Reputations were made and tastes were set. The samples went from the winemakers' barrels to the mouths of critics to the eyeballs and, occasionally, ears of consumers the nation over. In an era before the World Wide Web's search engines and self-blogging made everyone experts, the Four Seasons California Barrel Tasting was unavoidably influential. It allowed the industry to speak in one fell swoop "to the center of public relations of the world," as Robert Mondavi enthusiastically put it to the crowd at the second barrel tasting in 1977. Four Seasons owners Kovi and Margittai helped along the enthusiasm for it, too, by serving fantastic courses from star chefs and, most importantly perhaps, by insisting guests swallow the wine samples rather than spit them out. It was a binge that translated barrel access and critical expertise into money for the industry. From a winemaker's perspective, what wasn't to love?

There was nothing like the Four Seasons California Barrel Tasting for spirits in the United States in the early 1980s. Nor was there anything like the auctions or sommeliers or wine bars, or the *Wine Enthusiast* catalog selling George Washington–themed accessories, even though the first president once owned the nation's largest distillery. Nor did aspiring writers such as Paul Pacult move across the continent to cover spirits as they did to cover fine wine. There were no professional or widely published critics of spirits, American-made or otherwise in the early 1980s. Any discussion that might seep into consumer media regarding the industry and its products usually sprang from a business reporter or a publication's resident wine writer. That coverage, too, invariably centered around the boardroom machinations of Heublein, Seagram, and other large producers, or the rise and decline of individual drinks such as vodka and bourbon. If any of the coverage veered toward the bottles themselves, it was usually about the pricing, not the contents. The *Wall Street Journal*'s August 1980 front-page clarion on the slow-building success of Maker's Mark was a high-water point for the fledgling American craft spirits movement, but it showed little sign of being duplicated, much less surpassed. And never mind how it stacked up against wine; lowly beer drew more critical coverage than spirits. In April 1984, the *Oregonian*, the daily newspaper for the Portland metropolitan area, with a weekday circulation of nearly a quarter-million, began publishing the beer criticism of Fred Eckhardt, an ex-Marine turned photographer who taught homebrewing lessons and self-published a newsletter on the nation's smaller breweries. (He had in 1968 traveled to San Francisco to tour the Anchor Brewing Company with Fritz Maytag.) Eckhardt's first column dealt with the dearth of quality-made

US beers and ended with a list of "Twenty Beers with Class," including ones from Anchor and Sierra Nevada, a craft brewery that homebrewing enthusiasts started in Chico, California, in 1980. There was also 1977's *World Guide to Beer*, which English critic Michael Jackson wrote and a small publisher released in the United States following its publication across the pond. It was the first English-language book anyone could remember that critically assessed the statuses and whereabouts of the world's myriad beer styles. For Americans who could land a copy, *The World Guide to Beer* revealed in muscular prose and striking photographs that there was so much out there beyond the watery works of Anheuser-Busch and Miller.

Nevertheless, the American small-batch spirits movement continued to grow and change, even as it remained the proverbial palatal tree falling in a forest with no one around to hear it. In 1983 Miles Karakasevic, the Serbian immigrant who had helped start the distillery at Bill Baccala's Mendocino winery the year before, struck out on his own. For a decade, he and wife Susan, whom he met in Michigan after his arrival in the United States via Canada, had run their own small winery from a seventeen-acre ranch acquired in 1972 on Spring Mountain in Napa Valley, twenty-three hundred feet above sea level. It was a small affair focused on the burgeoning fine wine movement, with a special emphasis on Chardonnay. To pay the bills, Karakasevic worked as a consultant and an employee at larger operations, including generic wine kingpin Italian Swiss Colony, one of the few entities that could really compete with E. & J. Gallo. It was not his calling, though, to work at other wineries—or distilleries, for that matter. Born in 1941 in wartime Yugoslavia, he grew up in the northern Serbian town of Mol, where his father's family made white wines and eau-de-vie for their own enjoyment and for sales. It was said the House of Karakasevic could trace its commercial fermentation and distillation roots back to the seventeenth century. Karakasevic's mother's family was wealthy for the time. They owned thousands of acres of orchards that would have ballasted the clan's winemaking and spirits-making efforts had not the Communists taken over after World War II and, in Karakasevic's words, "brought equality." His prospects considerably dimmed, the twenty-one-year-old Karakasevic left Mol, the town where his father's family had lived for twelve generations, and traveled a well-worn path for Yugoslavian emigrants: first to West Germany for further academic work—he had studied viticulture and enology at the University of Belgrade—and then, in November 1962, over to North America at the first opportunity. By 1970 he was with Susan in Napa Valley, which was about to explode commercially because of fine wine—a perfect place and time for a trained enologist.

Spirits was another matter. The Karakasevics originally made brandy from an alembic still imported from Cognac. They mostly used Folle Blanche, one of the three traditional grapes that French distillers favored, along with Ugni Blanc and Colombard, but the family was not averse to experimentation. Miles Karakasevic would gain a reputation as a kind of moody, mad genius of distillation, eyes constantly dancing, a long, bushy mustache crowning a mouth that spoke in a heavy Slavic accent, isolated atop his mountain, making small batches of brandy, vodka, eau-de-vie, and more from whatever materials he thought might be worth a try. "No fruit is safe from Miles," Susan Karakasevic would tell people. There was clear method to the madness for anyone taking the time to look. Like Hubert Germain-Robin, generations flowed through Karakasevic's distillation. He had originally learned the trade in a master-apprentice system stretching back centuries. And, like Germain-Robin, he would have segued into the master role at a family firm had circumstances not intervened and launched him toward California. As it was, what the Karakasevics were doing would not become that well known for years as the brandy matured in French oak barrels—again, a touch of the old-world craftsmanship. They called the family firm Domaine Karakasevic at first and then Domaine Charbay, after a loose combination of "Chardonnay" and "brandy." Its first wines would not be released commercially until 1983, a full decade after the couple acquired the Spring Mountain property. In the meantime, Miles Karakasevic worked as a consultant elsewhere, distilling when he could, in the traditional ways and with both classic and new materials. This placed him amid the vanguard of the American small-batch spirits movement as 1983 bled into 1984, most of it clustered nearby in the still largely rustic counties north of San Francisco and none of its wares reaching much beyond.

The only distillery outside of Northern California in 1983 that might claim the small-batch mantle was Maker's Mark. Yet the tremendous interest that the *Wall Street Journal*'s coverage visited on the tiny Loretto, Kentucky, operation spurred a big change. In 1981 Bill Samuels Sr. sold control of Maker's Mark for an undisclosed sum to Hiram Walker & Sons, one of the world's biggest spirits conglomerates. Like a top competitor, Seagram, Hiram Walker could trace its roots to before Prohibition and back to Canada. The company was headquartered in Windsor, Ontario, just over the international border from Detroit. Maker's Mark simply could not keep pace with demand, and besides, a sale now would allow the Samuels family to end-run around potentially high inheritance taxes. In an unusual move, the new owner kept the clan in charge. Bill Sr., now seventy-one, in turn relinquished control to his son, who became sole head. Hiram Walker had bought the brand, its operations, and, especially, its potential. Sales of Maker's Mark bourbon would grow steadily throughout the 1980s with annual case runs soon measured in the hundreds of thousands, all at higher prices and after distillation techniques that the wider industry regarded as unnecessarily laborious and costly.

Maker's Mark was a comet-like bright spot in American small-batch spirits in the early 1980s. Otherwise, as Paul Pacult noticed upon his arrival in New York City from Napa Valley in 1982, the vast majority of liquor store shelves were still crammed with spirits understood more for their price than their taste or, certainly, background. Odorless vodka was still ascendant, and new craft entrants such as Jörg Rupf's St. George and the brandy concern of Ansley Coale and Hubert Germain-Robin were all but invisible beyond the Bay Area. The twin rises of fine wine and craft beer, the former already explosively underway, would change all that. Fine wine had already changed Paul Pacult. He could not have known it, of course, but he was on his way from college dropout to well-known wine writer and lecturer to groundbreaker in spirits criticism and writing. On the more technical side, barrels—the same sorts of barrels that fueled the famed Four Seasons gathering—would nurture major alterations in how Americans saw, bought, and talked about spirits. The stage was set; there were more actors than ever.

For now, though, it is time to exit the United States, cross the Atlantic, and scale the remoter reaches of the United Kingdom.

A SINGULAR IDEA

1978–1985 | Scottish Highlands—Santiago de Cuba

There was the whisky the Scottish drank themselves and the whisky they sold to the world. The Scots had been distilling the spirit since at least the 1400s, though it may have arrived as much as a millennium earlier with the first Christian missionaries in the northern reaches of what became the United Kingdom. Traditionally made with malted barley as the main ingredient, Scotch whisky came in two forms: from blends of different batches, sometimes from different distilleries; and from unblended batches from a single distillery. The former was often called Scotch or, in Scotland itself, simply whisky without the *e* as in the United States. And the latter was called single malt (or sometimes single malt Scotch). At the start of the 1980s, blends accounted for nearly 99 percent of all whisky sales in the United Kingdom and for the vast majority of Scottish whisky sales worldwide. Single malt was "a more unusual spirit," as the *New York Times* put it in December 1980, largely unfamiliar outside of its native land. Export-wise, Scottish distillers shipped 114 million gallons of blends and just under 2 million gallons of single malt.

Yet as many as 116 distilleries in Scotland made single malt, particularly those in impossibly bucolic graystone buildings in the more remote Highlands around the River Spey in the country's north. The distilleries and their employees kept a fair amount of this single malt production for themselves or their immediate markets, preferring the fuller, more concentrated, more complex taste to those of flavor-diluted blends, which were easier and quicker to make and which some in the industry mockingly called "cooking whisky." Such whisky paid the bills, though, and the corporate parents of many Scottish distilleries, including those behind major name brands in North America, saw to it that their holdings churned out blends for export, as well as whisky for blending elsewhere, at a much greater clip than they did single malt. This was the dual production approach for a majority of Scottish distilleries into the 1970s, as whisky, at least out of Scotland, continued to boom, taking ever more market share from flailing American bourbon and more than holding its own in Western Europe, where vodka had never penetrated that deeply outside of Scandinavia.

Then triple shocks arrived beginning in the late 1970s. First, two deep recessions struck much of the West, one starting in 1973 and the second in 1978, including in Scotland's home base. Average unemployment in the United Kingdom ballooned to double-digit percentages from below 3 percent, and entire industries, especially mining and transportation, were thrown into upheaval amid strikes and privatization. Rolling power outages were common, even in major cities, and garbage was sometimes not regularly collected. Things had grown that grim in a nation that had only the decade before emerged from post–World War II austerity. These economic conditions, of course, translated into less money for ordinary Britons to spend, including on their small pleasures such as blended Scotch and the odd single malt. The same went for other previously hot markets, including the United States. The volume of Scottish whisky exports dropped a full 10 percent in 1981 and 1982 as sales dried up. Such a sharp decline was potentially disastrous: Exports accounted for nearly 90 percent of the Scottish whisky industry's trades. A penurious domestic economy would never be able to pick up the slack.

Add to this recessionary shock the sudden rises in fine wine as well as two other spirits in the key American marketplace, and Scotland's vaunted whisky industry now faced not only a disastrous situation but also one that could easily turn fatal. In 1982 French vintners in that nation's storied Bordeaux winemaking region picked, pressed, fermented, and bottled what turned out to be one of the most phenomenal vintages of wine anywhere ever. That assessment came from the same phalanx of critics that had been talking up fine wine in the United States for the last decade, particularly Robert Parker Jr., a lawyer from suburban Baltimore turned founder, publisher, and editor of *Wine Advocate*, a newsletter of reviews self-published nearly every month. His unabashed praise for the '82 Bordeaux, first publicly expressed at the Four Seasons California Barrel Tasting in March 1983, coupled with the French region's need for a commercial hit after several so-so vintages, thrust fine wine further into the forefront of American cuisine. Magazines and newspapers carried their own raves about the '82 Bordeaux, and other critics and trade publications soon followed Parker's lead. Bottles of French wine in general started flying off shelves. The already fertile financial ground for fine wine in the United States grew that much richer. Just as spirits consumption was leveling off, that for fine wine was headed toward its own peak in the middle of the decade, with an industrial-consumer environment of media and events that spirits could only dream of.

As it was, spirits in the American marketplace increasingly meant two things: vodka and rum. In 1978 Smirnoff vodka surpassed Seagram's 7 Crown American, a blended whiskey from the Canadian giant, as the bestselling spirit in the United States. Smirnoff's ascent, and vodka's overall, had been so gradual yet so relentless that it seemed once it got to the top spot, it would never leave. Bourbon was in free-fall, and fine wine was picking off many potential consumers from other spirits. What could possibly take on the Russian-born Smirnoff but another vodka brand? The answer emerged from the Americas and from an entirely different libationary realm.

The family-owned Bacardí company dated from early 1864, when Don Facundo Bacardí Massó, an immigrant from Spain, bought a distillery in the eastern Cuban port city of Santiago de Cuba. He used charcoal filtration and a recipe that included Cognac yeast to create a lighter, sweeter, more drinkable version of rum, a spirit made from sugarcane by-products such as molasses. Before Bacardí, most widely available rum was heavier-tasting and syrupy. Don Facundo also proved a savvy marketer for the time, signing individual bottles and designing an open-winged bat as the distillery's logo. Within a generation, his signature rum was a hit not only locally but also with the

US military occupying the island after the Spanish-American War in 1898. Like Smirnoff vodka, Bacardí rum could be mixed with myriad other liquids. US soldiers were supposedly the first to mix it with Coca-Cola to toast what they regarded as a Cuba free from Spanish tyranny—thus the Cuba Libre. Soon Bacardí rum was selling so well in the United States that, like Smirnoff, it basically became synonymous with the spirit itself. "Rum is vodka with a sweet taste, whereas vodka has no taste," an analyst would note when the spirit conquered America in the late 1970s. "It's for people who want to know there's something in their drink besides orange juice."

Rum dated from at least the 1400s and really took off after Christopher Columbus brought sugarcane to the West Indies in 1493. From that point on, rum became a hefty part of a grim triangle of trade covering the Atlantic. Ships would exit northern European ports laden with goods such as firearms and other spirits to sell to slave traders on the west African coast. With the profits, Europeans bought kidnapped Africans, who would then be imported to the New World, where they would be driven to harvest goods to then sell back to the European market. One of the biggest goods was sugarcane, valued both by itself as a sweetener and for the use of its by-products, such as molasses, in making rum. As many as two-thirds of the estimated ten million Africans enslaved before abolition movements swept the Americas in the 1800s ended up harvesting sugarcane in the West Indies. This bleak statistic made rum perhaps the most influential drink ever, after the tea that fueled so much of the British empire's expansion.

Slavery's role in rum's rise, including in Bacardí's ascent—the Spanish crown did not abolish slavery in its Cuban colony until 1886—was largely ignored or conveniently forgotten by the late twentieth century. Rum was simply the spirit from the Caribbean, a sweeter, more delicate antidote to harsher whiskeys such as bourbon or a tastier alternative to vodka. And Bacardí, still family owned, was the world's biggest producer of rum. Not even being booted from its home base could shake its dominance. Shortly after the 1960 revolution in Havana, Fidel Castro appropriated Bacardí's assets, along with those of some three hundred businesses, for his Communist Party. The Bacardí clan resettled their concern in San Juan, Puerto Rico, once again under the protection of the United States. From there they expanded it rapidly, setting up thirteen different companies under the Bacardí umbrella, including one in the tiny, tax-friendly European principality of Liechtenstein, which handled the trademark and quality control, and ten entities, most in Latin America, to actually produce the spirit. This expansion went hand in hand with an advertising push, complete with celebrity endorsers such as actor

Telly Savalas and an endless supply of cocktail recipes, all in service of what was still Bacardí's only product: the lighter-tasting, lighter-colored rum that Don Facundo devised in the 1860s. The relentless dedication to the single spirit, coupled with the exile-turned-godsend, spurred phenomenal growth. Worldwide, Bacardí would control more than two-thirds of the rum trade at the end of the 1970s. In America, the dominance was just as pronounced. When Castro forced Bacardí out of Cuba in 1960, the firm controlled about 40 percent of the rum market in the United States, which in turn accounted for a mere 2 percent of the nation's spirits market. By the late 1970s, Bacardí's rum market share had grown to 55 percent, and rum itself had more than doubled in popularity. So when Bacardí rum overtook first Seagram's 7 and then Smirnoff vodka to become America's bestselling spirit, no one who followed such things was truly surprised.

Stunned was more like it, at least for the Scottish whisky industry. The Scotch now properly aged and ready for release in the early 1980s had gone into barrels in the mid-1970s, a time of seemingly ceaseless ascent for blended whiskeys in the United States as sales of bourbon nosedived and spirits consumption boomed. Now here came rum with its near-double-digit annual growth rate to, along with vodka, gobble up the suddenly shrinking marketplace of Americans who still drank spirits rather than fine wine. (To add insult to injury, neither rum nor vodka had to be aged like whiskey.) Distilleries up and down Scotland found themselves with unblended whisky they could not sell to the usual blending conglomerates who then sold it to America and the world. These distilleries also knew that selling it domestically was out of the question, given the gnawing recession. Besides, the United Kingdom by itself would never make up the difference. Some started operating under capacity, which sometimes meant never opening the distillery on some business days. What was the point? In places such as Islay, an island off the Scottish mainland's west coast that was, like the River Spey, a prime whisky-making area, talk turned to distilleries actually shutting down permanently, something that had not happened in a century. Then, in a tactical move that would reverberate down the decades and with a nod toward the barrel tastings already justly famed in the exploding fine wine world, several Scottish distilleries decided to pivot away from blends for a bit and toward marketing their smaller, more select batches of single malts for wider international sale.

The distilleries' corporate parents as well as their importers and distributors leaned heavily on what seemed to be working so well for fine wine. Just as a bottle of Robert Mondavi Cabernet Sauvignon retailed for more than one of Gallo Thunderbird, single malts would be more expensive for consumers.

A typical bottle might sell for nearly five times the $5.75 cost of a similar-sized jug of Jim Beam, still the nation's bestselling bourbon. They would not necessarily be more expensive to make, however. The single malt was there, listing in barrels at individual distilleries. It was more a matter of selling them to a new audience than any technical innovation. This, too, echoed fine wine. Higher-end grapes such as Cabernet Sauvignon had been growing in California for decades before the 1960s, and some smaller wineries had turned out fantastic vintages from higher-end grapes. When Mondavi sought to broaden their appeal and sales, he set out on a virtual crusade to educate and entice consumers, giving rise to an immensely successful fine wine culture, complete with media and events. The same could be had with single malt, complete with the heavily tutored tastings. Like fine wine nearly a generation before, here was something largely new and unfamiliar, with tongue-twisting Gaelic names and a deeper, thicker taste than even the experienced Scotch drinker was used to in his or her blends. As much as the average American tippler would have found a Chardonnay positively exotic in 1970, he or she found a Glenfiddich, one of the leading single malts, available in the United States even before the early 1980s, just as exotic. And, as with Chardonnay, our tippler might have stumbled over the name, pronouncing the last syllable as "ch" instead of as the proper "ck."

As so spectacularly with fine wine, this sense of connoisseurship soon melded with an equally strong sense of proprietorship: Single malt drinkers soon knew their stuff and wanted other people to know they knew. They likely also wanted people to know they could afford them. These were the perfect spirits for a flusher, postrecessionary America, one riding a bull stock market that produced that endlessly fascinating urban subspecies known as the yuppie—a young professional who wanted his or her consumption to be conspicuous. A pricey bottle of aged single malt presented the same opportunity as one of Cab Sav. As the *New York Times* noted, "single-malts seem to appeal to wine drinkers, particularly those who are young professionals over age twenty-eight." The industry picked up on this quickly. "There is a great deal of cachet with single-malts," a representative of the Scottish whiskey trade explained in 1985, after the first flush of the phenomenon had washed over the United States. "Not only can you drink them, but you can bore people's heads off with what you know about them." Like with fine wine, rituals soon arose regarding how to serve, store, and consume them. The almighty rule number one: Unlike omnipresent vodka and rum, single malts were never, ever to be used in a cocktail, the *New York Times* sternly instructed its readers. Instead, they "are usually sipped neat from a shot glass or snifter. They are appropriate after dinner and at cocktail time. Drinking a single-malt with water is an acceptable practice, and many people have water on the side. Asking for a cocktail with single-malt Scotch, however, is a pretentious waste." Here was the *Washington Post* to its readers in May 1983: "They should be drunk like a fine Cognac, in a snifter after dinner. No ice, no water." Finally, and simply, there was this inescapable factor tied to the rituals: Like fine wine vs. its generic predecessors, single malts tasted better. Or at least they tasted more complex and more interesting. There was a reason the Scots had for so long kept a lot of it for themselves. They were meant to be savored and to be bought based on that. This alone made single malts almost unique in the American spirits marketplace. One bought bottles of Bacardí or Smirnoff for the value and with the foreknowledge that their contents would soon mix with Coke, fruit juice, etc. Soon, higher-end restaurants throughout the land, never mind liquor stores, were stocking wide selections of the approximately forty-five single malt brands available in the United States—the City Lights bar on the 106th floor of the World Trade Center's North Tower stocked eleven, the exclusive 21 Club farther uptown stocked a respectable eight. Formal paid tastings, usually through retailers or restaurants, abounded. Coverage of the rise of single malts seeped from the few American trade publications into consumer media such as daily newspapers. By 1985 the United States was the world's third-biggest market for single malt Scottish whisky, behind the United Kingdom and Italy.

Although, to be sure, single malts still added up to a minority of the Scottish-made whiskey sold in the United States, their success in a few short years set an example for bourbon distillers. Some quickly drew a connection between the popularity of this Scottish whisky and the potential for a similar bounce in their flailing American whiskey. The notion was not that far-fetched. It could easily be argued that the Scots were ripping a page not necessarily from winemakers such as Robert Mondavi but from distillers such as Bill Samuels Sr. The approaches used to market single malts to Americans were the same ones Samuels used to market Maker's Mark three decades before. The higher prices, the different taste, the emphasis on savoring rather than inhaling and the rituals that that spawned, and, finally, the exclusivity and exoticness from knowing these were spirits more intimately produced in smaller batches—one could trace all of it back to tiny Loretto in the mid-1950s. Bourbon was more than halfway there; the sales rubric was already set. The industry just needed a pioneer to step forward with the American equivalent of Scottish single malt.

LIGHTNING IN A BARREL
1984–1987 | Frankfort, Kentucky

Elmer T. Lee looked and sounded straight out of central casting—even his name bespoke rural Kentucky, as did his backstory. Born in August 1919, Lee was the sole son of a tenant tobacco farmer who had to move the family often in central Kentucky in search of work. Typhoid killed his father when Lee was nine, and his mother took a job as a waitress at the old Southern Hotel in Frankfort, which gave her and her son some stability as the Great Depression set in. He grew up with a love of animals and thought he might be a veterinarian. The field was a popular one in horse-crazy Kentucky. Instead, he entered the University of Kentucky in 1940 with plans to study engineering. America's entry into World War II the following year interrupted his studies. Lee volunteered as a radar bombardier for B-29 bombers in the Pacific Theater, quite a ways from his rural roots. After the war, he returned to school intent on a degree and spent summers and other breaks working at the George T. Stagg distillery in Frankfort, which its namesake, a whiskey salesman in the St. Louis area, launched in the 1800s. Lee joined full time as a maintenance engineer after graduation in 1949. He was promoted a few years later to plant engineer and was entrusted with the entire operation's upkeep. This was the heyday of bourbon, with demand so insatiable that the Stagg distillery, like others in Kentucky, operated two shifts daily. Some parts of the plant operated around the clock, which might mean middle-of-the-night phone calls to Lee if something broke or slowed. He did not mind. He liked his work and his coworkers.

Lee was rapidly promoted up Stagg's ladder, even as the distillery changed owners and names, eventually becoming the Albert B. Blanton Distillery in the 1950s. In 1968 its current owner, the Schenley Distillers Corporation out of New York (headquartered in the Empire State Building), named Lee plant manager and then added what he considered a superfluous title: master distiller. Plant manager was one thing—Lee had already been working as plant superintendent, overseeing the mechanics and the upkeep of the distillery;

he was the go-to authority on how things should run and what to do when they stopped running. Master distiller? There already was one. Lee's title was, as he soon discovered, simply for marketing and advertising purposes. With big ears and a broad nose dominating a weathered face, not to mention his penchant for Balmoral caps from Scotland, Lee looked like how a consumer might envision a bourbon distiller. His courtly manner and soft Upper-South drawl helped, too. "Well" was "whale" and "bourbon" was "burr-bin" out of Lee's mouth. The move to make Lee master distiller would have profound effects on the American craft spirits movement. The title as it was understood for centuries was usually the product of years, perhaps decades, of training, an apprentice closely following the dictates and habits of another master distiller before assuming the mantle himself (for they were invariably men). Lee knew a lot about bourbon and how it was made. He was not a master distiller, however, in the usual sense, a fact that made him initially reluctant to take on the role. But take it on he did, lecturing visitors to the distillery and appearing in promotional materials. It was a desperate time in the industry as bourbon began its long fade into near-oblivion, a slide that accelerated into the 1980s—which is when Lee, by then perhaps as worthy of the title master distiller as anyone ever, looked around at the single malt phenomenon out of Scotland and realized America made some fantastic whiskey as well.

It all started with a conversation at the distillery with Bob Baranaskas. Baranaskas and Ferdie Falk had bought the Blanton distillery, now virtually synonymous with its Ancient Age bourbon brand, from Schenley and renamed it Age International. Falk and Baranaskas had been top executives at Fleischmann's Distilling, a subsidiary of food giant Nabisco (and Falk had worked at Schenley before Fleischmann's). They had left after their corporate parent's merger left them worried about job security. The name Falk and Baranaskas bestowed upon their new distillery spoke volumes about where they thought American bourbon whiskey was going: outside of America. Demand for whiskey in general had especially opened up in Japan, which had its own distilling traditions stretching back to at least the early twentieth century and which was still firmly in the midst of a nearly thirty-year economic boom that left many of its 120 million citizens flush with spending money. The Japanese had grown particularly fond of bourbon. The market there for America's signature whiskey grew 50 percent annually beginning in 1985, not only eating into blended whisky imports from Canada and Scotland but also forcing Japanese companies to scramble for the rights to import famed American brands. Theories abounded as to why the Japanese loved bourbon (and its close cousin Tennessee whiskey—Jack Daniel's was a huge seller there). Some said it was the macho image it conveyed. Others said it was par for the course, given that the nation had long embraced American products, if not America itself, Japan's conqueror in World War II and then its chief rebuilder. Still others hypothesized that, whatever its struggles back home against mighty vodka, bourbon was still that good and therefore that worthy. Falk and Baranaskas's Age International out of Frankfort wanted in on that Japanese market. The only question was how. Baranaskas talked it over with his master distiller.

"Elmer," he said, "we want to come out with a premium bourbon." This was in an era when such an idea seemed hopeless. Bourbon domestically was on the decline—a more exotic, more expensive brand seemed unlikely to catch on, but Baranaskas had the Japanese market in mind, not the American. "Give us your thoughts and ideas as to how we can develop a premium-price bourbon."

Lee told Baranaskas a story about Albert Bacon Blanton, the namesake of an earlier iteration of the distillery. Blanton was a Kentucky native who rose from office boy at the distillery in 1897 to its president before, through, and after Prohibition. He had for a time held a superintendent position similar to Lee's, and Lee had gotten to know Blanton before his death in 1959. Blanton would host parties quite often, Lee explained to Baranaskas. No fan of whiskey blends, Blanton would ask distillery workers to bring him samples that were at least eight years old from his favorite warehouse on the grounds, warehouse H, which he had constructed following Repeal in 1933, with metal walls instead of brick and mortar. The time-saving move ended up being fortuitous as well: the protection that the metal provided allowed the aging bourbon to expand deeper into the oak barrels during hot summer days and contract during cooler nights, which extracted more flavor from the wood. Blanton would sample the selections from warehouse H, each usually from a different barrel, and would pick one or two that he thought tasted best. "Bottle those for me," he would say. And those invariably would either end up with Blanton himself or with his guests.

Baranaskas understood exactly what Lee was saying. "We're going to go with that," he told Lee, "and we want you to select the bourbons that go into this Blanton. We're going to name it Blanton."

Blanton's Single Barrel Bourbon debuted first in Japan in the fall of 1984 and then in the United States. Age International pulled out all the stops in marketing the highly concentrated, small-batch creation from just what the name implied: barrels that Lee selected based upon their quality and character, with water to cut the alcohol level the only tweak. Packaging included a tag from the specially made spherical bottle that declared, "The finest bourbon in the world comes from a single barrel." The distillery provided no further explanation. The late Albert Bacon Blanton also featured prominently in the advertising, nattily attired in Victorian threads, complete with greatcoat and bowler—vintage all the way. Age International also marked each bottle of Blanton's with details such as which barrel and warehouse it came from, further accentuating its small-batch origin. Finally, the warehouse capped each with a stopper that itself was crowned with a racehorse and a jockey in various sporting positions. The distillery also included one of eight letters on each stopper—buy enough bottles and one might be able to spell B-L-A-N-T-O-N-S. But the content of the bottles was the main attraction. Here was not a whiskey blend; barrels that did not meet Lee's standards might be consigned to that fate. Here instead were bottles of bourbon directly from the source, a single barrel to a bottle to a glass: rich, complex, and undiluted, in large part precisely because of that single-barrel origin. Tasters picked up hints of everything from orange to vanilla, and, despite rye rather than wheat as the main secondary grain, Blanton's finished smoothly rather than harshly. The appeal was innate. Or at least Age International certainly hoped so—Baranaskas was very careful that the word *single* be included in the packaging and marketing. It was all the more insurance that an American tippler would understand right away what the distillery was going for, given the semantics, the product, and the approach. Single malt whiskeys from Scotland were riding an enormous wave of popularity, particularly in larger, flusher urban areas such as New York and San Francisco. And fine wine had forcefully established the romance of the barrel, whether it was through tastings such as the Four Seasons' heavily covered California Barrel Tasting or packaging that talked up a wine's gestation in oak barrels, a practice that Robert Mondavi popularized and evangelized starting twenty years before. Blanton's Single Barrel Bourbon, and the imitators that followed from other Kentucky producers, could not have happened without the rise of single malts from Scotland or fine wine from California.

Although Blanton's Single Barrel proved an almost immediate hit in surrounding Kentucky, it would be years before the spirit's influence was fully understood or felt in the United States. "It didn't do much the first year," as Lee recalled, and Baranaskas eventually felt compelled to flat-out invite competitors to release their own limited-edition single-barrel selections. No one did. So Age International kept releasing its own: Rock Hill Farms, Hancock's Reserve, and, finally, a single-barrel bourbon named after Lee upon his retirement in 1986. Along the way, to further drum up interest in this novel concept, Age International arranged through a local business magazine a blind tasting of Blanton's against Maker's Mark, the Kentucky favorite vaulted to prominence through that *Wall Street Journal* front-page piece a few years before. Blanton's won the annual tasting again and again, until, finally, Maker's Mark pointed out that its wheated classic was selected at random from a liquor store shelf each time while the Blanton's was specially bottled for the contest from a high-quality barrel. The yearly blind tasting ceased, "but not before," according to one analyst, "Age International had achieved its purchase—establishing a single-barrel bourbon and the Blanton's brand in consumers' minds in a way that traditional advertising could not." In that, of course, it echoed Bill Samuels Sr. and Maker's Mark itself thirty years before.

While Blanton's remained a commercial curiosity in the States, it really took fire in the Japanese market that the distillery originally aimed it at. Bottles routinely retailed for the yen equivalent of one hundred dollars, an unheard-of sum in American whiskey. (Blanton's was selling for around forty dollars a bottle in the United States.) That more than anything—more than the blind tasting, the clever packaging, the very concept of small-batch, high-quality—grabbed a struggling bourbon industry by the lapels and made it take notice. Soon other specialty, small-batch bourbons dropped on the domestic and international markets. Some were single-barrel like Blanton's. Others produced what they called small-batch bourbons, starting with the Jim Beam distillery. There, master distiller Booker Noe, a bona fide grandson of the original Jim Beam, selected various high-quality barrels to comprise an inaugural 1987 release called, simply, Booker's that retailed for around fifty dollars. The master distiller would explain to journalists who soon came calling that for years he had been bottling such selections for his own satisfaction or for gifts to industry insiders. Blanton's single-barrel inspired the commercial releases. Like with Blanton's, the Booker's label was an intimate affair, with cursive explanations of which batches were used and the lengths of time they had been allowed to age. Finally, there were also barrel-strength or cask-strength bourbon releases, though these predated both single-barrel and small-batch ones. These were bottlings straight from the barrel, with no water to cut the alcoholic strength of the bourbon, as distilleries typically did to get it to around eighty-five proof. Instead, barrel-strength bourbons clocked in at ridiculous strengths, often more than one hundred proof, meaning that the spirit within was more than 50 percent alcohol. The first widely available barrel-strength bourbon was likely Old Grand-Dad Special Selection from Frankfort's National Distillers Corporation. The *Washington Post* likened the 1980 release to "General Motors Corp. coming out with a 16-passenger Cadillac with fins," given the sharp decline in bourbon sales then. Old

Grand-Dad Special asked a scandalous sixteen dollars a bottle and boasted a throat-searing proof of 114—though aficionados would swear they detected a delectably concentrated taste that cut bourbons could not offer.

In the end, single-barrel, small-batch, and barrel-strength bourbons would not prove a panacea for America's once-vaunted whiskey industry. Bourbon sales continued to decline, each seeming plateau nothing more than a holding pattern before another drop. Domestic bourbon sales would in 1991 slide to their lowest since Prohibition, with a meager 15.6 million cases shipped. Sales of the specialty bourbons would not grow beyond 1 percent of all bourbon produced during the 1980s. Yet, these products—"the best bourbons ever made," according to one critic—would in time prove profoundly influential. The specialty bourbons of the early 1980s were a great leap forward in thinking about American spirits in general and the fledgling American small-batch spirits movement in particular. They created a homegrown context for understanding homegrown spirits, a clever and lasting answer to the twin ascents of single malts and fine wines, and proof positive that buying spirits need no longer hinge solely on alcoholic kick or the price tag. "These are bourbons for connoisseurs," the *New York Times* explained, "to be savored Cognac-style from a snifter." Fortuitously enough, right around the time that Blanton's Single-Barrel debuted, people would begin saying the same thing about another unlikely libation: American-made beer.

"YUPPIE BEER"
1982–1984 | Manhattan—Boston

In October 1982, a new brand of beer hit the streets of New York City. It was called New Amsterdam Amber Beer, named after the metropolis's old name under Dutch colonial rule and made from an all-malt recipe free of the adjuncts and chemicals often added to the wares of bigger brewers such as Miller and Anheuser-Busch. New Amsterdam was, at as much as nine dollars a six-pack, roughly twice as expensive as those beers and not nearly as ubiquitous. At first, only a handful of Manhattan restaurants carried it on draft or in bottles, and then some of the city's "toniest supermarkets and delicatessens." The beer's reach would expand throughout 1983 to more than

350 restaurants but still paled against the availability of Budweiser, Miller Lite, et al., which might be found at any corner bodega in all of Gotham's five boroughs. Matthew Reich, New Amsterdam's founder and driving force, did not mind. "It's the beer to have if you're having one. With dinner." That was how Reich would explain it to curious journalists and would-be retailers, the period-induced pause between "one" and "With" deliberate. It was a conscious spin off the old advertising tagline for Schaefer, a cheaper beer once brewed in huge quantities in Brooklyn: "Schaefer is the one beer to have when you're having more than one."

Schaefer was gone by the time of New Amsterdam's 1982 debut, as were the dozens of other breweries that had once dotted the New York City streetscape—Brooklyn alone had boasted nearly fifty at the start of the twentieth century. The rolling consolidation in American brewing since World War II and the perennial popularity of watery lagers such as Miller Lite had steadily eroded the number of breweries in the United States until there were fewer than one hundred at the start of the 1980s. There were simply few ways to really compete with national juggernauts that could quickly and cheaply make what Americans wanted—and then market it to them with massive advertising budgets. Reich's New Amsterdam was part of that crop of craft brewers that had arisen in the wake of Fritz Maytag's 1965 takeover of Anchor Brewing in San Francisco. Legal and tax changes in the 1970s, including a per-barrel excise tax cut in 1976, spurred a growth in the number of smaller breweries making beer from traditional ingredients such as hops and malted barley. It was by no means a boom—there were fewer than fifteen craft brewing operations at the start of 1984—but noticeable enough to have reached both coasts. (Save for Colorado and Michigan, the rest of the nation was devoid of craft breweries.) Reich, a trim, brown-haired Bronx native who went to college in Massachusetts and taught wine-tasting classes in Manhattan after a revelatory trip to France, created with New Amsterdam the first craft brewing concern not only in New York City but also the entire East Coast.

That presented an interesting challenge, one that would have been familiar to Jörg Rupf at St. George or Ansley Coale and Hubert Germain-Robin at Germain-Robin: selling when there was no real market for what you're selling. There were bottles of Anchor available on New York–area shelves, and there were plenty of potential consumers with living memories of a more diverse beer universe. Largely, though, a craft beer such as New Amsterdam, even in the nation's largest city, lacked a context for Reich to reference in quick sales pitches or public relations pushes. So he seized on connoisseurship, the idea that his beer was something special for a special event or a special someone, and therefore it might cost a little more and certainly would taste a little different. People could understand that, whether or not they had another craft beer to compare New Amsterdam with at the time. "This is yuppie beer, I guess," Reich told the *New York Times* in early 1985 for an article headlined A LOCAL BEER NOT FOR EVERYONE. Other craft beer pioneers ran with that same angle, happily defining themselves and their brands against the homogenized wares of the macrobrewers such as Miller. Charlie Papazian, a schoolteacher who had studied nuclear engineering at the University of Virginia, cofounded the American Homebrewers Association in 1978, a grandly titled organization that was at the time little more than his Colorado friends and himself talking, and making and drinking homebrew. In 1982 the association launched the Great American Beer Festival, again a rather grandiose title for what was little more than a five-hour gathering of twenty-four breweries and paying guests at a hotel in downtown Boulder. Still, the association and the festival clearly implied that American beer was worth the time, interest, and money of consumers in a way that it had never been before, at least for as long as most could remember. Beer, Papazian explained in 1983, was no longer "a workingman's drink—take a six-pack to the ballgame, or sit and drink in front of the TV." Instead, it was becoming "this connoisseur thing."

It dovetailed nicely with not only the explosion in Americans' fascination with fine wine but also the slow drip of their interest in all things "single" in spirits. The early 1980s proved an especially fertile time for American alcohol in general, perhaps the most inventive period in the nation's history since Prohibition, as the triple forces of fine wine, craft spirits, and craft beer gathered their tribes and gathered strength. Each still operated largely in its own network of producers, distributors, retailers, and trade media, though all clearly appeared to be working off the same idea of microproduction and exclusive (or at least exclusive-feeling) connoisseurship—and not desperately so. Fine wine had tipped into the mainstream with 1976's Judgment of Paris and Robert Parker's unabashed raves about the 1982 Bordeaux. Craft beer was itself poised to grow frenetically in the next few years, thanks largely to the exertions of a visitor to a New Amsterdam brewpub that Matthew Reich opened in 1986 in Manhattan's West Chelsea neighborhood.

Jim Koch was a successful management consultant in Boston and the descendant of several generations of brewers, first in what became Germany and then in the United States. His father, Charles, had worked in the brewery business, before leaving in the 1950s to help start a firm selling brewing and industrial chemicals. The younger Koch, who held undergraduate, law, and business degrees from Harvard, could have had a good life in his current

career—he was barely into his thirties, earning a solid six figures, and traveling widely—but then he read about Fritz Maytag and Anchor. And then he
read about the wider craft beer movement and sought out pioneers such as
Reich. Sensing an opportunity that might not come along again, Koch and a
secretary at his consultancy named Rhonda Kallman gathered investors and
retail accounts and, in late 1984, launched what they called the Boston Beer
Company. Its signature brand was Samuel Adams Boston Lager, a malty
sweet concoction born in part from an old Koch family recipe. Within a
year, the beer was all over New England, and then it went national, the first
breakout star of American craft beer. Koch himself, whose affable charm
masked an acute, sometimes ruthless business mind, became the closest thing
to a household name in craft beer. He was the gravelly baritone in numerous
radio spots; the suited, smiling figure in front of the White House, where
the Reagan mess served Sam Adams; the source at the end of loquacious
newspaper and magazine quotations on the joys of drinking craft beer; even
the target in dunking booths full of skunky lager, an idea Koch hatched to
show how much iffy beer his operation was willing to toss rather than foist
on consumers.

Jim Koch at the Samuel Adams Brewery in Jamaica Plain, Boston.
BOSTON BEER CO.

The rise of Koch and his Samuel Adams was not without controversy.
The biggest reason for the lager's rapid ascent was that Koch contracted

breweries to brew it rather than building or buying a facility himself. This lack of a physical brewery to look after freed him from mammoth financial constraints and allowed him to pour the savings into the marketing and distribution that made Samuel Adams so widely available. It also allowed him to quickly produce more beer through more contracts. Craft brewers shackled to the costs and the capacities of their physical breweries resented the ease contract brewing afforded Koch. Others faulted him for being a little too out there. No craft brewer had advertised like Koch advertised, nor set himself up as such an expert. That a Harvard-trained management consultant without an actual brewery had become the leading spokesman for craft beer grated on many nerves. "He's just an extremely aggressive salesman," sniffed Bert Grant, a Canadian immigrant who in 1981 had started the first American brewpub. That Koch's output of perhaps a couple million barrels of beer annually paled against the likes of Anheuser-Busch, which might produce fifty million just in the United States, mattered little. It just did not feel right to some that a rising tide of Samuel Adams should be lifting craft beer boats. There it was, though. David Geary, a former medical-supplies salesman who would in 1983 cofound Maine's oldest craft brewery, the D. L. Geary Brewing Company of Portland, remembered distinctly when Sam Adams landed on the city's supermarket shelves, beginning in 1988. "Now we have a category," Geary thought. Here was a context for consumers to think about "this connoisseur thing" that had largely been confined to the two coasts. The American small-batch spirits movement would soon find its own gateway brand from an unlikely source—not the first time it would starkly mirror the American craft beer movement.

THE NEW WHITE WINE

1985 | Manhattan

Michel Roux was quite pleased when Andy Warhol told him he really liked the Absolut vodka bottle. Since 1981 Roux had been the head of Carillon, the small northern New Jersey importer that the Swedish government enlisted to distribute its vodka brand, Absolut, in the United States. The Swedes debuted the brand during a spirits-industry trade convention at the Fairmont Hotel in downtown New Orleans in the spring of 1979, barely a year after Gunnar Broman, Hans Brindfors, and Peter Ekelund had presented the idea for it at the N. W. Ayer advertising agency in Manhattan. In the intervening several months, the Swedes had developed a grain-based recipe and gotten to work at a newly built plant outside of Stockholm, churning out the clear spirit that tasted slightly of black licorice and honey. The original Absolut certainly was not what would come to be called craft, nor was it particularly boilerplate in the vein of Smirnoff. For one thing, it would not leave a drinker breathless—this vodka had scent. For another, it was smoother going down, not rough firewater best cut in a cocktail. Finally, and perhaps most importantly in an American marketplace that often equated price with quality, it retailed for much more than other vodkas. A single two-ounce shot in New York City might run to four dollars.

Largely because the advertising budget for Absolut in 1979 was a relatively paltry $750,000, the Swedes concentrated on major cities such as New York in their marketing push. Conquer tastemakers in these places, the thinking went, and much of the rest of the nation would follow. Ekelund himself spent much of 1979 and 1980 schlepping Absolut from metropolis to metropolis, starting with that convention in New Orleans and including another industry trade show in Boston, where he belted out a Viking drinking song and then downed an entire mug of the spirit, its intoxicating effects becoming almost immediately apparent to onlookers. The Swedes had also switched advertising agencies, eventually ending up at what was then a small Paris house known as TBWA. To land the account, two recent TBWA hires, Geoff Hayes and Graham Turner, devised a simple though not simplistic pitch that worked unconsciously off the original epiphany of Jerry Siano at N. W. Ayer: The brand's name, Absolut, would be paired with one other word, whether that word was the name of a state, a city, a person, an industry, or even a concept or a movement. There would be an "Absolut Glasnost" before the decade's end to mark the historic opening of the Soviet Union. Then this verbal pairing would be reinforced with an illustration or photograph—in the case of "Absolut Glasnost," twenty-six works from Soviet artists that together formed the shape of the vodka bottle. The first idea Hayes and Turner pitched was "Absolut Perfection" with a golden halo crowning a photograph of the vodka bottle. The Swedes were hooked, and the idea of Absolut [Something] stormed forth into advertising immortality.

Yet, Absolut still lagged other vodka brands on the US market, despite a seemingly unquenchable thirst for the stuff in general. Absolut by the end of 1984 was not among the five bestselling brands in the United States, a list

Connecticut-based Smirnoff still topped. Nor was it even the number-one import. That spot belonged to Stolichnaya, the bona fide Russian vodka that Pepsi-Cola had been distributing since 1974. It was not as if there were not enough potential customers to go around. Vodka was the main alcoholic ingredient in more than one in five cocktails mixed in the United States by the mid-1980s. It just seemed that the Swedes' idea had petered out in the face of Smirnoff's decades-long head start. Absolut was destined for trendy bars in places such as New York and Los Angeles but not for a wider audience. One such trendy bar that the Swedes managed to place it, however, was Studio 54, perhaps the world's most famous nightclub in the late 1970s, a long-lined epicenter of disco music and a home away from home for a range of celebrities. It was within Studio 54's pulsating shadows off Midtown Manhattan's heretofore unfashionable West 54th Street that Andy Warhol first saw the Absolut bottle.

Warhol by that point was one of the world's most famous artists. He had exploded onto the scene in 1962, with twin exhibits in New York and Los Angeles, his images of soup cans and celebrities seamlessly—and, some said, shamelessly—turning commercialism into what came to be called pop art. "Being good in business is the most fascinating kind of art," according to the bewigged Warhol, a Pennsylvania native and son of immigrants from Czechoslovakia whose first artistic forays were of the deliberately commercial kind: as an illustrator for businesses such as the jeweler Tiffany and the magazine *Vogue*. The shape and appearance of the Absolut bottle itself, as well as the early ads pairing it with the brand name and another word, spoke to the abstemious Warhol, who was known to use Absolut as a cologne rather than as an intoxicant. He understood it in all its simplistic complexity. And the painting he produced for Michel Roux's Carillon in 1985 for $65,000 stamped the vodka with a cultural imprimatur most brands could only dream of. Here was one of the century's biggest artists immortalizing an advertising pitch. "People treated [Roux] differently after the Warhol ad," one journalist later noted. "He was no longer just another liquor dealer, but a patron of the arts." What had Warhol wrought? A sort of psychedelic painting of a black Absolut bottle against a bright background with the words ABSOLUT WARHOL underneath it. Carillon used it in yet another Absolut [Something] print advertisement, and from then on the brand was, well, absolutely unstoppable.

During its first year of sales in 1979, Absolut sold five thousand twelve-bottle cases. That number would balloon to more than two million within ten years. In 1979 the brand could claim perhaps 1 percent of the import vodka market. A decade later it held 60 percent and had belted Stolichnaya from the top import spot in 1985, the year of Warhol's painting. At one point, the Swedes literally "ran out of booze," unable to keep up with American demand. The plant producing Absolut had to kick into twenty-four-hour gear to replenish Carillon's East Coast warehouses, which Absolut's popularity had emptied. Smirnoff was still the most popular vodka in the United States as the 1980s went on, with ultracheap brand Popov eventually at number two. But Absolut had come literally out of nowhere—the brand did not exist when Gunnar Broman and company pitched it in 1978—to consistently soar sales-wise when the fortunes of other spirits were falling as the pool of American spirits drinkers dried up. And it had done so with a higher price tag and a remarkably different approach to packaging, never mind the marketing campaign that was already passing into legend, with various ad men and women vying to take career-making credit for its origins. The very phrase "premium vodka" entered the media's wider lexicon, as well as the minds of consumers paying attention. Absolut was very likely the first spirit, certainly the first vodka, that a large and demographically diverse number of Ameri-cans ordered at bars and restaurants entirely by name. Rather than a vodka tonic, for instance, it was an "Absolut and tonic" or an "Absolut tonic." Such an order might have been true before for certain bourbon brands—a "Beam and Coke," for instance—but not as widely executed.

This was important for the fledgling American small-batch spirits move-ment, with which, on the surface, Absolut otherwise had little to nothing in common. Here was a brand, priced at a premium and not so readily avail-able, at least at first, that consumers happily sought out and that conveyed a kind of knowing status on its purchasers. "A lot of yuppies come in looking for Absolut," a bartender at a hip watering hole in Manhattan's Greenwich Village told the *New York Times*. It was the name they wanted, too, not necessarily the contents behind it. "I think that if someone asked for Absolut and I poured them Stoli, they wouldn't know the difference," the bartender explained, using the shorthand for Stolichnaya. Even people who did not drink vodka not only recognized the brand but also were huge fans of it, some going as far as writing to advertising agency TBWA for copies of ads—an odd thing, given that Absolut [Something] soon appeared on everything from T-shirts to dorm-room posters to billboards to beach blankets.

With its tens of millions of bottles in circulation and its ads ubiquitous, Absolut served as a gateway for consumers into higher-end spirits in America. It was the same exclusivity conceit that steeled Bill Samuels Sr. until the world beyond Kentucky noticed his Maker's Mark. Traces of the novelty of single malt, single-barrel, and barrel-strength whiskeys could be found in

Absolut's smashing success, too. Absolut's ascent even contained hints of the context-creating role that Samuel Adams Boston Lager was beginning to play for craft beer around the same time. Things got so hot in the 1980s that some began thinking the unthinkable: that Absolut and premium vodka in general seemed poised to become the "white wine of the 1990s"—Americans' reigning tipple of choice. Might this quirky Swedish spirit rescue all others, small-batch included, from the Chardonnay they were drowning in?

OF PEARS AND BEARS
1983–1990 | Portland, Oregon

The late 1970s had been a lean time for the orchards that Steve McCarthy's family owned in northern Oregon's Hood River Valley. His great-grandfather and grandfather had cultivated the primarily apple and pear orchards at the turn of the twentieth century and then lost them in the Great Depression. McCarthy's father went into the more lucrative timber industry after World War II and rode a national building boom to affluence. The money allowed the elder McCarthy to buy up the orchards again, and they served for years as a staple of the family's income, along with other ventures. Then, through either poor crop quality or poor market conditions (it's not clear which), the family found itself unable to sell all the apples, pears, etc., that their orchards produced. One year the packaging firm that the family contracted with for distribution sent invoices rather than a check. Fellow Oregon orchardists were being wiped out. Something had to be done.

The younger McCarthy at this point was in his late thirties. He had graduated from Reed College in Portland, three hours north of his hometown of Roseburg, and earned a law degree from New York University. He had worked in the public sector, including as general manager of the Portland region's transit system. As the 1980s started, he was practicing law and running a family-owned company that manufactured hunting and shooting accessories. McCarthy himself was an avid outdoorsman. He could as a teenager, in his own estimation, "hike the legs off anyone in the State of Oregon." As a twenty-year-old, he embarked with two friends on a more than eighteen-thousand-foot climb in the Nepalese Himalayas; one friend died from a fall just as the trio reached their goal. (McCarthy later sold a story of this triumph-turned-tragedy to *Sports Illustrated* while a law student in Manhattan.) McCarthy's travels also took him to western Europe, including to the southeastern French city of Grenoble for six months during college in 1960. It was there that he first encountered eau-de-vie. When the family orchard started having trouble in the late 1970s, the bearded, bespectacled McCarthy realized that that distilled fruit juice might be the answer, an opportunity, he thought, to make "an elegant, expensive product" for sale in America—in North America—where there were no eau-de-vie distilleries. Even imported eau-de-vie was difficult to find, McCarthy discovered, mostly the provenance of upscale restaurants in major cities such as Seattle and San Francisco. Moreover, McCarthy also realized that the Bartlett pears his family had been growing off and on for nearly a century were one and the same with the Williams pears that undergirded the eau-de-vie de poire he had discovered in France. "It's just so logical," McCarthy thought. Besides, turning it into alluringly tasty alcohol "has to be the greatest way to sell fruit."

In the summer of 1983, McCarthy decamped for France to research his idea. He returned in the fall and heard through the winemaking industry grapevine that a German named Jörg Rupf was now making eau-de-vie in tiny amounts in Emeryville, California. McCarthy quickly tracked Rupf down. He was the one man on the continent who might be able to help him realize his plans. There was just one hitch.

"Look, I'm going to go out and compete with you," he told Rupf. "But, to be fair, I should pay you. Why don't I pay you seventy-five thousand dollars, and you teach me how to do seven or eight products?"

Rupf agreed. It was the first meeting of the minds in the American small-batch spirits movement, a watershed of information sharing. McCarthy's planning continued through 1984 and into 1985. He bought a small warehouse on the western bank of the Willamette River in downtown Portland. He got the necessary federal license, and he named the new operation Clear Creek, after the family orchard. He ordered a pot still from West Germany. It broke in transit, and the insurance company took it off his hands. A second one arrived, and Rupf came up from California. McCarthy proved an apt pupil, and, in the fall of 1985, they made a batch of poire that surprised McCarthy with its quality. He figured he had the right equipment, good fruit, and unique expertise in Rupf, yet he had not expected the first run to turn out so well. There would be some iffy goes of it in the future, but this inaugural poire came off without a hitch. Selling it and subsequent early batches was another matter.

Steve McCarthy at Clear Creek in the mid-1980s.
CLEAR CREEK

Luckily, McCarthy could not have picked a better city or a more promising state to commence the first small-batch distillery outside of California or Kentucky. Portland itself was by 1985 an epicenter of America's burgeoning craft beer movement. The city of just under five hundred thousand hosted two craft breweries, Widmer Brothers and BridgePort, both of which operated in the same gritty industrial area as McCarthy's Clear Creek. Cartwright Portland on SE Main Street, the first craft brewery in the entire Pacific Northwest, had already come and gone by 1985, its mild English-style ale, though of inconsistent quality, apparently enough to pique interest. Finally, Fred Eckhardt, a handle-bar-mustache-curating ex-Marine and professional photographer, started writing the first regular beer criticism column in a major American newspaper, the *Oregonian*, in April 1984. And in 1976, Don Younger, a long-haired corporate marketing refugee, created what became perhaps the most influential beer bar west of the Mississippi in his Horse Brass Pub on Belmont Street, which specialized in being the first to serve many craft beer brands. Although far from spirits technically, Portland's craft beer scene unmistakably fostered a culture of appreciation for small-batch alcohol made with traditional ingredients by independent producers, such as Steve McCarthy. Closer to spirits' technical wheelhouse, the wine industry surrounding Portland was undergoing its own explosive growth. It had all started in 1961 when San Francisco native Richard Sommer, a trained horticulturalist and army veteran, started the first winery in Oregon since Prohibition to make wines primarily from higher-end European varietals, including Pinot Noir, a notoriously finicky grape that winemakers farther south in California were having particular trouble with. Sommer's first Pinot Noir batch in 1967 proved exceptional, and the Oregon fine wine industry was on its way to becoming the nation's fourth-largest, after California, Washington, and New York. Several producers, including Sommer's HillCrest, formed a wine-promoting trade group in 1969, and the Oregon Wine Festival launched the same year. All the while, James Beard, at the time the nation's leading food writer and a proud Oregon native, talked up his state's winemaking potential to various audiences.

McCarthy was well aware of Oregon's fine wine success and Portland's craft beer growth. The state's reputation for fine wine by the 1980s helped him at least get meetings with higher-end restaurateurs and retailers, particularly in his old stomping grounds of New York City. Overall, though, McCarthy encountered the same arctic indifference other early small-batch spirits pioneers did. Most merchants just did not know what to make of an eau-de-vie from the Hood River Valley. Like Jörg Rupf, who also became an early investor in Clear Creek, McCarthy understood from the beginning that his market was infinitesimal against those for the likes of vodka and rum, never mind Chardonnay or light beer. "Producing wonderful eau de vie," as one critic noted, "is a little like being the greatest bouzouki player in America: regardless of your virtuosity, your audience will be small." Consequently, McCarthy never figured that his small-batch distillery would amount to anything similar to the promising reputations that some of the state's wineries and breweries enjoyed. For years, then, he operated alone—literally as Clear Creek's sole worker after Rupf helped on those first batches and as the only such distillery outside of California at that point. McCarthy produced sixty twelve-bottle cases that first year, and production would remain under one thousand cases annually for the rest of the decade. By 1990, he was grossing perhaps $100,000 in sales. His family's other business concerns provided McCarthy his income, not spirits. (He sold the hunting and shooting supply company in 1987, for instance.) Even after he added a second still and moved to a bigger warehouse in 1991, production did not creep much beyond perhaps one thousand cases annually. Distribution remained almost entirely in Oregon. The odd bottle of Clear Creek Poire might turn up in New York City for twenty-two dollars a pop, but otherwise the distillation remained more a labor of love, a personal and commercial curiosity in a late 1980s spirits landscape that trended as far from independent and small-batch as it seemed possible to get.

The relentless decline in Americans' spirits drinking—by 1984, per-capita consumption had declined five straight years and retail sales three—forced the industry's biggest players to both diversify their offerings and gobble up their competition. A dog-eat-dog ethos prevailed during this bear market for spirits as even gigantic concerns such as Seagram and Heublein struggled to maintain shares of a dwindling market. Rather than propping up flagging whiskey brands, Seagram test-marketed a no-alcohol wine and leaned more heavily on an existing lower-alcohol wine line. Heublein, too, looked more to wine than spirits for its bottom line, test-marketing a carbonated white wine soda and launching marketing campaigns to remind people that brands such as Smirnoff were better with cocktails than on their own. Other, smaller firms went the wine-cooler route, jumping on a juggernaut that already accounted for one in ten US wine sales after only a few short years. Heublein even had a lower-alcohol vodka, the approximately forty-proof Popov brand, introduced at the turn of the decade and quickly proving a smash hit as the second-top-selling vodka behind Smirnoff. If such gimmickry did not appear to be working, there was always the tried and true approach of hiring Wall Street advisers to hunt for acquisitions.

The spirits industry from almost the first days after Prohibition had always had its conglomerates, its large companies whose holdings might include a variety of foodstuff brands well beyond whiskey, vodka, etc. Heublein controlled Kentucky Fried Chicken, for instance, and Seagram and its new president in 1984, Edgar Bronfman Jr., were famously involved in movie and theater production. In the early 1980s, the sizes of these conglomerates grew, as did the number of new players. Guinness, the Dublin-based concern most famous for its signature dark beer, went on an acquisition spree in the mid-1980s that perfectly illustrated the often head-spinning brands within brands within brands approach that became the norm of an alcoholic beverage industry searching for steady profitability in a choppy market. Guinness partnered with Moët Hennessy, an importer and distributor that had itself recently acquired another importer and distributor, Schieffelin & Company, whose portfolio included brands such as Johnnie Walker blended whiskey and Tanqueray gin. Guinness around the same time purchased importer Schenley, one-time owner of the famed George T. Stagg distillery in Frankfort, as well as several other spirits producers. Finally, Guinness also partnered with Bacardí on the rum giant's operations in Spain, bringing yet another spirits brand under its corporate umbrella, where they operated alongside beer and wine. As for Heublein, Grand Metropolitan, a real estate company based in the United Kingdom, acquired it and its nearly one hundred labels in January 1987, after having just partnered with Martell, one of the Big Four Cognac makers, on an international distribution network. And Seagram set about in 1985 simply splitting its many spirits tentacles into four companies, two of them new, under the same corporate cloud. "The industry has been in trouble for five years," noted Marvin Shanken, an ex–real estate investment banker turned publisher of alcohol-industry trade publications such as *Wine Spectator*. "Seagram is the first to bite the bullet and reorganize the company to meet the problems they face."

If these problems, particularly the sharp drop in spirits consumption and the rocket-ship rise of fine wine, were nagging enough to rattle even hegemons such as Seagram, what hope had infinitesimally smaller operations such as Germain-Robin, St. George, Charbay, and Clear Creek? There were no more than five small-batch distilleries in the United States by 1985—all of them were in California and Oregon. The *notion* of small-batch spirits, if not yet the lexicon, was much more widely felt, thanks to the strange bedfellows of single malt, barrel-strength, and single-barrel whiskeys; the rapid rise of context-creating Absolut; and that similarly rapid ascent of fine wine and even craft beer in places. The stage was definitely set and the characters in their places. A small-batch spirits movement, personified in that mid-1980s connection that Steve McCarthy made with Jörg Rupf, could very well take hold and grow. It was no more improbable, really, than the fact that in 1985 the number of craft breweries nationwide was about to crest twenty after an identical number of years trying. Or that American fine wine increasingly dictated the tastes and textures of even ancient European styles. The travails of the wider industry might even prove a boon. Small-batch distillers would likely never overtake Seagram or Guinness, in much the same way the maker of Samuel Adams Boston Lager seemed unlikely to unseat the maker of Miller Lite. But during the previous decade Bill Samuels Sr. had patiently led tipplers to a better bourbon made in smaller amounts. Maker's Mark was no longer independently owned, but its charging growth during a time of general decline in bourbon sales pointed to the potential of small-batch distilling as the latter half of the 1980s dawned. Yet the biggest challenges lay just ahead, ones titanic enough to drown the entire movement.

PART III

"AN AFTER-SCHOOL SPECIAL BROUGHT TO LIFE"

1986 | College Park, Maryland—Washington, DC

Just after 6:30 in the morning on Thursday, June 19, 1986, a 911 dispatcher in Prince George's County, Maryland, took a call from a dormitory at the flagship state university in College Park. The young male voice on the other end of the line was slurred and hesitant, though the information it imparted seemed to demand more panic: "This is Len Bias," Brian Tribble said of his friend. "You have to get him back to life. There is no way he can die."

Tribble repeated Len Bias's name over and over, as if to spur the ambulance that much faster toward him.

"It doesn't matter what his name is," the dispatcher finally said.

It would. For Tribble's friend and classmate was at that moment one of the most famous figures in America and, because of what the 911 call set in motion, he would become even more well known, a legend for all the wrong reasons before the age of twenty-three. Just two days before Tribble's call, the Boston Celtics had selected Bias as the number-two pick in the NBA draft. The six-foot-eight University of Maryland forward who led the Atlantic Coast Conference in scoring his final season was about to join professional sports royalty, with all the trappings that entailed, including money. The Celtics were then in the midst of an epic run of world championships (1981, 1984, and 1986), conference titles (four straight from 1984 through 1987), and accolades for their star, Larry Bird (NBA MVP 1984, 1985, and 1986). Bias himself was already seen as the anointed successor to Bird, a forward with potentially even more power and surer shooting. A Celtics scout on draft day even compared Bias to the Chicago Bulls' young star, Michael Jordan, who was a few years into what would turn out to be the greatest professional basketball career ever. "He's a great athlete," Red Auerbach, the legendary ex–Celtics coach-turned-team president, told a reporter that draft day of Bias. "He's got good work habits. He's a good kid." Bias himself took it all in stride, saying he would be happy just to be the "sixth man" behind the five starters. "It's a dream within a dream," the twenty-two-year-old Maryland native told a reporter from the *Washington Post*. "My first dream was just to play in the NBA. To get drafted by the world champions is an extra one." Asked what he might do first with the millions the Celtics were expected to offer him, the son of a repairman simply replied, "A car. A Mercedes."

Bias was dead within forty-eight hours of that statement. What happened? In events that the police would record in the following days, and that filmmakers and journalists would re-create for mass audiences in the years to come, Bias went partying with his friends to celebrate the Celtics' decision. He and three others ended up after midnight in a dorm room on Maryland's College Park campus, where they broke out some cocaine. Bias by most accounts partook freely, pronouncing himself "a horse" before doing one last line off a mirror. He then got up to use the bathroom, tripped, and sat back on the bed, where he soon sputtered into a seizure that thoroughly alarmed his friends. One stuck the handle of a pair of scissors in Bias's mouth to prevent him from swallowing his tongue. Another held his legs. Tribble called 911. The paramedics came and went, and Bias's trio of friends cleaned up the dorm room as best they could. Bias died shortly before 9:00 AM, just after his mother arrived at the hospital.

The details, which flashed through newspapers and television news programs over the next several days, were beyond compelling: a young man, full of promise and potential, from a good family and in seemingly perfect health—a pro athlete in a popular culture that worshiped pro athletes—cut down suddenly; and at a place of learning, no less, not in some seedy bar or back alley. "This was a moralistic passion play," one sportswriter would remember decades later, when Bias's death could still conjure up fresh shudders of fear, especially through parents, "an after-school special come to life." That was because it was not so much that Bias had died, or even that he had died fewer than two days after one of the world's greatest sports franchises drafted him into a bubble of wealth and fame—it was how he died. Even more specifically, it was the perception of how he died, the narrative that some in power and in the media seized upon that shook Americans following along at home. Bias very likely indulged in cocaine regularly or at least regularly enough for investigators to later find several grams of it under the front seats of his car. His buddy Tribble was a well-known, small-amounts drug dealer on campus who would go to prison on unrelated drug dealing charges the following decade. And, while Bias and his mother were born-again Christians and Bias obviously possessed a strong work ethic to have gotten him where he was athletically, he, like young men since time immemorial and especially like those who have just scaled a professional mountain, liked to party at nightclubs, to spend money on nice clothes and other accoutrements, and to flirt with young women. Yet the picture of him that emerged was one of near princely perfection. "Bias, a student leader and born-again Christian, had no record of drug use or abuse," one reporter told his readers. "He had passed every random drug test at the university and had been tested by four NBA teams and found to be drug-free and in perfect health," according to the *Washington Post* editorial board (which conveniently ignored the ease with which drug tests could be doctored or simply ignored). "Len Bias was a born-again Christian," the nation's third-largest daily went on, "a spiritual leader of his team at a religious retreat. He wrote poetry.... His worst confirmed transgression: missing a team curfew at an away game when he visited old friends."

What had done Bias in, then, the media agreed, was a single, freakish bout with cocaine. His parents, in an interview with the *New York Times*, dismissed as "innuendo" the idea that their oldest son could be a regular user. His mother said he might even have taken cocaine accidentally that tragic night or been poisoned. "He made a bad decision to try cocaine for the first time," Lefty Driesell, Bias's coach at Maryland, assured a reporter (though, given that news soon emerged that other Maryland players had used drugs, it seems likely Driesell was either being charitable or simply lying). Toxicologists would conclude not only that Bias did cocaine more than once in the hours leading to the fatal dose but also that he had used it before. That and other behaviors such as the nightclubbing faded. What emerged after the initial shock wore off was the narrative of the healthy, focused young man who tried drugs only once and died because of it. This phony narrative smashed head-on into political realities that made Len Bias's death in June 1986 "the most socially influential moment in the history of modern sports." And the moment, as detached as it may first appear, had profound effects on American small-batch spirits.

Tip O'Neill had been the speaker of the US House of Representatives for nearly nine years when Bias died. The bulbous-nosed Democrat with wavy silver hair was perhaps best known outside of Washington's power corridors as the cagey operator who coined the adage "All politics is local." That was true for O'Neill himself in the case of Len Bias's death: O'Neill's congressional district covered a sizable chunk of the Boston area, the same metropolitan region Bias was due to decamp to for the Celtics. Constituents and local media demanded some sort of forceful response to the circumstances that led to the rising star's death. At the same time, the speaker saw an opportunity to one-up the Republican-controlled Senate and White House with a forceful—and very public—condemnation of illegal drugs. On July 24, roughly a month after Bias's death, O'Neill staged a press conference with eleven chairmen of various House committees to announce sweeping antidrug legislation. "Drug abuse is no longer a problem for a few localities or a few communities to handle," he intoned. "It has spread like wildfire to become not only a tragic national menace but a threat to our domestic peace and security." Not to be outdone, House Republicans hastily cobbled together their own calls for legislative action on drugs and urged their counterparts in the Senate to move, too. Finally, the Reagan White House announced a few days after O'Neill's press conference that it, too, had a plan to combat the sorts of substances that doomed Bias—though it was careful to deny its moves had anything to do with O'Neill's. Almost overnight, fighting drugs became the key issue in Washington, bumping aside all others despite a tight congressional calendar as the summer recess loomed. Acting with a speed and a level of bipartisan cooperation rarely seen, then or since, Democrats and Republicans passed the Anti-Drug Abuse Act of 1986. President Reagan signed it into law in October. The legislation budgeted huge amounts of money for drug prevention and enforcement, though it would become most famous, or infamous, for imposing mandatory minimum sentences for certain drug offenses, particularly possession of even small amounts of heroin, cocaine, and crack. The act, which the death of twenty-two-year-old Len Bias sparked, was the single loudest crescendo yet in a drug war that was then more than a decade old. He became "the Archduke Ferdinand of the Total War on Drugs," one journalist later wrote, comparing the basketball star with the Austrian royal whose 1914 assassination touched off World War I. In this beefed-up fight against narcotics, the government would open a front against spirits, too, dusting off familiar Prohibition-era weapons and trying out new ones with near-fatal accuracy.

CRUSADE

1986 | Washington, DC

On September 14, 1986, a Sunday, President Ronald Reagan and wife Nancy greeted primetime television viewers nationwide from a couch in the West Hall of the White House. As the president explained in a folksy tone that gradually turned more and more somber, he normally addressed his fellow Americans from some part of the West Wing administrative hub, such as the Oval Office. Instead he was in the residential portion of the mansion afforded the First Family

> because the message this evening is not my message but ours. And we speak to you not simply as fellow citizens but as fellow parents and grandparents and as concerned neighbors. It's back-to-school time for America's children. And while drug and alcohol abuse cuts across all generations, it's especially damaging to the young people on whom our future depends.

The president went on to invoke Abraham Lincoln's fortitude in the same White House during the Civil War, the waves of immigrants from times past, the nation's mobilization during World War II, and the liberation of Europe from Nazism, as well as to implore the help of every entity from the clergy to union bosses to the media, and all toward one goal: ending drug and alcohol abuse. It was not merely a matter of mitigating the abuse, as the first couple explained, but of ending it for all time. The Reagans' address painted narcotics such as cocaine and perfectly legal alcohol with the same broad, menacing brush: "They're threatening our values and undercutting our institutions," the president said. "They're killing our children." Drugs, alcohol, and the abuse of both were positively un-American to boot: "Drug abuse is a repudiation of everything America is. The destructiveness and human wreckage mock our heritage." He assured viewers that the following day he would lay out a multipoint plan to combat drug and alcohol abuse, one that followed on the heels of congressional efforts in the wake of basketball star Len Bias's death that June. First Lady Nancy Reagan, who had been campaigning against drugs long before Bias's death leapfrogged it to the political front-and-center, was even blunter. Her concluding remarks brooked no dissent and gave no quarter, couching it all in quasi-religious terms—on the Christian Sabbath, no less. "Now we go on to the next stop: Making a final commitment not to tolerate drugs by anyone, anytime, anyplace. So, won't you join us in this great, new national crusade?"

The First Couple's primetime address dealt mostly with illegal drugs. They did, however, reference alcohol repeatedly and unmistakably lumped in its abuse with that of the likes of cocaine and its smokable form, crack. It was this verbal and psychological linkage, and the very real fallout from it, that presented American craft spirits with its single biggest set of challenges. The industry at large was already reeling from a shift in drinking habits that led to a sharp drop in sales and consumption in the 1980s. The rapid ascent of fine wine, particularly American-made brands, did not help matters in the marketplace, nor did a health craze that seemed determined to exercise away that hangover from the overindulgent 1970s. The 1980s saw hundreds of exercise videos debut, designed in part to take advantage of the proliferation of the VCR, and some so popular they spawned sequels. President Reagan's surgeon general, C. Everett Koop, intoned humorlessly in radio and television messages against sloth and overindulgence. Fitness chains such as Bally Total Fitness, Crunch, Planet Fitness, and Equinox opened hundreds of locations nationwide throughout the decade, and a "perpetual stream" of diet books flowed onto bestseller lists. Weight Watchers, the fat-fighting organization launched in Queens, New York, in 1963, reached its membership peak in the 1980s and spread to more than two dozen countries. The nonprofit Center for Science in the Public Interest, which an acolyte of crusading consumer-rights lawyer Ralph Nader started, flooded eager newsrooms with reports on the dire consequences of too much of pretty much anything, whether it was beer or Chinese takeout. There was an unmistakable climate of healthy—or at least healthier—living in the United States, one spirits clearly did not fit into. "There is a fundamental attitude change about health and alcoholic beverages," one leading spirits executive noted in 1984, and it was colliding with the creeping neo-Prohibitionism that peaked in late 1986 with the federal government's reaction to Len Bias's death.

The creep had begun in earnest in 1980 with the formation of Mothers Against Drunk Driving, a nonprofit that advocated exactly what its name implied. MADD grew from the experience of its founder, Candy Lightner. A drunk driver hit and killed Lightner's thirteen-year-old daughter near Sacramento in May 1980. Although the culprit was a repeat drunk-driving offender, he escaped any sizable prison term under California law at the time. Lightner then started MADD to advocate for tougher laws, as well as to educate the public about the dangers of mixing drink and a drive. Lightner's own story proved powerfully compelling. NBC even broadcast a primetime movie in March 1983, based on her tragic experience, entitled *MADD*, and her group's effectiveness was almost instantaneous. State legislatures and highway patrols snapped to attention, stiffening their own oversight and sentencing. Lightner's home state of California recorded a 43 percent drop in New Year's holiday traffic deaths from December 1981 into January 1982, a plunge officials attributed to tougher drunk-driving laws. MADD's specific push against drunk driving, like Nancy Reagan's Just Say No campaign against illegal drugs, which she launched in 1981, took on a psychological force well beyond the intended target, much as Len Bias's death a few years later gong-rattled well beyond College Park, Maryland, and even professional sports. (And, by the way, as media reports later noted, had the basketball star not bought a bottle of Hennessy Cognac only a few hours before his overdose?) Simply put, attitudes had changed. "It's almost stylish not to have too much to drink," an executive at the Houlihan's restaurant chain told a reporter. "It used to be no big deal if you got blind drunk. Now it's sort of disgusting." Some of this had to do with that shift in drinking habits away from spirits. "We used to figure a half-bottle of wine per person when ordering for a party," a caterer in the DC area explained to a *Washington Post* columnist just before the holiday season in 1984. "Now we order at least a case of white wine for every thirty people. That's just for the bar. Not counting wine with the meal. We find that booze is relatively untouched at parties, but the white wine goes." The attitude shift away from overindulgence, though, in the end had more to do with the efforts of MADD, the Reagans, and others, as well as the newfound national jones for exercise, or at least cleaner living.

All of which might have been fine for the wider spirits industry in the long run. The big brewers, including Anheuser-Busch and Miller, found ways to promote responsible consumption of their products while selling more of it than ever before—domestic beer production hit an all-time peak in 1982. In the realm of fine wine, no less a gregarious personage than Robert Mondavi hosted symposia on the drink's supposed health benefits, ones the media, including its phalanx of wine critics, were only too happy to tout. Besides, fine wine had the sales wind at its back still. The problem for American spirits, big and small, was that consumption had already been dropping in the short term. For some parts, such as bourbon, it had been dropping pre-cipitously for years. The newfound aversion to overindulgence and the focus on higher-alcohol drinks as taboo did not help matters in the least, nor did the fact that the Reagan administration, with congressional blessings, bared some serious teeth to back up its highly publicized bark. Congress passed legislation withholding a crucial percentage of highway-maintenance funds from states that did not raise their drinking ages to twenty-one. All fifty states would fall into line by 1988. Federal officials tied grants and money for student loans to colleges' and universities' implementation and enforce-ment of "no-use" drug and alcohol policies. The new Drug Abuse Resistance Education Program (DARE) taught elementary and high school students that "alcohol is a gateway drug that can lead to other, stronger chemical dependen-cies." Its scolding posters popped up on school walls nationwide seemingly overnight in the mid-1980s. Finally, the federal government in 1988 began requiring alcoholic beverage packaging to carry a forty-two-word warning listing the potential consequences of consumption, including the risks to pregnant women. While nobody of any consequence talked seriously about another widespread alcohol ban, these legal actions, coupled with the health craze (and scares), created a climate that the spirits industry just did not need after years of decline already. During the 1980s, according to legal scholar Richard Mendelson, "Americans came closest to re-creating the moral panic that had accompanied the march to Prohibition."

And the industry could not do thing one about it—an impotence that drove its members mad. "The industry feels intimidated," a top executive with Rémy Martin said. "It should be trying to mobilize public opinion to fight this stuff. Alcohol is not an evil; it's something that makes life a little bit more pleasant. I think the industry should not act like we're bad guys trying to push demon rum on people." But all the industry could do was chip away at the edges of this "moral panic." Distributors and producers slapped appeals to moderation on packaging. Big-time players such as Seagram phased out promotional events on campuses. Retailers, including restaurants and bars that had long been the biggest accounts for distillers, warned patrons in post-ers and placards to please not drive drunk. Meanwhile, the hits kept coming. There was serious talk of making the spirits industry's longtime voluntary ban on television and radio advertising involuntary—and of requiring counter-commercials to run after those touting beer and wine. And Ronald Reagan's successor in the White House, his vice president, George H. W. Bush, con-tinued the crusade against drugs that often linked up with a crusade against alcohol. During a primetime address from the Oval Office on September 5,

1989, the first time Bush had addressed the nation like so, the president held up a bag of crack cocaine he said had been seized in a park just across the street from the White House. "All of us agree that the gravest domestic threat facing our nation today is drugs," Bush intoned in that clipped New England accent. The answer, like with his predecessor, was more money for "more prisons, more jails, more courts, more prosecutors," as well as for additional education for the young, including a forthcoming taped presidential address to students that Bush said would be played at schools nationwide in the coming days. Unlike Reagan three years before, Bush did not reference alcohol in his speech, though the linkage was clear enough. "But drug education doesn't begin in class or on TV," Bush explained. "It must begin at home and in the neighborhood. Parents and families must set the first example of a drug-free life." Bush set his own example. Though known to not be averse to vodka martinis and the odd beer, the president made it a point to be seen jogging, buff secret service agents in tow. He also resurrected the Presidential Council on Physical Fitness and Sports under the leadership of Arnold Schwarzenegger, a Kennedy in-law and the world's highest-paid movie star. Millions of schoolchildren were soon condemned to compete yearly through pull-ups and sprints for certificates from the White House. Through it all, "increasingly vocal anti-alcohol advocates" continued to connect bourbon and Cognac to crack and cocaine.

It all seemed so conclusive, so set in stone. The health and consumption shifts in the 1980s, especially after the fallout from Len Bias's death, were talked about in the spirits industry as irreversible, ones that producers would have to adapt to, perhaps through lower-alcohol offerings, rather than alter. For the tiniest of the tiny, the fledgling small-batch distillers clustered on the West Coast, the abstemious climate of the 1980s could not have been a bigger setback. Jörg Rupf at St. George and Steve McCarthy at Clear Creek had enough trouble convincing restaurateurs to carry their eau-de-vie without the news chockablock with near hysteria over the evils of alcohol. As for Hubert Germain-Robin, Ansley Coale, and Miles Karakasevic, their aged brandies were only just now making it to a public that increasingly did not care for higher-proof alcohol, however well crafted. The "moral panic" of the 1980s seemed to dump salt on the fertile grounds that developments such as single-barrel and single malt had just opened up, along with the rises of craft beer and fine wine. The landscape for American small-batch spirits appeared barren as the decade slouched toward its close. Then, things began to happen and fast, changing everything.

CIGARETTE MACHINES

1987–1988 | Ukiah, California—Washington, DC

For Ansley Coale, the academic turned distillery owner turned salesman for that distillery's products, the reaction was invariably the same. He would pour a bar, restaurant, or store owner a neat glass of russet-colored Germain-Robin brandy from the sleekly cylindrical bottle, which was not unlike the standard-sized ones used for most fine wines. He would explain that Hubert Germain-Robin, scion of generations of distillers back in his native France, had crafted the spirit himself using a hand-cranked alembic still in a converted shed in the mountains of Mendocino County north of San Francisco. The distillery was one of only a handful in the United States independently owned and making small batches of spirits in traditional ways. Though there was a catch with Germain-Robin: the distillery leaned on Pinot Noir grapes from California for its brandy. The Cognac kings back in France used Ugni Blanc or perhaps Colombard, or maybe Folle Blanche, as the main grape. Not Germain-Robin or its master distiller; he preferred Pinot Noir, which produced in his and Ansley Coale's modest opinions a phenomenal, perhaps one-of-a-kind brandy—and which they could not call Cognac because of legal restrictions that France imposed, even on an operation eight thousand miles away. The squat, white label read simply CRAFT METHOD BRANDY DISTILLED IN UKIAH, CALIFORNIA over two lines, above a sepia-toned photo of the distillery and a further two-line explanation of the "varietal grapes," "antique cognac still," and "Limousin oak" used in the distillation and aging. All of this was immaterial to Coale's sales pitch, though. That hinged on the tasting.

"God, this is fabulous." That was invariably the response to tasting Germain-Robin—happened a million times, according to Coale.

Not that it did him and his outfit any good. That was why he carried a bottle of Rémy Martin VSOP, a popular number from one of the Big Four Cognac producers, to serve as an easy touchstone. That was also why a blank stare usually followed the praise for his brandy. "What am I supposed to do with this?" That was the question Coale faced as he schlepped the bottles to potential accounts nationwide beginning in April 1987, including in the San Francisco Bay Area, Miami, New York, and Atlanta. It was not simply that the brandy was rare or unusual. Nor was it that spirits consumption was on the decline amid a national health craze and a skittishness about stronger alcohol. (Germain-Robin clocked in at eighty proof.) It was that few restaurateurs, bar owners, and retailers stocked their menus and shelves based on taste. They certainly did not do so based on pedigrees. Who cared that it came from a small, independent distillery on a Mendocino mountain? And what was an alembic still anyway? No, Coale likened it all to a cigarette machine at a bar: Cigarette brands were carried based entirely on sales. When a stack of a particular brand ran low, it was restocked. It was the same way with spirits: when a bar or a store owner ran out of a certain spirits brand, it was time to re-up on that brand. New equaled uncertainty. Except for pockets such as single malt whiskey aficionados or bourbon fans left over from that spirit's heyday, there was no culture nor context in America for caring about the origins and the vagaries of a freshly introduced spirit—unless, like with Absolut vodka or Bacardí rum, a massive marketing effort flexed behind it. Or unless perhaps there was a larger operation behind it as well. Rémy Martin Schramsberg, the Napa Valley partnership between the Cognac giant and the Schramsberg Vineyards, released its first brandy in 1986. Confronted with the same legal constraints as Germain-Robin and wanting the brandy to be understood as distinctly Californian, the distillery labeled it as RMS California Alambic Brandy. It ended up being distributed and sold much more widely than its Ukiah competitor. Germain-Robin had about fourteen thousand cases aging by 1987 and around $1 million in new financing thanks to Coale's fundraising efforts back east. Rémy Martin Schramsberg could produce twenty thousand cases annually in its $10-million Napa facility. For smaller-time producers, then, such as Germain-Robin, which did not advertise and which relied more on word of mouth, there was little hope of breaking through.

It was just like with the earliest craft brewers, Coale thought. He knew the people behind Sierra Nevada, the craft brewery started in Chico, California, in 1980. Pour a bar owner a glass of their signature pale ale, and he or she might enjoy the citrusy sweetness or the novelty of a beer made only from traditional ingredients. But a typical bar's beer selection still turned on a Budweiser-Miller-Coors axis by the late 1980s, even as more craft breweries opened, including in far-flung outposts such as Alaska and Hawaii, and Boston Beer's Sam Adams spread across the land.

In the end, Germain-Robin's only early sales accounts came via places where customers were used to asking for recommendations and staff were used to giving them. These included the Sherry-Lehmann wine store on Manhattan's tony Upper East Side and MacArthur Liquors on the outer reaches of Washington, DC. The latter had since 1986 organized an annual tasting of some of California's most sought-after wine vintages straight from the barrel, before they were released. These sorts of places kept Germain-Robin alive in those first years. Them and the White House.

David Berkley, the son of an alcohol-averse fundamentalist minister, was pursuing a career in medicine when a medical mishap in 1971 changed his life. He slipped a disc in his back and had to spend two weeks in traction. His wife bought him an introductory textbook on American wines to fill the time. This was the period just before the Judgment of Paris blew that industry and culture wide open, but there was more than enough information to hold Berkley's attention and to never let it go. Soon after his recovery he got a part-time job at Corti Brothers, a fine wine and gourmet food shop in Sacramento, California's capital. One of his regular clients was Ronald Reagan, the state's governor from 1967 to 1975. Reagan continued to follow Berkley's advice on wine, and drink in general, after his move to the White House six years later. One of the earliest accounts that Ansley Coale landed for Germain-Robin was Corti, and soon Berkley was recommending the brandy to the president's men, who brought cases of it eastward throughout the last two years of Reagan's second term. It was said that the president, proud of his state's alcohol industry whatever his public stances, served Germain-Robin privately to luminaries such as Mikhail Gorbachev, including when the Soviet Union's last leader visited Washington in December 1987.

The White House nod in turn caught the attention of Frank Prial. Prial was a beat reporter at the *New York Times* covering everything from the United Nations to street crime when he started writing the newspaper's first-ever regular wine column in 1972. Initially worried he would not have much to write about, Prial soon found himself drowning in vinous information by that decade's end. Occasionally he turned his attention beyond fine wine. In the early 1980s, Prial was one of the first domestic journalists with a wide audience to pick up on American craft beer. And, in the late 1980s, he picked up quite forcefully and consistently on American small-batch spirits, starting with a column about Germain-Robin on Sunday, September 4, 1988.

Prial delved into the background of the distillery's two principals, including that chance meeting on the 101 nearly a decade before. He also schooled his readers in the legal vagaries of Cognac as the reigning French saw it and on the innovative grape decision Germain-Robin made. Prial described how the brandy "already graced the White House table." And he also noted something that Coale himself pretty much held privately sacred: that to survive and thrive, Germain-Robin's output had to be not just as good as the larger producers such as Rémy Martin but better.

> But it is Cognac the two men plan—not to emulate—but to surpass. "And why not?," Mr. Coale asks rhetorically. "Most modern Cognacs are made in vast quantities, by commercial methods. Everything here is done by hand."

It was that notion of hand-crafted quality, that devotion to small-batch production of something novel, that would not only power the American small-batch spirits movement in the coming decades but sharply divide it as well. For now, as the hourglass turned over on the 1980s, a quietly impactful decade for the fledgling movement, Germain-Robin typified the tininess of small-batch spirits in America. Frank Prial noted that annual sales would likely not surpass three thousand cases—and they didn't. Prial's Sunday *Times* column did not do for Germain-Robin what David Garino's *Wall Street Journal* front-pager did for Maker's Mark in 1980. Then, again, bourbon was a different animal in the American marketplace than brandy and Germain-Robin a different operation than the Loretto, Kentucky, distillery. What mattered was that the likes of the former were even on the radar of major media. Such attention might help answer that question Ansley Coale kept facing in 1987: "What am I supposed to do with this?"

THE WRITE TIME
1987–1992 | Manhattan

"This is 1988. Nobody wants to know about whiskies, much less write about them."

That was the response Paul Pacult kept getting from his wine-writing acquaintances in Manhattan when he told them about an offer from the business side of the *New York Times Magazine*: pen a major advertising supplement on whiskey. It had all started with Pacult's increasingly popular wine-tasting classes, still held in the Tribeca loft he had first rented upon arriving in Gotham in 1982. The wine industry itself was enduring the same health-craze, neo-Prohibitionist crucible as the spirits industry, though sales and consumption numbers continued to bend upward. The stock market crash of October 1987—the Dow Jones Industrial Average lost 508 points in a single day—was already in the rearview of many of Pacult's Wall Street students, who continued to work hard and play harder, spending freely on an increasingly variegated kaleidoscope of wines. There were more styles of wine from more places and producers available in cities such as New York than ever before. The same might be said of spirits, whiskey in particular, though neither the number nor variety was anywhere near the same league as wine—just that there were more brands available than years before. Moreover, the single malt, single-barrel, and barrel-strength fads of the early 1980s had grown into bona fide trends, their rarity and expense gelling nicely with the yuppies' yen for all things conspicuously consumed. Yet, there was not nearly enough information about spirits available to consumers of whatever financial strata as there was about fine wine. It was not unusual in the late 1980s to see a fine wine book on the *New York Times* bestseller list. When *Wine Advocate* founder and editor Robert Parker did a signing at an Upper West Side bookstore for his 1985 Bordeaux guide, the line of autograph seekers stretched around the block. Too, every major publication, including the *New York Times*, had at least a part-time writer covering and criticizing fine wine. And at least two newspapers, the *Portland Oregonian* and the *Seattle Post-Intelligencer*, had someone writing regularly about craft beer. There was no journalistic equivalent in spirits, small-batch or otherwise. The only writers covering it commercially in the United States were those moonlighting from their steadier wine- and beer-writing gigs. There were also no spirits equivalents of consumer-friendly wine publications such as the newsletter *Wine Advocate* and the magazine *Wine Spectator*—or even of the nearly ten-year-old *All About Beer*, a trade magazine designed to appeal to consumers, too. (Its inaugural cover featured Hollywood legend Paul Newman in the uniform for his Budweiser-sponsored Formula One racing team.) If there was spirits coverage in these and other publications, it invariably piggybacked on the coverage of wine. By themselves, "distilled spirits were considered, in editorial circles at least, as impolitic, passé and therefore journalistically radioactive."

Into Paul Pacult's lap, then, fell a remarkable opportunity. Rich Colandrea, an executive on the business side of the weekly *New York Times Magazine*, approached Pacult after the conclusion of one of his more advanced wine-tasting classes. Colandrea and two colleagues had wanted to broaden their enological knowledge because they sold ad space to liquor stores in the New York City area.

Pacult and Colandrea shook hands. Colandrea and his coworkers mentioned that they had read some of Pacult's recent work, including in *Wine & Spirits*, a six-year-old magazine published out of New York six times a year. (*Wine & Spirits* might have provided the most regular consumer spirits coverage in America by the late 1980s, usually publishing three or four features on the subject yearly, as well as tasting guides to particular types of spirits.) Then, Colandrea got to the point.

"Paul, how'd you like to write about Scotch whiskey for the *Times* Sunday magazine?"

The blood drained from Pacult's cheeks. He knew nothing about whiskey or about spirits in general. Who did? He thought of spirits as something consumed "only by people who were making arrangements for their retirement in communities with names like Whispering Pines or Sheltered Meadows." But this was the *New York Times*, with some three million readers, the most influential newspaper in the English-speaking world—if not in the world, period. Pacult had decamped from the bucolic splendor of the northern San Francisco Bay Area to the mean streets of pregentrified Manhattan with the very goal of writing for publications such as the *Times*. Decision time, then. Colandrea and his colleagues were waiting.

"Scotch whiskey?" was all Pacult could manage, his voice running off with the last syllable.

Never blessed with an implacable poker face, Pacult quickly came clean. Like most Americans, even those who wrote about alcohol, he knew little about spirits, at least in any critical sense. He had noticed that people tended to choose their spirits based upon the bang for the buck, not upon things such as taste or origin or the traditions behind the distillation. It did not seem to matter to consumers that Smirnoff was about as Russian as Abraham Lincoln—it had been made in the United States for decades—only that it was inexpensive, ubiquitous, and consistent wherever it was found. And consumers, by and large, certainly did not care about taste, not beyond the diehards into trends such as single malt whiskey or single-barrel bourbon. Pacult was intimately familiar with the rituals behind wine tasting and the fanaticism that sometimes seized enological initiates craving the latest bottles and styles. There was no such current running through American spirits. Beyond Absolut, really, there was little context for understanding spirits as anything other than the kick for the next cocktail.

Pacult voiced his reservations to Colandrea, including his ignorance of the subject. Not wanting the opportunity to slip away, however, Pacult stalled for time. Spirits were a "tipple from my parents' generation," he explained.

Colandrea walked right around the superfluous comment. Pacult's ignorance might be an asset, he said. They wanted him for his writing chops, besides, and he did know about wine—that would be an asset, too, according to the *Times* admen. They had done their market research and knew that no other major US publication had covered a non-wine alcoholic beverage the way the *Times Magazine* planned to cover it. The special advertising section, scheduled to drop on the first Sunday in December 1989, would hit the industry and the drinking public like a bolt of brown lightning. Colandrea and team were sure of it. Was Pacult in or out?

He would have to sleep on it, but he kind of knew the answer already. He called Colandrea the next morning and took the assignment: five thousand words on whiskey by July.

The then-clubby world of food journalism in New York—a fraternity that in those pre-Web days set many of the nation's culinary trends and anointed many of its culinary trendsetters—soon got wind of Pacult's fresh gig. Instead of that natural writerly reaction of barely veiled envy, the transom buzzed with misinformation and disbelief, even pity. Some fellow writers were convinced the *Times* had assigned Pacult a piece on wine, or maybe even a new wine column for the magazine. Others got it slightly more correct. He would be penning a piece on some spirit or another—whiskey, perhaps? Cognac, maybe? Finally, in hushed tones that reminded Pacult of the confessional at his boyhood Catholic parish back in Illinois, a well-connected senior member of the foodie press corps warned him about the new assignment. "Let me just say that writing about a thing like whiskey won't do much to advance your wine-writing career," he said. "Whiskey is . . . is unfashionable and, well, brown."

That reaction in particular confirmed in Pacult's mind that he was on to something. There really was a vacuum in serious spirits writing. Fill it and profound things might happen. Look at wine writing. In the early 1970s, an entire phalanx of writers, most based in and around New York City and San Francisco, arose to not only cover the industry and its wares but also proselytize about them, a mix of reporting and cheerleading that would go a long, long way in lifting the American fine wine movement to international renown. In 1972 alone, the *New York Times*, *New York* magazine, and *Gourmet* all launched regular wine columns. Also that year, Robert Finigan, a Harvard alumnus turned critic, started what became the most popular paid-subscription newsletter about wine. Finigan and others, including the *New*

York Times' Frank Prial, were pals with many merchants, distributors, and importers and would suggest, and be called upon to suggest, certain styles and vintages. A major reason Paris merchant Steven Spurrier decided to host the earth-rattling Judgment of Paris in 1976 was that so many American wine writers kept coming into his shop, talking up their nation's newer wines. A similar though much more low-key evangelical movement was under way in American craft beer as well, with Portland *Oregonian* columnist Fred Eckhardt often cajoling his city's brewers to reach beyond the most common beer styles then in the United States to nearly extinct ones such as porter and wheat. Other beer writers had penned popular guides to homebrewing, which often served as guides into the wider world of beer. (Few homebrewers wanted to mimic Budweiser in their kitchen, after all.) *The Complete Joy of Homebrewing* by Charlie Papazian, the schoolteacher turned American Homebrewers Association cofounder, was well on its way to more than 1.2 million copies in print after its 1984 release.

No beer writer, though, approached the status of Michael Jackson. He was born in Yorkshire, England, in 1942, the son of a truck driver who was himself the son of a Lithuanian-Jewish immigrant. After dropping out of the English equivalent of high school, Jackson began writing about beer for a West Yorkshire newspaper at the tender age of sixteen through a column he thought up called This Is Your Pub. He would visit a local pub and profile its people, foods, and beers, this at a time when English beers might be distinct from region to region or even from village to village. In the early 1970s, he took over a contract from another writer for a history of the English pub in general. That book came out in 1976 and was followed the next year by what many would regard as the most important beer book in the English language: *The World Guide to Beer*. Jackson had had his epiphany about the true variety of beer the previous decade during a writing assignment in Belgium, then the world's leader in terms of more traditional beer and brewing. In the direct and descriptive prose of *The World Guide to Beer*, Jackson unpacked the styles, customs, and techniques he had discovered since that Belgian foray, ones that were nearly lost to history or at least obscure to most readers in the United Kingdom and the United States. In America especially, drowning as it was in the likes of Budweiser and Miller Lite, to learn about the likes of bock, Dortmunder, Kölsch, India pale ale, porter, etc., was a revelation for those who could get a copy. (*The World Guide to Beer* would not enjoy wide circulation until a revised edition in the late 1980s.) Charles Finkel, a bow-tied wine importer and merchant in Seattle, compared absorbing Jackson's book to "a heathen discovering the Bible. It answered all those questions that I had about top and bottom fermentation, about hops, about yeast, about the nature of beer and the history of beer, and traditions of beer and beer culture." Finkel would soon add beer, especially from Belgium, to his importation repertoire, one of so many whom Jackson inspired to delve into beer beyond Budweiser. Throughout the 1980s, Jackson would continue to write about beer at length for a variety of publications and publishers and would travel widely, especially to the United States, where what brewers were doing was "so much more interesting," as he told an English reader annoyed at what he regarded as Jackson's neglect of his homeland's beers.

Michael Jackson at the time of the 1977 publication of his *World Guide to Beer*.
COURTESY PADDY GUNNINGHAM

In the 1980s Jackson also started writing about another subject dear to his palate: whisky. After all, as he never tired of pointing out, did not whisky distillation spring from the malted-barley mash typically used for beer? Take away the hops as bittering agent, and the two libations—whisky and ale, especially—were quite similar, if vastly different in alcoholic kick. Jackson discovered the joys of whisky shortly after he began writing that pub column in West Yorkshire. He was eighteen and had moved on to a bigger masthead in the Scottish city of Edinburgh, in an era when an Englishman relocating northward was still a relatively big deal. He became enamored of single malt whiskys in particular, which in the early 1970s were virtually unavailable

THE WRITE TIME 119

south of the Scottish-English border. As with beer, writing authoritatively about whisky just kind of fell into Jackson's lap. During a press push for his first book on the subject, 1987's *World Guide to Whisky*, an offended journalist from the Scottish city of Glasgow asked why an Englishman should be writing about what was basically Scotland's national drink. Another Scottish journalist piped up before Jackson could answer: "Because none of us did, dummy!" Jackson's 224-page *World Guide to Whisky*, which included sections on distilleries in Pennsylvania, Maryland, Virginia, Tennessee, and, especially, Kentucky, was the first major work on the subject in the English language. A subsequent book on Jackson's favorite subsector of the spirit, *Malt Whisky Companion*, became the bestselling whisky book ever after its 1989 release. It was, as one Canadian journalist put it, "the first to take a hard-headed look at the distilleries in terms of quality and try to capture in prose the elusive nature of the highly individual spirits they produce." Powerful and groundbreaking stuff, but not in the United States—Jackson's first two whisky books would not be published Stateside until the 1990s. He would remain primarily known in America as a beer critic, including through a six-episode show called *The Beer Hunter*, which the Discovery Channel began airing in 1990. Jackson's genial personality and unkempt appearance, complete with a thin beard, a circlet of loose hair, and a penchant for colorful ties, seemed the perfect match for the subject in a country that still regarded beer as a laid-back, far-from-serious beverage. Jackson's criticism regarding whisky, however—the most widely read and influential writing of the day on any spirit—stopped at the water's edge in the late 1980s. It was another stroke of luck for Paul Pacult.

Armed with the *Times* assignment, Pacult decamped in May 1989 for a press tour of the distilleries of Scotland. He was surrounded by writers who, like him for the present, focused on wine. Something about the distilleries, though, grabbed Pacult and did not let him go. They were almost always remote, certainly from the perspective of a visitor raised in the Chicago metropolitan area and then living in überdense Manhattan, the surrounding silent glens often coming complete with babbling brooks and wispy morning mists. The industry itself was collegial, as were the Scots with whom Pacult dealt. The actual "nuts and bolts of distillation and the mysteries of maturation" appealed to him, harkening as they did to his time working in Napa Valley in the quieter pre–Judgment of Paris days. It was all so bucolic and serene, yet precise and distinct, individual distilleries' whiskeys tasting different even if only short distances separated them. Such distinctiveness—and the people and the processes that went into crafting it—struck Pacult, even with his wine expertise, as foreign in the most literal and figurative senses. He had no idea spirits could be like this, and he had a strong suspicion neither did his fellow Americans. "It was obvious from the beginning," Pacult recounted later, "that one aspect could not possibly be addressed without full inclusion of the others. This was unusually rich writing material that simply wasn't being told to Americans."

Paul Pacult at a tasting in New York City in 2015.
DANIEL SILBERT

Back in New York, the article for the *Times* poured out of Pacult in "torrents, not sentences," with the writer eschewing a lot of punctuation in earlier drafts in order to get down what he had seen, heard, and tasted while the memories were freshest. What resulted was a twenty-one-page piece running to more than ten thousand words. Pacult submitted it in July 1989, expecting that Rich Colandrea would request a serious round of chopping—the *Times* had contracted for only five thousand words. Pacult called Colandrea to query about cuts. "You kidding me?" the adman responded. "Don't even think about. This story has been passed around and nobody wants you to cut a word. We're going to use all of it."

The magazine did. On Sunday, December 3, 1989, Pacult's effort, headlined SCOTCH WHISKEY—A CONSUMER GUIDE, ran over twenty-eight pages in a special advertising section of the *New York Times Magazine*. It was divided into four sections designed to handhold the reader through this curious product: "An Elegant Beverage for Today," "History in the Making," "The Journey from Spring to Bottle," and "More Than a Matter of Taste." With history, tasting notes, buying guides, even a "Scotch Whisky Trivia Quiz," the guide represented the single most impactful piece of spirits writing in the United States since David Garino's front-page *Wall Street Journal* report on the success of Maker's Mark. It was not so much the information that Pacult imparted, though the article was meticulous and lively in detail, but the fact that he imparted it so thoroughly at all. There had been little like it before, and certainly nothing to that length or in a publication as widely seen as the *Times'* Sunday magazine. Pacult's piece, and subsequent ones he would do for the *Times* and various other publications over the next couple of years, marked a turning point in writing about, even in thinking about, spirits in the United States. It provided a further context, in much the same way that fine wine and craft beer had, or the rapid ascent of Absolut, or the rise of single malt whiskeys and single-barrel bourbon. The criticism of Pacult, and later Michael Jackson, once his books were available in the United States, were another necessary piece of the puzzle for boosting the notion of traditionally crafted, small-batch spirits in the minds of American consumers. And consumers were responding, as Pacult's own expanding workload made clear. In 1990, just after the first *Times* piece, editors at other publications began requesting articles as short as two hundred to three hundred words. By 1991, the year Pacult transitioned mostly to spirit rather than wine writing, the editors wanted stories of five hundred to one thousand words. At the same time, distilleries, eager for serious coverage of their wares, inundated Pacult's Manhattan office with samples and preview bottles. To capitalize on this demand and to clear a bit of the sample inventory, he launched his own quarterly review called *Spirit Journal* in 1991. Subscriptions drove it financially, with its founder refusing advertising so as to help maintain its editorial independence.

The year after Pacult launched *Spirit Journal*, none other than the *New York Times* approached him as an expert on none other than whiskey, in this case bourbon, a subject he had known so little about in 1989. Food writer Florence Fabricant asked Pacult to comment on that unlikeliest of spirit trends: a bourbon revival driven by single-barrel batches. "These bourbons were invented as the American answer to single-malt Scotch," Pacult explained. "But the reality is that these are the best bourbons ever made." He would know.

VIRGINIA LIGHTNING

1988–1993 | Culpeper County, Virginia

I t was the mid-1980s when Chuck Miller decided to plant grapes on part of
the Culpeper County, Virginia, farm that he and wife Jeannette bought in
1975, about seventy miles southwest of Washington. They had been using the
land primarily to raise Jeannette's championship racing horses, but the market
for commodities such as livestock and corn, which the couple also raised,
had all but collapsed at the start of the decade. Investors and their brokers
instead rushed to stocks amid Wall Street's bull run. The grapes, and the
brandy Miller hoped to craft from them, would bring in the money that the
corn and livestock were not bringing in. Yet, like many Americans in Virginia
before him, stretching back to at least Thomas Jefferson at the turn of the
nineteenth century, Chuck Miller soon discovered that the commonwealth's
climate and topography were not that hospitable to grape growth, even for
the lower-end Concord and Niagara varieties he was trying to harvest. The
vineyard and the brandy were a bust, and commodities prices showed no
signs of a steady climb. What to do?

Miller thought of his paternal grandfather, whom he had known as a
boy and a teenager. The man owned only one milking cow on his Maryland farm, yet several dairy tanks. After a while, Miller figured out what his
grandfather used the extra tanks for. And then the stories came: the time
his grandfather smashed through a police barricade on the Fourteenth Street
bridge during a delivery run into Washington, DC, and the revenuers shot
his back window out; or the one where agents raided his house and missed
the entrance to the secret cellar beneath a carefully placed rug and rocking
chair. Miller's grandfather was a moonshining bootlegger during Prohibition.
Moonshine was the tipple of choice for many along that ribbon of Appalachia
during Prohibition and the lean years of the Great Depression that followed.
Relatively easy to make—an unaged combination of lots of sugar and lots of
corn—and generally much stronger than anything that could be had legally,
moonshine was a quick way to both get drunk and make a buck. "Well,"

Miller thought when the vineyard wouldn't yield, "my grandfather made corn whiskey; why can't I do it?"

He had the supplies, or at least the makings of them: literally tons of corn that weren't selling, dairy tanks, and enough land—two hundred acres nicknamed Belmont Farm since the early 1800s—to make a small distillery plausible. He also had the know-how, including an old recipe from his then-deceased grandfather and his own engineering training. Plus, commercial distillation was legal now, even of the equivalent of moonshine. Miller seemed the perfect fit for the venture. Then in his early forties, he looked every bit the backcountry boy in what seemed to be a uniform of blue jeans, a plaid shirt, and a floppy, weather-beaten cowboy hat. With his bushy mustache that would whiten with age, a folksy Upper South accent, and a wide grin that came easily, he even bore a striking resemblance to Jed Clampett, the genial patriarch of the fictional *Beverly Hillbillies* family. As it was, though, Miller had earned an aviation-engineering degree from the University of Maryland and flown sorties over Vietnam in F-100 supersonic jets, segueing into commercial piloting after the war. That job as well as the income from the horse-breeding would afford him the time needed for distillations. Finally, Miller had the added benefit of a product that would not have to be aged, unlike the brandy he might have made; it could hit shelves as fast as he could produce it.

Or at least that was the plan in 1988, when Miller applied to the Bureau of Alcohol, Tobacco, and Firearms for a distilling license. He soon ran smack into the labyrinth of rules and regulations that persisted from his grandfather's day and that the neo-Prohibitionists then were doing their best to keep as onerous as possible. At the federal level, things went relatively smoothly, though the license took about two years. (He also needed approval from the Food and Drug Administration.) The ATF even helped Miller locate a two-thousand-gallon solid copper still. A neighboring landowner had discovered the still on a newly purchased tract. It dated from just after Repeal in 1933 and would do just fine. The ATF also hooked Miller up with some aged outlaws, men who like his grandfather had made what was then illicit moonshine and who had advice to impart. The Commonwealth of Virginia was not as helpful as the ATF. Like many states, Virginia acted within its borders as the sole spirits retailer, stepping into the middle of the distribution chain between the producer and the consumer. A distiller such as Miller would need a sales contract from the state liquor authority or there was no point in starting production. What's more, the state required that a distiller present each new product at a formal hearing to win approval for sale. Add to this the needed federal approvals for products, as well as state and federal OK's for labels and packaging, and Miller's notion of simply cooking up some corn and sugar and selling the results for extra cash took on a whole other dimension. Never mind that his still in an old shed behind the barn in Culpeper County, home to perhaps thirty thousand souls total, would be one of a kind east of the Rocky Mountains: an independently owned distillery making small batches with (very) traditional ingredients. That in itself might present its own challenges when Miller brought his products to market. For now, starting in 1989, it was a matter of assembling things and nailing the recipe.

The first results were not good. Miller thought it would just be a matter of cooking up the corn like it was Cream of Wheat. What he got were giant gobs of unusable corn. He kept at it, took the advice of the old-timers, tweaked his grandfather's recipe proportionally, and soon had a suitable mash to build on with the copper still. He worked in between his commercial-piloting jags, and usually alone, in the quietude of a countryside that once popped with the burps and clanks of illicit stills like the one he was now legally using. The first offering from the Belmont Farm Distillery was a crystal-clear corn whiskey clocking in at a throat-searing one hundred proof. (It actually exited the still at 150 proof, but Miller cut it with water.) Miller used corn he had grown and ground himself, as well as other ingredients culled from his grandfather's recipe. For all its ethanol punch, the whiskey could go down smoothly sip by sip, with a clean sweetness tasting very much of fresh corn. Miller called the finished product Virginia Lightning, after the old moniker for moonshine, white lightning, and, of course, after the state in which the spirit was born. Belmont Farm's initial production run was three hundred cases of a dozen fifth-sized bottles, which Miller personally drove the approximately ninety miles to the Virginia Alcoholic Beverage Control warehouse in Richmond, the state capital, for distribution.

That was in December 1989, though it would not be until late in the following year that bottles of Virginia Lightning actually hit shelves. Sales were modest, at $8.95 a pint, and Miller made about a dollar per bottle in profit, which might translate into $3,600 for that first three-hundred-case run. It was not until the *Fredericksburg Free Lance-Star* dropped in a year later to profile the new outfit that Miller and Belmont Farm's reputation began to spread to the four corners of Virginia. Miller himself proved an irresistible character for writer Rusty Dennen. In an article that appeared three days before Christmas in 1990, right next to one about local children's fears surrounding the looming Gulf War, Dennen, the daily newspaper's business editor, painted Miller as a kind of folksy craftsman, learning by trial and error to resurrect a spirit that was once ingrained, literally and figuratively, in the life of that region of Virginia and in the United States; though, as the article also noted, corn whiskey made up an infinitesimal share of the American spirits market every year. It was an irresistible portrait, really, and Miller seemed to play his role to the hilt, complete with his homespun anecdotes about discovering his still "in a barn that was about ready to cave in" and the humor splashed on the Virginia Lightning label (GUARANTEED TO BE AT LEAST 10 DAYS OLD— "We're not talking aged Scotch here," as Dennen put it). The article ran below a photo of Miller stirring the corn-and-water mash, cowboy hat firmly on head. Orders for Virginia Lightning were soon coming in from package stores throughout the commonwealth, and Miller hired a distributor to make the rounds to the state authority warehouse in Richmond. By 1993, he was producing one hundred gallons of Virginia Lightning, from about ten times the amount of corn mash, during a typical week, enough for eight hundred bottles or about sixty-six cases. The *Washington Post* visited that year, taking Belmont Farm national, at least in reputation.

Chuck Miller with the original still for Belmont Farm.
CHRIS HARRIS

Distribution in the early years remained mostly Virginia-bound, though there were sales in North Carolina, Maryland, and West Virginia. Other media would follow, including the History Channel, the Discovery Channel, and National Geographic's cable-television vehicle. Soon, Miller, still an airline pilot just trying to make more money from the family farm, found himself a breakout star of the American small-batch spirits movement. Not that he realized it, per se—Miller himself was not aware of the West Coast pioneers. He was barely familiar with Virginia's nascent craft beer scene, which kicked off in the Tidewater region in the early 1980s with the launch of the Chesapeake Bay Brewing Company. Miller did realize that his fame translated into visitors to the Culpeper farmstead, people eager to see what all the handcrafted fuss was about and who might otherwise have not cared for a super-alcoholic whiskey. They sought out Miller's autograph on their bottles of Virginia Lightning and snapped his photograph, floppy cowboy hat and all.

This attention was the only thing that really separated Miller from the small-batch spirits pioneers on the West Coast, such as Jörg Rupf at St. George, Ansley Coale and Hubert Germain-Robin at Germain-Robin, and Steve McCarthy at Clear Creek. Like them, Miller toiled virtually alone and in relative obscurity compared with the reach of a Seagram brand or an import such as Absolut. He approached distillation traditionally, with a copper pot still rather than a column one. Like McCarthy in particular he used material he himself grew—in this case, corn. And his distribution was limited, in no small part due to the vagaries of Virginia's Prohibition-era alcohol laws—the state's distribution-dominating liquor authority dated from 1934, just after Repeal. Miller's Belmont Farm also echoed an earlier pioneer of American small-batch spirits, one similarly rural—Bill Samuels Sr.'s Maker's Mark. It was all there in Culpeper County: the remote location; the novelty of the product; the folksiness, complete with a healthy helping of American lore; the desire to make a sipping version of a spirit normally knocked back as quickly as possible; and, finally, the sales-spurring attention that a newspaperman's coverage generated.

YOUNG BLOOD FROM AN OLD BREWERY

1993–1996 | San Francisco

In a November 9, 1996 column for the *Independent* newspaper of London, Michael Jackson raved to his British readers about a particular American spirit: "Old Potrero represents a wholehearted return to tradition." He explained:

Old Potrero is also made wholly from rye, without the usual addition of corn and barley malt. Furthermore the rye is all malted; in other whiskies it is raw. In my view, these differences create a richer, rounder, deeper flavor, despite the somewhat raw youth of the whiskey. It is only one year old, as it might have been in the pioneering days when there was little time for aging.

What spirit, what whiskey, had smitten Jackson so thoroughly? Old Potrero, a rye whiskey produced in small quantities at the Anchor Brewing Company's brewery on Mariposa Street in San Francisco's Potrero Hill neighborhood. Fritz Maytag, the pioneering force behind much of American craft beer up to that point, who had rescued Anchor from ruin in 1965 and nursed it back to robust health, launched the Anchor Distilling Company in 1993 in back of the brewery's bottling line, in a single pot still brought over from West Germany. The company's distiller, Bruce Joseph, came from the brewhouse. This tiny operation in what remained a relatively tiny brewery, compared with the likes of Anheuser-Busch and Miller, was more than enough to mark a dramatic entry into the American small-batch spirits movement.

For Joseph, the journey really began in late 1980. He grew up in Modesto, California, the Central Valley city that E. & J. Gallo, the nation's biggest winery, famed for relentlessly nondescript brands such as Pink Chablis and Thunderbird, dominated. He went to college in San Francisco. Two college friends had a brother who decided one day to get a job on the bottling line at the Anchor Brewing Company, which in 1979 had moved to a roomier location on Mariposa Street that an old coffee roastery once occupied. The brother, though, was just kind of passing through, and after six months he told Joseph that he was moving on. "They need someone to take my place." Would Joseph be interested? At the time, Joseph was just into his twenties and working rather unenthusiastically as a proofreader at an accounting firm. Here was a chance to jump into one of the more curious, if not popular, local businesses. Maytag had resolutely maintained Anchor Brewing as a San Francisco animal, when he could surely have relocated it in 1979 beyond the city to a cheaper location. Joseph said yes to the offer, and, like the majority of the approximately dozen Anchor employees then, started on the bottling line in mid-October 1980. He had no brewing experience, save for some stabs at homebrewing in high school with cans of Pabst Blue Ribbon malt extract. (The results were predictably unmemorable.) As it was, then, Joseph learned on the job and by the early 1990s was a brewer at what was then one of the largest craft breweries in the nation and certainly its oldest, the only surviving craft beer link between the early 1970s—a time before the legalization of homebrewing, before Michael Jackson's style-rescuing *World Guide to Beer*, before the advent of so many imitators—and the present.

That present was busy beyond what few could have imagined a generation before. The movement that Anchor had kicked off in the 1960s was now growing sales-wise by double-digit percentages every year. The success of brewpubs, those breweries that served their beers on-site, often along with food, and of the contract-brewed brands Samuel Adams and Pete's Wicked, both unconstrained by the costs of a physical brewery, had introduced more Americans than ever before to small-batch beer made with traditional ingredients at independently owned breweries—the very hallmarks Maytag had unwittingly gifted the movement during his early, treading-water days with Anchor. Make no mistake: Anheuser-Busch and its ilk dominated domestic—and, increasingly, world—beer sales. Anchor's annual output of perhaps fifty thousand barrels absolutely paled in comparison to that of the macrobreweries, which might churn out several million barrels from a single plant. More than 80 percent of the beer sold in the United States in the early 1990s was made by a handful of the biggest brewing companies. But craft beer had enough of a toehold, with nearly six hundred breweries and brewpubs, that it clearly was not going away anytime soon. The bigger brewers, in fact, would soon co-opt a sizable chunk of the Maytag-inspired movement's ethos, developing what came to be derisively nicknamed "phantom crafts." These were beers, sometimes entire brands, that looked like craft beer, with similar packaging, though that packaging usually contained no hint of the beer's corporate parentage. The phantom crafts might even taste similar to the real deals, and they certainly made use of the stylistic nomenclature. The Coors Brewing Company's Blue Moon was the most successful of these phantom crafts, a wholly created wheat-beer brand of the Colorado-based macrobrewer that would roll out to twenty-two states virtually overnight in the fall of 1995. The name *Coors* was nowhere to be found on Blue Moon's soft-blue packaging, which was the point. The ethos of craft beer—small, traditional, independent—was in the ascendant in American brewing in the early 1990s. The business of it might tarry, might even drop off down the road, but the principles were set as if in granite.

Anchor Distilling's 1993 formation built the most unmistakable bridge yet between the American craft beer and the small-batch spirits movements, the company and its inaugural product reflecting that craft beer ethos spectacularly. Little noted at the time, or since, was the connection between Old Potrero and the American fine wine movement, which was just then shaking off the hangover from the same neo-Prohibitionist assault that had gummed up the works for distilleries and preparing for another run of record growth. Maytag and a Stanford classmate named Paul Draper had invested, together with other friends, in a vineyard in Chile beginning in 1959. The grape yields were "unbelievably good," but political unrest in the South American nation drove the young would-be vintners back to the United States. Draper would go on in 1969 to become the winemaker at Ridge Vineyards, a groundbreaking winery a group of Stanford academics started in the Santa Cruz Mountains west of San Jose. Maytag, in addition to saving Anchor Brewing, also bought York Creek Vineyard on Napa Valley's western edge. It would become the sole grape source for Ridge. Maytag, then, found himself in 1993 one of the few Americans with a major hand in all three alcoholic beverage industries, and perhaps the most fiscally independent one at that.

The stills at the Anchor Distilling Company in San Francisco.
COURTESY ANCHOR DISTILLING COMPANY

As for the spirit that provided this trifecta, it enjoyed, as Michael Jackson alluded to, a long tradition on the continent. Rye whiskey was the spirit George Washington made at his Mount Vernon estate beginning in the 1790s and that allowed the nation's foremost leader to also become its foremost distiller. Born in eastern Pennsylvania in the 1640s, it was the whiskey that predated that other great American whiskey, bourbon, with its copious use of corn. Rye whiskey, on the other hand, leaned mostly, if not entirely, on its namesake grain, creating a sharper, more piercing taste. The relatively rapid rise of bourbon throughout the nineteenth century to its pinnacle in the mid-twentieth, together with the introduction of vodka and the enduring popularity of whisky blends from Canada and Scotland, pushed rye into obscurity. With the Jim Beam–distilled Old Overholt brand perhaps the sole domestic exception, rye "survived only vestigially in rare labels" that were rarely widely available, according to Michael Jackson. That was primarily why Maytag had picked it as his distillery's first offering. His brewery over the last nearly thirty years had resurrected a variety of beer styles in the United States. These included the signature Anchor Steam, which had fallen into disrepair and disrepute under the brewery's previous regimes. There was also that first modern porter, the first craft beer seasonal (Anchor Christmas Ale), the first American beer to call itself "summer," the first American wheat beer since Prohibition, and, of course, the monumental Liberty Ale of 1975, an inspiration for the legions of bitterer American-made India pale ales that followed. Regarding the rye whiskey, Maytag knew about Washington's work two centuries before—and about the disappearance of the style. Like so many Anchor beer offerings, this spirit offering would be a groundbreaker: the first pot-distilled rye whiskey in the United States since Prohibition. "It was a category waiting to be reborn," Maytag figured. So Anchor Distilling midwifed it.

It was a curious decision—and not because rye remained "a small niche" in the whiskey marketplace. It was that Maytag, Joseph, and company did not really know how to make it. They were enamored of the history, really, before they learned the science, which they did from books on the subject, some available only at the Library of Congress, which Maytag visited, and all published decades before. Throughout 1993 and 1994, until the first batch for commercial sale went into barrels for aging, Maytag and Joseph essentially experimented using that lone still behind the brewery's bottling line. There was little urgency to fill a distribution quota or satisfy sales accounts. The brewery paid the distillery's way initially. At one point, Maytag secured from his beer distributor a palette of screwtop quart bottles—Anchor Brewing's wares required a bottle opener. Joseph and he filled the bottles with the early batches of the spirit at different points during its distillation. They spent a considerable amount of time then tasting the iterations to see what was working and what was not. Finally satisfied, in 1995, they filled charred oak barrels with what turned out to be 1,448 bottles of rye and commenced aging it in the beer cellar.

The Old Potrero label that would go on the 750-milliliter bottles was a veritable lesson in small-batch distillation, the most detailed packaging yet for any American-produced small-batch spirit. There was the brand name, of course, and then below that, on either side of a pot still with a giant "A" in the middle, the words TRADITIONAL and POT DISTILLED. Then, in lettering almost as big as the brand name, the words 18TH CENTURY STYLE SPIRIT and a further explanation that Anchor had used only malted rye and no other granular addition in crafting the bottle's contents. Finally, there were multiple references to San Francisco, tapping into a local vein that had served Anchor's line of beers so well. Maytag had long insisted that Anchor Brewing remain a San Francisco–based company, no matter the rising costs of doing business in the rapidly gentrifying city, a stance that won loyalty from beer drinkers who appreciated the difference between an Anchor Steam brewed and bottled on Mariposa Street vs. a Budweiser of nebulous origin. It was an adherence to locality that had helped not only the brewery survive and thrive but American craft beer as well. The same would hold true for Anchor Distilling's products, Maytag decided—their San Francisco origin would be a big part of their packaging.

And of their sales. Anchor Distilling released most of those first bottles of Old Potrero to restaurants and bars in the Bay Area that were already likely familiar with the Anchor name because of its beer. Some were shipped to New York City. In another nod to history, some found their ways to Northern Virginia and the Washington, DC, area, the old sales territory of George Washington's rye, not to mention a hub of rye distillation centuries before. This deliberately limited distribution virtually guaranteed that few beyond the Bay Area and the craft beer movement, never mind the still-toddling small-batch spirits movement, noticed the early 1996 rollout, Michael Jackson in London the most notable exception. (Paul Pacult's *Spirit Journal* did not review Old Potrero until years after its release.) Or, if people did notice, they sniffed at the fact that Anchor had aged Old Potrero only thirteen months, well short of the typical aging lengths for other whiskeys such as bourbon. Maytag and Joseph stood by the decision to release Old Potrero without a longer aging time. "We sell our whiskey as soon as we think it is nice," Maytag explained (to a leading trade magazine for the *brewing* industry). "I don't apologize for one minute for not aging the whiskey." He added that he found the newfangled single-barrel bourbons too oaky, besides, and single malt scotches too peaty. Besides, small-batch, traditional rye was uncharted territory in modern America. Who was to say what it should taste like? When Joseph and Maytag tasted their own early batches before the 1995 barreling, they also sought out and sipped other rye whiskeys, almost all of them of foreign origin. There simply were not many American-made brands on the shelf—and zero that used rye as the sole grain. That made Old Potrero one of the most unique spirits released in the American marketplace in decades, however few and far between its availability.

Bill Owens and Maytag, right. The pair were pioneers in craft beer and then in small-batch spirits.
ANDREW FAULKNER

"It is significant that someone with such catholic interests in food and drink should carry the torch for rye," Jackson wrote of Maytag in that piece on Old Potrero. "American whiskies powered the racy cocktails of the Jazz Age, but in more recent times have been deemed the drink of the redneck, or the urban cowboy. Now their qualities are being rediscovered." This was no accident, according to the critic. "To some extent, this is part of the rediscovery of traditional and regional drinks and food throughout the Western world." Jackson himself would host a whiskey-tasting at Denver's Wynkoop brewpub on October 1, 1995. The time, location, and the venue were significant. Launched in 1988, Wynkoop was part of that crop of brewpubs that had grown up in the late 1980s and early 1990s, introducing more and more Americans to craft beer. And Denver hosted the annual Great American Beer Festival, which since its debut in 1982 had quickly grown into the largest beer festival outside of Germany, with some twenty-five thousand ticket holders sampling 1,450 beers from 365 American breweries. Bruce Joseph saw Jackson's whiskey tasting as a relaxing cap to the often-frenzied beer tasting weekend and dropped in after seeing his beloved San Francisco Giants lose to the postseason-bound Colorado Rockies at Coors Field earlier in the day. The Wynkoop served a Scottish buffet of mushroom soup, smoked salmon, grilled lamb chops, wild rice salad with walnuts and gorgonzola, fruit and cheese, fresh-baked bread, and Scottish shortbread. As for the whiskeys that Jackson would talk about, Old Potrero was not on the menu that Sunday evening—that first batch had not finished aging—but three vintages of the classic Scottish single malt whiskey Macallan were: a twelve-year-old, an eighteen-year-old, and a rare twenty-five-year-old. To Joseph, at least, the eighteen-year-old tasted far superior to the twenty-five-year-old. Older, he thought, does not necessarily mean better.

MAKING MARKS

1994 | Fairborn, Ohio—West Point, New York—Loretto, Kentucky

To Dave Pickerell, it always seemed that his father got lost every Sunday without fail, driving the family around in their powder-blue-and-white 1959 Bel Air. The passing scenery, bits of southwestern Ohio suburbia, would look familiar, and then the familiarity would cease after a while; and they were lost again, another Sunday for the Pickerells to spend finding their way back home. Only later would the son realize that his dad was simply taking the family for a drive for relaxation and a touch of adventure.

During one of those drives in 1961, the five-year-old Pickerell spied a billowing smokestack, not exactly an unusual sight in the Upper Midwest, then churning with industrial output of all sorts. He excitedly peppered his father with questions: "What's that smokestack? What's that billowing stuff?"

"The only one who understands that is a chemical engineer," came the response from the front seat.

Years later, too, Pickerell would realize that his father, a letter carrier who rose to become a postmaster before retiring, was probably joking or at least trying to stop the cascade of queries interrupting the Sunday drive. The five-year-old Pickerell took him completely seriously and decided right then what he wanted to be when he grew up: a chemical engineer. To do that, though, would require a college education, and Pickerell was well aware he and his family would likely not be able to afford that. Plus, he would be seventeen when he graduated high school, too young to sign for a loan. Xenia, the Ohio town near Dayton where Pickerell was born in

1956, was most famous for a tornado having pretty much destroyed it in April 1974, killing nearly three dozen and rendering some ten thousand homeless. The Pickerells had thankfully moved away by then, to another solidly working-class Dayton suburb called Fairborn, where Pickerell took every science and math course the local high school could teach and then some, bothering his teachers for extra work, his mind set on a full college scholarship—half wouldn't cut it; it had to be full. He also began picking sports to play with the same scholastic goal in mind. He tried baseball. He was a good first baseman, by his own recollection, but his batting average was in the low hundreds. He swung at everything, knowing that, if he connected, his then-sizable frame would force the ball over the fence. He did not always connect. He tried wrestling and golf, too, and those did not really work out, either. Then he tried track and field and soon rose to become one of the best shot-putters in Ohio. He played football as well, and made the first All-State team as an offensive tackle. The athletic scholarship offers started coming in—full ones, at that. But Pickerell picked West Point, the United States Military Academy on the Hudson River about fifty miles north of New York City. The school offered a full ride in exchange for several years' military service afterward—and Pickerell got to play football on a nonvarsity squad, to boot—but West Point in the mid-1970s did not have a chemical engineering curriculum. So Pickerell majored in chemistry, with a minor in physics and some engineering on the side, his childhood plan inching that much closer to fruition. He would finish his chemistry degree, serve five years in the army as an officer, and then pursue a master's in chemical engineering.

Then the academy stepped in with an offer Pickerell could not refuse. As part of his service, would he teach chemistry at his alma mater? His independent research, particularly as part of a team investigating the causes of acid rain, as well as his academic record, which placed him year after year toward the top of his class, spurred the school's offer. In exchange, West Point would underwrite the pursuit of that all-important chemical engineering master's. Pickerell said yes and decamped from New York for two years at the University of Louisville in Kentucky, where another institutional hand of fate intervened. Pickerell took a thermodynamics class with a professor named Charles Plank. That branch of physics, which covers the relationship of heat and temperature to energy, encompassed so much of the distillation process. What was distillation, after all, but the heating of mash and the capture of the resulting vapors? The class changed Pickerell's life and set him on course to become the most sought-after consultant in the

American small-batch spirits movement, if not the most well-known distiller in America. Through Plank's thermodynamics class, Pickerell discovered what he would later call his "stupid human trick," after television host David Letterman's segment: the preternatural ability to visualize molecules within an active still. Pickerell could not explain it, though he would quickly add it did not necessarily mean he was smarter than the next chemical engineer. It was that he simply could not seem to avoid it. He would close his eyes and the interior of the still would be there. The ability helped him score a ninety-nine on Plank's thermodynamics final. The next highest score was a thirty-five.

Pickerell would call on Charles Plank several years later, when he finished his teaching commitment at West Point and needed references for a job search. "I will do you one better," Pickerell's old professor told him. "I'm going to tell you where you're going to work. I've never done this in forty years, but it's the best match I've seen, and I know it's perfect." The match was a consultancy in Louisville specializing in the alcoholic beverage industry. Specifically, the four-person operation needed a distillation-system designer right away, and in Plank's mind Pickerell fit the description exactly. The student soon turned professional, a chemical engineer at long last, and took his stupid human trick on the road. Pickerell worked on projects throughout the world, big and small, designing individual distillery parts and entire, multimillion-dollar distilleries. He would sometimes spend months at a time on projects in countries as disparate geographically as China and Mexico, though another sudden turn would ensure that the man met his moment in Kentucky.

One of the consultancy's clients was Maker's Mark. The now-legendary distillery in still-tiny Loretto, Kentucky, was a survivor by the time Bill Samuels Jr. contracted with Pickerell's consultancy for some engineering work in 1994. It had chugged along through the bourbon crash of the 1970s, the twin rises of vodka and rum in the early 1980s, and the gustatory triumph of fine wine over spirits around the same time. It had now weathered much of the inhospitable, neo-Prohibitionist climate of the late 1980s and seemed poised for another growth spurt similar to the one at the start of the previous decade following that August 1980 *Wall Street Journal* rave. Pickerell, then, could not have found himself at a better place and time. Unhappy with the consulting work and itching for a change, he ran into Bill Samuels Jr. one day in October 1994 just outside of the Loretto distillery.

"Hey, Dave, come here," Samuels said. Pickerell walked over. "Did you know we're looking for our next VP of operations and master distiller?"

"No, sir, I didn't." The two men, though raised on opposite banks of the Ohio River, spoke with a similar Southern drawl.

"Well, we are," Samuels replied. "We've exhausted the entire candidate pool and couldn't find anybody we liked. But we like you. And, if you want it, the job's yours."

Pickerell stammered for a few seconds before finding the words to accept the offer. He put in his two-week notice at the consultancy and started at Maker's Mark before Thanksgiving. On his first day, he marched up to the distillery's chief financial officer and asked him to write down the cost of crafting one case of Maker's Mark. The CFO wanted to know why. Because, Pickerell said, he would never make a case that expensive again. He would make cost-cutting his hallmark at the distillery, a way of pruning away the wasteful to create a more competitive Maker's Mark in a more competitive spirits market. These cost-cutting measures included a recycling program that extended not just to reusing certain parts and materials but also to such innovations as the installation of an anaerobic digester that separated spent grain so that its fiber could be sold to cattle farmers as feed and its methane used as fuel for the distillery. Along the same lines, Pickerell got rid of Maker's Mark's fuel tanks and started buying cheaper natural gas on the commodities market. These were small changes that struck the engineer in Pickerell as obvious; he would describe their implementation not as plucking low-hanging fruit but as tripping over watermelons. What was less obvious, at least at first, was Bill Samuels Jr.'s vision. Pickerell learned from him that it was not just a matter of making a tasty bourbon (and bourbon was all that Maker's Mark would continue to produce—Pickerell's brief did not include new products). Instead, Samuels pushed the notion that a spirit, even one as already storied as Maker's Mark bourbon, had to be relevant, something eminently interesting and engaging to a consumer confronted with dozens of brands at his or her local liquor store. "You have to give people a reason to drink your stuff," he told Pickerell. That notion, the idea that taste alone could not power a smaller spirit brand to success, would prove as revolutionary as anything Maker's Mark had done.

GOOSING SALES

1996–1999 | New Rochelle, New York—New Orleans

Early one summer Sunday morning in 1996, just before dawn, Sidney Frank, a spirits tycoon who conducted a sizable chunk of his business from bed in one of his four palatial homes worldwide, phoned the number-two executive at his Sidney Frank Importing Company. "I figured out the name," he cried into the receiver. "It's Grey Goose!"

The seventy-six-year-old Frank had set irreversibly in motion the creation of what would become America's bestselling vodka. It would take square aim at Absolut and would share many characteristics with that phenomenally successful Swedish brand. For one thing, the creation story: Frank and his firm pulled the concept and the name, as well as much of the backstory for Grey Goose, from what was often described in the media as "thin air"—and well before there was an actual spirit to sell. And, like Absolut, everything would deliberately hinge on the marketing, not the taste. "Go to France and come back with vodka," Frank told his subordinates, figuring that the cachet of the nation long associated with fine wine, Champagne, and Cognac would help sell what he planned as a "super-premium" vodka. His firm contracted with Cognac distilleries in the Charente and Charente-Maritime regions to switch some of their stills to producing Grey Goose, a much quicker process than producing the storied brandy. As for the name itself, there was just something about it, according to Frank, who knew a thing or two about spirit salesmanship.

Born in 1919 in rural Connecticut to a pair of hardscrabble farmers, he got his first taste of business at age twelve during the early days of the Great Depression. He fashioned a ladder to climb a local hump called Mohegan Rock and charged tourists a dime for the privilege. A good and gregarious student, he gained admission to Brown—Frank's firm handshake with the admissions dean was said to have sealed the deal. His next-door dorm neighbor was Edward Sarnoff, the son of David Sarnoff, the founder of the National Broadcasting Corporation. Sarnoff introduced Frank to a friend of his, Louise

Rosenstiel, the daughter of Lewis Rosenstiel, founder and head of Schenley, the major distillery conglomerate based in the Empire State Building. Frank proposed to Louise six times before she said yes, and the two married. Then Frank's fortunes dramatically changed. He had had to drop out of Brown earlier because he could no longer afford the Ivy League school's tuition and had gone to work for an engineering firm that specialized in airplane design and maintenance, a not inconsequential field given the world war then raging. He got into spirits through his father-in-law, who originally asked him to use his engineering prowess to gin up an alcohol-based fuel. That didn't work, but Frank proved adept at increasing productivity, and profits, at certain Schenley holdings. This and the familial connections helped elevate Frank to Schenley's presidency, though his tenure at the firm proved rocky nonetheless: he was fired, rehired, and ultimately blackballed from the spirits industry, his hard-charging ways, however profitable, clashing with Lewis Rosenstiel's own more measured management style. Louise Rosenstiel's 1972 death ensured an irrevocable break between Frank and Schenley.

From that professional nadir, Frank began an at-first slow but later meteoric rise. He founded his eponymous importing firm and gained his first toehold in the alcoholic beverage industry, connecting sushi restaurants with Japanese producers of the rice wine known as sake. His real break came during a stroll through the Yorkville area of Manhattan's Upper East Side. Such outings from his firm's New Rochelle headquarters in Westchester County were common for Frank, a way for him to scope out what people were drinking. It was the late 1970s, an uncertain time for spirits in America, and Frank's new firm was not doing so well despite the sake sales. An attempt to popularize Liebfraumilch, a sweet white wine from West Germany, had flopped early on, and Frank found himself selling off personal assets just to stay afloat. The stroll through Yorkville, then still an enclave of Germans and German-Americans, introduced him to another Teutonic beverage: Jägermeister. Germans had long prized the syrupy, herb-laden spirit for its supposed medicinal properties, ensuring a steady consumer base despite Jägermeister's acrid, black licorice–like taste. Frank secured the importing rights in 1974. For more than a decade it seemed that Jägermeister would continue to be exactly what it had been: an eccentric digestif for the Germanic set amid a slumping overall spirits market. Then, in 1985, media in southern Louisiana noted the curious trend of college students in the region drinking "Jäger" and seeming to enjoy it. One student described the drink as "liquid valium" to a reporter from the *Baton Rouge Advocate* and others swore it was an aphrodisiac. Frank saw the coverage and immediately commenced a promotional blitz that would have been familiar to anyone who followed the rise of Absolut in the preceding half-dozen years. The blitz included eight billboards in the New Orleans area. They featured a giant bottle of Jägermeister on one side and a wincing man on the other, holding a full bottle and shot glass. In between were the words JÄGERMEISTER . . . SO SMOOTH—an ironic play on the drink's acquired taste. The man and the slogan soon found its way on to all manner of paraphernalia, including T-shirts, posters, and coasters. Frank also loosed squads of attractive young women, dubbed Jägerettes, to go from bar to bar, first in southern Louisiana and then in major metropolitan areas nationwide, to dispense free or steeply discounted shots of the stuff. (Phalanxes of Jägerdudes were eventually enlisted, too.) Sales of Jägermeister went from around the six hundred cases Frank's firm unloaded in 1974, the year it acquired the importation rights, to the hundreds of thousands and then millions. In particular, Jäger became *the* party accoutrement for the college set. While much of the spirit's initial success had to do with that early media coverage—yet another instance of newspapers in particular goosing the sales of a spirit brand or distillery—the industry gave Frank all the glory. "It's a liqueur with an unpronounceable name," a marketer explained at the time. "It's drunk by older, blue-collar Germans as an after-dinner digestive aid. It's a drink that on a good day is an acquired taste. If Sidney Frank can make that drink synonymous with 'party'—which he has—he can pretty much do anything."

Enter, then, Grey Goose. Contrary to the creation myth he developed after the spirit's smashing success, Frank did not come up with the name out of thin air one summer Sunday morning (though the phone call to his number-two was true). Instead, he had long owned the worldwide rights to the name, which he slapped on that doomed attempt at Liebfraumilch sweet wine in the 1970s and resurrected for Grey Goose vodka in 1996. As for everything else beyond the contents of the bottle, that would be about one thing: luxury. Grey Goose, a not particularly tasty vodka and one virtually indistinguishable from the Absolut it was intended to dethrone, was targeted toward "the hottest clubs on the hottest nights, in the hands of the hottest people . . . the obsessive arbiters of taste who like to tell their friends what to buy." To that end, Frank did ensure that complementary bottles were placed in popular clubs as well as at noteworthy charity events and into the swag bags of limos spiriting celebrities to and from the Academy Awards. Frank's firm stressed the vodka's French origins, including the use of Champagne limestone to filter it. In fact, the $3 million that the firm made selling Grey Goose that first year went toward advertising it in subsequent years. In the end, though, the most important thing Sidney Frank did was set the price of a bottle of Grey Goose about ten dollars higher than that of Absolut, the bestselling vodka in America and right up there with Bacardí white rum as the dominant player in the spirits market. The move seemed counterintuitive, crazy even, but it worked: Grey Goose soon did dethrone Absolut as the nation's most popular vodka. Drinkers simply equated the higher price with better quality, another echo of Absolut and one that would reverberate throughout the small-batch spirits movement. Most significantly, the success of Grey Goose in the mid-1990s helped lead a resurgence in spirits consumption in the United States, one that not only ballasted the bottom lines of major players but also raised the prospects and expanded the potential consumer base for smaller ones, too.

The year 1994 turned out to be the lowest point for per-person spirit consumption in the United States since the nagging decline began in the late 1970s. From then on, the average amount of spirits an American drank yearly would inch up nearly every year, until by the new century it was increasing steadily toward one gallon per person per year. There were several theories as to what was causing the turnaround. One of the biggest bandied about was that Grey Goose and its imitators had won over younger drinkers more susceptible to luxury marketing. Longtime vodka presence Smirnoff, for instance, released what it called Smirnoff Black, essentially the spirit in a differently hued bottle, and, taking a cue from Sidney Frank, priced it at nearly ten dollars more than a regular Smirnoff. It and other superpremium spirits—a term that came into widespread use in the mid-1990s—found ready homes in the hands of the children of the very baby boomers who had so widely rejected spirits. "In bars and restaurants in the USA's major cities, young adults increasingly are forsaking mass-market beer and wine to imbibe brands with image," went one USA Today article in July 1995. "They're ordering high-end mixed drinks, straight tequila and designer martinis. And they're paying $8 to $9 a glass, or more." Others saw the creeping rise in spirits consumption as a counterreaction a long time coming to the neo-Prohibitionism and antidrug crusade of the previous decade. These newer spirits consumers in particular were "tired of being told not to drink, smoke, eat fatty foods or forget to exercise." Having come of age amid the antidrug DARE program, Mothers Against Drunk Driving, and the presidential fitness tests, they saw a bracing drink with an equally strong price tag as a liberating experience. They also undoubtedly saw a beefier new president, Bill Clinton, who clearly enjoyed heavier dishes.

Or maybe it was the slow reemergence in the popularity of cocktails, which popular media abetted. The independent movie Swingers debuted in

October 1996. Written by Jon Favreau, the plot tells the tale of young, struggling actors in Los Angeles enamored of midcentury pop culture, with its swing music and cocktail habit front and center in the film. Advertisements for the movie included the blocky tagline, "Cocktails First. Questions Later." Made with a budget of just $200,000, *Swingers* grossed more than $4.5 million domestically and launched the film career of Vince Vaughn. It also helped spur a renewed jones for cocktails among younger consumers, as did the six-season HBO series *Sex and the City*, which debuted in 1998 and which grew out of an identically titled column written by Candace Bushnell for the *New York Observer*. In the show, four female friends, and their friends and lovers, routinely bonded, plotted, and self-medicated in Manhattan with cocktails, especially vodka-infused cosmopolitans and fruit-flavored martinis. (The cosmo was perhaps *Sex and the City*'s biggest nonhuman breakout star.) At a time when the larger alcoholic beverage industry and its marketers assumed women leaned on white wine as their preferred libation, the cosmo-swilling of Carrie Bradshaw and company was truly trendsetting. So were new cocktail-centric bars, especially Milk & Honey, which Sasha Petraske, an ex-Communist who had bartended elsewhere, opened on Manhattan's Lower East Side in late 1999.

Finally, the rise in spirits consumption coincided with rises in fine wine and craft beer consumption throughout the 1990s. Fine wine's increase commenced in earnest after a November 1991 segment on the hugely popular CBS television program *60 Minutes* entitled "The French Paradox." It sought to explain the relative health, and slenderness, of the French as a result of their moderate intake of red wine (never mind the high rates of cirrhosis and heart disease relative to the United States). A follow-up piece in July 1992 concluded with avuncular correspondent Morley Safer smiling into the camera and saying, "The evidence of the benefits of alcohol in moderation keeps growing." That was all many would-be tipplers on the sidelines needed to hear. Per-capita wine consumption in the United States had dropped below two gallons in 1991 for the first time since 1979. By the end of the decade, it would bounce to well above that two-gallon mark as consumers besieged retailers for "the same wine the French drink." Concurrently, revenue for the wine industry, particularly those now-many wineries specializing in higher-end grapes, grew by double-digit percentages annually.

Craft beer saw similar percentage leaps for sales, though that segment of the alcohol trade never ascended to the same dizzying heights as fine wine. Still, steady growth and a plethora of entrants, including in many areas of the country that had not seen a new brewery in decades, ensured in turn a steady growth in consumers. At some point in the not too distant future, it seemed that craft beer would tip into the majority of beers sold and consumed in the United States, wresting that distinction from macrobrands such as Budweiser and Miller Lite. Fine wine had done the same a generation ago, toppling long-reigning generics. More portentously for craft beer, a lot of this consumer growth was organic. The vast majority of the approximately six hundred craft breweries did not advertise, and many did not pursue any active public-relations agenda. Fine wine, on the other hand, did advertise and had gregarious unofficial spokespeople such as Robert Mondavi, who went as far as taking credit for spurring *60 Minutes'* "French Paradox" segment, something the show and Morley Safer denied. Craft beer instead grew through word of mouth as well as through festivals and sporadic media coverage, a kind of up-from-the-people culinary movement with little precedent in American history—and one small-batch spirits might mimic.

As the calendar ticked toward the end of the twentieth century, the most momentous one for spirits in America, not least because of Prohibition and the industry's long slog back, small-batch distilleries such as St. George, Charbay, Germain-Robin, Anchor Distilling, and Belmont Farm made up an infinitesimal slice of the industry. Even the nearly 10 percent market share that craft beer had eked out over the last thirty years seemed comparatively unimaginable. The signs were definitely there, though, the momentum long building. The rise in overall spirits consumption that Sidney Frank's Grey Goose spawned vanquished the neo-Prohibitionists once and for all and set the table for a remarkable fin de siècle and beyond. Or so it seemed.

LITTLE BERT AND THE BIG IDEA

1997–1998 | Houston—Travis County, Texas—Napa Valley

The Texas Alcoholic Beverage Commission did not know what to make of Bert Beveridge's request. It was a kind of Catch-22, the commission explained: the Lone Star State had never licensed a distillery, much less one that a single person would run, because Texas law did not permit it to do so. Beveridge, a mortgage broker in the Austin area who often gave homemade vodka-infused drinks as gifts, disputed the commission's line of logic. It was 1996, and he wanted to turn professional. There was no such legal statute against new distilleries, including solo operations, he argued. The state, after consulting with federal authorities, agreed. Beveridge had his distillery license, the first one since Prohibition in America's then third-largest state.

Beveridge grew up in San Antonio with a boyhood dream of being a horse trainer. (He played polo.) Instead, he studied geology and geophysics, first at Vanderbilt and then at the University of Texas in Austin, and took a series of jobs in those fields after graduation in 1984, most of them having to do with oil drilling and exploration. He traveled widely, often to South America, and worked hard, harder than he preferred given the instability of the oil and natural-gas markets. A friend of Beveridge's was working in the infinitely easier mortgage-brokering business. "You wear Italian suits, hang around a bunch of girls, and there's air-conditioning," the friend told an anxious Beveridge. He was in. For a while, the money rolled in after him, and he dived into dining out and partying. Then the housing market in Texas collapsed, and Beveridge found himself with little do but watch late-night television, a bottle or a glass of something often in hand. It was during one of these late-night jags that he came across a motivational speaker on the small screen. Find the intersection of what you love to do and what you're good at, the speaker said. A lightbulb went off in Beveridge's brain. "I'd been working my whole life just so I could go to restaurants and hotels and resorts," he would recall years later. "And I'd been making infusions of cheap vodka as gifts." He enjoyed drinking, and he might just be able to writ his gift-making hobby commercially large. Soon, the hunt for the state and federal distilling licenses began, the three-inch-thick codebook of the Texas Alcoholic Beverage Commission becoming Beveridge's bible.

His prophets were not fellow distillers. They were craft brewers. Beveridge, in his travels and at home in Houston, had encountered America's burgeoning craft beer movement. That movement came to Texas, to Houston, in fact, in a big way when Brock Wagner and Kevin Bartol, two former investment bankers, raised $400,000 and used another $500,000 of their own money to open the Saint Arnold Brewing Company in the city in the summer of 1994. Named for a Roman Catholic patron of brewers, Saint Arnold was the second craft brewery in Texas since Prohibition and the first to really take hold. (A smaller operation out of the Dallas suburb of Plano went out of business in 1990, after six years.) The operation faced formidable odds, not least the indifference of Texans to its products, which included what it called Fancy Lawnmower, a dig at the watery pilsners then dominating the American market, perfect supposedly for quenching thirst during yard work. Texas may have had as many as sixty breweries in the decade following the Civil War, but the number dwindled to single digits before 1900 and pretty much stayed there after Prohibition ended in 1933. There were only six breweries in Texas by the early 1980s, and outside forces owned most of them, including Anheuser-Busch's 126-acre Houston plant and Miller's in Fort Worth, with its capacity for nearly six and a half million barrels annually. Even the beloved Lone Star brand was owned by G. Heileman out of La Crosse, Wisconsin. Bartol and Wagner pressed on, tapping into Texans' formidable thirst for beer of any kind—some thirty gallons per Texan per year—and riding the rising tide of craft beer nationally in the 1990s. Their beers, Fancy Lawnmower in particular, caught on especially with younger professionals such as Bert Beveridge, those perhaps most familiar with the wider world of beer beyond Texas's often-insulating borders. By the time Beveridge was getting his distillery papers in order, Saint Arnold was pushing the ten-thousand-barrel capacity of its original Houston location. It would soon start planning an expansion.

For Beveridge, success would come a little slower—but the example was clearly there. If a small-batch brewery could survive, even thrive, at least among the urban sophisticates in Texas's larger cities, why couldn't a distillery making small batches of vodka? The term *craft distillery* was not commonly used at the time, and Beveridge operated largely in a vacuum as he started out, unaware of other smaller-scale distilling efforts in Virginia and on the West Coast. He, of course, knew of the Swedes' Absolut and the more recent stonking success of Sidney Frank's Grey Goose, vodkas produced and sold on scales he could not hope to replicate. Although he would later tell people the idea early on was simply to intersect what he loved and what he was good at, and try to grow, it was clear from the start that Beveridge had bigger goals in mind, perhaps ones as grandiose as Sidney Frank's and the Swedes' years before. There was the matter of his new distillery's physical size. Beveridge ran up around $90,000 in debt on nineteen cards to buy thirteen acres off State Highway 130 in Travis County, just outside of the Texas capital of Austin. The land came relatively cheap: $33,000 with a down payment of $3,000 using a credit card check. Plus, Beveridge acted as his own real estate broker, saving on a commission.

It would take him a decade to pay off the self-financing, but Beveridge had his land before he had an operation in need of so much space. He named his new company Fifth Generation because that was how many generations his family had lived in Texas, and his vodka brand Tito's, a spin off his nickname: named after his paternal grandfather, relatives called him Bertito, as in "little Bert," a nickname eventually shortened to Tito. He then set about cobbling together his equipment. Here he echoed the earliest days of American craft brewing. Just as brewers then would use old soda or dairy equipment, Beveridge rigged his sixteen-gallon pot still from a pair of old soda-making tanks, with a deep-fryer for heat. Beveridge used corn as his primary grain and water from a local aquifer, and spent a lean year beginning in 1996 tweaking his vodka. By early 1997, he figured he had the recipe just right; he bottled by hand what he had and began distributing the first one thousand cases to bars in major Texas metropolitan areas. His friend from the mortgage-lending industry would toss him some work sometimes, but otherwise Beveridge during this period crashed on couches and floors of people he knew and awaited a break. It came in the form of a brief but glowing mention in the May 7, 1997, food section of the *Houston Chronicle*—the largest newspaper in Texas, with around 450,000 subscribers. Michael Lonsford, the newspaper's veteran wine writer, used the 173rd anniversary of the first public performance of Beethoven's Ninth Symphony to segue into a quick few sentences about Beveridge's efforts:

> Well, here's a home-grown symphonic spirit to applaud:
> Tito's Texas Handmade Vodka, a corn-distilled spirit made outside Austin by a native Texan with an appropriate name: Tito Beveridge.
> The spirit is clean, with a slight, almost sweet aftertaste, "like a liqueur," said Brennan's bartender Richard Hazzard. "I like it."

Lonsford then noted the cost of a bottle of this newfangled spirit, unlike anything else that had rolled out of a Texas operation in decades. Its fifteen or sixteen dollars a pop meant it was "about a pack of smokes less than Stolichnaya or Absolut." That quotation came from Beveridge himself and presaged a knack for marketing that would grow Fifth Generation and its Tito's from that modest deep-fryer beginning into the first breakout success story of the American craft spirits movement, one that would quickly need all that acreage in Travis County.

Newer spirits brands, vodka in particular, helped Beveridge's ascent. In the late 1990s, Absolut, which Seagram now owned, rolled out four flavored iterations, including the phenomenally successful Absolut Mandarin, an orange-infused vodka. This was a direct response to Russian-owned Stolichnaya's earlier debut of Stoli O. Both vodka companies, too, were looking over their shoulders at fast-rising Grey Goose. The Absolut rollouts were typically grandiose, featuring massive advertising using the already iconic

"Absolut [Something]" tagline as well as the bottles colored to reflect the flavors within. Absolut had introduced lemon and pepper flavors in the 1980s, but the newer entrants and others from competitors represented "a fruit-filled tidal wave" as the *New York Times* put it, one that maybe was getting a little out of hand. Flavored vodkas became virtually ubiquitous, straight versions shunted to the sides of bar and store shelves. "Banana vodka is fact, not theory," the *Times* reported. "It is legal in all 50 states. And it poses the same moral question as human cloning: just because scientists can do it, must they?" Consumers, especially younger ones, could be forgiven in the late 1990s for thinking that vodka was supposed to come flavored. The market had journeyed a long way since Smirnoff's roaring success touting its vodka as odorless and flavorless.

Marko Karakasevic noticed the tidal wave. He had grown up under his father Miles's tutelage at Domaine Charbay, the distillery and winery launched in the 1970s near the top of Spring Mountain in Napa Valley. While the mercurial Miles might not leave the mountain for days or even weeks, his son was much more outgoing, dining in the valley and traveling the country, all the while noting the new spirits on the market. The bottles of flavored vodka were unavoidable, and soon Marko was trying to convince his father that Domaine Charbay could make its own flavored vodkas—and that it could make them that much more flavorfully. Miles had been making straight vodkas for nearly twenty years, though not with any particular enthusiasm. The idea of flavored ones seemed positively bizarre. Yet he assented, and, in 1997, the first three hundred cases of a Domaine Charbay vodka infused with Meyer lemons from Napa Valley rolled out of the tiny distillery. Seagram in the same year distributed four hundred thousand cases of its lemon-imbued Absolut Citron alone. Marko Karakasevic's idea was a small one in practice, then, but a pivotal moment for American small-batch spirits. It marked the first time a small-batch distillery had chased a trend in the wider market rather than operating virtually parallel to it. This was not Jörg Rupf making something as domestically esoteric as eau-de-vie in virtual anonymity in Emeryville or Chuck Miller trying to take moonshine national from Virginia's Belmont Farm or even Fritz Maytag and company resurrecting 100 percent rye whiskey as a style. This was a small-batch distiller noticing the popularity of a style—for flavored vodkas might be considered as distinct an American style, for better or worse, as bourbon whiskey—and making it his own.

In the end, Bert Beveridge could not have picked a better time to launch a vodka line, small-batch or otherwise. Total US vodka sales would bounce 17 percent during the 1990s, and dozens of new brands, imports and domestics, would launch just at the turn of the century. Beveridge had a jump on a lot of them. The growth of Tito's only confirmed Beveridge's decision to ditch the mortgage-lending business and pioneer the first small-batch distillery in Texas—in the South outside of Virginia, for that matter. The growth, though, would spawn the loudest, most protracted controversy in small-batch spirits in the new century. And the craft beer movement that inspired Beveridge's early efforts foreshadowed this controversy, just as he made those first batches of Tito's that were good enough to sell.

CRAFT VS. CRAFTY

1996–2000 | Manhattan—Bra, Italy

S hortly after 7:00 PM Eastern time on Sunday, October 13, 1996, the sonorously smooth voice and chiseled-chin good looks of Stone Phillips introduced eight million households to the next segment of *Dateline*, a four-year-old news show on NBC that broadcast out of the network's Rockefeller Center headquarters in Midtown Manhattan. *Dateline* had debuted as a Tuesday-only show but had quickly spread to four nights, including this Sunday edition that was meant to go head-to-head with CBS's *60 Minutes*. It had yet to come anywhere close to besting that venerable program's numbers, having tripped out of the gate with a disgraceful 1992 segment in which *Dateline* got caught rigging the fuel tanks of General Motors pickup trucks to explode to prove the vehicles were unsafe. The show's marquee names, including Tom Brokaw, Jane Pauley, and Bryant Gumbel, kept *Dateline* afloat, and its documentary-like, confrontational style was eventually seen as something almost entirely new in primetime news, a precursor even to reality TV. Like spectators at a racetrack, those millions of households could not help but tune in to perhaps catch the next wreck.

On this particular autumn Sunday, the wreck would be craft beer—and the impact of the collision would reverberate down through the next decades into small-batch spirits. For now, the driver was Jim Koch, the cofounder and chairman of the Boston Beer Company, the concern he had grown from a few dozen sales accounts in and around its namesake city to a national, even international juggernaut that churned out nearly two million barrels of lager and ale annually. This paled in comparison to the tens of millions of barrels that Anheuser-Busch and the other few macro operations produced. But it was more than enough to make Boston Beer's Samuel Adams brand pretty much omnipresent by the mid-1990s, particularly in bigger cities. Samuel Adams and its main craft competitor, Pete's Wicked from the Pete's Brewing Company based in Palo Alto, California, accounted for around one in four craft beers purchased in the United States. There were myriad smaller competitors now, too. The United States had between five hundred and six hundred craft breweries and brewpubs, whereas in the mid-1980s it had fewer than twenty (never mind that in the mid-1970s the nation had fewer than three). So Stone Phillips's opening line to introduce the *Dateline* segment was inarguable: "When it comes to beer, you've never had more choices on tap."

To drive home the point, images filled the screen of colorful pull taps and glasses full of multihued beer. An unidentified man at an unidentified bar pronounced his verdict upon something called Rhino Chasers Peach Honey Wheat from a craft brewing company in Culver City, California: "It's got a hint of berry flavoring." The setup was clear: This was not your father's American beer scene—no watery, thin pilsners the color of an ill man's urine here. Flavorfulness and craftsmanship were key. Yet, here was Phillips again: "But do you know where some of those exotic and expensive specialty beers are really being made?"

Phillips soon ceded the cameras to *Dateline* correspondent Chris Hansen, who took viewers into his taped report entitled "Brew-Haha" with another remark on the sheer diversity of beer in the United States. "They're called craft brews, or microbrews," Hansen explained, "because, we're told, the beer is carefully crafted one small batch at a time." His first interviewee was Koch from Boston Beer. The exchanges between journalist and brewer started innocuously enough. Koch got to explain that he came from a long line of Koch family brewers stretching back several decades, and Hansen explained in a voiceover that Koch sampled every batch of beer that his company bottled. Then Hansen lowered the boom using a label on a bottle of Samuel Adams:

> The bottle invites you to come visit their small traditional brewery in
> Boston. So we did, and found a small brick building, a photo tribute
> to previous generations of Koch brewers, and, just as you see in the
> Sam Adams commercials, the small copper kettles and equipment
> used to brew the beer. But there's one small problem with this pic-

ture: At least 95 percent of all Sam Adams beer isn't brewed here—or anywhere even near Boston, for that matter.

The screen then cut to far less bucolic scenes than the quaint-looking brewery in Boston, which Koch's company had opened in 1988 as primarily a tourist attraction and research facility. Viewers now saw breweries that resembled Dickensian factories: billowing smokestacks, drab warehouses, their locations clearly at the margins of cities. These, Hansen explained, were larger, more industrial breweries in western Pennsylvania and upstate New York, where, in fact, the vast majority of Boston Beer's wares were brewed, bottled, and shipped from. These same breweries made much cheaper brands, too, the correspondent went on, including Old Milwaukee and Stroh's, adjunct-filled, alkaline-tasting brews much less flavorful than a Samuel Adams. What's more, Koch's company was "far from alone," Hansen said. "Many of the expensive boutique beers that promote themselves as 'handcrafted' or 'micro-brewed' are actually made in larger commercial breweries like this one; it's called contract brewing."

The *Dateline* segment then cut to a representative of Anheuser-Busch complaining to Hansen about a supposed lack of transparency on the part of Boston Beer and its competitors, particularly Pete's Brewing, also a contract operation. The scene was improbable, laughable even: the world's biggest brewer—the biggest brewer ever in terms of sales and volume—playing the aggrieved victim of a much, much smaller and younger competitor. Although most viewers likely did not know this, and *Dateline* never connected the dots for them, the pose was especially egregious because Anheuser-Busch had tried to co-opt much of the craft beer movement with phantom craft brands such as Elk Mountain Amber Ale and Pacific Ridge Pale Ale, beers that looked and sounded like craft offerings but tasted not quite so. Other macrobrewers had gone the same route in the early 1990s, though most, including Elk Mountain and Pacific Ridge, had flopped commercially. Anheuser-Busch and its main competitors, especially Miller, had also tried squeezing distribution channels so tightly as to cut off the supply of craft brands to much of the country. While that had a more detrimental effect than the phantom crafts ever did, the distribution vise impacted smaller craft brands more than bigger ones such as Samuel Adams and Pete's. Those continued to find their ways into newer markets and were easily available in all fifty states by 1996. The *Dateline* segment, then, was the latest and perhaps last card Anheuser-Busch could play against craft beer. The macrobrewer was one of NBC's biggest advertisers—Anheuser-Busch had bought 175 commercials for the Olympics in Atlanta that summer. Plus, a subsidiary of the network's corporate parent,

General Electric, had invested with Anheuser-Busch in the former craft brewery behind the Redhook brand. Hansen disclosed this latter connection, but not the former one about the Olympics. His segment ended amid smaller craft breweries denouncing contract brewing—they assumed tremendous costs for physical breweries, after all—and Koch stammering a defense of it: "We tell them who brews the beer. If Julia Child comes to your house, brings her own ingredients and her own recipe, goes into your kitchen, and makes dinner for you, who made dinner, you or Julia Child?"

It was a clinic in gotcha journalism—and Koch had been got. In a larger sense, *Dateline* had gotten craft brewing and craft beer in America. That sector of the industry, which had been growing sales-wise by double-digit percentages for years, found itself painted with a profoundly broad brush of inauthenticity and chicanery, and in that most public of American forums, primetime network television. To drive home the point even further, Anheuser-Busch launched a radio, print, and television advertising campaign almost in tandem with the public relations of the *Dateline* piece, one of its ads ending thus: "Time to stop tricking beer drinkers, Jim." Craft brewers who absorbed the piece and the ads felt they made all of their efforts look fake and fleeting, not just Boston Beer and Pete's.

The numbers soon reflected this feeling. From 1996 through 2000, nearly two hundred US craft breweries and brewpubs went out of business; 1999 would be the first year when more craft breweries closed than opened. That double-digit growth of the previous several years ceased almost overnight. Craft beer sales suddenly flatlined, brands drifting off shelves and tap lines like loose garbage in a stiff city wind. Much more than the *Dateline* piece had caused this. There was the distribution squeeze, the phantom crafts, and Anheuser-Busch's ad campaign. There were also quite a few craft brands that were admittedly not that good, sorry imitators of Jim Koch's Boston Beer, who thought it was only a matter of contracting out a generic recipe and slapping some folksy label on it. Some consumers did crack open one too many iffy craft beers before wandering away from the sector completely. Finally, impassioned disagreements, particularly over contract brewing, had riven the American craft beer movement, dirty laundry the *Dateline* piece aired as well. It really did seem as the new century dawned that craft beer was over, a fad. There were still several hundred such breweries and brewpubs in operation. It would surely never grow like it had in the 1990s, though, and would certainly never pose a sales threat to Anheuser-Busch and its ilk, nor a taste threat to the likes of these bigger brewers' watery pilsners. And it looked like nothing could change that.

GETTING A TASTE FOR IT
1996–1999 | Lehigh Valley, Pennsylvania—Manhattan

John Hansell would tell people he dreamed the event before he ever planned it. He was in a fancy ballroom, and before him at tables were the best whiskeys in the world. And behind the tables were experts who could tell him all about the whiskeys that—and this was the best part—he was free to sample. On November 18, 1998, a Wednesday, in a ballroom in the massive Marriott Marquis hotel in Manhattan's Times Square, Hansell turned this reverie into reality. What he called WhiskyFest was the first large-scale tasting festival for the storied spirit in the United States, and perhaps the largest ever held in the world. That it happened was a near miracle, and that miracle had its origins in beer.

Hansell grew up in the Lehigh Valley of eastern Pennsylvania and studied environmental science at Penn State. He then earned a master's in occupational health from Drexler University in Philadelphia and began working for a utility company, specializing in the delicate enterprise of disposing of toxic and hazardous waste, some of it the by-product of nuclear power. Shortly after his 1982 graduation from Penn State, the scientifically inclined Hansell also picked up a new hobby: homebrewing. While he loved a good beer, the avocation was born more of necessity than anything else. Pennsylvania was one of those states that had long inserted itself in the distribution channels of alcohol. One of the obnoxious vagaries of that was that beer came only in twenty-four-count cases at state-run stores. In that era just before the first full flowering of craft beer in America, Hansell found himself buying one too many cases of beers that he did not like—yet there he was, stuck with the other twenty-three cans or bottles once he drank the initial off-putting offender. Plus, the imports available in eastern Pennsylvania then tended to taste stale because they had been shipped so far and sat so long on the shelf. As for the domestically made beers available, Hansell took a pass on the vast majority, at least initially. They bored him. By the close of the 1980s, however, several craft brands were available in the Keystone State, and Pennsylvania boasted at least a few craft breweries of its own, beginning with the Stoudt Brewing Company in Adamstown in 1987. The greater variety and his own desire to avoid having to buy cases of beers he ended up not liking led Hansell to host tastings at his house in Emmaus, just south of Allentown. He invited coworkers to the first one held in 1992 in his garage. He bought twenty-four cases and mixed up the beers so every guest got his or her own twenty-four-count case, charged them the cost of a case, and came out ahead with a free two dozen of his own.

His coworkers started asking questions about the beers, which gave Hansell an idea. For subsequent tastings, as well as beer dinners he would host at his house, he typed up tasting notes on the individual beers; just simple descriptions of what to expect in drinking each. Soon he had an informal beer club going, and his tasting notes were more in demand. The entrepreneurial bug having bitten, he took the notes to local restaurants and bars with decent beer menus, and they in turn asked to advertise in the de facto newsletter. Hansell was happy to take their money and to expand what he called *On Tap*, beginning in 1992. Soon he was distributing the newsletter in parts of New York State, too. It was a fortuitous time to be publishing a craft beer newsletter, however limited the distribution. The growing numbers of both craft breweries and sales naturally spawned a subculture of craft beer fans, which in turn laid fertile ground for a wave of media, both online and in print, to cover the movement. *All About Beer*, the leading trade magazine for the industry, expanded around this time under new ownership out of Durham, North Carolina. Other magazines and newspapers, including *Southern Draft Brew News*, *Brew Your Own*, *Celebrator*, and *Ale Street News* joined *All About Beer* in the late 1980s and early 1990s. Bill Brand, a reporter and editor at the *Oakland Tribune*, launched the *What's on Tap* newsletter for the San Francisco Bay Area, and Jack Erickson, a former congressional aide and speechwriter, launched a national newsletter covering the craft beer industry, which, by that time, warranted national coverage. Websites such as RealBeer and the precursor to BeerAdvocate launched from locations on both coasts, each a mix of reviews and news. The critic Michael Jackson even had a CD-ROM beer guide called *The Beer Hunter* and a brief television series of the same name on the Discovery Channel starting in 1990. As for wine publications, several of those had been going since the 1970s and had long gained national, even international reach. John Hansell's *On Tap* efforts, then, fit snugly with the times.

The slim, lightly bearded Hansell, then just past thirty, kept his day job as he continued to write and distribute *On Tap*. He also continued his libationary evolution, which led to further evolution in his brief publishing career. In early 1991, an old college buddy bought Hansell a bottle of Johnnie Walker Black, the popular blended whiskey from Scotland that was usually aged for a dozen years. They cracked it open on a Friday night and "put a serious dent in it." It was the first time Hansell, a consummate beer man, had really tasted whiskey. "This is pretty good stuff," he thought. That Saturday he checked out the latest edition of *BusinessWeek*—he was a subscriber—and saw an article on the rising popularity of single malt whiskeys in particular. That piqued his interest further. He hit the nearest package store for every single malt he could get his hands on, which in those days, in his location, meant about four bottles. Soon, too, Hansell and his wife were on a three-week jaunt through the distilleries of Scotland, Michael Jackson's single malt guide in hand. As fervently as he tossed himself into writing about craft beer, Hansell soon did the same with whiskey. Unlike his previous foray, however, there was not really any context beyond books such as Jackson's *Complete Guide to Single Malt Scotch*, which came out in the United States in the same year Hansell experienced his Johnnie Walker epiphany. There were no whiskey-specific newsletters of any import. Aside from Paul Pacult's *Spirit Journal*, which also debuted in 1991, there were no meaty spirits newsletters, period, and certainly no magazines or bulky American-penned guides like there were for beer and wine. Hansell pitched a whiskey piece to *Wine Spectator*, then already the glossiest publication for that beverage, and was turned down cold. The magazine did a bourbon piece every year around the Kentucky Derby and maybe one on Scottish whiskey in the fall—otherwise, it was not interested in wider coverage. Hansell realized he stood before virgin territory. In 1994, then, *On Tap* became an expanded quarterly magazine called *Malt Advocate*, with one half dedicated to beer and the other to whiskey, malted grain the common root of both. At the same time, whiskey consumed Hansell's life—vacation days, weekends; on business trips, he would hit local libraries to scour the Yellow Pages for liquor stores that might carry particularly choice brands.

All the while, Hansell encountered souls, including craft beer aficionados, who did not share his passion for whiskey. The indifference baffled him: "What's up with everybody?" To counter this dearth of knowledge, never mind the lack of appreciation, Hansell and wife Amy Westlake, who ran much of the business side of *Malt Advocate*, began devising what would turn out to be the first large-scale spirits tasting in the country since Prohibition. Hansell had been to the Great American Beer Festival in Denver, which had grown since 1982 from a single evening with twenty-four breweries in one hotel ballroom to a three-day bacchanalia featuring hundreds of breweries in a convention center. He had a sense of the etiquette involved, the sizes of samples, the way attendees were supposed to conduct themselves, the possibility of bringing competing companies together for the mutual benefit of introducing their wares to a paying audience. Yet, what Hansell and Westlake were calling WhiskyFest ran into challenges from the start. Distilleries, and their corporate parents especially, did not see the benefit of appearing at a tasting festival with competitors. Hansell found himself on the phone a lot trying to convince distilleries to attend. A big part of that was financial: He had booked a ballroom in the New York Marriott Marquis, which unfolded over half of a long block of Midtown Manhattan. Hansell and Westlake were on the hook for the venue, regardless of whether they could fill it. The festival could turn out to be an existential threat to the magazine. "No way it will work or be successful," a top spirits critic told Hansell.

The couple pressed on. In the end, they filled the ballroom and made money. *Malt Advocate* poured more than 150 whiskeys from Kentucky, Tennessee, Ireland, Canada, and Scotland to at least six hundred attendees paying fifty dollars a pop. Tickets, in fact, sold out a month before the November 1998 event, with a waiting list quickly ascending past an additional two hundred. Those eager to get in the door were asked to call 1-800-810-MALT, though most had no luck. As for Hansell's dream, the festival fulfilled it. Several experts, including master distillers, showed to lead seminars and explain various whiskeys as they poured them. Those pours, too, were kept at a quarter-inch, with plenty of water available. That had been the number-one concern once the ballroom was paid for: people not getting too drunk. In the end, Hansell was pleased to see a healthy respect for the spirit among attendees. Here was a tribe that Hansell had not thought existed, at least not in the United States or on such a scale nor in a city as cosmopolitan as New York. They were out there, though: fans of distinction and taste in their particular spirit of choice.

Other annual WhiskyFests would follow, starting with one in Chicago in 1999 and another one in New York that same year. Although Hansell and Westlake occasionally still confronted indifference from the industry, WhiskyFest became within a few years, in the words of one journalist, "the Holy Grail of whisky events," something "no respectable retailer or distiller would turn down." Other whiskey-tasting festivals soon followed. In 1999, Rhiannon Walsh, who had grown up around her father's passion for whiskey in Ireland and Wales, organized the Whiskeys of the World Expo in San Francisco, which soon surpassed WhiskyFest in attendance. It would be years

WhiskyFest in 1999.
WHISKY ADVOCATE

before other organizers arranged major American tasting festivals for other spirits. Whiskey had a head start in the United States that other spirits did not—namely, the popularity of whiskeys from Scotland, particularly single malts, and the long history of bourbon. Still, it was only a matter of time before other tasting festivals caught on, for WhiskyFest and Whiskeys of the World Expo were but signs of a much larger trend in American culture.

RISE OF THE FOODIES

1990–2000 | Venice, Italy

The first night of the first International Slow Food Congress in December 1990 ended with a grand banquet at the Palazzo Pisani Moretta, a late-fifteenth-century palace along the Grand Canal in Italy's Venice. The venue for the 250 delegates, press, and assorted guests, most of whom arrived by motorboat, was no accident: according to one organizer, the grandly isolated palazzo, a rare example of Gothic floral style, was meant to evoke an "earlier, slower" time.

The Slow Food movement was born in Rome four years before during a protest against the opening of a 450-seat McDonald's near the Spanish Steps. Italians angry at the "degradation of Rome" and the "Americanization" of their nation's culture cooked heaping plates of penne pasta al dente in giant skillets and carried placards reading, CLINT EASTWOOD, YOU SHOULD BE OUR MAYOR. The Hollywood legend had recently been elected mayor of the Northern California city of Carmel and had made it a point to crack down on the proliferation of fast-food restaurants. This particular Spanish Steps McDonald's would be the eighth to open in the area in recent months, not to mention the single biggest outpost of the fast-food behemoth on Earth. Worse perhaps, a Frenchman owned the franchise, and it was replacing a popular café and coffee bar. The McDonald's, then, represented all too perfectly what some Italians, particularly in the republic's larger cities, regarded as the homogenization of their famed cuisine, which was so much a part of their culture as well. It was all so impersonal, so giant, and so unforgivably bland. "We don't want fast food," the protesters chanted that April day in 1986, "we want slow food!" The McDonald's near the Spanish Steps survived—and thrived, its hundreds of seats often completely filled—but from that opening-day protest was born what came to be called Slow Food or the Slow Food movement. It was one of the more extreme and illuminating examples of an approach to food and drink that first swept parts of Europe and then America throughout the 1990s.

"I am not a foodie," the comedian Jerry Seinfeld declared in a bit to introduce a June 1991 episode of his hit NBC sitcom. "I don't, 'Oh, this is too rare. Oh, it's too salty.' Just eat it and shut up." That one bit, delivered with the decade's signature detached irony, captured both this new approach and the reaction to it perfectly. For one thing, Seinfeld dropped *foodie* itself, a word that appears to have gradually supplanted *gourmet*, *gastronome*, and *gourmand* by 1990, though media references stretched back to at least 1980. For another thing, the word did describe a certain somewhat involved, some would say persnickety approach to eating and drinking, one that an attention to origin, preparation, and presentation, including the actual eating, came to define. And, in perhaps the surest sign of its omnipresence, this foodie movement grated on the nerves of those who did not approach their meals and libations the same way—yet who found during the decade that, no matter what they did, they could not escape it. An entire ecosystem sprang up in the 1990s to support and to encourage foodies and their interests.

There was Slow Food, with its 248-word manifesto speaking for many, especially in defining what foodies were against: "We are enslaved by speed and have all succumbed to the same insidious virus: Fast Life, which disrupts our habits, pervades the privacy of our homes and forces us to eat Fast Foods.... Our defense should begin at the table with Slow Food. Let us rediscover the flavors and savors of regional cooking and banish the degrading effects of Fast Food." Slow Food's membership numbers—for it became a dues-paying organization—grew in the United States throughout the 1990s, with the Slow Food USA wing launching out of San Francisco in 1998. Slow Food often walked hand-and-hand with what came to be called locavore or locavorism, a sometimes fanatical desire to eat and drink goods made close to a consumer's home. An increasing number of restaurants, especially in larger cities, latched on to locavorism, and enthusiasts started their own groups to facilitate the purchase of locally produced foodstuffs. Also growing during this period was the number of Americans traveling overseas, where they might sample culinary wares they'd never experienced or at least had never had in the foods' natural habitats. Nearly twenty-seven million Americans traveled overseas in 2000—roughly 10 percent of the nation—up dramatically from sixteen million in 1990.

At the same time, new media launched to capitalize on this fresh fondness for food and drink. The Food Network debuted in 1993, reaching fifty million households by the decade's end with its all-cooking-and-eating shows, all the time. Major publications such as the *New York Times*, the *Wall Street Journal*, and *USA Today* expanded their culinary coverage, even adding entire weekly sections devoted to food and drink, especially wine. Niche publications such as *Saveur*, *Cook's Illustrated*, and *Fine Cooking* launched, as did ones dedicated to fine wine and craft beer. Finally, the World Wide Web, which English programmer Tim Berners-Lee created and launched in 1992, busted the Internet wide open. Long the preserve of academics and government workers, it now became the domain of anyone who could establish a proper Internet connection. Browsers such as Marc Andreessen's Mosaic, launched in 1993, made it idiot-proof simple to upload graphics and photos. Foodie coverage went online, and the first foodie bloggers were publishing by the end of the 1990s. Moreover, "thousands and thousands" of Americans began to "frequent kitchens in cyberspace" through such revolutionary software as the AOL Cooking Club chat room, which facilitated, as one publication described it, "a cadre of food aficionados from around the country who chat about recipes and food at all hours by exchanging comments they type in and transmit with the tap of their fingers."

Finally, the free market responded to the foodie movement in big ways in the 1990s, not least through the proliferation of retail chains selling what came to be called artisanal (or artisan) products, a somewhat ironic turn given the products' supposed small-batch nature. The most prominent of these was Starbucks. The original coffee house opened in Seattle in April 1971. A gradual expansion began after an ownership change, and in 1987 there were some fifteen Starbucks in the Seattle area. Fifteen years later, there were more than fifty-six hundred outlets in twenty-eight countries. Starbucks, along with competitors such as Caribou and Peet's, revolutionized how millions of Americans ordered and consumed their coffee, never mind how much they were willing to pay for it. During the 1990s, too, artisanal bread became briefly "the next food craze," with upscale bakeries and cafés populating metropolitan areas such as San Francisco and New York, and chains such as Au Bon Pain and the St. Louis Bread Company (later Panera) rising.

The American marketplace also made veritable rock stars of chefs. They were the main characters in major motion pictures and the stars of more and more cooking shows. The Food Network routinely received fifteen thousand requests for one of the fifteen hundred audience seats available for its *Emeril Live*, starring chef Emeril Lagasse. A main character in the NBC sitcom *Friends*, one of the most popular primetime shows of the 1990s, was a chef, as was a character on *The Sopranos*, the HBO mafia drama that debuted in 1999 and became the next decade's most critically acclaimed television production. (A *Sopranos* writer named Matthew Weiner began honing his own dramatic vehicle in the late 1990s, one centered around spirits-inhaling advertising executives.) Chefs such as New York maestro Anthony Bourdain wrote national bestsellers—and not necessarily via cookbooks or other how-to arcana. In the case of Bourdain's *Kitchen Confidential*, the book was a dishy confessional about the sometimes raucous rigors of higher-end commercial cooking. Fellow New York chef Marcus Samuelsson found himself on the cover of *People*, one of the world's widest-circulating English-language magazines, as among the nation's one hundred most eligible bachelors. Such homages to and vehicles for chefs would only amp up in the next decade and a half. Julia Child, America's first true celebrity chef, whose *The French Chef* ran on dozens of public television stations in the 1960s, saw the rise in popularity during the 1990s as all but inevitable: "You've had so many other people become celebrities," she told a reporter in 2000, "why not chefs? And we have so many good-looking chefs around now." Child would find herself in a particularly bright spotlight at the end of the 1990s, when France bestowed upon her its highest civilian award, the Legion of Honor, for her help in promoting French cuisine.

Nearly all of these celebrity chefs—and all of these newfangled artisanal coffee houses and bakeries, for that matter—operated initially in the nation's larger cities and metropolitan areas (and Child received her medal in a ceremony in Cambridge, Massachusetts, where she had retired amid the bustle of the nearly four-million-person Boston region). The chefs' presence in places such as New York, Boston, San Francisco, Chicago, and Houston was a byproduct of the remarkable changes these and other cities experienced in the 1990s. Crime, especially violent acts, dropped precipitously throughout the decade. At the same time, manufacturing continued to decline in urban areas, emptying warehouses of their original business uses and neighborhoods of many blue-collar workers. Vacant lots and other developable sites shot up in value, spurring fresh residential construction. Into these newer or converted spaces in these safer neighborhoods moved white-collar professionals, as well as artists and students. Cities, especially New York, saw their populations begin to grow steadily for the first time in nearly a generation. The largest metropolitan areas, those with at least two million residents, outpaced smaller areas in resident growth in the 1990s, and among the ten largest cities only Philadelphia and Detroit saw their populations fall. Cities were hot, the suburbs were not—at least among younger baby boomers and their spawn, what would come to be called Generation X. It was no accident that John Hansell and Amy Westlake picked major cities, starting with New York and Chicago, to host their WhiskyFest tastings. The idea of people paying a sizable amount of money to swirl, sniff, and sip pricey spirits fit the urban milieu of the 1990s perfectly. These cities' newcomers moved in first for jobs, particularly in fledgling fields such as new media, but stayed for accoutrements such as hot restaurants and bars. A famous chef, even one locally famous, added to the allure of a particular joint and the surrounding neighborhood. The same could be said for craft breweries, which often harbingered change in the areas in which they built or rented space. Operations such as the Brooklyn Brewery in New York, the Wynkoop brewpub in Denver, the Mass. Bay Brewing Company in Boston, and the Anchor Brewing Company in San Francisco became major draws as well as drivers of gentrification. Once a distantly made product shipped far and wide, beer was increasingly becoming that much more local as the number of craft breweries ballooned through the 1990s. This shift heralded one that would sweep the American small-batch spirits movement in the next decade as cities continued to grow in popularity and the foodie culture embodied in Slow Food claimed ever more converts. An increasing number of urban consumers wanted handcrafted, smaller-scale products—including "better-quality drink" as spirits pioneer Jörg Rupf put it to a reporter at the turn of the century—rather than ones from humongous, industrialized producers. "That is what real culture is about," the Slow Food manifesto read, "developing taste rather than demeaning it."

MULTIPLE SINGLES
1995–2000 | Alameda, California

I t was a cold and rainy February day in 1996 when Lance Winters knocked on the door of the St. George distillery in Alameda County just north of San Francisco. He had a bottle of homemade whiskey in his hand and a plan in his head. The muscular, goateed, thirty-year-old Winters had served as an engineer in the navy, including aboard the USS *Enterprise*, the world's first nuclear-powered aircraft carrier. He had then transitioned from homebrewing to working in nearby Fremont, where he had grown up, as a brewer at two of the hundreds of brewpubs that had opened in just the last few years. It was as a brewer that he experienced a twin-tiered epiphany about spirits, whiskey in particular, which intrigued him because of the potential for aging, as opposed to beer, which for the most part was meant to be drunk as young as possible. The first part of the epiphany was that whiskey distillation was similar to beer brewing—both started with, and hinged on, a fermented grain-based mash. The second part was that there was not much out there knowledge-wise regarding whiskey distillation. There was plenty out there by the mid-1990s on how to taste whiskey and what it was supposed to taste like. There was virtually nothing, however, on how to actually make the sort of small-batch, handcrafted whiskey that attracted Winters, who had already become very familiar with a similar approach to what the newspapers were starting to call craft beer.

Jörg Rupf's reputation was out there, though.

The founder of St. George Spirits had hung on through the 1980s and early 1990s, through the neo-Prohibitionism and the hegemony of white wine, never mind the indifference of the marketplace. He now enjoyed a bit of a cult-status reputation amid industry types who paid attention to what the newspapers certainly were *not* yet calling craft spirits. There had even been cause for a physical expansion in 1989, from the tiny shack by the old

Emeryville railroad tracks to a capacious 60,500-square-foot building near the shuttered Alameda Naval Air Station on the east end of San Francisco Bay. Still, St. George, like the handful of other small-batch distilleries nationwide, flew largely below the larger marketplace's radar. There had been some media attention. A reporter from United Press International filed an October 1987 missive about "the nation's first and only producer of eau de vie" that large newspapers such as the *Chicago Tribune* picked up. The *New York Times*' Florence Fabricant had stopped by, too, writing in December 1990 about not only Rupf's background but also his influence so far. Stephen McCarthy at Clear Creek in Portland, Oregon, had consulted Rupf, as had Fritz Maytag at Anchor Distilling and Randall Grahm, who briefly added eau-de-vie and grappa to the lineup of his Bonny Doon winery south of San Jose, which already pioneered lesser-known grape varieties such as Grenache, Syrah, and Mourvèdre. Rupf had also joined forces with other small-batch distillers in the Golden State, including Ansley Coale and Hubert Germain-Robin at brandy producer Germain-Robin, to form the Artisan Distillers of California, an informal group with the very formal idea of expanding the fledgling sector's consumer reach. To this end, they hosted blind tastings for restaurateurs and retailers and produced explanatory literature for the public. The group, though, had grown to a grand total of only five within a year, including Germain-Robin, Bonny Doon, and what was then called Jepson Vineyards, the successor to William Baccala's Napa Valley operation, started by Georgia tycoon Robert Jepson Jr. in 1985. Rupf and his fellow West Coast small-batch distillers, including McCarthy in Oregon, produced fewer than fifteen thousand cases altogether at the start of the 1990s, a veritable "trickle," as the *Times*' Fabricant saw it, compared with the "millions of cases produced in Europe every year," never mind the oceans of spirits that domestic macro-producers churned out. Small-batch spirits in America was still a small club. Crucially, however, it was not a closed one.

Lance Winters felt supremely comfortable, if not confident, knocking on Rupf's door after a twenty-five-minute drive from his Fremont home that February day in 1996. Rupf was expecting him. Winters had been by a week or so earlier, but Bill Manshardt, a navy vet, too, and the distillery's sole employee, had told him Rupf wasn't in. Now the younger man got right to his résumé: the bottle of homemade whiskey in his hand. "You don't know me," Winters quickly said, "but I know you by reputation. I think you do amazing work. This is what I'd like to do with my life."

He showed Rupf the bottle of whiskey he had made in a still that Winters rigged in his home. His homebrewing hobby, brewing experience, and engineering work in the navy had made the process fairly easy for him. He was confident in what he had produced. He poured samples for himself and Rupf as the rain beat against the distillery walls. Rupf sipped it.

He pronounced Winters's whiskey "inoffensive."

Only later would Winters realize that that was high praise from Rupf, who had not lost his German accent after more than fifteen years in the States. He cut Winters a deal on the spot: Come work for him for one month and see if this works out. Winters the next day put his notice in at the brewpub and started with St. George shortly thereafter. Fate intervened in the form of Manshardt's long-planned retirement, and Winters soon found himself full-time at the distillery. It was a homecoming of sorts given that he had been stationed at the old naval base nearby before it closed in 1997.

Lance Winters at the St. George Distillery.
BEN KRANTZ

Rupf and Winters quickly developed a master-apprentice relationship. The first spirit the pair worked on was a whiskey, using the same pot still used for the eau-de-vie. It was a sharp departure from St. George's hard-won reputation for eau-de-vie, sharper yet because of the type of whiskey they decided upon: barley-based single malt in the grand tradition of Scotland. It was positively heretical in some ways. Single malt was bound up in Scottish lore and tradition, and dozens of Scottish single malts were now available in the United States. American whiskeys had generally broken down into a handful of categories: bourbon; blends, mostly imported, especially from Canada and Scotland again; and rye, like the one Maytag's Anchor first released in 1996 to bafflement and muted applause. Here came American single malt, though. Rupf and Winters dubbed the release St. George Single Malt Whiskey, putting it in 1997 into barrels once used to age other spirits such as bourbon and the fortified wine sherry. St. George released five hundred cases in mid-2000, with another five hundred held back for further aging. Priced at fifty dollars per standard 700-milliliter bottle, St. George Single Malt found its way mostly to shelves and restaurants in larger cities, where critics struggled to make sense of it for consumers awash in vodka, white rum, and, if whiskey, then single malt from Scotland, blends from Canada, or bourbon from Kentucky. "This single-malt is not your smoky, honeyed, amber Highlands dram, but a light quaff, closer perhaps to Irish and with a personality all its own," Florence Fabricant explained to *New York Times* readers in December 2000. "In the glass, it's the color of oaky Chardonnay.... The first whiff suggests dried apricots." Like with Anchor's rye, what most critics paying attention could not get away from was the relative youth of St. George's Single Malt. "It has the exuberance of a young spirit not quite reined in by its three years in oak," Fabricant wrote, "which is the minimum allowed in Scotland."

Another youthful single malt on the American market in 2000 was McCarthy's Oregon Single Malt from Steve McCarthy's Clear Creek. It was the first such domestically produced whiskey since Prohibition, a true groundbreaker in both approach and marketing. It all started with a vacation McCarthy and his wife took to Ireland in the summer of 1992. The trip started promisingly enough. The couple rented a car in Dublin and drove into the republic's sparsely populated western reaches, staying at delightful hotels and enjoying the food and the surprisingly solid wine selections on offer. The pair eventually reached the area around Galway on the Atlantic shore. That's when heavy rains set in, gumming up their travels and those of fellow tourists. Their next hotel was full of guests unable to move on, so McCarthy and his wife found themselves hunkered down north of Galway. To pass the rainy hours, he ran through the hotel's whisky selection, particularly many richer single malts yet to land in faddish glory on American shores. "This is fabulous stuff," he thought. And he brought the feeling back to Oregon, to his now seven-year-old Clear Creek distillery, where he set about making whiskey. For help, he enlisted a fellow Portland pioneer. Kurt Widmer was one-half of the fraternal duo behind Widmer Brothers, one of the oldest craft breweries outside of Northern California and occupying real estate on the same west bank of the Willamette River as Clear Creek.

"Let's make some whiskey," McCarthy said.

To start, McCarthy imported from Scotland barley that had been roasted over peat, the dense, boggy soil common to the United Kingdom and Ireland, and which distillers there often used to give single malts an earthy richness. Widmer then used that to brew a smoky beer. McCarthy took back over and, using the same pot still he used for his eau-de-vie, distilled from Widmer's brew a whiskey that he then put into three types of barrels: two made from distinct species of Oregon oak trees, with one barrel kiln-dried and the other air-dried, and a barrel used to age sherry. The Oregon barrels were particularly easy to come by—wineries eschewed the coarser wood, which left a supplier McCarthy knew with a surfeit of barrels on hand. Around Christmas 1997, after barely three years of aging, McCarthy released a limited amount of McCarthy's Oregon Single Malt, holding back some to see the effects of more time in the wood.

As with Anchor's rye and St. George's single malt, the critics paying attention could not look beyond the youth of McCarthy's groundbreaker. Nor, naturally, could they escape comparisons to the European model—it had centuries of history at its back, plus McCarthy's label prominently mentioned the use of "peat-malted Scottish barley." "How good is this Oregon malt whiskey?" John Hansell's *Malt Advocate* asked rhetorically in March 2000. "It's a darned sight better than you would imagine any three-year-old whiskey could be. Although this isn't an overly complex dram, it bears a buttery palate and is reminiscent of an Islay malt in character, bringing a deep peatiness to the mouth, and a smooth, gentle, long-lasting finish."

Like Anchor Old Potrero and St. George Single Malt, McCarthy's Oregon Single Malt barely registered commercially, even amid the sorts of people who would be paying attention. A January 1999 *New York Times* piece that legendary gourmand R. W. Apple Jr. wrote about the rise of small-batch distilling in Northern California mentioned McCarthy's Clear Creek, but only its eau-de-vie and not the single malt whiskey that had by then been on the market for more than a year—at the same time noting that Lance Winters at St. George was "tinkering obsessively" with that type of spirit as well. Case runs for these newer whiskeys were small and distribution limited. (McCarthy released around fifty cases annually for those first three years of his single malt.) Even the better-known eau-de-vie and brandy did not make it that far from the source. Or, if they did, the sales were targeted toward larger metropolitan areas such as New York and Los Angeles or toward overseas markets. The Japanese took a particular liking to McCarthy's whiskey, as they did to so many other brown spirits from America. In the late 1990s, retailers in Germany were importing about 80 percent of St. George's annual eau-de-vie output, a surely satisfying development for expatriated son Jörg Rupf, but one that all but insured St. George's anonymity beyond certain circles, both geographic and gastronomic, in the States.

Yet these developments in the late 1990s, set as they were against a rising and unmistakable cultural desire for small-batch, handcrafted products, signaled a profound shift in the fortunes of American small-batch spirits. Survivors such as St. George and Clear Creek—and, it would turn out, others—had the equipment, the knowledge, and the networks in place to produce spirits well beyond their signatures. Moreover, there was an ecosystem developing to boost these and other wares, as Lance Winters's hop from craft brewing to small-batch spirits, and the coverage of both in consumer and trade media, evidenced. People were paying attention—and there were people to pay attention to. As John Hansell explained to *USA Today*, the nation's largest newspaper, at the very start of the fresh century: "We are on the verge of this really cool exploration."

TEQUILA FROM A BRANDY SNIFTER

1995–2000 | Irwindale, California—Jalisco, Mexico

James Busuttil picked the spot in Irwindale, a city of perhaps fifteen hundred people eighteen miles east of Los Angeles and best-known for a failed bid to lure the National Football League's Raiders from that much larger neighbor, because it was near his day job as a biology teacher at Mountain View High School in nearby El Monte. There, in Irwindale, in an industrial park amid the city's quarries, some of them in disuse, and across from a mobile-home repair shop, Busuttil launched in 1995 what he called the Saint James Distillery. It was the years-long fulfillment of a passion, one that he knew would likely not make him wealthy and one that would consume his free time as surely as homework did his students'. In this, Busuttil followed a pathway that many of the newer entrants to the American small-batch spirits movement would now traverse and one that would not necessarily have been familiar to earlier arrivals. People such as Chuck Miller at Belmont Farm in Virginia or Steve McCarthy at Clear Creek in Oregon had come from food-related pursuits—in Miller's case, raising the corn that ended up undergirding his whiskey and in McCarthy's the fruits of his eaux-de-vie and brandies. Ansley Coale at least had plans to cultivate grapes by the time he picked up Hubert Germain-Robin by the side of Highway 101. To come from so far afield, as Busuttil did, was fairly novel.

It started with an epiphany during Busuttil's 1987 honeymoon, when he and his new wife traveled to her family's farm in Switzerland. It was late spring, during the annual cherry harvest, and a truck was going from farm to farm with a pot still to distill the cherries and other fruits into eau-de-vie and brandy. Kirsch, the sweetish Central European cherry eau-de-vie, struck Busuttil in particular—here was something you did not see too often back home. Distillation, too, fascinated him, though he himself was not much of a drinker. It was all like a "big science project," something that appealed to the educator in him. Busuttil grew up in Southern California, the son of immigrants from postwar Britain. He went to California State University in Long Beach, graduating in 1981 and securing his teaching credentials afterward. He would earn an MBA from Azusa Pacific University, in that same municipal patchwork in Los Angeles's orbit, teaching high school the entire time, including during the summers. Fitting in his newfound passion for distillation meant weekends, evenings, and vacations, which Busuttil invariably spent visiting distilleries in Europe, especially the whisky distilleries of Scotland—he drove around with his mother, who grew up there. He spent years saving the money and, in anticipation of the 1995 launch of Saint James, bought a pot still made in Germany.

Busuttil initially attempted to replicate the kirsch that had so enthralled him during that Swiss trip eight years before. He worked with his father, whose family had made wine on Malta, the Mediterranean archipelago once a colony of the United Kingdom. But when his father died, Busuttil, shaken, set the kirsch aside, never bottling it. Instead, he turned to two other spirits, both fairly rare in American craft spirits: single malt whiskey and tequila. First released in 1999, Busuttil's Peregrine Rock California Pure Single Malt Whisky was one of the first single malts to be released in the United States, along with Clear Creek's McCarthy's Oregon Single Malt and St. George's Single Malt. All carefully avoided the internationally protected "Scotch" reference on their packaging, though Busuttil did use the Scottish spelling of *whisky*. Peregrine Rock, like the others, leaned on peated barley from Scotland and was produced in Busuttil's usual forty-gallon pot still. Although media as disparate as the *Malt Advocate*, the *Los Angeles Times*, and *Newsweek* wrote about Peregrine Rock, most of the attention—like with Clear Creek and St. George, and with Anchor Distilling's rye whiskey, for that matter—focused on the short aging time. "Aged only two years (most malts age at least eight), Busutill's [*sic*] Peregrine Rock label appears as single-malts have become the fastest-expanding category in the booze business," *Newsweek* reported in late October 1998. "Connoisseurs say, however, that the raw product shows promise.... To make sure, he'll let his malt age another year before releasing it nationally."

Busuttil's other major craft spirits offering of the late 1990s was already on the market in late 1998. What he called California Gold Agave was a hand-made version of tequila, the Mexican spirit whose circuitous life had seen it evolve from little more than collegians' binge-drink of choice on spring break into a sipping spirit often compared with Cognac and single malt whiskey. "Tequila in America was taken almost exclusively as a means to get plas-tered," according to historian Chantal Martineau, with pop-culture references repeatedly reinforcing this. "One tequila, two tequila, three tequila, floor," went the joke that comedian George Carlin popularized. Singer-songwriter Jimmy Buffett's biggest hit, "Margaritaville," hinged on the similarly named tequila-infused cocktail.

It had not always been so. Tequila was centuries old when the Mexican government in 1949 created the first official standards for distilling it. The most important stricture was that the spirit be made from 100 percent blue Weber agave, a cactus-like plant that grew widely in the western Mexican state of Jalisco. The spirit shares its name with the Jalisco town of Tequila, about forty miles northwest of Guadalajara. Soon, though, a cycle of agave gluts and shortages drove the government to drop the minimum thresh-old, first to 70 percent agave by the mid-1960s and then to a bourbon-like 51 percent in 1970s. Geographic borders, too, were changed, with the essential agave no longer having to come from Jalisco but from a variety of areas of Mexico. These alterations made making tequila that much easier, as did a rapid industrialization in the Mexican spirits industry throughout the twentieth century. Like north of the border, pot stills were out and column ones in, as were industrial shredders for the plant itself. Large companies such as the family-owned Jose Cuervo began producing macroamounts of tequila using 49 percent corn or cane sugar, and shipping much of it to the United States, where pop culture had primed the public to receive it as that surefire way for a quick and powerful buzz. Tequila had been steadily gaining in popularity in the United States since Prohibition in the 1920s, when it became a ready replacement for banned domestic spirits. World War II only bolstered that popularity as the conflict largely cut off the flow of Cognac, Scotch, and other European spirits. It was in the 1970s, though, that things really began to take off. "Before 1970," *Time* magazine told its readers in January 1976, "liquor stores used to stock tequila—if they carried it at all—on a back shelf alongside ouzo and grappa. In the past five years, however, annual imports have increased more than four hundred percent; where only a handful of brands were available north of the border ten years ago, some two hundred fifty labels are now registered." That amount would double, then triple, then quadruple in the next century. Like with vodka, tequila benefited commercially from cocktails concocted for it, especially the margarita, which dated from at least the 1960s and which grew staggeringly in popularity after a Dallas restaurateur, inspired by a Slurpee machine at a 7-Eleven, created a contraption in 1971 for cranking out frozen versions fast. Also, "one unknown genius" along the way invented the superfluous ritual of inhaling tequila by the shot glass with a lick of salt beforehand and a slurp of lime wedge afterward—"which had the dual benefits of promoting heavy consumption while masking the bone-rattling bad taste of many tequilas on the market." For a lot of the tequila then on the American market in particular was foul-tasting, very much living down to its reputation as what one drank to get drunk. And, in an echo of American beer, two companies, Jose Cuervo and Sauza Tequila, made the vast majority of this tequila, almost 90 percent.

That started to change in the 1980s, just after that time of frenetic growth. Robert Denton and Marilyn Smith were business partners in a spirits importing company and had been working in the industry for years when they discovered small-batch tequilas made from 100 percent blue agave sugar—a dying, or at least faded, art amid the echoing boom in mass-produced tequilas made with nearly half cane or corn sugar. Beginning in 1983 with tequilas from the family-run Chinaco distillery, Denton and Smith imported, distributed, and promoted higher-end tequilas in the United States. It became their passion, in fact, one they shared in simple yet profoundly influential ways. For one thing, they were careful to be seen at spirits and wine trade shows drinking tequila from brandy snifters. This simple act was bound to draw attention, and it did, during a time when tequila was invariably pounded by the shot glass. They also gave talks and distributed materials about the qualities that comprised a higher-end tequila, particularly the small-batch creation in pot stills and the use of as much agave as possible to undergird the spirit rather than substitutes such as corn sugar. The idea was to change the perception of tequila first—to make it something worthier of esteem and a heftier price tag—and then to get the actual small-batch, higher-end spirit in front of the consumer. It was a challenge unique in the American small-batch spirits movement to that point, one that simple prejudice and rank unfamiliarity made more difficult. "They didn't mind it when it was Scotch," Denton explained to the *New York Times'* Florence Fabricant in 1998, when his and Smith's efforts were finally paying off. "But one of the hardest things we've had to overcome is the image of top quality coming from Mexico."

Overcome it they did, as did other evangelists from the industry. By the late 1990s tequila was the fastest-selling spirit in America, with premium brands retailing for upward of one hundred dollars per bottle helping drive those sales. Make no mistake: tequila even at this pace still accounted for no more than 2 percent of the American spirits marketplace, and cheaper—and more cheaply made—brands comprised most of that share. But tequila had clearly rounded a corner in terms of regard. "The finest tequilas, meant for brandy snifters, not blender drinks, are listed along with single-malt Scotches and rare Cognacs in top restaurants," Fabricant noted in 1998. Tequila received an especially august imprimatur in 2002, when Austrian glassware maker Riedel, famed for its wine and spirits vessels the world over, created for tequila a snifter all its own—a finely blown stem with an elongated, narrow bowl at the top, better to capture and hold the spirit's aroma; no lime wedges nor salt required.

James Busuttil's California Gold Agave fit well with this newfound respect for the spirit. Like its Mexican counterparts, Saint James's tequila-in-all-but-name was made with 100 percent blue agave sugar, producing a slightly sweet taste and a clean finish. California Gold Agave retailed by late 1998 for $21.75 per slender 375-milliliter bottle. Its distribution reach was neither wide nor far—mostly to upscale restaurants and grocers in Southern California—but Busuttil's spirit marked the first domestically produced small-batch tequila in America since Prohibition. It would be one of many firsts for a suddenly invigorated movement at the turn of the century.

MIXING IN GIN

1996–1998 | Bend, Oregon—San Francisco

Jim Bendis, a red-haired, superfit salesman at a local central Oregon television station, was running through what was perhaps the world's largest juniper tree forest when a thought struck him like a streak of lightning: so much juniper and yet no gin from Oregon. In 1996 he began laying the plans for what became Bendistillery, after his surname and after the distillery's location in Bend, an Oregon city of perhaps seventy-five thousand people straddling the Deschutes River and just to the east of the lush Willamette National Forest.

Juniper berry is the animating ingredient in gin, a clear spirit dating from at least the seventeenth century and thought to have been developed in the Netherlands when that tiny European kingdom was building one of the world's largest empires. The European nation with the biggest empire, the United Kingdom, discovered gin through the Dutch, including its late-seventeenth-century Netherlands-born king, William of Orange, and the spirit soon rivaled rum and vodka in popularity worldwide, though nowhere more than in the United Kingdom itself. Gin became so popular in the eighteenth century, particularly in London, that it caused widespread social ills and a counterreaction among the governing classes, including new licensing laws for distillers and penalties for disreputable ones. It was estimated that the average Londoner put away a ripping fourteen gallons of the spirit annually in the mid-1700s, most of it cheaply made and therefore of poor, even dangerous quality—turpentine sometimes took the place of juniper as a flavoring agent. One much later observer would call the gin of eighteenth-century London "the crack cocaine of its day," likening it to the narcotic that ravaged so many US inner cities two and a half centuries later. In this, gin mimicked the vodka craze blighting the Russian empire around the same time, where what the masses were inhaling was not always what they thought and the consequences, for them and society, were often dire. The fresh government regulations did clean up the gin trade a bit, but the lack of cheap sources caused a sharp dip in consumption levels. Britain and its empire largely returned to alcoholic staples such as beer, whiskey (the Scottish stuff in particular), and claret (what the rest of the drinking public called red wine from France's Bordeaux).

Then, in the early nineteenth century, gin received a massive boost from an innovation in health care. British soldiers and administrators in colonial India started using quinine powder, the active ingredient in the bark of the cinchona tree, to treat and to prevent the then-common tropical disease malaria. The Spanish had discovered the bark's medicinal attributes in one of their own colonies, what became Peru, centuries before. Yet quinine powder, which had to be taken every day for proper effect, was especially bitter and hard to ingest straight. Many British took to mixing in water and sugar with their daily tonic of malaria-fighting quinine powder. Thus was born tonic water, which European firms began churning out commercially in the middle of the century—a Swiss named Johann Jacob Schweppe added carbonation to his "Indian Tonic Water"—and enterprising tipplers started mixing with gin. The gin and tonic, one of the most popular cocktails of all time, boosted the spirit to consistently healthy sales and cemented a hard-won respectability following the dangerous overindulgence of the century before. Other gin-based cocktails joined the G and T, including the Negroni, the Tom Collins, and the martini. The latter, traditionally a mixture of gin with the fortified wine vermouth (and usually an olive or three), dates from at least the turn of the twentieth century, with its genesis either on the West Coast, in modern-day Syria, or in Italy. The upper echelons of British society adopted gin as a particular favorite around the birth of the martini, in much the same way Hollywood elites later took to vodka. Elizabeth Bowes-Lyon, King George VI's wife and the mother of the current British monarch, became especially fond of gin cocktails, and the press let the public know it.

This newfound respectability via cocktails and the popularity it brought had one unintended but not that surprising side effect: a lot of gin produced became homogenous and barely indistinguishable brand to brand. The United Kingdom, including Scotland, became the epicenter of the gin-producing world, with most of the world's largest brands, including Beefeater, Gordon's, and Tanqueray, either started or headquartered there, some of them survivors of the mid-eighteenth-century government crackdown. British distilleries produced the vast majority of these twentieth-century gins with column stills, rather than smaller-batch pot ones, and often hurried along production through soaking the juniper berries and other flavoring agents—everything from tree barks to cinnamon—in the earliest version of the distillate and then simply redistilling it, without extracting the aromas and tastes of the flavoring agents for another round of distilling. These made for drier, stronger gins with little nuance in taste. Because gin did not have to be aged, the faster these distilleries could produce the spirit, the faster they could get it out the door and into a thirsty world marketplace that included the United States in a prominent role. Gin in America would never ascend to the same heady sales heights as vodka or rum, though as with those spirits and with whiskey, the United States would remain one of the leading markets for the spirit through much of the twentieth century. Per-person consumption in America never rivaled that in Britain, either, or, interestingly enough, Spain and the Philippines, which drank more gin per person than any nation, but it always seemed to rank among the top five. Gin consumption in the United States rose steadily throughout the 1900s, peaking in 1975 at forty-four million gallons and then precipitously dropping at the start of the 1980s to around twenty million, or by more than half in under a decade. The reason for the cliff-drop was familiar: the rise of fine wine, white wines such as Chardonnay in particular. That and the popularity of vodka and rum, in the spirits' sphere at least, may have ensured an almost-terminal decline for gin in America.

Enter Absolut, the premium vodka brand that had played such a major role in shifting perceptions not only of that particular spirit but also of spirits in general in America. Michel Roux had since 1981 headed Carillon, the small northern New Jersey importer behind the domestic success of Absolut. He was the man who arranged Andy Warhol's famed portrait of the vodka bottle, and his firm's portfolio had understandably expanded in the wake of Absolut's success, Roux's own reputation as a marketing man with a golden touch only increasing. One entrant on Carillon's ledger was Bombay Original, a gin with recipe roots in the 1760s and produced in the United Kingdom by the independently owned Bombay Spirits Company. In 1985 Roux and Ian Hamilton, Bombay Spirits' master distiller, commenced a two-year trial-and-error process to develop a new kind of gin. Hamilton infused it with botanicals that Bombay Original did not have—and infused it in a more delicate way. Rather than steeping the flavoring agents in the alcohol base, he laid them in racks above, so that the vapor from the distillation would pass through them. As one later fan of the gin would point out, it was the difference between boiling vegetables and steaming them. This and the new ingredients left Hamilton and Roux's experimental gin with a lighter, less herbal taste, one deliberately designed to compete with premium vodka brands, which, whatever their distillations, invariably came out with less flavor because of the very nature of the spirit.

The new gin's recipe settled, Roux moved to the marketing. Like with Absolut, the emphasis would be less upon the taste of the spirit itself—though its unspoken similarity to vodka was important—and more upon its provenance. It had to stand out in an alcohol marketplace drowning in white wine, rum, and vodka, where even older, more established gin brands such as Beefeater and Gordon's barely registered any recognition with the average consumer—or, if they did, it was as the accoutrement to a G and T. Roux started where the Swedes behind the original Absolut started: the bottle. He made it sky blue and he called the new gin Bombay Sapphire, a reference not only to the company behind it but also to a 182-carat gemstone known as the Star of Bombay, which film star Douglas Fairbanks gave to his wife, fellow actor Mary Pickford, and which Pickford bequeathed to the Smithsonian. Right there, Roux had a tantalizing backstory, one that combined history with the exclusivity inherent in pricey jewels and the exoticness of an Indian destination that many consumers in the West were likely unfamiliar with. To bolster the backstory, the front label referenced the original 1761 recipe as well as a pendant that included a representation of the sapphire and at its center a portrait of a dour-looking Queen Victoria, the British monarch who reigned during gin's last heyday in the nineteenth century. Roux also listed Bombay Sapphire's ten botanicals on the side of the bottle, a novel move for gin, one meant to imbue it with a certain sophistication. Here was a spirit sippable on its own and not necessarily with tonic water, etc. The botanicals included that juniper berry mainstay but also more esoteric fair such as liquorice, cassia bark, and West African grains of paradise. Finally, in the grand tradition of Absolut and of its later Grey Goose competitor, Roux went long on the price: Bombay Sapphire retailed for more than twenty-five dollars for each rectangular bottle, several bucks more than other bottles of gins. In cities such as New York and Los Angeles, a cocktail with Bombay Sapphire might go for an astronomical nine dollars.

Released in the United States in 1988, Bombay Sapphire proved an instant hit. It would not, and never would, rocket gin to a sales level on par with vodka or even rum; but it opened up a path for gin producers fretting the decade's steep sales decline. Described as "the first new premium gin for decades," Bombay Sapphire "provided the model for dozens of subsequent boutique gins." The spirit did so not only through its distillation—"about as far from industrial mass production as a mainstream distiller could get," including the use of Welsh spring water—but also through the same sort of lifestyle marketing that boosted the success of a certain vodka brand a short decade before. Everyone who followed such things recognized the parallels with Absolut, and not just because Michel Roux helped popularize that vodka and Bombay Sapphire. The higher price, the unabashedly sophisticated and subtle packaging, the stylish bottle, marketing that included print advertisements with the tagline "Pour something priceless"—it all screamed to consumers that what they beheld was not their parents' or grandparents' G and T ballast. Like with Absolut and vodka, Bombay Sapphire was a gin to be savored on its own or to be added conspicuously to any cocktail, a ninety-four-proof status symbol. "The first crack in the ice doubtless was Bombay Sapphire, with its light blue bottle," one Utah-based importer told the critic Paul Pacult for a *Wine Enthusiast* magazine article on renewed interest in gin. "Packaging became just as important as product quality. Credit where credit is due. Sapphire offered both." And it had the US premium gin category to itself for years after the 1988 release.

It was not until Jim Bendis's Bendistillery that another premium gin— this one made in America in small batches in a pot still at an independently owned distillery—dropped on the US market. What Bendis called Cascade Mountain Gin debuted in Oregon for $18.95 per 750-milliliter bottle just after the start of 1997. State authorities were so taken with the new product and its local juniper berry roots that they authorized what legal parlance called "forced" release, meaning the fifty busiest of Oregon's 234 liquor stores received at least three bottles. The allure of the localness was no accident. To Bendis, his gin and a Crater Lake Vodka rolled out around the same time were a mere extension of those other great libationary trends in Oregon and the Pacific Northwest. "It seems like the next logical step to what's been going on with Oregon wines, micro-brewed beers and coffee," he told a reporter from the Associated Press that March. The Beaver State's wine renaissance dated from 1961, when a man named Richard Sommer ignored those who thought he was wasting his time and planted Cabernet Sauvignon, Pinot Noir, and Sauvignon Blanc vines on an old turkey farm in Roseburg, in the state's southern reaches. Within two years, what Sommer called HillCrest winery was in production, and in 1967 it produced a Pinot Noir, the first in Oregon of the wine style that would become most associated with the state. Sommer quit his day job as an appraiser the same year, and by the end of the decade there were several Oregon wineries in production. Moreover, Oregon State University soon joined the University of California at Davis, near Sacramento, as the sole four-year school offering accredited training in winemaking. Some of the owners of the wineries following in Sommer's wake branched out into craft beer in the spring of 1980. Charles and Shirley Coury debuted the Cartwright Portland brewery—Cartwright was Shirley's maiden name—with a 150-case run of a mild English-style ale retailing for one dollar a bottle. Dogged by iffy quality, Cartwright Portland did not last long. In 1982 two other winemakers, Dick and Nancy Ponzi, picked up its craft beer mantle, launching what became the BridgePort Brewing Company, also based in Portland. By the start of the 1990s, Oregon was one of the top states in terms of craft beer production, sales, and appreciation. Ex-Marine-turned-photographer Fred Eckhardt had started writing his Portland *Oregonian* column in 1984, the first such regular criticism of beer in an American newspaper. And Bend itself, where Bendis launched his distillery in the city's downtown, hosted the Deschutes Brewery, which restaurant-industry veteran Gary Fish launched in 1988 and which was destined to become one of the nation's biggest craft operations. Finally, there was that gourmet, or premium, coffee that Bendis mentioned, the sort that Starbucks, born in the Pacific Northwest, embodied for most Americans stepping beyond macrobrands such as Folgers and Maxwell House.

Taken together, these wineries and breweries, and the coffee shops and their culture, laid a framework for Bendis and other Oregon small-batch distillers, including Steve McCarthy's Clear Creek, to build upon. Such framework would repeat itself in states and regions nationwide in the new century: The context that one drink forged helped ease the entry of another, different one into a particular marketplace. This was particularly true out West and in the Northeast, where there was a relatively long tradition of higher-end winemaking and craft brewing, but also in areas where there may not have been too many such operations. The commercial presence of these brands from the wineries and breweries, and the subculture they engendered, were sometimes enough. "Southern distillation of craft spirits has lagged behind the rest of the country," a writer for the *Atlanta Journal-Constitution* would explain. "That's changing, however, as homebrewers discover that corn beer is one step removed from corn whiskey." Simultaneously perusing the consumer media coverage of small-batch spirits around the turn of the century and of craft beer fifteen or twenty years before is particularly helpful in understanding how this framework worked—and worked so effortlessly after a while.

Small-batch spirits did not necessarily fit the craft beer storyline as neatly as some would have wished. Distilleries that giant corporations controlled crafted some of the best small-batch whiskeys, for instance, and the influence of macrobrands on the marketplace appeal of their smaller brethren was much more acutely felt with spirits than with beer. Budweiser was not a stepping stone to Samuel Adams Boston Lager the same way a consumer might cotton to Cascade Mountain Gin after having tried Bombay Sapphire. Sam Adams was an alternative to Bud, not a conceptual godchild. No matter, though. On the outside, the craft beer and small-batch spirits' respective rises looked so similar, right down to some of the locations of the earliest pioneers, including Oregon's Willamette Valley. Writers like the one for the Atlanta daily could not seem to avoid taking refuge, then, in references to craft beer and its subculture, including homebrewing, when it came to explaining these newer spirits, just as writers in the 1980s had used fine wine to tell readers about this newfangled microbrewing trend. "During the last two decades, a legion of microbrewers have thrilled suds buffs with handmade pale ales and stouts that are remarkably more flavorful than mass-produced varieties," ran another report, this one in the much larger *USA Today*. "Now, grassroots craftsmen like these are applying modern methods and an artistic sensibility to making whiskeys, gins, vodkas, Cognac-style brandies, eau de vie (fruit brandies), grappas and other high-powered potables."

One distillery in the entire nation understood the power of craft beer context more than any other: Anchor in San Francisco. That operation, after all, had grown in the early 1990s from the oldest craft brewery in America, a vibrant example of the symbiosis, if not synergy, between craft beer and small-batch spirits, one journalists could not stop citing once they stumbled upon it in the 2000s. And it was Anchor Distilling that chose gin as its second spirit offering, to follow the 1996 debut of Old Potrero rye whiskey. Anchor's Junípero debuted in 1997, shortly after Bendistillery's Cascade Mountain. Like that one, distiller Bruce Joseph and his assistants crafted it virtually by hand from a pot still, the secreted recipe heavy on juniper berry and the resultant spirit bracing and herbaceous. Unlike Cascade, which did not at first make it beyond Oregon (Bendis kept his day job in ad sales), Anchor Junípero made it across the continent, to liquor stores and restaurants in major cities such as New York and Washington. The critic Michael Jackson, whose own career thus far also exemplified the easeful connection between beer and spirits, raved about his discovery of Junípero in a 1999 piece for a London newspaper. A friend of his in New York had bought a bottle for one hundred dollars (it actually retailed for slightly less than that) and mixed Jackson a martini with it. "It was big in body, powerful in flavor, and extraordinarily long, and I later noticed it on sale in some of the hipper places in town."

Such a resurrection for gin was remarkable. On its commercial deathbed in America when Michel Roux's Bombay Sapphire came along and still a spirituous also-ran when Jim Bendis had his epiphany in the juniper forest, the drink had come roaring to life, in terms of both style and popularity. "Gin Fights Back," read a *New York Times* headline in April 2000, over an article by food—and, later, wine—critic Eric Asimov touting the rise of "superpremium" gins. Its unlikely success was proof positive of the potential audience for a decently crafted spirit, even one more obscure. Luckily, there were plenty of performers warming up.

PART IV

NO NEED FOR A SMUGGLER'S TREE

1997–2001 | Ashford, Connecticut—Barnet, Vermont—Cincinnati —Bend, Oregon—New Orleans—Kelso, Tennessee

Louis Chatey's grandparents, Hungarian immigrants, had deliberately hollowed out the old chestnut tree on their northeastern Connecticut farm. It was called the smuggler's tree, and for good reason: the farmers used it to hide illicitly made apple brandy during Prohibition. There was plenty of the stuff. That area of New England had long been one of the nation's best areas for cultivating apples of various varieties, with brandy as a natural by-product given the frequency of large harvests—best to distill some of the fruit lest it rot. This approach echoed that of eau-de-vie distillers in central Europe. As it was, Chatey's grandparents used their two-hundred-acre farm in Ashford mostly for raising cattle, pigs, and chickens. Their grandson had other ideas after he inherited it in the 1980s.

He and his wife, Margaret, intended to turn the farm over to the cultivation of higher-end grape varieties. It seemed the sound thing to do that decade. Fine wine sales were booming, particularly those of whites. Farm owners and vineyardists nationwide were replanting tens of thousands of acres with such varieties, hoping to capitalize on the American public's seemingly insatiable thirst. Per-capita wine consumption, most of it of the finer kinds, reached a post-Prohibition high in 1986 of nearly two and a half gallons. The sky seemed the limit, and the grapes that the Chateys selected reflected that. They picked the great German variety Riesling as well as the French-American hybrid Seyval Blanc for their abilities to grow in colder climes, and they chose Chardonnay, the French-born stalwart that fueled so much of the American fine wine boom and that was well on its way in the 1980s to becoming the most popular wine style in the United States. Chardonnay grapes were known to not grow particularly well in colder climates, and New

England's early-autumn frosts might wipe out entire harvests just as the grapes were ready to pick. The Chateys' decision, then, was a risky one. Succeed in cultivating Chardonnay, and their Westford Hill farm-slash-winery would become one of the few such successful operations in the northern latitudes. It was all so bold and invigorating.

And it turned out to be a detour. The Chateys discovered eau-de-vie on a trip to Europe and the epiphany quickly followed. "We lived in the oldest fruit-producing area in the U.S.," Margaret Chatey realized. "We could make something special out of our local produce." In this realization they unwittingly mimicked Steve McCarthy on the other side of the American empire. Like the Chateys, he, too, had inherited a working farm, one where fruit, especially Bartlett pears, grew in abundance. McCarthy had also realized the family farm's spirits potential during a trip to Europe. A pivot to distillation did not seem all that far-fetched, whatever the distribution and sales challenges afterward. Clear Creek was up and running in Portland by the time the Chateys were planting Chardonnay et al. at Westford Hill. The couple did not know this—there was no traditional, small-batch commercial distillation in all of New England. Their home state of Connecticut was best known spirits-wise as the remarkably incongruent home of the Smirnoff vodka brand, that Russian import (by way of France) that had become since 1934 one of the biggest spirits brands of all time in the United States.

To turn their European epiphany into reality, then, the Chateys again unwittingly copied McCarthy: they sought out Jörg Rupf at St. George, the first eau-de-vie distillery in the nation since Prohibition. Following a visit to Rupf's distillery in Alameda, California, the Chateys hired him as a consultant for their start-up. Rupf relocated cross-country for a week and advised the couple on equipment and techniques. They soon acquired a fruit-crushing grinder called a hammer mill, stainless steel fermentation tanks, and a sixty-five-gallon copper pot still made in West Germany, one that looked like "a cross between a driver's helmet and a traditional espresso machine," according to one early visitor. The federal government granted a license to Westford Hill in 1998, and the Chateys were soon producing an eau-de-vie from Bartlett pears they grew and a kirsch from Montmorency cherries grown over the border in New York. Two big red barns that topped a grassy hill near the couple's early-eighteenth-century house served as the distillery. Other spirits would follow, too, including vodka and brandies from various fruits, again from either their own acres or from farms and orchards nearby. This was a key component for the Chateys, Margaret in particular, who took the lead on Westford Hill and became the first woman to prominently lead a small-batch distillery in the United States. It was almost a religion, one rooted in quality as much as in neighborliness. Margaret Chatey saw their distillation and the constant need for fruity material as "opening up a whole new market for New England fruit growers." Indeed, the Chateys could not hope to grow all the fruit they needed. The distillery by the new century would require about one hundred thousand pounds of fruit to make twenty thousand slender bottles of assorted eaux-de-vie. There was also the simple aspect of hands-on work toward the end of a locally crafted product (that for a time was only available locally: Westford distributed solely in Connecticut those first few years). The Chateys' operation would become a particular favorite of the Slow Food movement, bottles of their brandy eventually ending up at that organization's biennial trade show in the northwestern Italian city of Turin.

The Chateys' Westford Hill was the first stand-alone small-batch distillery in not only New England but also the entire Northeast. And along all of the East Coast it had just one contemporary in 1998: Chuck and Jeannette Miller's Belmont Farm Distillery in Culpeper County, Virginia, another farm-turned-distillery that had first tried its hand at grape cultivation. Yet there were stirrings in other, often disparate parts of the country, enough for national consumer media to now talk in broad terms about "a burgeoning, loose-knit movement called micro-distilling." In December 1999, Ann Fazendin filed incorporation papers with the State of Hawaii for Aloha Distillers, the maker of a locally popular coffee-infused spirit her father David Fazendin developed in the 1980s with Rod Dvornik, a German whom he met while Dvornik was vacationing on the islands. The Oahu-based Aloha made its Kona Gold with no additives, just coffee beans—unlike the popular Kahlúa liqueur it was often compared with, which included corn syrup and vodka. Duncan Holaday, an anthropologist with a doctorate from the University of Pennsylvania and with experience studying how indigenous peoples in Indonesia and Malaysia lived off the land, started what he called Vermont Spirits in 1999 on a nineteenth-century farmstead near the Connecticut River town of Barnet. Channeling his experiences overseas, Holaday built the distillery pretty much from scratch, using the wood from hemlock trees to construct a building by hand on the stone base of an old barn. Holaday chose vodka for his initial offering—one made with the lactose from milk and the other made from the sucrose of that Vermont staple, maple syrup. Like with the Chateys' Westford Hill, Holaday's Vermont Spirits did not initially distribute beyond the boundaries of its tiny New England state. The Green Mountain State audience was enough, however, to sustain the distillery and the interest of Holaday, who basically worked alone until it came time to bottle and ship the vodkas. It was while celebrating Vermont Spirits's first such shipment in 2000 that a cat knocked over a hot still, sparking a fire that burned the original distillery to the ground. Holaday soon built a new one.

Such were the early adventures of this new crop of small-batch distillers. There were some twenty-three such distilleries in twelve states by the end of 2000. That was not a huge number—there were around six hundred craft breweries, for instance, even as an industry shakeout culled their numbers. But relative to where the spirits numbers were a decade before, twenty-three was positively remarkable. In 1990 there were six small-batch distilleries in three states, four of them in California. Ten years before that, there was one: Maker's Mark in Kentucky. The growth during the 1990s, especially the latter half of the decade, was, then, steady and promising. Still, the vast majority of these newer distilleries operated in geographic and cultural isolation. Or they were barely operations at all. Peter Paisley ran a brewpub called Local Color in the Michigan city of Novi, just west of Detroit. In 2000 he started distilling Michigan-grown grapes and blueberries into vodka and selling the result at his pub for three dollars per half shot—voilà, the first small-batch distillery in the Upper Midwest. In New York State, Douglas and Suzanne Knapp, who had launched an eponymous winery in the central Finger Lakes region in the early 1980s, added an alembic pot still in 1995 and began making brandies for sale at the winery—thus the first small-batch distillery in New York (and what some would consider the first in the Northeast, though the Knapp operation was not stand-alone like Westford Hill in Connecticut).

Not all inaugural small-batch distilleries in their respective areas were so narrowly conceived. Inspired by his wife's home winemaking, James Michalopoulos, an artist in New Orleans best known for his painted posters of the city's architecture and fellow artists, wanted to start a winery but realized that "Louisiana is not the best place to grow grapes." The state was famed for its sugarcane, its per-acre production levels hefty enough to rival more tropical locations in the Caribbean. "Why not rum?" Michalopoulos thought, and thus was born Celebration Distillation in a nineteenth-century cotton-processing warehouse off Frenchman Street in New Orleans' Gentilly neighborhood, about three miles inland from the famed French Quarter. Michalopoulos started production in 1995, using sugarcane from Louisiana, though it would take a while of trial and error for the amateur distiller to perfect a recipe. That original recipe, for a white rum, led to one for a dark rum, aged up to three years in charred whiskey barrels, and what Michalopoulos called a Cajun spice rum—all under the Old New Orleans Rum brand. While distribution would not make it much farther than the Big Easy in the late 1990s, by the decade's end, Louisiana's oldest small-batch distillery, and the only one in the United States focusing solely on rum, was gaining national attention critically. *Saveur*, one of those niche publications launched in the 1990s to capture some of that burgeoning foodie culture, named Old New Orleans Rum its favorite domestic spirit of 2000.

The nation's second strictly rum distillery also launched in the South, in a tiny Tennessee hamlet of not even one thousand residents near the Alabama border—and a short drive east of Lincoln County, where the Jack Daniel's distillery pumped out its omnipresent Tennessee whiskey. Phil Prichard was the son of a dentist who himself worked as a dental technician for some thirty years, fabricating teeth and making braces. In the mid-1990s, in need of a hobby, he tapped into some family history: Generations back, one of his paternal ancestors distilled whiskey and occasionally bottled his wares for sale. The tall, powerfully built Prichard, whose face seemed perpetually on the verge of a grin and whose eyes twinkled when he talked spirits, at first dabbled in distilling whiskey, in a setup so rudimentary he stacked the condenser for the boil on an ironing board next to the kitchen stove. When he decided to take a commercial leap in early 1997, however, he picked rum, which he had also been making. Part of it was the historic romance the spirit held—there had been hundreds of rum distilleries in the United States in the nation's earliest decades, the sugar plantations of the Deep South and the Caribbean providing voluminous raw material. The marketplace was a bigger factor in Prichard's rum route: The US whiskey trade was still in decline, and standing out in the vodka market would be next to impossible for a tiny outfit. Tequila, which Prichard also considered, could not be legally made in the United States. So rum it was. He knew he was on to something when in the same year he went to his fortieth high school reunion. Prichard ran into a fellow alumnus named Victor Robilio Jr., whose family owned a Memphis-based wholesaler famed for pioneering distribution of fine French wines in Tennessee in the 1970s.

"What're you doing, Phil?"

"Matter of fact, Vic, I'm making rum."

It was not something one did in Tennessee in the late 1990s, at least not independently and on a very small scale. Robilio, aware of his family's role in popularizing then-novel French releases, was intrigued. "Bring me some."

Three weeks later, Prichard's phone rang.

"Phil, this is Victor." In high school, he was Vic; in adulthood, Victor. "I let my sales staff taste your rum today, and I have two questions: When are you going into business, and what is this going to cost me?"

"Vic, are you serious?"

The wholesaler was. "You're making one of the best rums in the world. You need to pursue this."

It was all the motivation Prichard needed. He filed incorporation papers for Prichard's Distillery with Tennessee in October 1997, his eponymous operation growing from that phone call with Robilio into one of the nation's best-known smaller spirits concerns. In 1999 the fifty-nine-year-old Prichard rented part of Kelso's community center, which itself had been the crossroads' lone schoolhouse until 1979. In the fall of 1999, he began making rum, using sugarcane from Louisiana. Prichard did all of the distilling himself, his still a converted gas-fired turkey deep-fryer. He worked even when the adjoining community center hosted Saturday night dances. Prichard released that first rum in the spring of 2001 and sold about $35,000 of it initially. In 2002 he bought the entire community center building, and the dances stopped. Prichard left the old schoolhouse's chalkboards and wall maps up, as well as the basketball hoops of the community center, and used the enameled-steel teacher's desk as his own, the top eventually buried in the sample bottles and general clutter of the somewhat grandly titled chief executive officer of Prichard's Distillery. Numerous rum flavors would follow the original—from Key lime to spiced to cranberry—as would a Tennessee whiskey meant as a direct challenge to Jack Daniel's nearby. Prichard would call that offering Benjamin Prichard's Tennessee Whiskey, after the ancestor who distilled in the same area at the start of the nineteenth century, when such corn-based spirits, including bourbon from Kentucky, were king.

Not even four hundred miles north from Phil Prichard's start-up, Don Outterson was taking his decades of experience as a professional brewer and brewery consultant, particularly for brewpubs, and translating it in early 1999 into Ohio's first small-batch distillery, renting space from a winery forty minutes' drive north of Cincinnati. He and wife Linda's Woodstone Creek also operated as a winery in what before Prohibition had been nicknamed America's Rhineland because of its high concentration of people of German descent and its production of wines from Central Europe–born grapes such as Riesling. Their first spirits offering was Cincinnati Vodka. To Don Outterson at least, that spirit was simply a way to learn the legalities of being the state's first small-batch distillery—as well as a mere placeholder for the bourbon the couple planned to craft, age, and release. By 2001 Woodstone Creek had outgrown its more suburban digs and resettled in a warehouse a few blocks from Xavier University near downtown Cincinnati.

These pioneers in their respective states illustrated where the movement was, and was going, in the new century. First the entrants, including those who came just after them, shared approaches to their distillation. All were hands-on and had entered the field with the expectation that they would be doing most of the work themselves. This was different than, say, craft brewing, where many newer arrivals had hired experienced brewers rather than dived in themselves to the vats and tuns. The same went for wineries specializing in higher-end wines. Those often began through investors either starting up an operation or taking over an existing one, and hiring the skilled labor to handle production. When it came to small-batch distilling in the late 1990s and very early 2000s, a kind of all-hands-on-deck mentality prevailed, regardless of the state or region. So did a dedication to and an awareness of tradition and traditional ingredients and techniques. Pot stills were the norm; column stills were too big and too pricey anyway for the small batches these distilleries produced. Adulterants, such as artificial coloring, were out. Local ingredients, where they could be had, were must-haves—and if they boosted marketing, all the better. Several of these entrants, including Westford Hill in Connecticut, Vermont Spirits in that New England state, Celebration Distillation in Louisiana, and Local Color in Michigan, built their brands around the very notion that they used locally sourced ingredients; and Prichard's Distillery in Tennessee *wanted* to do so—with sugary sorghum from the Volunteer State—but federal law that stipulated rum come from sugarcane prevented it. Moreover, if they could not produce from local ingredients or if it did not really matter the ingredients' provenance, then these toddling distilleries at least nodded to their places of birth; note Woodstone Creek's Cincinnati Vodka, about as non-Russian-sounding a vodka brand as had ever yet sprung up in the United States.

These new entrants were also by and large just that: new. They came to spirits from beyond the field, some through an epiphanic trip or conversation, others a familial connection or through a brush with the wider industry. Few came from other alcohol trades such as wine or beer, Don Outterson's Woodstone Creek perhaps the most prominent example. This inexperience helped explain the monolithic nature of many of these concerns. They more often than not each produced only one kind of spirit, with fruited spirits such as brandies and eaux-de-vie the narrow favorites over vodka and whiskey. While they might craft variations on the same theme, like Prichard's Distillery's many flavors of rum, these newcomers generally focused on one particular spirit, at least at first. Financial necessity also surely played a role; for all the growth in American small-batch spirits and cocktail culture, at the turn of the century the sector accounted for an infinitesimal slice of the nation's total spirits sales in any given year. The collective production of all smaller distilleries likely totaled well under one million cases by 2000. By comparison, the likes of Seagram or Bacardí might sell several million cases of a single brand. Newer arrivals invariably kept their day jobs, distilling at odd hours and on the weekends, packaging with the help of family and friends.

Plus, these small-batch distilleries invariably faced the same challenges at the federal level, in terms of both geography and legality. They remained largely isolated, for one thing, with no large-scale trade-group representation and very little in the way of traditional wind at their backs. Government regulations, particularly at the state and local levels, still worked decidedly against distilleries in a way they did not against breweries and wineries. By the 2000s, craft brewers had a powerful voice in Washington in the Brewers Association trade group, and craft brewers in individual states had formed craft brewing booster groups as well. John Hickenlooper, cofounder of Wynkoop, Colorado's oldest brewpub, and an investor in several more, would be elected Denver's mayor in 2003, on his way to the state's governor's mansion. Craft brewing also benefited from a government-sanctioned perk that distillers could only continue to fruitlessly pine for: the legality of homebrewing. Home winemaking had been legal since Repeal in 1933, and homebrewing ever since a concerted, California-based lobbying effort in the late 1970s. Home distilling? That was still moonshine as far as the authorities were concerned, subjecting perpetrators to up to $10,000 in fines and five years in prison for each offense. And, while federal authorities appear not to have busted any homebrewers engaged in the hobby before its 1978 legalization, home distillers had been targeted, arrested, and punished.

Small-batch distilleries also stood on one side of a gnawing chasm between federal excise taxes on beer and wine versus spirits. The government had long taxed the former two libations at a much lower rate. Winemakers paid $1.07 in federal excise tax per gallon. If the wine was particularly strong—greater than 14 percent alcohol by volume—winemakers paid $1.57. These rates translated into per-bottle tax totals of only around $0.20. Contrast this with distillers, who paid $13.50 per usable, or proof, gallon. Worse still for small-batch distillers, the regulations made no distinction between them and macroproducers. The rule did distinguish between craft brewers and larger brewers. Since 1976 the federal government taxed the first sixty thousand barrels that a brewery produced every year at seven dollars per thirty-one-gallon barrel, so long as the brewery did not produce more than two million barrels annually. That seven dollars was a sharp discount off the eighteen dollars that larger producers paid on every barrel (and that those making fewer than two million barrels paid on each one after the sixty thousandth). And, since every craft brewery at the start of the twenty-first century produced fewer than two million barrels a year, each one enjoyed that discount. That initial 1976 reduction was credited with helping unleash the growth in the number of craft breweries to begin with. There had been one, the Anchor Brewing Company, in operation at the time of the cut; twenty about ten years afterward; and now hundreds. The lower excise tax had slashed the cost of doing business for a generation of small-batch brewers and would do so for all those who followed in their footsteps. Like with the unrealized legalization of home-distilling, small-batch distillers could only dream of such a deregulatory shot in the arm.

Finally, for all their relative growth, small-batch distilleries still saw the future through a glass darkly. Wineries that started up in the early 1970s were able to tap into an entire ecosystem of producers, distributors, critics, and consumers that ran back, however thinly at times, to at least Prohibition. Even craft breweries, more than three hundred strong at the start of the new century, had pioneers to reference going back to the 1960s, Fritz Maytag at Anchor the most prominent example. Small-batch distilling had no such history at its back. Analysts and journalists discussed these distilleries, when they discussed them, almost entirely in terms of these other alcohol competitors, fine wine and craft beer. Individually, newer distilleries might hit up Jörg Rupf at St. George for advice or paid consultants or subscribe to Paul Pacult's quarterly *Spirit Journal* or John Hansell's *Malt Advocate*, but otherwise the economic and social framework was just not there for what they were doing and selling. It was all so novel, whatever the growth, motivated more by magical thinking than cold, hard reality. "We wanted to make traditional American rum," Phil Prichard would explain to a reporter as the century wore on. "The idea wasn't to run Bacardí out of business. I just figured that if we made something hand-distilled and hand-bottled, people would pay more for quality." Would they? The answer was coming faster than anyone could have imagined only years earlier.

BREAKOUT STARS

2001–2004 | Alameda, California

One day in August 2001, Ansley Coale and Jörg Rupf sat down in Rupf's house in Oakland to discuss a long-simmering idea: crafting a flavorful vodka through their respective distilleries using traditional methods and equipment.

The spirit itself seemed a natural choice. Vodka sales in the United States continued to march steadily forward. Neither Coale nor Rupf could know this at their August 2001 sit-down, but domestic sales of vodka were about to spike: from about thirty-nine million cases in 2003 to nearly forty-nine million three years later. Premium brands, such as Absolut and its usurper Grey Goose in particular, were priming such strong sales. Both men certainly knew that, which is precisely why Coale and Rupf met when they did. They had always known that they could never make the vodka they wanted to make without then selling it for more than thirty dollars a bottle. Sidney Frank's Grey Goose, which had grown from a few hundred thousand cases of sales in 1997 to well over one million just a few years later, was a particular inspiration, at least from a business standpoint. Here was a vodka that had out-Absolut-ed Absolut, and did so solely through a higher price. One, then, could trace a straight line from the rise of Absolut to Grey Goose to what Coale and Rupf had in mind. To be sure, Grey Goose's spectacular sales were nothing compared with sector leader Smirnoff, which might turn around fifteen million cases a year in the United States, but its climb was certainly impressive to two of the oldest small-batch distilleries in the country. Coale's Germain-Robin and Rupf's St. George together sold not even twenty thousand cases of their various offerings, mostly eaux-de-vie and brandies, annually. Plus, the resurgence in fine wine sales in the 1990s, following those *60 Minutes* "French Paradox" segments on the supposed health benefits of red wine in particular, was eating into the distribution channels of smaller distilleries such as theirs. The number of California wineries crossed the one-thousand threshold for the first time ever in 1997 and, nationally, the two-thousand mark a year later. It wasn't that St. George or Germain-Robin were losing customers so much as ways to get to them. Distributors preferred carrying bigger-selling brands from the many boutique wineries popping up. Their bottles, after all, sold for as much as if not significantly more than those of St. George and Germain-Robin.

Not that both distilleries did not have some momentum by the new century. St. George's growth had been steady enough to justify that 1989 physical expansion in San Francisco Bay's east end, and Rupf himself was in high demand among newer distilleries as a consultant. Moreover, he had taken his spirits to their—and his—birthplace to compete against Europe's finest offerings through an annual competition organized by an Austrian magazine. St. George's kirsch, poire, and grappa all won gold medals in the competition in the 1990s, and in 1997 the distillery as a whole won the contest's top nod. As for Coale's Germain-Robin, it received the sort of press in February 1993 that most companies, distilleries or otherwise, would crave. Dan Berger, the *Los Angeles Times*' wine critic, journeyed to the still-remote sheep ranch off the 101 two hours north of San Francisco and returned to rave about every aspect of the operation, from the "beautiful" ride to it, "the noses of new wildflowers barely visible in the soft earth" along the way, to the "modest" distillery itself, still a one-room shed that could be "traversed in three giant steps," to, of course, the finished product, which Berger pegged as "arguably the best brandy in the United States and one of the best in the world—Cognac included." The equation of an American distillery in the backwoods of Mendocino County with the vaunted, centuries-old houses of the French area that gave the spirit its name would have been inconceivable a few short years before, certainly when Coale and distiller Hubert Germain-Robin started in late 1983. There it was, though, ten years later, in one of the largest daily newspapers in the United States, at a time just before the World Wide Web when most Americans got most of their news from newspapers. Similar critical encomiums would follow for Germain-Robin and St. George as well, the two distilleries often mentioned in the same editorial breath, but invariably as much because of their novelty—there were fewer than two dozen such distilleries nationwide by 2000—as for their unmistakable quality. How, then, to break out a bit? While possibly drawing the attention of distributors wooed by the numbers fine wine was posting?

Rupf and Coale would call the vodka Hangar 1, after the World War II–era airplane shelters at the closed naval base near Rupf's distillery. Rupf would handle the actual distillation and Coale the marketing and sales, for which he formed another company called Craft Distillers. Each of them took out an initial $500,000 loan to fund the start-up and then saddled themselves with an additional $1.5 million in financing from Wells Fargo right before Hangar 1 launched. Rupf, with Lance Winters's aid, spent about six months experimenting with different vodka recipes before settling on one that relied on Viognier grapes and wheat. Viognier was a rarity in the American fine wine scene, which was awash in Chardonnay and Cabernet Sauvignon. A somewhat more delicate white wine varietal, Viognier did not produce much usable pulp and therefore had to be harvested at just the right time. It was a level of difficulty that no large-scale distillery would have willingly accepted, but Rupf felt the Viognier smoothed the often harsh alcoholic edge found in most straight vodkas. The first slender, cylindrical bottles of Hangar 1 rolled out of St. George in April 2002, and it was clear almost from the start that the spirit marked a turning point, not just for Coale and Rupf but also for the American small-batch spirits movement.

The pair did get to charge their price of at least thirty dollars per bottle, if not nearly forty in some markets. But their brand did not owe its success to the premium pricing that Absolut and Grey Goose had so effectively employed. Instead, it was the taste and marketing that helped relatively tiny Hangar 1 stand out in an ever more crowded vodka market—more than 270 brands would launch between 2001 and 2006 alone. The original Hangar 1 and its subsequent fruit-infused variations met with unvarnished critical acclaim. "Extraordinary," Paul Pacult wrote in his *Spirit Journal*. "Unlike anything I've experienced in thirteen years of professional spirits evaluation." Much of the acclaim stemmed from Rupf crafting the vodkas with actual fresh fruit, rather than the fruit flavoring that larger vodka producers preferred, a shortcut that guaranteed the fruity smells and tastes lasted longer than in their fresh counterparts. Hangar 1 Buddha's Hand Citron was "a bit lemony-sharp," Florence Fabricant explained in the *New York Times*, its tropical lime "an intriguing citric flavor," and the mandarin blossom version had "honeyed, floral overtones." "And if flavored vodka is not your drink, consider the plain version," Fabricant wrote, "which is silken, with exceptional lightness."

Such high-profile plaudits only boosted the largely word-of-mouth campaign that Coale ran for Hangar 1. "Where are the girls, the limos and the free money?" distributors would ask him. Vodka in particular had a long-running reputation for a certain insouciant sauciness going back to those "Smirnoff leaves you breathless" ads in the 1960s, and that reputation had grown more louche as the decades wore on. Skyy, a brand introduced in the early 1990s and made with bulk railroad deliveries of ethanol to a San Jose distillery, perhaps pushed the envelope further than any concern, eventually featuring a print ad with a pair of shapely feminine legs, stiletto heels pointing northward,

The St. George distillery in the old hangar.
BEN KRANTZ

wrapped around a Skyy bottle. Coale went in a decidedly different direction for Hangar 1, relying essentially on the relentless retelling of a tale that hinged on "quality, taste and our story." That story was of small-batch craftsmanship, a process unhurried and with the end product in mind, rather than the sales afterward. It was a compelling sales pitch, all the more so because it happened to be true. St. George and Germain-Robin had grown pretty much organically since the 1980s, relying on high-quality products made largely by hand with traditional equipment and the best available ingredients.

And Rupf and Winters crafted Hangar 1 the same, slow way. "In distillation, most of the technological advances are geared toward increasing efficiencies," Winters explained during a segment on a Yahoo! Finance Web series. "And we don't like to be efficient here, we like to be tasty. And efficiency doesn't necessarily taste good. But when you're looking for a touch of artistry, a pot still is the only way to go." Coale's campaign for Hangar 1 was supposed to generate some thirty thousand cases' worth of sales annually within a decade of the 2002 launch. That was the plan, at least. In reality, Coale would within five years be selling nearly forty thousand cases annually in forty-nine states,

Singapore, Malaysia, and Europe, with revenue far exceeding $8 million. The vast majority of these sales would be to restaurants and others in the hospitality industry, but liquor stores and even supermarkets were starting to pick up Hangar 1. As for the distiller, Rupf would find himself physically expanding tenfold in 2004, moving into sixty-five thousand square feet of capacious space at one of those hangars at the old Alameda Naval Air Station, his St. George distillery having come a long, long way from the shack by the old railroad tracks. Hangar 1 was a breakout star in American small-batch spirits.

It was not the first. That distinction belonged to Tito Beveridge and his own vodka. Demand for the Tito's brand had grown from about one thousand cases annually in 1997 to fifty-eight thousand in 2004, a staggering rise unprecedented in American small-batch spirits. A few key turns, and the publicity Beveridge wrung from them, helped the Travis County, Texas, operation immensely. In early 2001 Tito's won the Double Gold Medal at the San Francisco World Spirits Competition, which Anthony Dias Blue, a wine and spirits critic, launched the year before and which involved expert judges tasting dozens of different brands in a variety of spirits categories. Tito's finished second overall in the vodka category to a small Polish brand, which also won a double gold. The year before, in 2000, Paul Pacult awarded four stars to Tito's in his *Spirit Journal*. Finally, around the same time, regulators from the Bureau of Alcohol, Tobacco, and Firearms declared Tito's to be the "cleanest and purest spirit ever tasted" from the bureau's viewpoint.

These plaudits soon found their ways into not only Tito's marketing material but also numerous articles about the success of the vodka—and the chisel-chinned man behind it. Intentionally or not, a fuzziness often fogged the facts. An April 2002 rave about Tito's in a hometown newspaper, the *Austin Chronicle*, told readers that the spirit "beat . . . every other vodka entered" in the San Francisco competition, which was not true. (It had whipped every other *domestically* made vodka, though those were few and far between.) The *Dallas Morning News* would make the same error three years later. Also, Paul Pacult's four-star review was often presented as unprecedented for a vodka, even though the critic had awarded four stars, even five, to others before. In the same year as Tito's four-star assessment, Pacult awarded five to a quartet of brands, including the domestically produced Smirnoff Black. Finally, that original *Houston Chronicle* assessment of Tito's from May 1997, just after the spirit's launch, showed up everywhere paraphrased and out of context. Wine critic Michael Lonsford had used a tidbit about Beethoven's Ninth Symphony to segue into "a home-grown symphonic spirit to applaud."

Other writers, looking for quick adjectival ballast, either dropped or never bothered to find out about the Beethoven lead-in. Thus, Tito's became "a symphonic spirit" from pretty much day one, foreordained to triumph in the marketplace because it had already charmed critics.

Tito's, distilled as it was six times for a particularly clean appearance and made with yellow corn for a smoothly sweet finish, was unmistakably a solid entrant in the burgeoning small-batch pantheon. It probably did deserve the top domestic rating that the judges at the San Francisco World Spirits Competition bestowed upon it. Plus, the industry and consumer media regarded Paul Pacult as the leading spirits critic, and he had awarded those four stars to Tito's. And, it should be noted, both he and the San Francisco judges did so through blind tastings. But what really set Tito's apart—and set it upon its rapid rise, such that sales started to double each year in the new century—was its creator's willingness to put himself out there in a way no small-batch distiller had yet done. The only possible precedent was Bill Samuels Jr. at Maker's Mark, but he had put the distillery's bourbon front and center, through public relations and advertising firms, rather than himself. Tito's was different. The spirit and the man often seemed one in the same. This was because Beveridge tapped into his experience in real estate, as well as in oil speculation, to unleash an easygoing yet forceful salesmanship that placed his own story front and center. Journalists making the pilgrimage to the expanding Travis County headquarters of Fifth Generation, the distillery behind Tito's, could not help but be charmed. "I'm tempted to describe Tito as a singular eccentric oddball in the great tradition of Texas iconoclasts and mavericks," one correspondent reported in 2002. "But he's really much more complicated." This particular article presented Beveridge as simply a very dedicated distiller eschewing fancy advertising in favor of making quality vodka, one who launched his company by "applying for every credit card he could get." (The amount of debt that Beveridge took on began to vary in these profiles.) Another newspaper piece three years later noted that Beveridge had expanded production tenfold, to more than five thousand cases of Tito's yearly, far and away the most output of any smaller distillery in the United States. Despite this production and the demand it clearly suggested, Beveridge demurred about expanding into other spirits or even into the flavored vodkas that were all the rage. He was once again presented as just a craft distiller trying to make it in a Smirnoff world. "I had plans to do about sixteen different liquors when I started out," he told the reporter, "but have found it to be hard enough to do one thing really right."

Journalists in the early 2000s could be forgiven for not contextualizing Beveridge's position or for not even fact-checking the plaudits his vodka had earned. For all the growth in the last few years in the number of small-batch distilleries, the spirits they produced simply were not that widely available compared with those of much larger companies. Plus, there was no agreed-upon definition of what these distilleries actually were or were producing. Early on, the media usually let the term *microdistillery* do the explanatory trick. Later terms such as *craft spirits* and *craft distilleries* did little to help define matters, accompanied as they often were by clumsy attempts to wedge these spirits and distilleries into the same rubric as craft beers and craft breweries, despite dissimilarities. There was no national trade group speaking institutionally, either, and most states' laws actually worked against the notion of a start-up distillery of any stripe. Consumers were apt to learn about a spirit such as Tito's from local news outlets rather than trade media such as Pacult's *Spirit Journal* or John Hansell's *Malt Advocate*, which together paled in total circulation against even daily newspapers in midsize cities. Therefore, a lot of craft spirits information arrived only after passing through a prism of reporters themselves unfamiliar with the trend—or only familiar with it as it might relate to craft beer or, more likely, fine wine, which was more ubiquitous.

Beveridge, then, could often sculpt his own story interview to interview (thus the fluctuations in just how many credit cards he maxed out by just how much). Again, it did not hurt the narrative that his vodka was exceptionally smooth, worthy of drinking straight rather than as part of a cocktail. Those who sipped it, including journalists with little stomach for vodka and more experienced critics such as Pacult, could tell Tito's quality right away. In both the self-made narrative and the product quality, Beveridge had a ready counterpart in the craft beer movement that had so inspired him in the beginning: Jim Koch, cofounder and chairman of the Boston Beer Company, maker of the now-omnipresent Samuel Adams brand. Koch also needed only a few years to become the biggest craft beer name in the United States, and he, too, proved a solid salesman for not only his own product but also the very notion of beers made in small batches in more traditional ways. The backstory Koch told to reporters and recounted in first-person essays and radio spots sometimes, like Beveridge's, played loose with the specifics. And, just like Beveridge, it did not hurt Koch that he had a fantastic product to sell, his Samuel Adams Boston Lager a particular hit with critics and consumers. (Michael Jackson had declared it "an American classic.") Yet Koch had sown controversy pretty much from the launch of Boston Beer in the mid-1980s, much of it self-inflicted, including that time he tried and failed to trademark the phrase "the best beer in America" after Boston Lager won a string of taste-test victories. In such controversy, Tito Beveridge would be similar to Jim Koch as well.

BUFFALO BILL AND THE LEGAL STAMPEDE
2000–2003 | Hayward, California

For Bill Owens, it really started with Elton John. In 2000 an agent for the English music legend discovered some of Owens's photographs at a gallery in San Francisco and made a sizable offer for an assortment of them. The photographs were originals used in Owens's 1973 essay *Suburbia*, which charted in gorgeously alluring black and white just what the name implied: the rise of post–World War II suburbia in America, in all its pleasures and rituals—specifically, suburbia in Livermore, California, about twenty miles east of Hayward, where Owens lived. "Never before had the mass exodus to the suburbs been documented so intimately," one critic noted. The book, and the sensation in the contemporary art world that it caused, turned out to be the peak of a photojournalism career that stretched back to the 1960s and included a stint as a stringer for the Associated Press, during which Owens ended up capturing the fatal violence at the free Rolling Stones concert at the Altamont Speedway near San Francisco. All the while, Owens, a self-described "kid who liked to drink beer," though with no particular scientific chops, had homebrewed. This was before the 1978 legalization of the hobby at the federal level and during a time when ingredients were scarce, often makeshift, and the resultant beers pretty iffy. It was just fun, and Owens, an easygoing, long-haired type who drove a Volkswagen Beetle and absolutely loved to talk, liked trying new things.

So when a friend suggested on Owens's fortieth birthday in 1978 that he start a brewery, the idea did not seem all that absurd. There were by then at least three small breweries in the San Francisco Bay Area, including the Anchor Brewing Company, which now distributed as far as the East Coast and which was searching for a bigger brewhouse to expand production. Besides, the photojournalism assignments were coming fewer and farther between. The only hurdle Owens could see was money. He visited his accountant and asked him how small businesses raised funds. The accountant reached into a desk drawer and pulled out a form meant for another client. "White out 'almond farm,'" he told Owens, pointing to a space on the form, "and put in 'brewery.'" Thus was Owens able to form a limited partnership, which allowed him to start recruiting investors, a skill he turned out to be adept at, even in an era when what he had in mind was virtually unprecedented. In 1977 California had enacted legislation allowing breweries to sell a certain annual amount of beer on premises. It did not, in other words, have to be distributed through bars or stores. Also, unknown to Owens, a former brewing consultant and hops grower named Bert Grant had filed incorporation papers with the State of Washington in late 1981 to open what he called the Yakima Brewing and Malting Company in an old opera house in downtown Yakima. The following year Grant's operation became the first brewpub in post-Prohibition America: a brewery that sold its beers on-site, usually with food as well. Owens would do the same in Hayward, opening Buffalo Bill's Brewery in early September 1983 in rented space in—coincidentally—a former camera store. Owens used about $90,000 he had raised through the limited partnership to renovate the shop and purchase secondhand equipment from a dairy, a candy manufacturer, and a food-processing firm to outfit the actual brewing apparatus. The two key pieces turned out to be sixty-two feet of pipe for running the beer from the brewhouse to the bar, which Owens hand laid with the help of an investor who normally worked on nuclear bombs, and a picture window in front of the brewhouse, which allowed patrons at the bar to see where their beer was coming from.

It was all so novel. Buffalo Bill's was only the third brewpub in the entire nation and the second in California, behind one in Mendocino County that staff from the now-defunct New Albion Brewery had launched in the summer of 1983. (New Albion, the first start-up craft brewery since Prohibition, had been unable to get financing for an expansion.) Owens was soon doing brisk business in the San Francisco Bay Area, which had long been ground zero for the American craft beer movement. He cut his hair into a salt-and-pepper flattop, sold many of his cameras and the Volkswagen Beetle, and became quite the ethanol entrepreneur. "For one hundred, thirty dollars' worth of ingredients, I can make a two thousand, five hundred dollar profit," Owens explained to a visiting journalist. "A glass of lager—that's all I brew now—costs seven cents. I sell it for a dollar and a half." Soon Owens opened two more brewpubs and was grossing $1 million annually. He also wrote a canonical guide to opening a small brewery and for years published two magazines about the nascent craft beer movement, including *BeeR*, a graphically ambitious glossy that featured some of his own photography. Soon,

Owens found himself "like a grandfather" in a fast-growing craft beer industry, his brewpubs but a few of the approximately four hundred nationwide by the early 1990s. Yet, for all the gross profit, the net takeaway proved paltry. Owens tried a public stock offering to raise funds for a stand-alone brewery dedicated solely to production, not sales as well—several craft breweries, led by the Boston Beer Company, were going public in the 1990s—but Owens's offering never got off the ground. He sold off the brewpubs one by one, the original Buffalo Bill's going in 1994. He stopped publishing the magazines in the latter half of the decade and then faded away from the craft beer movement he had helped spearhead. Owens's exit came as the whole thing started to teeter anyway, with around one-third of the craft breweries and brewpubs nationwide closing in the late 1990s. He worked in an antique shop during that period, scouting items to sell, but that was never going to be long term.

Enter Elton John. Owens received $15,000 from the star's purchase of his *Suburbia* photographs. Owens promptly went to his children and asked them if they needed a cut from the windfall. Keep it, Dad, they told him. With little tethering him to Northern California, the former photojournalist and brewpub mogul set off on a three-month, cross-country trip in a newly acquired used Lexus, a cardboard box full of clothes in the trunk. He would stay with friends or in motels and would try scrupulously to keep his expenses under one hundred dollars a day, including gas and food, and he usually succeeded. Owens was not sure of his exact itinerary as he rolled away from Hayward—that was kind of the point. He started with a northward trek through the vast upper veld of California, into Oregon and Washington State, and then he turned right, dipping slightly through Montana to Kansas and then back up to Indiana and over to the East Coast. The return trek brought him farther south, through Texas and then northward back home. Owens made it a point to visit breweries and distilleries on the way. The visits to smaller distilleries were particularly illuminating, starting right nearby with Jörg Rupf's St. George and including Steve McCarthy's Clear Creek in Portland. Owens saw in them what he had seen in the early days of craft beer: relatively tiny operations using techniques and equipment—and, in many cases, ingredients—that seemed almost quaint. And there were so few of them. Yet there was a fervency about their owners and their clientele, a real potential there. The number of craft breweries was on the march northward again in the new century, and the number of wineries, especially those specializing in higher-end grapes, continued to boom. But these distilleries seemed so fringe. Owens realized by the end of his trip that he had the potential to get in near the ground floor of another major culinary movement in America.

Starting his own distillery was out of the question—too many memories of too many headaches from the brewpubs. Owens mulled other options and continued to work unenthusiastically in the antique trade. Occasionally, a writer or a novice brewer would call him to talk craft beer, but that life grew more and more distant.

Until one day in 2003, when Owens noticed a casually dressed young man in a coffee shop in downtown Hayward. The man was reading a book on flipping property. Residential real estate in particular was booming nationwide amid a slow, steady economic recovery from the recession at the start of the decade and the terrorist attacks of September 11, 2001. Low interest rates and loose credit were making it increasingly easier for even those with limited income to trade houses and condos almost like stocks. Still, to Owens, now past sixty-five, the scene looked irreconcilably incongruous. He turned to the youngster. "All the guys I know who sell real estate have neck ties on and wear suits," he said. "You don't look the right role for this job." Owens loved that. He walked out of the coffee shop and drove to Hayward city hall, where he started the process for incorporating a new business. It would be called the American Distilling Institute, and it would be dedicated to boosting the prospects of the smaller distilleries that Owens had encountered during his trip around America. He used one hundred dollars to open a bank account for the new business.

Realizing that the first and third words of the American Distilling Institute were more magical thinking than reality, Owens set about organizing a conference to foment interest. He approached that first distillery he had visited, Jörg Rupf's St. George, about hosting the spring 2003 conference, the itinerary of which was about as loose as that for Owens's continental drive three years before. Owens rented seventy-five chairs and set them up in the airy distillery in Alameda. Every seat was filled, with eleven people standing in the back—Owens therefore noted eighty-six people at the first ADI conference. Most of them, fifty-eight, were interested in the industry and not actually involved in it yet. Then there were a handful of vendors, including from as far away as the United Kingdom, and the distillers themselves. Tickets were fifty dollars each, and little happened at this inaugural American Distilling Institute conference other than an address from Owens and a lot of mingling by everyone else. Still, the one-day conference marked the largest concerted gathering yet of those involved or interested in traditionally made spirits in tinier batches at smaller distilleries. In this, the ADI was a watershed, different from WhiskyFest or other such festivals—a gathering dedicated not to tasting craft spirits but to making them.

An early American Distilling Institute conference at St. George in Alameda, California.
ANDREW FAULKNER

Owens realized he was on to something with his newly formed ADI. He began laying the groundwork for a proper office and a staff, as well as for a publishing wing that, like with his foray into craft beer, would include glossy magazines. Being privately held and not a nonprofit, Owens's ADI could not lobby government in the same way a nonprofit trade group could. The ADI could gather the tribe, though, and rally it. Lucky for Owens, just as he had picked a fortuitous time to jump into craft beer, he had picked the perfect moment to embrace its spirits counterpart. The tribe was about to balloon.

HURDLES FALL

2000–2003 | Schoharie County, New York

It wasn't just the distilleries themselves that John Torgersen noticed. It was the symbiosis they fostered. A Long Island native who grew up in East Asia, Torgersen had graduated from the State University of New York Maritime

College in the Bronx, earned a master's in quality management from Loyola University in New Orleans, and taught at the Maine Maritime Academy for four years. Then, beginning in 1984, he took various positions over the next dozen years with oil tankers and rigs in Europe's North Sea, between the British Isles and Scandinavia, working twenty-eight days at a time and then getting twenty-eight days off. He would spend this ample terrestrial free time visiting distilleries in Scotland. In 1986 Torgersen visited every distillery the region had to offer. Merely a curious tourist at first, he soaked up not only the sought-after single malts and blends but also the culture surrounding that land's legendary whisky. Part of the culture sprang from the attendant industries that fed into the distillation process: the farms for grains and other ingredients, the cooperages for barrels, the distributors, even hospitality businesses such as hotels that serviced tourists doing what Torgersen was doing, and, of course, construction firms that built the necessary structures, including housing. These industries often existed only because of the distilleries, too, a kind of build-it-and-they-will-come ethos holding forth, especially around more isolated distilleries in the Scottish Highlands. Without the distilleries, Torgersen noticed, there would not have been much to see or to do in these areas, much less any work to be found.

Torgersen relocated to the States in 1996 to work as a safety director for private companies and for a trade group representing firms that worked on most federal dredging and marine construction projects. Able to work from home when not on the road, he settled with his family in Middleburgh, New York, a town of around three thousand people forty-five miles west of Albany and 150 miles north of New York City. Middleburgh, however, and its surrounding Schoharie County might as well have been worlds away from either, especially Gotham to the south. A steady decline in population and manufacturing jobs, the two trends often reinforcing each other, had rocked upstate New York during the last several decades. Young people especially were moving out to chase employment elsewhere, and near-constant government promises and proposals to revitalize upstate usually did nothing but highlight the gnawing decline. Well over half of the state's nineteen million residents by 2000 lived in New York City or its immediate environs, including Torgersen's native Long Island. That left areas such as Schoharie County as virtual ghost towns, sparsely peopled by an aging population and with little prospect for economic growth. To Torgersen, this "dead" upstate economy spurred recollections of the Scottish Highlands from years before.

It also gave him an idea: He would make white whiskey from the copious amounts of corn in the area and create a distillery that would serve as both a production facility and a tourist attraction. The interest in spirits that the Scottish sojourns had piqued had only intensified over the years. Torgersen distilled (illegally) at home and read up voraciously on distilling in general, especially as it applied to New York State, which probably hosted dozens of distilleries—legal or otherwise—before Prohibition. In this reading, he discovered a cocktail called "flip" that had been particularly popular in the early nineteenth century with cadets at the US military academy at West Point, on the Hudson River. A man named Benny Havens ran a tavern at different locations near the academy, and his flip became the stuff of legend, the libationary focus of an often raucous pub. Flip was essentially an amalgam of alcohol—rum, ale, and hard cider, usually—mixed with a sweetener such as molasses or sugar, spices, and eggs, and then brought to a froth by plunging a hot poker into it. Torgersen would recreate his own version of flip, complete with the hot poker, for local fairs and other events. But he wanted to take things further. He wanted to recreate the lore of New York places such as Benny Havens's tavern for modern audiences, and, in turn, perhaps revive a bit of the fortunes of the upstate New York he had fallen in love with. He would do that with a distillery.

With agricultural researchers at Cornell University in Ithaca, Torgersen even isolated the type of white corn he would use, one pollinated naturally through birds, bees, and wind. He began laying the groundwork for what he called Storm King Distilling, after a prominent mountain north of West Point, even going so far as to file incorporation papers with the state in January 2002. He planned to call the inaugural offering Benny Havens Old New York Whiskey, and he picked a motto that said it all: "Distilling the Spirit of New York." The Middleburgh-based operation would be the sole stand-alone distillery in New York and likely the first since Prohibition. An industrial-scale operation in Queens held a federal license but was not distilling at the time. And while the Knapp winery in the Finger Lakes had been distilling brandies since 1995, and other New York wineries had added such operations, Storm King would be spirits and spirits only, a major benchmark food-wise for what was then the nation's third most populous state.

Then Torgersen hit a wall. A three-year distillation license for New York operations wishing to make spirits other than fruit-based brandies cost $39,575. That was too much for Torgersen without him seeking investors, which he did not want to do. He simply wanted to distill whiskey from local corn for local sales. The start-up costs for that alone were enough for him working solo. The added licensing fee, a vestige of Prohibition-era oversight meant to curb supposed vice, seemed an insurmountable hurdle—and an arbitrary one, given the relatively low state fees for wine and beer start-ups. Torgersen, who was now working as a consultant in the commercial maritime industry, approached the staff of a local state legislator as well as the New York Farm Bureau, a lobbying group for agricultural businesses, including farmers. Both saw his conundrum immediately, as well as the potential economic impact the distillery could have on Middleburgh and Schoharie County.

Moreover, there were two powerful precedents, both statewide and nationally, for cutting red tape when it came to alcoholic beverage producers. In the mid-1970s New York's grape growers faced a severe, weather-driven glut that threatened to harm not only their bottom lines but also the wider winemaking industry in New York, which was then the nation's second-biggest wine producer after California. Simply put, New York winemakers in regions such as the Finger Lakes and eastern Long Island could not turn grapes into wine fast enough to prevent the fruit from going to waste through spoilage. To spur production, New York lawmakers in 1976 introduced the Farm Winery Act, which not only allowed small producers, including grape growers, to sell wine directly to consumers on-site but also drastically reduced the licensing and sales fees related to such small-scale operations. The number of New York wineries ballooned in the wake of the 1976 legislation, from around twenty to several hundred, and wine-related tourism became a major economic boon, especially upstate. While New York was not the first state to legalize farm wineries, its size and its rip-roaring success made its act the most influential of its kind in the nation. Others copied it, and soon it became apparent in the new century that New York itself would copy the law when it came to smaller breweries. Those smaller breweries had already been helped on a national level in the same year as the Farm Winery Act enactment. In September 1976 Congress chopped the federal excise tax on beer from nine dollars a barrel to seven dollars on the first sixty thousand barrels annually—as long as a brewery produced no more than two million barrels annually. The industry had long championed the tax cut, and Stroh Brewing chairman Peter Stroh nudged fellow Michigander Gerald Ford to sign the legislation without any fuss. When President Ford did so, in September 1976, there were fewer than one hundred breweries in the United States, craft or otherwise, with experts predicting only two or three by the century's end. The exact opposite happened, with the number of breweries skyrocketing, the cost of doing business that much lower for smaller producers. The first craft brewery in New York opened in 1979 in Albany.

For distilleries, there seemed little hope in the early 2000s of replicating such a cause and effect. The Farm Winery Act rankled Torgersen in particular.

Why should upstate grape growers have gotten such an economic lifeline and not corn farmers around Middleburgh? But there simply were no small-scale, stand-alone distilleries in New York State and therefore no industry clamoring for help—nor were there viable examples for hard-up corn producers to see as a plan B as grape growers had found in existing wineries. On a national level, too, there was no trade group speaking forcefully for the industry as the United States Brewers Association had in the mid-1970s—and certainly no group speaking forcefully for smaller producers, who were still scattered geographically far and wide. A handful of conglomerates produced most of the spirits on the market, and they had no trouble hurdling such barriers to entry as a $40,000 licensing fee.

Yet fostering small business and fomenting economic growth were powerful arguments, especially coming out of the national economic recession of 2000–2001. Torgersen and his newfound allies wielded these arguments very effectively. Who could be against small business and economic growth—in a depressed area, besides? "Prior to Prohibition, New York state produced several varieties of locally distilled whiskies, all grown from New York corn and rye," read a letter from the Farm Bureau on Torgersen's behalf. "This economic venture assisted New York farmers by providing another alternative market for their crops." The state legislature in Albany responded, passing a bill that lowered the nearly $40,000 three-year licensing fee to as low as $250 for producers making fewer than thirty-five thousand gallons of spirits annually. Governor George Pataki signed the bill into law in September 2002. A significant obstacle to small-batch distilleries in America's third-largest state had come tumbling down.

New York's experience in 2001 and 2002 is illustrative of similar fights in other states that ended in victories for distillers and their supporters. These victories invariably lowered fees for start-ups; allowed more direct sales to consumers, often at the distillery; or simply eased the way for opening a small-batch, more traditional distillery in the first place—or a combination of two or all three of these effects. What's more, it was a kind of house-to-house conquest, no president's pen bringing sweeping changes. Nationwide, it remained illegal to distill in the home and the federal licensing process for distilleries had not changed much since the 1980s. While it was not illegal to actually own a still or the individual supplies for distilling spirits, there was not a home-distilling infrastructure that might seed the industry with amateurs turning professional—as was the case with craft brewing, where myriad operations grew from homebrewers making the leap to commercial brewing, especially after legalization of homebrewing at the federal level in 1978.

In the end, the fights for small-batch distilleries were all at the local and state levels, and there the struggles generally unfolded along the same pattern as in New York: A lone soul or business looking to open or to expand would discover a Prohibition-era law meant to prevent just that; the individual or company would approach lawmakers; legislation would then be drafted, passed, and enacted, with everything couched in terms of economic development and small-business assistance, no one daring to defend alcohol consumption itself or any supposed benefits of it; and all of this usually took years and by no means seemed assured of a happy ending. If such a legal odyssey did end happily, it usually proved a tipping point that rippled change far and wide. "In the case of U.S. craft distillers, state-level differences in licensing requirements may lead to a profusion of entrants in one state, and few or none in a state next-door," wrote Michael Kinstlick, an executive at a New York craft distillery called Coppersea, in a widely cited analysis of the industry's growth during the 2000s. "Generally, the entry of the first craft distillery in a state has led quickly to more and . . . favorable changes in licensing requirements have been 'trigger events' in individual states."

For John Torgersen, the New York victory proved bittersweet. In 2002 he lost his consultancy's biggest customer and had to take a full-time job again, this time down in New York City, which meant weekly commutes back and forth from Middleburgh. In 2003 he invited state regulators and representatives of New York corn farmers to a hotel in West Point, where he presented his plans. The presentation included a visit to one of the sites of Benny Havens's early nineteenth-century tavern. (Hounded by authorities, Havens had had to switch locations.) There, on the banks of the Hudson, Torgersen explained the spirit behind his spirits idea—a resurrection of an industry once intimately entwined economically and socially with large parts of New York.

But the commuting and the day-jobbing proved too much. He basically ran out of time fighting the regulatory ghosts of Prohibition and soon left the state for Texas and another role in the commercial maritime industry. Torgersen's pioneering work on behalf of lowering New York's licensing fee would inspire similar movements in other states and pave the way for dozens of New York distilleries—just not his own.

THE GOLDEN AGE BEGINS

2003–2010 | Gardiner, New York—Milwaukee —Denver—Spokane, Washington

Ralph Erenzo had grand plans for his thirty-six acres of newly acquired land in upstate New York, about seventy miles north of his native New York City. The slim, compact Erenzo, a navy veteran, had gotten into rock climbing in the early 1980s after covering the subject for a newspaper in Portland, Maine. He was "thrilled to find a sport that favored the skinny, little guy," and eventually took his new hobby from New England to New York City, where he climbed Central Park's deceptively squat rocks and headed a local climbing club for similar urban enthusiasts. Soon, though, Erenzo decided to push his passion that much further and in 1991 started a company that made and managed indoor vertical-climbing walls. These included a fifty-foot-high faux-rock wall in a gym near Manhattan's Lincoln Center, as well as two that stretched to thirty and fifty feet, including through a glassed-in atrium, at Sixty-Second Street and Broadway. The cable-sports juggernaut ESPN even commissioned Erenzo's firm to stage the first few rock climbing segments of its extreme-sports franchise in the late 1990s. He would also take his more adventurous clients on approved climbs of New York City bridges and buildings. As straightforward as these ventures might seem—installing a fake massif and supervising short climbs—Erenzo often confronted skeptical government officials and private landowners unsure of just what he was proposing. The taller wall at Sixty-Second Street and Broadway, for instance, led right onto the sidewalk. Erenzo had to convince the city, the police, and the owners of two adjoining buildings that it was perfectly safe. He eventually replicated his New York success in other locales, including Colorado Springs and Philadelphia, and then decided to branch out from simply gyms to an entire complex, a kind of rock climbing nirvana for enthusiasts such as himself.

That was what led Erenzo back to upstate New York (he had grown up in Westchester County, just north of the Bronx). The Shawangunk Mountains represented the East Coast's greatest rock climbing area, with hundreds of possible routes for even novices to conquer. Erenzo's idea was to open a campground and hostel in the nearby town of Gardiner for climbers who wanted a secure, clean home base for their rocky adventures. Some Gardiner residents had other ideas. "My only goal," one told Erenzo, "is to stall you long enough so you run out of money and have to sell the place, and move away." Neighbors feared disquiet from the climbers traipsing and trafficking through and quickly bogged Erenzo down in a protracted legal fight that cost him years of lost income and escalating legal fees. He eventually sold off dozens of acres to keep his fight for the campground alive, the total dwindling by 2003 to a mere eight from the original thirty-six. Fed up and fretful, Erenzo asked a local zoning official to walk the remaining acreage with him and explain what Erenzo might use it for—that did not involve an OK from the neighbors. "The place is an agricultural district," the official told him, "and under the New York state constitution you have a right to farm." What's more, a winery on such land was considered farm use, thanks to the state's landmark 1976 Farm Winery Act. Perhaps that was the direction Erenzo would like to go in? He did some research and realized that he would like to go in a similar, though not identical direction. There had not been a new distillery in New York State since Prohibition. Erenzo would start the first, in Gardiner.

He partnered with Brian Lee, an engineer and MBA from Columbia University whom he had met through selling off some of his land. That land included the oldest continuously operating gristmill in New York State, a water-powered contraption dating from the 1780s that made Kosher matzo flour for Hasidic Jewish communities in Brooklyn. Lee's engineering work centered around developing television facilities and technologies—he had consulted on ESPN's move to high-definition broadcasting—and he thought he might pivot to engineering flour the old-fashioned way, with the superannuated mill. A couple of days at the mill changed Lee's mind. "It's not a career change," he told Erenzo, "it's a death sentence." Erenzo countered with the distillery proposition, and, two day later, having had time to mull it over, Lee e-mailed: "OK, let's build a distillery."

Both knew "less than amateurs," according to Erenzo, versed more in drinking than actually making the drinks. Nevertheless, in December 2003, they filed incorporation papers with the state for what they called Tuthilltown Spirits, after that water-powered mill. Soon they became the first New

York distillery licensed under the 2002 fee reduction that John Torgersen had championed. More than that, Erenzo and Lee's Tuthilltown was the first *applicant* for a distillery license in New York State in roughly eighty years. Erenzo realized that no one had been asking the questions they were asking in four generations. Aside from asking government officials questions, they also sought advice from the handful of small-batch producers nationwide, and Erenzo visited smaller, farm-based distilleries in Europe. Those visits convinced him the model might work in the States. In a pot still acquired from Germany and inside a converted granary near the gristmill on the Gardiner property, Erenzo and Lee began in 2004 producing vodkas from local apples and a corn whiskey from local corn. In particular, Tuthilltown saw the apple-based vodka as a service to the surrounding area, as foreign producers and those in the Pacific Northwest were then cutting significantly into the sales of upstate New York orchards. A Tuthilltown bourbon would soon follow in the summer of 2006. In 2008 Erenzo orchestrated a distribution coup that helped expand Tuthilltown's presence. Tonier establishments in Manhattan, including higher-end restaurants and hotel bars, had hesitated carrying this new arrival. So Erenzo contacted an old high school friend living in Paris. "Get me the best liquor distributor in Paris." The friend set him up with La Maison du Whisky, a leading distributor in France. Erenzo flew over with some bottles and flew back with a seventy-five-case order and the cachet of being able to tell reluctant American retailers that Europeans, those discerning sophisticates who had originated so many spirits styles, sipped Tuthilltown at finer eateries and other establishments. To Erenzo, it mimicked in a smaller way the success of artists such as the singer Ella Fitzgerald and the trumpeter Louis Armstrong, who had to go to the Continent to foster stardom in their home country.

Aside perhaps from the French sojourn, Erenzo and Lee's tale was repeating itself nationwide in the middle of the first decade of the twenty-first century. The stories were obviously not always the same, but regardless of geography the basic characters and plot twists were. Just as with legal changes wrought around the same time, the debuts of newcomers in certain areas otherwise bereft of craft spirits often proved the only catalyst necessary for more to join. In New York itself, for example, the number of small-batch distilleries reached double digits within ten years of the incorporation filing of Tuthilltown, the state's first stand-alone craft distillery. That New York number would leap even higher after the state enacted a farm distillery law modeled after its Farm Winery Act, which rewarded distilleries that used substantial amounts of locally produced ingredients with lower fees and the ability to sell on-site.

Ralph Erenzo with his son, Gabe, at Tuthilltown.
TUTHILLTOWN

In Wisconsin, Guy Rehorst sold his successful DVD- and CD-manufacturing business to open that state's first small-batch distillery in Milwaukee in late 2004. Rehorst, a homebrewer, had considered a craft brewery instead but realized that "just about every decent beer that the bars around here had were made locally," and so he switched to spirits, his Great Lakes Distillery releasing its inaugural Rehorst Premium Milwaukee Vodka in 2006. Great Lakes' sales rose from about two thousand cases annually in 2007 to seven thousand a few years later—and the number of Wisconsin small-batch distilleries reached six. There were also a half dozen such distilleries in Ohio by 2010, eleven years after Don and Linda Outterson started Woodstone Creek in the Cincinnati area. Out in Colorado, volunteer fireman Jess Graber responded to a call about a burning barn and ended up meeting the immolated property's owner, George Stranahan. Stranahan, a rancher and an heir to the Champion Spark Plug fortune, had started a brewpub in Aspen in 1991 and cofounded the Flying Dog Brewery shortly after. Graber's passion for whiskey convinced Stranahan to partner with him on Stranahan's Colorado Whiskey. The Centennial State's first small-batch distillery launched in Denver shortly after its late 2002 incorporation and quickly became locally famous for its namesake whiskey. By 2005 Colorado had four such distilleries, and five years after that, in 2010, it had fifteen. In Texas there would be eight by the same year, less than fifteen years after Tito Beveridge launched his eponymous vodka line near Austin.

Such aggregate leaps were the most pronounced along the West Coast. In early 2007 fellow fly-fishing enthusiasts Don Poffenroth and Kent Fleischmann launched Dry Fly Distilling out of an old coffee shop space in downtown Spokane, becoming Washington's first distillery, small-batch or otherwise, since Prohibition. The pair focused on a vodka made with wheat harvested in state and gin made from Washington juniper and other botanicals. Dry Fly proved a smash right from the start. Poffenroth and Fleischmann had five months' worth of orders for those initial spirits by March 2008 and a second pot still on the way. Their operations were helped along immensely when Washington State amended its Prohibition-era distilling laws to allow for on-site sales, a change Dry Fly's founders helped spearhead. Within three years of that distillery's launch, and within barely two of that legal change, there were thirteen small-batch distilleries in Washington State. In neighboring Oregon, where such distilling stretched back to Steve McCarthy's Clear Creek in 1985, there were twenty-one, the vast majority opening between 2005 and 2010. And, in immense California there were twenty-five such distilleries by 2010, more than double the number from five years before and accounting for roughly one in seven small-batch distilleries in the United States. Even in far-flung Hawaii, the movement's presence was growing dramatically, from Aloha Distillers at the very end of the 1990s to at least four operations by 2010.

These were small numbers in total but represented huge leaps growthwise. The growth in the number of Washington State distilleries, for instance, represented a nearly 770 percent increase in just three years. In the end, the geographic creep of these distilleries may have mattered more than the total number. Distribution was obviously key to any successful operation, and the various state-by-state legal changes often opened or widened those channels, either by making it easier for smaller distilleries to launch in the first place or by allowing things such as sales at the distilleries themselves. The mere presence of a tinier, more traditional distillery, then, translated into the presence of that company's product on local shelves and menus. In 2010 forty-three states had at least one small-batch distillery, the only holdouts Alaska, the Dakotas, Minnesota, Oklahoma, Alabama, and New Jersey. In 2005 twenty-five states had at least one. In 2000 only twelve did. That growth rate in itself reflected the changes wrought by both early pioneers and the legal changes they often helped drive. These newcomers in the middle and late 2000s were thoroughly more cognizant and prepared than their small-batch distilling forebears from earlier eras. Whereas those start-ups in the 1990s and certainly the 1980s usually operated in geographic and commercial isolation, the only such distillery in not only their states but perhaps their region of the vast nation, the start-ups of the middle and late 2000s were very much aware that they functioned within a wider movement, one that certain standards had started to define, unwittingly at first and then very much consciously.

There were also business and political frameworks for these newer pioneers to work within that were not available to earlier entrants. Ralph Erenzo, for one, baffled New York authorities when he presented the idea for Tuthilltown in the early 2000s. Within a few years, though, the distillery and the same authorities had formed a smooth working relationship. In Chicago, husband and wife Robert and Sonat Birnecker, who chucked positions in diplomacy and academia, respectively, to start Koval, the first new distillery since Prohibition in America's third largest city, encountered similar bafflement on the part of local and state lawmakers. An alliance with a Chicago alderman straightened the licensing labyrinth, and Koval opened in early 2008. Soon after, the Birneckers were running a brisk consulting business on the side, helping other start-up distilleries navigate the necessary legalities. Pioneers such as Erenzo and the Birneckers deserved credit for such governmental evolutions. But the twin rises of fine wine and craft beer had a lot to do with it, too, as did the rise of artisanal versions of staples such as coffee and bread. These provided a context in which smaller distilleries could mature. Ancillary industries, such as distributors, restaurants, and retailers, more quickly and easily understood what these distillers were peddling based on the context that fine wine, craft beer, and higher-end coffee provided. Similarly, government officials, including elected leaders, could better understand a pitch for a small-batch distillery because they or their predecessors might have encountered one for a craft brewery twenty years before. Finally, consumers could more readily comprehend the idea as well, trained as they were for nearly two generations by the likes of Robert Mondavi on fine wine and Jim Koch on craft beer. Simply put, small-batch spirits had started to lose its novelty for significant swaths of America. This familiarity—and the numbers and the changes behind it—would only continue to grow. Soon the movement would step completely around those of fine wine and craft beer and create a context all its own.

DON DRAPER ORDERS AN OLD FASHIONED
2007–2010 | Manhattan

The man in the gray flannel suit sits in a booth in the smoky, dimly lit Manhattan bar, scribbling furiously in black ink on a white napkin, two Lucky Strike cigarette stubs in a transparent ashtray on one side of him, an empty highball glass with a maraschino cherry at the bottom on the other. A waiter approaches the man, who pauses from his scribbles and asks for a light for his next cigarette. He asks the waiter what his own favorite brand of smokes is—and what would ever make him switch to another.

Thus did more than 1.2 million American households meet Don Draper, the protagonist of the new television series *Mad Men*, which debuted on Thursday, July 19, 2007, on the cable network AMC. Played by the actor Jon Hamm, the handsome, imperturbably smooth Draper is an advertising creative director in his thirties in early 1960s Manhattan, a California transplant from a troubled childhood with a talent for selling flush post–World War II America all manner of products, from cigarettes to automobiles to detergent to hamburgers. His is a stylish world of smoothly run pitch meetings in boardrooms and long client lunches in classy restaurants, aggressive assignations in Gotham's higher- as well as lower-end addresses and quick confabs in sprawling offices in Modern skyscrapers—with cocktails or straight spirits thoroughly lubricating all of it. *Mad Men*, which would routinely draw more than one million viewers per episode over the next seven years and amass a slew of Emmys and Golden Globes, placed alcohol, spirits in particular, front and center in a way no successful television drama had to that point. The prominence was neither accidental nor incidental, according to series creator Matthew Weiner, who had developed the premise for *Mad Men* while writing for *The Sopranos*, another phenomenally successful cable television drama. "I'm trying to tell a story about that time," Weiner explained. "It's not done for glamour. People drank more and all the time. They drank in their cars, at work, in the morning at work." Many of *Mad Men*'s pivotal scenes take place either after much casual imbibing—bottles and drink carts were staples of the offices of Draper's firm—or in some of the more notable restaurants and bars of 1960s New York. In that very first scene broadcast in July 2007, Draper ordered a whiskey-based old fashioned—or another old fashioned, as it were, the latest in a string clearly easing him into another run of creativity as the napkin scribbles evidenced. Any deleterious effects of such drinking were mined for laughs, quickly shaken off, or shunted to sad-sack characters with little going for them anyway (or to the later seasons, when the effects of Draper's own drinking became dismally clear).

And therein lay a key appeal of the show, the so-called "*Mad Men* effect" that bartenders and other alcohol vendors started noticing: spirits, and the cocktail culture they ballasted, were depicted in the show as par for the course, something as common and unremarkable as the midcentury modern furniture or fear of the Bomb back then. Drinking was something a hip, enterprising professional did and knew how to do: pour the proper spirits in the proper way, drink them, and repeat. This was the time, too, right before the steady rise of American fine wine and also during the period of domestic beer's rapid homogenization. Those drinks made only sporadic appearances in *Mad Men*, their brands generic, their use more props than plot drivers. Weiner's creation instead focused on spirits in a prelapsarian age that they dominated commercially. In the 1950s and 1960s, bourbon sales were still brisk, everyone knew Smirnoff left a tippler breathless, and the ability to precisely mix a G and T was a sign not of dotage but of style. *Mad Men* reached back beyond the intervening decades of profound marketplace change and became "a piece of pop culture that's basically credited with reviving public interest in stylish drinking."

Nowhere did this revival echo louder than with younger viewers. The show consistently drew its biggest chunk of viewers from the eighteen to forty-nine cohort, and the innumerable magazine, newspaper, and Web features about *Mad Men* and its aftershocks targeted this age group as well. "The show not only introduced us to the impossibly suave, lantern-jawed Don," went one take from National Public Radio's *The Salt* blog, "it also introduced a new generation of TV viewers to old-fashioned cocktails like Manhattans and martinis, gimlets and sidecars." The influence manifested itself in the marketplace, including for small-batch spirits, which while obviously not featured on a show that wrapped chronologically in 1970, benefited from renewed interest in spirits in general. Bartenders in major cities such as New York and San Francisco reported copious daily requests for cocktails, including the ones mentioned on the show. Sales of whiskey, the preferred spirit of Draper et al., jumped by double-digit percentages. Online cocktail guides arose referencing *Mad Men*, as did guides to drink pairings. The show was even credited with a rise in spirits consumption among younger women in particular. "The 'Mad Men effect' is widely talked about among whiskey sellers" in Kentucky, as one report from that bourbon-soaked state put it. Sellers and manufacturers on the clearer end of the spirits spectrum were also discussing the show—though they were more concerned with the worrisome consequences for vodka and gin since many fans of the show seemed to be imitating Don Draper's affection for whiskey.

Mad Men's influence represented a kind of zenith for what critics and other journalists often called a cocktail renaissance. This was different than false starts during the preceding two decades. "One day a federal death squad will hunt down and eliminate every loser with thick-rimmed glasses and a smoking jacket," read a chart in satirical news magazine *Spy* in the summer of 1997. Under the headline "Lounging Towards Gomorrah," the chart pinpointed various media declarations of a cocktail renaissance in America going back to the mid-1980s. The editorial eye roll was understandable. During that period the ascent of vodka had spawned flavored vodka, which in turn spurred the rise of treacly sweet cocktails such as every iteration of the martini but the classic gin and dry vermouth. The popularity of sweeter, usually vodka-infused cocktails continued into the 1990s, in part due to the influence of HBO's *Sex and the City*, where a favored tipple was the apple-and-vodka appletini, and also partly due to the very sweetness of the mixtures themselves. America had long been comfortable with sugary sodas and coffees. The hegemony of this "alcoholic candy," as one critic put it, belied changes subtly running underfoot, however. As the 2000s dawned, bar owners and bartenders (sometimes persons one and the same) were resurrecting older recipes, some not widely formulated since the last undisputed cocktail renaissance right before Prohibition. "The first half of the decade saw a wave of creativity and experimentation come crashing through barrooms in cities like New York and San Francisco and Portland, Ore.," according to critic Jonathan Miles, who wrote a drinks column for the *New York Times* in the later 2000s. These bars were careful, too, to showcase the creation of these concoctions—among them, sazeracs, bourbon daisys, rusty nails, knickerbockers, Manhattans, Brooklyns, juleps (mint or otherwise), salty dogs, Harvey Wallbangers, white Russians, black Russians, and vintage versions of martinis and gin and tonics. Bartenders often wore Jazz Age garb, tutored patrons on their machinations and measurements, and pointed them to cocktail menus that could be positively wine-like in their verbosity. That was part of the fun and the foundation of bartending as an "art form," another phrase, along with "cocktail renaissance," batted frequently around during the 2000s. And those declarations of bartending as an art form often came with reminders that the United States, perhaps more than any other nation, perfected and popularized legions of cocktails. The heritage just got lost amid and around the inhospitable wilderness of Prohibition.

There were a few theories as to why cocktail culture finally took on a wide scale. The biggest was probably that *Mad Men* effect, with its nod to a time when a well-made old fashioned was not so old fashioned. Indeed, unlike the false starts in the 1980s and 1990s, a fashionableness seemed to undergird the newly ascended culture. It was sleekly cool to dig cocktails—and to be seen digging cocktails. "Surrendering your drink choice to the bartender," Jonathan Miles wrote, "the way diners at sushi restaurants request whatever is freshest, became the '00s hippest drink order." The 1996 sleeper hit *Swingers*, in which the movie characters' cocktails went beyond flavored vodka, may have proved more durable in this regard than *Sex and the City*. The ubiquity of social media, particularly Facebook and Instagram, helped as well, with experiences and recipes easily shareable on a wide basis. And cocktail guides and other books abounded during the decade, both online and in print. In 2007 a guide-slash-history by David Wondrich, a comparative literature PhD and English professor turned jazz writer turned *Esquire* magazine drinks critic, became the first cocktail book to win a James Beard Award, the highest accolade for food and drink writing in the United States. Wondrich at the time of his win was living in Brooklyn, one of several urban areas in America that had changed dramatically in the past twenty years, with previously gritty neighborhoods dominated by manufacturing plants and shoddy housing morphing through public- and private-sector efforts into gentrified playgrounds for moneyed baby boomers, generation Xers, and now millennials. Along with pricey condos, spin-cycle studios, and coffee shops, seemingly obligatory features of these neighborhoods included fashionable bars offering a range of spirits, small-batch included—and a staff knowledgeable about how to mix them. There were also concomitant booms during the decade of interest in more esoteric beer and wine styles. This was the decade that the India pale ale, once an obscure curiosity even in its English homeland, became the bestselling style among craft beers and the decade when natural wines, those made with as little adulteration as possible, stood athwart the juicier, brawnier, stronger wines, often deliberately doctored to make them that much more oaky and buttery, that dominated the market.

The cocktail renaissance seemed to feed on simple nostalgia during a difficult period for the United States, one marked by the historic events of the terrorist attacks of September 11, 2001, and the Great Recession, which started in 2008. Just as bartenders and bars resurrected older recipes, so too did distillery owners and spirits enthusiasts resurrect older drinks and accoutrements, absinthe, bitters, and liqueurs perhaps the most noteworthy. In 2007 federal regulators approved four brands of absinthe for sale in the United States. The intensely alcoholic, anise-flavored spirit had been a bit of a sensation in Europe throughout much of the nineteenth and early twentieth centuries, infamously coveted for its supposed hallucinogenic properties and often ritualistically consumed, including after pouring ice water over a sugar cube to turn the often green-hued drink a milky white. "What difference is there between a glass of absinthe and a sunset?" Oscar Wilde was said to have written rhetorically. The legendary wit was one of many absinthe devotees during the spirit's heyday, before that very mind-bending effect led one Western nation after another to curtail either its production or importation. The United States banned imports of absinthe in 1912 and then outlawed it altogether—unless it was made with extremely low levels of thujone, the compound derived from the wormwood plant that was thought to cause the hallucinations. Absinthe enthusiasts carried a candle for the spirit throughout the twentieth century, and after the European Union scrapped myriad prohibitions in the 1990s, it became only a matter of time before the United States followed suit. New research, too, into the chemical composition of preserved absinthe bottles from the nineteenth century showed that the level of thujone in the spirit was never as high as authorities assumed and feared. Ted Breaux, an American chemist working in New Orleans and, later, France, showed that the thujone levels were, in fact, much lower than the legal threshold that US regulations had long required. The hallucinations that tipplers experienced probably had more to do with consuming too much of a very strong drink—pure ethyl alcohol might comprise more than 50 percent of a properly distilled absinthe. Or, in the case of fans such as the painter Vincent van Gogh and the writer Ernest Hemingway, undiagnosed mental maladies that sometimes sparked paranoia were instead blamed on prodigious absinthe consumption.

After much regulatory back and forth, the federal government approved imports from Switzerland and France. In March 2007 the brand Lucid Absinthe Supérieure became the first genuine absinthe to go on sale in America since at least 1912. Viridian Spirits, a Manhasset, New York–based company started by former corporate lawyer Jared Gurfein, marketed Lucid, which Ted Breaux developed from a base in the western France city of Saumur. Viridian did nearly $10 million in sales in its first full year, a bevy of articles about the American reemergence of the once-illicit drink ballasting distribution. Journalists could not seem to get enough of the backstory, especially the witticisms that famous absinthe imbibers uttered under the influence or shortly after. The success capped years of effort on the part of Gurfein, who had long realized the potential for absinthe amid the general renewed interest in all things cocktail-related.

That interest included bitters, concentrated infusions of flowers, herbs, barks, roots, and spices once standard in cocktails such as the Manhattan, the Sazerac, and Don Draper's preferred old fashioned. There had at one time been hundreds of brands of bitters, but they then fell out of favor with the decline in whiskey consumption and the rise of clear spirits, especially vodka. By the start of the twenty-first century, there were two brands of bitters in wide use: Angostura for old fashioneds and Manhattans and Peychaud's for rye whiskey–infused Sazeracs. The cocktail renaissance, however, made them must-haves again as essential ingredients in new and resurrected recipes. The number of brands of bitters multiplied exponentially during the 2000s to the point where they became "a cottage industry, taken up by every cocktail fancier who wanted to get in the game." Suddenly, once "bitters-starved" bartenders were able to experiment with offerings as disparate in flavor as grapefruit, chocolate, rhubarb, and tobacco. And patrons were asking for bitters not by flavor, but by brand name, so deeply went the interest. Some journalists even referred to "craft bitters" to differentiate the newer, more eclectic flavors from older standards.

Timing also played a key role in the resurgence of small-batch liqueurs, those lower-alcohol cousins to spirits that are flavored and then bottled with added sugar (hence the sweetness). It appears that few wrote or spoke of "craft liqueurs" or "small-batch liqueurs" until 2007, when a young entrepreneur introduced an elderflower liqueur called St-Germain. Rob Cooper was twenty-four in 2001 when he saw a bartender in London use homemade elderflower syrup in a cocktail. Intrigued, he began experimenting with bitters back at the family liqueur company in Philadelphia. After years of tweaking, he released St-Germain, which became "the breakout liqueur of the cocktail revival." Soon it was so omnipresent in the industry that some called St-Germain "bartender's ketchup." Such demand for liqueurs for cocktails opened commercial doors for other, smaller liqueur producers, including small-batch spirits pioneers. Steve McCarthy's Clear Creek was likely the first small-batch distillery in the country since Prohibition to turn serious attention to liqueurs. He did so in 1998 and 1999, though it would be many years before there was much of a marketplace response. In 2006 McCarthy moved from his original warehouse location in Portland, Oregon, where he had already expanded to take over the entire space, to a much larger location in the city. He added two stills and introduced more liqueurs, including ones flavored by cassis, cherry, pear, and loganberry. St-Germain's success helped ensure a market for them, as did the continued vitality of the cocktail renaissance, its resurrected recipes sometimes in turn inspiring the resurrection of effectively extinct liqueurs. Cherry-infused maraschino, for instance, went into the aviation, a gin-powered cocktail dating from at least the early twentieth century and voguish again by 2010. That cocktail recipe in turn required the rejuvenation of a largely extinct liqueur, crème de violette, which a Minnesota importer acquired via an Austrian producer.

Such a turned-on-its-head symbiosis was not uncommon, with newfound demand for cocktails feeding the development of supply. And, unlike previous consumer dalliances with cocktail culture in the 1980s and 1990s, this round seemed more durable. A titanic part of that was *Mad Men* and the ingenuity of the spirits and the hospitality industries.

Another big reason for the durability of this cocktail renaissance was similar to one for the rise in small-batch spirits: Americans were paying particular attention to what they ate and drank. Small-batch spirits were not necessarily integral to the renewed interest in cocktails—a skilled bartender could make the latter just as deftly with a macrobrand as with the former—but they benefited from a new and persistent way of thinking about spirits generally. "What had once merely lubricated conversations became the subject of conversations," the *Times*' Jonathan Miles wrote in 2010 of cocktails, "in much the same way that dinner parties, with the rise of foodie-ism in the '90s, became more about the dinner and less about the party."

POURING OUT WORDS

2000–2010 | Nationwide

In 2008 Robert Burr, the well-traveled publisher of a scuba diving magazine, organized a tasting of fifty rums in Coral Gables, Florida, just south of Miami, for 150 friends and associates. He felt the gathering went so well that the following year he launched the Rum Renaissance Festival in Miami Beach. That inaugural festival drew more than one thousand paying attendees, with that number increasing tenfold in the next decade. Burr's gathering became "a central stage for what you might call the rum revolution—the recent ascent of high-end, premium rum," according to a National Public Radio report.

The Renaissance Rum Festival became that spirit's national answer to John Hansell's WhiskyFest, which routinely drew more than one thousand attendees with tickets starting at around one hundred dollars. Smaller festivals for whiskey, rum, and other spirits, particularly tequila, started in the 2000s as well, offering curious consumers a chance to sample wares well beyond the big brand names—and for newer distilleries to showcase their products.

Media coverage usually accompanied these festivals. Such coverage invariably started out explaining the novelty of tasting spirits generally and referenced the concomitant rise in craft beer, reassuring readers and listeners (and sometimes viewers) that these tastings were not sources of easy inebriation but opportunities to savor the fruits of smaller-batch, more traditional distillation. "It's not a college-beach bacchanal," NPR explained of Burr's Renaissance Rum Festival. "It's rum for grown-ups, for people who know that most aged rums today are distilled as masterfully as fine cognacs and single malt Scotches." It was a contextual leap many consumers would not have made on their own—or would have known they *had* to make. However different the storylines of craft spirits and craft beer might be otherwise, in this case, one had set a precedent for the other. Craft brewers had had to do the same convincing twenty to thirty years ago, with the organizers of events such as the Great American Beer Festival and the World Beer Cup assuring potential ticket buyers that these were not raging keg parties but gatherings for aficionados and those who would join their ranks. They also had to make it clear that there was a wider galaxy of beer available in the United States, that the macrobrands were not the only options, however ubiquitous they seemed. "That's a great idea, Charlie, but what will you serve for beer?" was the critic Michael Jackson's response to GABF cofounder Charlie Papazian when the latter first broached the idea of a grand tasting for American beer. The intimation was clear: Wouldn't it all be Budweiser and Miller Lite in 1982, the GABF's first year? Potential small-batch spirits consumers needed the same sort of reassurance: "If your knowledge of Scotch begins with Johnnie Walker and ends at 'on the rocks,' a weekend spent tasting expensive single malts at whiskey bars around the city might seem pointless, even intimidating," began a *New York Times* piece from 2007 on the city's better bars for the brown spirit, one that teased the tenth annual WhiskyFest, coming to Manhattan that October. "If it turns out that you still can't tell Cutty Sark from Glenlivet, no problem: Halloween is the next day, and you can at least masquerade as a Scotch connoisseur."

There were plenty of real connoisseurs emerging during the decade, happy to help consumers along their spirits journeys. The rise of the World Wide Web helped this growth mightily along, affording critics a cheap and fast way to reach potential readers. No exact statistics exist as to the number of American spirits critics arising during the 2000s, but several became prominent enough to warrant the courtship of distilleries themselves, comped samples included, as well as actual written feedback from readers, as sure a sign of reach as any in the Internet age. The 2000s, particularly the decade's latter half, represented an unprecedented flowering of American spirits criticism, comparable to what arose in wine in the 1970s and beer writing in the 1990s. Disparate in their backgrounds and locations, these new critics did share some features. They were overwhelmingly men; they came to spirits writing from or through other pursuits, gradually becoming interested rather than a stark epiphany turning them on to the subject; they benefited from technological innovations to disseminate their critiques; and they invariably wrote partly as evangelists, if mostly as critics. Early to the pop cultural party, especially when it came to small-batch spirits, these writers wrote with a realization that their readers sometimes had to be turned on to the very idea of a particular spirit, never mind a particular brand. The vocabulary these critics marshaled, too, did not at first include the likes of *craft spirit*, *craft distillery*, or *small-batch*— and many would expend considerable ink questioning the terms anyway.

Chuck Cowdery grew up in north-central Ohio. In 1978 the twenty-six-year-old relocated to Louisville, Kentucky, where he worked as a freelance commercial copywriter, putting together sales and marketing materials for companies such as Brown Forman and other major spirits producers. The work familiarized Cowdery with the spirits industry, particularly its bourbon producers (no accident, given his location). He was taken specifically with the culture of bourbon and its rich history in the state and the nation, and not so much with the idea of tasting notes or connoisseurship, at least not at first. As Kentucky's 1992 state bicentennial approached, Cowdery collected his knowledge and his contacts for a documentary on the history of bourbon for KET, Kentucky's public television network. Two years after that documentary aired, and after relocating to Chicago for work, Cowdery launched the *Bourbon Country Reader*, a newsletter he published six times a year and that was among the first independently produced publications nationwide focusing on a single spirit, a kind of blog before there were blogs. Blogs did flow from that newsletter beginning in 2005, and Cowdery would also write books on bourbon and bourbon culture.

Fred Minnick was a photographer with the US Army's public affairs wing for a year in Iraq and, before that, a print journalist who got his start in his native Oklahoma. In 2006 he turned to freelance writing full time, making a list of the topics he would ideally like to cover. Bourbon was on that list. From a home base in Louisville, Kentucky, the very heart of American bourbon country, Minnick started writing books, blog posts, and articles on the subject, breaking particular ground on the contributions of women to the success of whiskey in the United States.

Minnick also wrote about Mark Gillespie, who in November 2005, while working as a broadcast producer for the Gallup polling organization, launched *WhiskyCast*, a regular podcast on Apple's iTunes, which only a few months before had added the ability to independently upload (and download) such podcasts. Gillespie would grow what Minnick called "the NPR of whisky" into a going concern with forty thousand listeners in dozens of countries. In 2009 Gillespie quit his last day job, as an assignment editor at Bloomberg News, to focus full-time on *WhiskyCast*. Wayne Curtis would also, when he wasn't writing books on other topics, turn his efforts full-time toward spirits coverage at the end of the decade. He had been a travel writer for the Frommer's travel guide series, with a particular focus on eastern Canada and New England. But the regular visits to hundreds of venues so he could update the guides began to wear thin. Curtis in the mid-2000s started writing regularly about the burgeoning small-batch spirits movement for a variety of outlets, particularly the *Atlantic* magazine. Clay Risen also wrote about spirits, whiskey in particular, for the *Atlantic*. He grew up in Nashville, where his paternal grandfather introduced him to Blanton's, the revolutionary single-barrel bourbon that seemed all the more revolutionary because of the omnipresence in Tennessee of native brand Jack Daniel's. By the mid-2000s, Risen was working as a journalist in Washington, DC, around the corner from a store that had a decent collection of bourbons in particular. He was writing regularly about small-batch spirits, and craft beer, by the end of the decade and would continue to do so on the side while working as a staff editor for the *New York Times'* op-ed section.

Lew Bryson came to spirits coverage much earlier through longtime work as a top editor at the *Malt Advocate*, now mostly a magazine about whiskey rather than half about beer, and one that marked its tenth year of publication in 2004. Bryson, who would continue to be a force in beer criticism, would also write well-received whiskey guides beyond his work at the *Malt Advocate* (which he left in early 2016). In one of the surest signs of the ascendancy of spirits criticism in the new century, John Hansell sold control of the *Malt Advocate*, along with the annual WhiskyFests, to Marvin Shanken, head of the eponymous publishing house that also had produced the glossy *Wine Spectator* magazine since the late 1970s. Under Shanken's ownership that publication had become less about wine per se and more about a kind of aspirational wine-infused lifestyle. (Shanken had taken the same approach in the 1980s with another sanctioned vice and another magazine, *Cigar Aficionado*.)

Amy Westlake would still manage WhiskyFest, and Hansell retained editorial oversight of the magazine—and its headquarters remained in Erasmus, Pennsylvania, rather than in Shanken's Manhattan hub—but the deal signaled new potential in spirits coverage in the United States, as did a slew of tasting and travel guides and histories of individual spirits that started regularly rolling out in the decade's latter half. The readership of *Malt Advocate*, which Shanken renamed *Whisky Advocate* in 2011, grew to 225,000 readers, with thousands more online.

There was an audience out there thirsty for knowledge about not only what spirits to drink but also from which distilleries and how to drink them once purchased, an appetite that *Mad Men*'s cocktail-soaked reach whetted significantly. Indeed, a whole phalanx of cocktail writers arose in seeming tandem with these spirits critics. Several cocktail writers, some of whom bartended as their day jobs, launched blogs, and publishers large and small felled a forest's worth of books on the market in the new century at a frequency never before seen in cocktails. Most of these blogs and books tackled not only cocktail recipes but also the often pre-Prohibition origins of these recipes, adding a dash of history to a reader's next round. This demand benefited the new small-batch spirits entrants, whose wares found a much wider audience when featured in consumer or trade media and in the recipes of these cocktail books. Meanwhile, foreign writers and more general alcoholic beverage chroniclers routinely toe-dipped now into the American small-batch spirits movement. Steve McCarthy's recently expanded Clear Creek received more than sixteen hundred emails from consumers following an August 2007 *New York Times* article written by Eric Asimov, the newspaper's chief wine critic, praising the more than twenty-year-old distillery's output. Jim Murray, a British whiskey writer, wrote about Clear Creek's single malt around the same time, and subsequent sales proved so brisk that McCarthy worried his distillery would become known for that libation alone.

This same formula—coverage equaling sales, praise clearing obscurity like the sun slicing through fog—had worked way back in August 1980, when the *Wall Street Journal* raved about tiny Maker's Mark and its traditional approaches in lonely, little Loretto, Kentucky. Such success would repeat itself manifold as the first decade of the twenty-first century bled into the second and the American small-batch spirits movement entered its period of sharpest growth. Shame, then, that, around the same time, the movement confronted a mortal challenge, one largely of its own making.

CRAFT BEFORE THERE WAS CRAFT

2007–2010 | Loretto, Kentucky

The staff meeting in the Loretto, Kentucky, offices of Maker's Mark was only partway through when Bill Samuels Jr. said he had to take a phone call. On the way out of the conference room, he turned to Dave Pickerell, Maker's Mark's master distiller and vice president of operations.

"Dave, can you wrap this up?"

"I got it," Pickerell told Samuels.

The meeting continued until noise at the conference room door interrupted it. In barged Gary Roedemeier, one of the leading news anchors in Louisville, with a cameraman in tow. The pair made a beeline for Pickerell, the lights of the camera sinisterly bright and Roedemeier's microphone jammed inches from Pickerell's mouth. The anchor wanted answers and right away: Someone had died after drinking Maker's Mark. Was the world-renowned bourbon safe? Should consumers be turning their bottles in to the distillery to be trashed? Well?

Pickerell spoke slowly and calmly. "This is the first we've heard about this," he told the microphone and the camera. "This is obviously a tragedy, but we really don't know anything about it. We don't really know if this person passed away from Maker's Mark consumption or if something else that was somehow related might have been the case. We really don't know anything." Pickerell added that it was too early for the distillery to make an announcement. He promised an exclusive interview to Roedemeier if he gave him until four that afternoon to investigate.

The room fell silent—and the camera lights quickly dimmed. Samuels walked back in with a public relations consultant whom Pickerell had been working with to develop his chops as a distillery representative. They congratulated Pickerell on a job well done and told him he was now authorized to speak on behalf of Maker's Mark without permission.

Such was Maker's Mark in the new century: a carefully calibrated, smoothly run operation reaping decades of experience in every aspect of distillation and distillery management, all toward crafting what had become since Pickerell's late 1994 start the number-two-selling bourbon brand in the world (behind Jim Beam). Maker's Mark was selling about three hundred thousand cases annually at the start of the 2000s and would move past one million at the decade's end. It could be found in every state, several countries overseas, including Japan, and, as of 2001, it had recorded thirty straight years of sales growth. As after the *Wall Street Journal* article in August 1980, Maker's Mark could have satiated the steadily growing demand with an expansion fueled by the latest computerized gadgetry and stainless-steel equipment. Instead, in 2000, when it did double its production capacity, the company replicated its original distillery—a more laborious and expensive process but, as Pickerell explained to a reporter, necessary to keep quality consistent. "We're not trying to be technologically innovative," he said. "We're trying to do the same thing over and over again."

Bill Samuels Jr. had hammered home this mantra of consistency during his more than twenty years at the distillery's helm, dedicated as he was to "not screwing up Dad's company." He launched what the distillery called an ambassador program, in which volunteers pledged to tout the bourbon online and in person to friends, family, coworkers, etc., in exchange for perks such as Christmas gifts and special tours of the Loretto operation. Half of the distillery's output went to bars and restaurants anyway, perfect spots for getting people to try something new. It was how Samuels had gotten the *Wall Street Journal's* David Garino to visit the distillery in 1980, through what Samuels described as "managed discovery"—setting people up to (hopefully) be wowed by his product, which he then guaranteed would never change, no matter which way the winds of the market were blowing. "We measure success as we've never lost control of the product," Samuels explained in 2005. "Our number one marketing goal is not to alienate our existing customers and always try to make new friends."

As the decade wore on, though, it looked like Maker's Mark might miss out on a lot of potential friendships. The distillery had long ceased to resemble what would come to be called, for better or worse, craft distilling, in both its ownership and its production levels. It had undergone two additional ownership changes since the Samuels family sold it in 1981 to Hiram Walker & Sons out of Canada. The latest trade was in mid-2005, when Fortune Brands, a conglomerate based in the Chicago area, bought Maker's Mark and a slew of other alcoholic beverage brands. Fortune also owned Jim Beam and companies in fields as varied as hardware, home security, and golf. The Samuels family, Bill Jr. in particular, retained effective day-to-day control, but the corporate oversight was unmistakable: Dave Pickerell might make the magic happen over and over in little Loretto, but major decisions had to be run up the chain to Chicagoland. And, however modest Maker's Mark's production might be compared with larger producers such as Jim Beam and Johnnie Walker, its hundreds of thousands of cases annually, and counting, dwarfed the output of even larger small-batch operations such as the vodkas Tito's and Hangar 1.

It was precisely that sector, though, that was emerging as the fastest-growing in the American spirits market, particularly when it came to bourbon. These consumers most definitely did not prefer bigger, better-known brands. If they could not have small-batch spirits from independently owned distilleries, then they at least wanted pricier brands produced in limited quantities. From 2002 to 2006, the sales share of premium and superpremium bourbon increased roughly 7 percent and 12 percent, respectively, while demand for other brands dropped nearly 4 percent. These premium and superpremium bourbons included single-barrel selections from bigger producers, as well as the newly arrived small-batch bourbons. Maker's Mark had made the same bourbon the same way in the same place under the same family's tutelage for half a century, using ingredients from the same area farmers—yet many of these new consumers considered it run-of-the-mill, even hegemonic, a brand one could find just about anywhere. It was nothing like the bourbons from smaller-batch producers, never mind that it could be considered the original small-batch bourbon of postwar America.

To compete, then, Samuels executed that most radical of marketing approaches: He and the distillery did nothing. Or almost nothing. In mid-2010 they introduced a stronger, sweeter, pricier take on the original bourbon called Maker's 46, after the number of recipes that master distiller Kevin Smith tried before hitting on what he and Samuels felt was the right one. (Smith in 2008 succeeded Pickerell, who became the leading consultant for small-batch start-ups.) The distillery would produce only twenty-five thousand cases of the new arrival—a clear if very belated nod to the single-barrel releases that competitors had been producing since the mid-1980s. That output was "a drop in the bucket" compared with the distillery's signature bourbon, for which Maker's Mark continued to gradually ramp up production, using the same ingredients and the same techniques as ever before. Samuels himself took often to the road in the 2000s, recounting before any reporter who would listen and before trade-group audiences the genesis of Maker's Mark back in the 1950s and the distillery's strict adherence to not growing too fast nor changing its approach to suit a thirstier market. He continued throughout the decade to dispatch brand ambassadors and to advertise in print media and on billboards. Samuels was often charmingly folksy in person, a kind of archetypal, aw-shucks Kentuckian, his discourses on the family firm carefully avoiding the distillery's corporate parentage as well as the wider distributive reach of Maker's Mark compared with the typical smaller arrival. In many ways, Samuels simply continued the marketing approach he had started in the mid-1970s with his father's blessing, one that emphasized a focus on small-batch distillation using traditional methods and equipment as well as ingredients sourced close to home—micro vs. macro, in other words, craft before it was craft, small-batch before it was cool.

This surging sector, it seemed, had merely caught up to the approach Samuels used to make his father's wheated creation a world-renowned representative of that most American of spirits. It was a kind of transferable mythology, wrapped in the twin ideas of small equaling authentic and indifference to the larger market signaling integrity. Emphasizing both continuously, rather than adopting some snazzy new marketing approach every so often, ended up working for Maker's Mark—annual sales growth continued into the next decade, the bourbon riding a rising bibulousness in America. Samuels had done it again. Thing was, it was not all an act for Maker's Mark. The distillery could actually draw from a half-century-deep well, and critics considered its signature bourbon one of the best ever crafted.

What happened if a distillery simply embraced the mythology, without a track record?

THE MOVEMENT'S DEFINING MOMENT

2010–2015 | Nationwide

Ralph Erenzo was sitting back one sunny summer day in 2009 in his Tuthilltown Spirits office in rural Gardiner, New York, his bare feet propped up, dangling out the window in the warmth of the Hudson Valley.

The phone rang.

It was a representative from William Grant & Sons, the largest family-owned spirits company in the United Kingdom and the world's sixth-largest producer of whiskey in particular, with brands such as Glenfiddich single malt and Tullamore D.E.W. Irish whiskey, never mind Stolichnaya vodka and Hendrick's gin. We've been following your progress, the representative said, and we'd like to talk about a possible deal.

Erenzo sat up. "This is that phone call," he thought. "This is it. Somebody noticed us!"

What did they notice, exactly? Tuthilltown's four-year-old Hudson whiskey brand, including a couple of bourbons, a single malt, a corn whiskey, and a rye, had made inroads throughout the United States and in Europe, beginning with those first Paris bottles that Erenzo himself cannily placed to spur interest in his native land. Otherwise, though, it was highly unlikely that William Grant & Sons noticed the distillery itself, still a primitive affair in Erenzo's own opinion, one with no pavement for the parking lot, nor siding on the walls, and open plastic fermenters for distilling.

Yet the finished products were the finished products. They were good enough to have kept, as Erenzo's caller put it, "popping up" on William Grant & Sons' radar. Executives from the family-owned firm were soon in Gardiner, offering a wholesale purchase of the distillery. Erenzo and partner Brian Lee turned it down. They had sunk so much money, time, and effort into Tuthilltown that they were in no mood to sell it. Plus, as they told their visitors, William Grant & Sons could probably build a better distillery for less money than Erenzo and Lee were willing to sell it for. The suitors quickly agreed after a look around, and the two sides settled on a counteroffer: the UK company would buy for an undisclosed sum Tuthilltown's Hudson whiskey brand, including all marketing and distribution rights, while the Gardiner distillery would continue to produce them. Within five years of the June 2010 deal, Hudson whiskeys were being sold in a dozen countries, including the United States, and were so relatively ubiquitous compared with other craft spirits brands that the business news channel CNBC nicknamed Tuthilltown "the Samuel Adams of whiskey." The network saw little need to explain the link, either.

The Hudson deal rippled through the small-batch spirits industry, as did one around the same time for Ansley Coale and Jörg Rupf's Hangar 1 vodka brand. In April 2010 Proximo Spirits, a firm based in Mexico that would become best known for its Jose Cuervo tequila, acquired the Hangar 1 brand. The deal included a caveat that Craft Distillers, the company Coale and Rupf set up to manage the vodka, would continue to produce it for four years at St. George's Alameda location. Like with the Tuthilltown-Grant deal, the terms were not disclosed, and Proximo's entry led to even greater reach for the already successful Hangar 1. In May 2011 the firm would launch a national promotional tour for Hangar 1, complete with a 120-foot-long blimp and cocktail contests. Such effects of such brand deals were not lost on other smaller distilleries. Here were macroproducers taking notice of much smaller com-petitors—and then taking their signature brands in mutually beneficial deals. (Indeed, the publicity alone surrounding the 2010 deals served up oodles of free marketing for Tuthilltown and St. George in general.) More than anything, the brand buys seemed to signal that the sector had arrived as a going business concern. It was just in time to capitalize on that growing consumer interest spurred in large part by *Mad Men* and the resurgent interest in cocktails.

For Tom Mooney, the realization of small-batch spirits' business potential also involved Samuel Adams. Like Jim Koch, principal founder of the Boston Beer Company behind the beer brand, Mooney was a Harvard Business School graduate, and he had worked since the early 1990s in various marketing and branding positions with major firms such as Procter & Gamble, Kellogg's, and Booz Allen. In 2009 Mooney was managing the marketing and international expansion of Fiji Water, a brand he first started working with in 2005, through consultancy work with Fiji's corporate parent, the Wonderful Company out of Los Angeles. It was through Fiji that Mooney became thoroughly acquainted with the beverages industry, and he liked what he found. The work was chal-lenging, and the people were interesting. Mooney decided he wanted to strike out on his own in the industry. Mooney partnered with an old business-school friend named Arturo Litwak. In the late 1990s Litwak had cofounded Milagro, a distillery in Jalisco, Mexico, that was part of the vanguard of small-batch producers in that nation trying to turn around the American perception of tequila as simply a cheaply made way to get quickly drunk. The pair was not sure which beverage, or even which beverage sector, they might launch a business within. Enter a late 2009 phone call with Jim Koch.

Mooney had e-mailed the Boston Beer chairman, explaining that the two had mutual friends, and asked if he might seek Koch's advice. Koch told him to call, and when Mooney did, Koch matter-of-factly brought up small-batch spirits (which he, like most people, called craft spirits). To Koch, a keen observer who had noticed craft beer's potential long before most people, this relatively young spirits sector seemed to teem with promise. A lot more people were going to jump into it, Koch told Mooney, and the sector would certainly grow. (Koch himself had no plans to jump in.) Those who knew what they were doing could really do well, he said. Koch did have one caveat: Qualified as Mooney and Litwak might be to launch their own spirits concern, they might seek out one already in existence, one that perhaps needed their management expertise or the capital they could raise. If they could find such a distillery, then Mooney and Litwak would be two to three years ahead of others entering the sector,

Koch said. He then signed off with a jocular request: "I'm sure you guys would do great in beer, but I don't need more competition."

Koch's advice was the most specific that Mooney and Litwak had yet received. And it was all the more remarkable because of the obviousness. There were relatively few small-batch distilleries in the United States in 2009. Finding one that perhaps did need that capital infusion or that management expertise did not seem all that far-fetched. At least they could run through possible candidates quickly and then move on to another idea if none bit. That is exactly what Mooney did in the fall of 2009, traveling from his Los Angeles base to Portland, Oregon, for the Great American Distillers Festival. Jack Joyce—a former attorney and executive at athletic apparel giant Nike, who cofounded the Rogue Brewing Company in Oregon in 1987 and, in the mid-2000s, its distilling wing—launched the festival in 2005. The Portland gathering resembled the early Great American Beer Festivals in its grandiosity; whatever its introductory adjectives, the two-day affair was far from national in scope, attracting a couple dozen distilleries, most from the surrounding Northwest. The crowds were mostly local, with patrons paying between ten and twenty dollars a person, depending on how much an attendee wanted to sample. Still, a gathering was a gathering. Mooney went from table to table, pitching himself as a partner. He struck gold with House Spirits, a small-batch distillery launched in 2004 in Corvallis, in Oregon's hop-growing region. It relocated to Portland the following year as part of an expansion and, also in 2005, launched Aviation gin, a well-received interpretation of the juniper-dominated spirit. Aviation soon became available throughout Oregon and Washington State, but little beyond. Christian Krogstad, the cofounder running House Spirits, brought on Mooney and Litwak as partners to grow the business side while he focused on production. The 2011 move proved remunerative for both sides as distribution expanded with a new wholesaler and with new investors, including three-time Super Bowl MVP Joe Montana, who also became a director of the company. Aviation gin in particular found itself spreading across more of the United States.

And Mooney found himself immersed in a movement that he had known little to nothing about only a few short years earlier. That immersion led him to Bill Owens's American Distilling Institute, the privately owned trade group representing the interests of small-batch producers. That representation, Mooney and other members realized, could only go so far, given the private nature of the ADI. Legally, the group simply could not lobby government officials and agencies, including for such pined-for changes as a reduction in the federal excise tax for spirits. That excise tax, high as it was compared with ones for beer and wine, hoovered up huge amounts of revenue—more than two dollars per 750-milliliter bottle in some cases, a deceptively tiny amount that could quickly add up to a potentially fatal deficit for any fledgling start-up. Distribution and licensing challenges varied from state to state, too, sometimes from city to town to city within different states. Mooney and other distillery principals felt that the ADI needed to be not only promotional but also overtly political to confront these challenges. And being overtly political meant being a nonprofit, not a for-profit organization such as the ADI. These distillers started meeting, including at ADI conferences; their discussions led to an offer: Would Bill Owens consider selling them the ADI?

He would not. Owens, who had done so much to move craft beer into the mainstream and who was beginning to do so for small-batch spirits, declined to seriously entertain an offer from a group of about fifteen distilleries. On April 9, 2013, four days after the close of the annual ADI conference, held that year in Denver, these distillers announced from the same city the formation of a nonprofit that they called the American Craft Distillers Association. Rory Donovan, the owner of the eight-year-old Peach Street Distillers in western Colorado, would be its first president, and Penn Jensen, who had just left a similar post at the ADI, would serve as its day-to-day executive director. The new organization would focus on lobbying all levels of government, especially Washington, on matters related to smaller distilleries, particularly the federal excise tax, which the group called for cutting substantially. The decision to focus on lobbying was an easy one for the American Craft Distillers Association. The other matter that dominated a lot of early discussion and time was defining exactly who and what the group represented. What was a craft spirit or a craft distiller? And were those even the correct terms to use? It was the single biggest issue facing smaller distilleries, one that ACDA members—and ADI members, for that matter—realized had to be confronted head-on before an increasingly fuzzy marketplace decided for them. The marketplace was well on its way to doing so by the ADI-ACDA split in the spring of 2013.

During the previous winter, the critic Wayne Curtis visited a new distillery in the ground floor of an aged industrial building in a grittier part of an unnamed American city—"exactly which city doesn't matter," Curtis wrote in the *Atlantic* magazine, "because I guarantee there's a building just like it near you." What he encountered on that ground floor encapsulated what was shaping up to be the American small-batch spirits movement's most vexing challenge and insidious threat. Curtis wrote:

> The distillery's operators, a trio of agreeable, Oliver Twist-ish young men, had just launched a new vodka, which I'd seen in local bars and

on liquor-store shelves. But when I looked around, I didn't see any of the equipment one might expect to find at a vodka distillery—no gleaming column still, or storage bins for grain or potatoes, or even tanks for fermentation.

It was a clear sign to Curtis of what had become an inescapable trend: The operation was pretty much a small-batch distillery in name only. It had adopted a common and quick business model, as Curtis explained: buy alcohol in bulk from an industrial supplier, sometimes by the railcar-load; run that alcohol through a charcoal filter or some other apparatus to rid it of impurities; bottle it; and then, and this was key, slap on a label bespeaking a kind of artisanal origin. Only a careful consumer might think beyond the explanation BOTTLED IN X LOCATION to consider where the spirit was actually *distilled*. As stealthy as this practice appeared, it was all perfectly aboveboard legally. State and local authorities invariably only cared about the end result: where and how the spirit was sold. Federal regulators required certain font sizes on the forty-two-word warning that alcoholic beverages had had to carry since a 1988 legislative change in the wake of Len Bias's death. Washington also required the spirit type be clearly delineated and the alcoholic content percentage as well. Beyond that, "you can tell whatever story you want," Nicole Austin, a distiller and blender at Kings County Distillery in Brooklyn, New York, told Curtis.

Kings County, the first small-batch whiskey distillery since Prohibition in America's largest city, dated from 2009 and occupied an approximately 330-square-foot second-floor warehouse space near the Brooklyn waterfront. It epitomized the brick-and-mortar start-ups of the era, the busiest of the American small-batch spirits movement so far. It had real equipment, including a pot still, and real distillation talent producing small batches of spirits—initially, in this case, white whiskey from organic upstate New York corn so as to qualify for that state's business-friendly farm distillery act. To give a sense of the growth rate of American small-batch spirits at the turn of the new century's first decade, Kings County was one of several such distilleries starting up in just the borough of Brooklyn beginning in 2009. A competitor included the New York Distilling Company, cofounded by a founder of the Brooklyn Brewery, started in the same borough twenty-five years before.

These types of technically astute, truly small-batch, locavore-oriented distilleries stood in stark contrast to the operations getting most of the ink. Curtis's *Atlantic* piece typified the majority of coverage of small-batch distilleries and spirits, at least in the consumer media. Trade publications such as the recently rechristened *Whisky Advocate* might still drill down into the nitty-gritty of the business, its equipment and techniques, its individual personalities and products. But the wider media could not help but dwell on what this supposedly new distilling sector was or was not, each dispatch from the movement striving to define it for readers, listeners, and viewers, each leaning on the adjective *craft* like a crutch. "Although there's no across-the-board production cap," *Time* magazine reported during this period, "craft distilleries are usually considered to be those that make under 100,000 gallons of spirits in a year. Outfits like Bacardí, by comparison, can produce more than 100,000 gallons in a day."

The American Distilling Institute and the then–American Craft Distillers Association both initially adopted this one hundred-thousand-gallon cap. So did the Distilled Spirits Council of the United States, a trade group for larger distilleries that traced its origins to the early 1970s and that in February 2010 announced a membership program for tinier concerns, the advisory board chaired by Fritz Maytag of Anchor Distilling. Beyond an uppermost production limit, none of the groups or the critics could agree on other parameters, which only sowed doubt as to what, exactly, "craft" distilling was—and whether, really, there was such a thing as craft distilling in the first place, beyond size. Owens's ADI, for instance, stressed that a distillery had to "physically" produce its spirit on-site. The ACDA, in its first year at least, did not even go that far, just asking that members be transparent in their marketing and packaging. In 2014 the group would spell out membership prerequisites requiring that members not distill more than 750,000 taxable gallons annually and own at least 75 percent of the distillery. Given the private ownership structure of nearly every small-batch distillery, the key theme careening through this and other definition attempts was self-policing. "Every producer wants the definition of craft to describe what they do," said a distiller at an early ACDA convention. This self-policing, in turn, left the door wide open for the sorts of stealth operations like the unnamed one in Curtis's *Atlantic* piece. It was virtually impossible to tell how many such distilleries had sprung up in the last several years, unless one ripped a page from Curtis's book and visited a new arrival or did similar digging one brand at a time. The critic Chuck Cowdery called them "Potemkin distilleries," after the fake villages of contented Russians that authorities threw up in the eighteenth century to impress visiting empress Catherine the Great. The distilleries might boast "shiny new copper stills" to wow tourists, as Cowdery put it, but in the end it was just factory-made booze eased into carefully labeled bottles. Of course, more legitimate small-batch distilleries could turn this chicanery to their advantage. Koval, Chicago's oldest distillery, which actually did distill in house, prominently displayed Distilled in Chicago or Handmade in Chicago on its front labels. Again, though, it was a matter of consumers knowing what to look for and why looking for it even mattered.

It is important to note, too, that none of these definitions attempted to define a craft *spirit* beyond where it was made. So long as it came from a distillery defined as craft, the spirit itself apparently qualified as craft. This stood in sharp contrast to generally accepted definitions for craft beer and various fine wines. Ingredients mattered immensely in those. Wines had to be made with certain percentages of grapes to call themselves Merlot, Cabernet Sauvignon, etc. And craft brewers rarely used additions such as rice and corn, never mind artificial preservatives. Individual states, such as New Jersey, New York, Illinois, and Washington, might bestow a special craft distillery license on operations that made their spirits from a sizable amount of locally produced products. Beyond these licenses, though, ingredients appeared to play little to no role in defining craft spirits. Size and ownership were apparently what mattered.

Further muddying the definitional firewater was a gulf between the "Potemkin distilleries" and the truer start-ups. This gulf included blenders and blending concerns that bought spirits from third parties and then crafted and aged them to produce distinct offerings, as well as distillers who contracted space, equipment, and sometimes labor to make their products, much in the same way that contract brewers did. Nearly all of these operations were small compared with the larger small-batch distilleries, and these efforts involved a level of technical skill that elevated their executioners to "authentic artisans" in the words of Chuck Cowdery. Bottle fillers these operations were not. Nor did they simply filter someone else's finished product before bottling it behind a bucolic label. Perhaps the best example of these sorts of operations, or at least the most famous, was Shoreham, Vermont–based WhistlePig. Raj Bhakta, a serial entrepreneur who moved to a five-hundred-acre farm in the Northeast Kingdom after an unsuccessful run for Congress in Pennsylvania and a stint on the Donald Trump NBC vehicle *The Apprentice*, launched the WhistlePig brand with a whiskey made entirely from rye in 2010. Bhakta hired Dave Pickerell as a consultant on the spirit, which was made from whiskey distilled at a Canadian distillery, WhistlePig itself being too young to have already produced a rye. The whiskey soon won plaudits—Paul Pacult gave it five stars in his *Spirit Journal*, and *Wine Enthusiast* magazine scored it a ninety-six out of one hundred. In July 2012 a character on the hit AMC series *Breaking Bad* poured glasses of WhistlePig, the label clearly visible on camera. Eventually, the true Canadian roots of the rye seeped into media coverage. "Look, I'm a salesman with a bit of P.T. Barnum in me, and I like it," Bhakta told a critic in 2014, seeming to suggest he never intended to deceive. The revelations in the end did little to hurt the WhistlePig brand. The industry held Pickerell in immensely high regard, and his work on the Canadian distillate, including finding it in the first place, had made the finished product so laudable. Besides, construction was underway on a real working distillery in Stoneham by the end of 2015, Bhakta, dressed "like an English country gentleman," presiding over the whole affair. To sweep more exacting distilling companies into the craft fold, the ACDA, now led by Tom Mooney as its president, enacted a brief, straightforward code of ethics, albeit one that again relied upon self-policing more than anything:

> We operate in an honest, transparent and non-deceptive fashion. We inform consumers truthfully and accurately about the sources and methods used to make our spirits through our labels, materials and communications. We expect fair dealing and respect amongst members. We obey all federal, state, and local laws.

In other words, the trade group expected its members to tell the truth about what they did, how they did it, and where they did it. Rebottling was fine, so long as packaging made clear that the finished spirit was distilled somewhere else. Blending was fine, too, so long as it was clear the distillate originated at a certain distillery. Transparency was the order of the day, meant to enlarge the craft tent to include all manner of producers. In 2016 the trade group would also ask that its members "market themselves as craft" and not be "openly controlled by a larger supplier," in addition to the earlier 750,000-gallon limit and 75 percent independent owernship threshold. Moreover, in a clear sign of the self-policing necessary for the definition, especially the ownership threshold, the organization announced it had "set up a process that asks industry members to notify [it] of all ownership or strategy changes away from craft so the changes can be reflected accordingly in the database." All of this suggested that who got to call themselves craft depended a lot on who saw themselves as craft—unless it was blindingly obvious they were not small, independent, and more traditional. The ACDA would even change its name to in part reflect this larger welcome mat. The American Craft Distillers Association became in May 2014 the American Craft Spirits Association, though controversy swarmed around even this simple gesture.

In June 2013 Craft Distillers Inc., the company that Germain-Robin and St. George formed a decade before when the distilleries launched their Hangar 1 vodka, sent a cease-and-desist letter to the ACDA, claiming that the *C* and the *D* (for *Craft Distillers*) would confuse consumers and hurt the earlier entity's bottom line. Besides, Craft Distillers Inc. had trademarked the term in 2003, an eternity ago in the movement. "The reason we did it," Ansley Coale of Germain-Robin explained to a journalist, "was because we knew craft distillers or some phrase like it was likely to become meaningful, in the sense that if somebody used it they meant what they said." Coale was right, and the trademark was an attempt to stop macroproducers from co-opting the term, even for less voluminous production runs. He did not seem to have foreseen in 2003 the rise of faux small-batch distilleries or the definitional controversy that engulfed the movement. The trademark was instead intended as a bulwark against "the big guys," as Coale put it, a way to ensure that "Diageo or Pernod Ricard can't put 'craft distillers' on a bottle." Yet, Craft Distillers would end up challenging at least a half dozen small-batch entities in the subsequent decade-plus, as well as the ACDA, which initially ignored Craft Distillers' cease-and-desist letter. The company sued the trade group in federal court in California. In January 2014 the ACDA filed a counterclaim, saying that the term *craft distillers* was a "generic phrase that generally refers to a distiller who uses quality ingredients and artisanal techniques to create distilled spirits." Not being able to use it, the group said, would hurt its ability to run its own affairs. Eventually, though, it appeared the ACDA relented and changed its name later that year. The reconstituted American Craft Spirits Association claimed that the change was due to the widening definition, not to the lawsuit.

As for that widened definition and the ethics statement, and the ADI's own definition, never mind the media reports of the *lack* of an agreed-upon definition—it all did little to neutralize the major threat confronting the American small-batch spirits movement by 2015: namely, the perhaps dozens, if not hundreds, of stealth operations, and the controversy around them, that kept getting most of the attention. Worse, the controversy came amid that unmistakable pop cultural and marketplace breakthrough, right when small-batch distilleries could be racking up the most repeat customers. First-time customers, instead, might be turned off on spending forty or fifty dollars for a bottle of something that could be just macrospirits in craft spirits clothing. It was difficult enough to draw new customers in the spirits industry in general. Nielsen, the consumer behavior tracking firm best known for its television ratings, also tracked what it described as the inertia levels of products—how difficult it was to get a consumer to switch from one brand to another. Spirits was the top inertia category, according to Nielsen, the hardest product within which to get consumers to switch. Customers instead overwhelmingly purchased the same brand that they entered a store or a bar to buy. Moreover, research showed that many younger consumers, the children and grandchildren of baby boomers, limited their spirits' consumption to a handful of types. One in five members of the so-called generation X, those Americans born from the mid-1960s through the late 1970s, drank only either rum or vodka when they drank spirits at all. Turnover in brand loyalty, then, was positively herculean in the best of conditions. Nagging doubt did not help.

It was a challenge unique to the movement, at least when it came to alcoholic beverages in the United States. Controversy over contract brewing had riven the craft beer movement in the 1980s and 1990s. "Those people are just top-notch salesmen," Bill Owens himself had sniffed back then when talking about the likes of Jim Koch and his Samuel Adams brand. But at least Koch and other early contract brewers had their beer produced from raw ingredients to their own specifications, even if they used someone else's brewery and brewery labor. The stealth distilleries simply trucked or rolled in bulk amounts of whatever spirit they intended to market, particularly whiskey and vodka, flavored it if need be, and bottled it, any further filtration doing little to alter the ultimate taste. In this, small-batch spirits were similar not to craft beer, which is what journalists covering the lack of a definition seemed to mention without fail, but to fine wine, those offerings at various price points made from higher-end grape varietals such as Cabernet Sauvignon and Chardonnay. By 2010 none of America's thirty bestselling wine brands grew, produced, or bottled their own wines. Instead, the large-scale conglomerates behind them crafted the wines from bulk grape or grape-juice orders in factorylike wineries far removed from the rustic image many Americans had of winemaking. The marketing was key. Labels in particular, resplendent as they often were with heraldry or with scenes of sweeping vineyards, moved the wines, as did price points that put these thirty brands within the reach of most consumers. "Those bottles may look beautiful, implying a bucolic wine-y setting," wrote one industry consultant in 2009, "but the cold, hard fact is that the juice within is just a trademark coupled with a savvy marketing plan."

Again, though, similar to contract craft brewers at least providing the proper hops and malted grains for their beers, at least the wine within these brands' bottles came from higher-end grape varieties such as Chardonnay and Cabernet Sauvignon. Government regulations had a lot to do with that, the same sort of regulations lacking in the spirits sector. The federal government had long required that a wine be composed of at least 75 percent of the grape variety on its label. A Chardonnay, in other words, had to come mostly from Chardonnay grapes (otherwise, it was labeled a blend or a generic term). Some states, most notably Oregon with its prized Pinot Noir, required an even higher percentage. No such thing with spirits, craft or otherwise. This further freed the stealthy craft spirits to foist their wares on a public just becoming acquainted with the notion. More experienced consumers might be able to tell the difference between a brandy or a whiskey carefully made from choice ingredients and with a pot still and the harsher, "moonshiney" wares that came from brands that were craft in name only. Besides, thanks in large part to the *Mad Men* effect, a lot of these new spirits were being mixed into cocktails and their taste therefore diluted.

Some of these stealth distilleries argued that their purchase and turnaround of bulk alcohol allowed them to fund their salad days by cutting start-up costs. Rather than having to wait years for a bourbon to age before it hits the market, for example, a new craft distillery could buy one already ready from a much larger producer, including companies that might also make other grain-based foodstuffs such as cereals and breads, and release it under its own label following relatively minor tweaks such as filtration and blending. Those sales could in turn fund the same distillery's in-house distillation of other spirits. Or so the theory went. In practice, many of these distilleries merely kept cranking out the original spirits with which consumers associated them, perpetuating the threat to the larger movement. "All that they do is hire salespeople, make up a BS story, and, boom, they look like a distillery," groused one master distiller at a small-batch operation in Denver. Moreover, this and the even stealthier approach of simply bottling bulk alcohol prolonged the dearth of true distilling talent, including those in that most vaunted of ranks, the master distillers. Unlike with winemaking and brewing, there were relatively few academic options for learning how to distill—certainly no four-year college degrees like the ones that the University of California, Davis, offered for winemaking and brewing. (Oregon State and Appalachian State in North Carolina also offered brewing degrees.) Much of the training came through special community college courses or the odd symposium that a trade group such as the American Distilling Institute offered. More often than not, it came on the job. The rapid rise in the number of small-batch distilleries in the last decade had drained the already shallow talent pool. Trained distillers in their twenties found themselves offered sixfigure salaries, even for part-time work. As with the earliest days of American small-batch spirits, it was often all hands on deck at newer start-ups, with principal founders working solo until operations were up and running. If the training was there—or if a consultant such as ex–Maker's Mark master distiller Dave Pickerell was there—the results could be sublime from the first batch. Otherwise, and at the stealth distilleries especially, the lack of training often translated into that "moonshiney" hooch that tarnished the wider movement. Even something that might seem as straightforward as blending, particularly for whiskeys, required training, for blending was practically a science demanding attention to taste, aroma, mouthfeel, and other tactile measures, never mind the chemistry of spirits themselves, including alcohol content. Blend wrongly and a release might taste off to aficionados or like so much overpriced firewater to newcomers. "There's no reason to think anyone knows how to make whiskey or can learn how to make whiskey based on buying whiskey," Chuck Cowdery told yet another journalist parachuting into the movement's biggest controversy. The lack of expertise did especially show in grain-based spirits such as whiskey. "The stuff made by the guy who just started last year won't be quite as good as the stuff that's been made for over a century by the people who invented it," according to one bar owner in the spirits (and beer) mecca of Portland, Oregon.

Further muddying things was the bestowment like candy at Halloween of the title "master distiller." Once meant to connote someone who had trained on the job for years, if not decades, master distiller now became mere marketing fodder in some cases. The practice stretched back to at least 1984, when the George T. Stagg distillery in Frankfort, Kentucky, named its plant manager, Elmer T. Lee, master distiller during the rollout of Blanton's Single Barrel Bourbon. Lee at least had decades in the industry and played the pivotal role in selecting the pioneering Blanton's. The newer crop of master distillers taken all together could not claim as many years in the industry as someone such as Lee alone. "Hell, I could call myself a master distiller right now," the critic Fred Minnick wrote in frustration in September 2014. "Buy six cases of bourbon and blend them for the 'Old Minnick, America's Smoothest Fake Bourbon,' and nobody would stop me." Again, the frenetic twenty-first-century growth of American small-batch spirits fueled this fast and loose wordplay. Who had time to spend years, as Hubert Germain-Robin did in France and California or Dave Pickerell did in Kentucky and all over the world, to become a master distiller? Especially when the title mattered little beyond the gravitas it might impart for a new operation seeking media salivation? Dave Scheurich was a master distiller best known for resurrecting the Woodford Reserve bourbon brand for spirits giant Brown Forman, whose lineup included Jack Daniel's. Scheurich, not entirely tongue in cheek, described the qualifications of a master distiller in 2014 for a publishing offshoot of Bill Owens's ADI:

This individual should have a working knowledge of the following: microbiology, chemistry, mechanical aptitude, quality assurance, quality control analysis, lab testing, yeast propagation, environmental control, sanitation, budgeting, accounting, finance, human resources, personnel, legal, sensory judgment and analysis, agricultural, planning, forecasting, procurement, maintenance, power generation, boiler and waste management, security, contracting, leadership, fire protection, safety, OSHA, local, state and federal government regulations, emergency procedures and others.

This breadth of training on a wide scale was not going to happen. There was no time.

THE CHALLENGE AHEAD

2014–2015 | Travis County, Texas

It was a scorching hot June day in 2014, and yet another reporter had trekked to Travis County, Texas, to check out Tito Beveridge's eponymous vodka operation. The distillery was in its seventeenth year and producing a phenomenal amount of Tito's Handmade Vodka: 850,000 cases annually, a 46 percent climb from just three years before and worlds away from Beveridge's first output in 1997, using the sixteen-gallon pot still rigged from old soda kegs and a turkey fryer. Beveridge had housed that still in a shack. Those days had long passed into legend. His company now covered twenty-six acres, the shack and its contents more museum piece than production hub. The real hub could bottle five hundred cases of vodka an hour via ten column stills, though Tito's also now used distillate made elsewhere and shipped in.

To illustrate to the reporter the challenges he had overcome to get to this voluminous point, Beveridge grabbed a frayed binder brimming with federal regulations. He began to tell the story of how he convinced officials twenty years ago to approve his distilling license, Texas's first since Prohibition. Just then, a scorpion jumped from the binding and plunged its stinger in Beveridge's palm.

"Shit." He interrupted the interview to find Benadryl and baking soda.

Beveridge's stonking success had stung in a less literal way. Several plaintiffs in California, Florida, Illinois, and New Jersey sued Beveridge's Fifth Generation distillery, beginning in September 2014, alleging that its "handmade" claim was erroneous and had led them to spend money on what was essentially a vodka more like Smirnoff than any small-batch distiller's product.

The distillery shot back that it had been making the "handmade" claim for nearly two decades without such scrutiny and that, besides, "no consumer would reasonably conclude that a distilled spirit can be made without the use of machines." The federal judge hearing the lawsuits eventually tossed most of their claims, citing federal regulators' approval of Tito's "handmade" assertion. The judge did note, however, that Tito's assertion of being "crafted in an old fashioned pot still," as its label clearly said, might be construed as misleading. As 2015 drew to a close, however, the label remained the same as ever, and Beveridge's Fifth Generation was petitioning for the claim to be tossed along with the others. Maker's Mark had faced similar legal scrutiny over its "handmade" claim and with similar results—the same federal judge, in fact, rejected plaintiffs' assertions of false advertising in May 2015. Another judge tossed another case a couple of months later.

A lawsuit against Templeton Rye Spirits, a ten-year-old distillery in Templeton, Iowa, was much more successful and, according to one critic, put "the fear of God" into those distilleries that were not being fully upfront with consumers regarding their products' origins. A Chicago resident who had since 2008 bought more than a dozen bottles of Templeton's signature rye whiskey, at around thirty-five dollars a pop, sued the company after reading in a 2010 *Chicago Tribune* article that the spirit was actually made in relatively small quantities at a plant in Indiana and then shipped to the Iowa facility for bottling. What's more, the lawsuit pulled back the curtain on a bit of the alchemy that such stealthy distilleries used. Templeton's president revealed that his company blended the distillate it received from the Indiana producer with an "alcohol flavoring formulation" that an engineering firm in Louisville, Kentucky, made. That artificial flavor helped Templeton achieve the taste of what its label described as a "Prohibition-era recipe." Post-flavoring, Templeton simply cut the rye with water to achieve a suitable proof and then bottled it. Under a settlement announced in early July 2015, Templeton agreed to remove from its labels the Prohibition-era recipe reference as well as the words SMALL BATCH—and to add DISTILLED IN INDIANA. Customers who had bought Templeton since 2006 were also due refunds of up to six dollars a bottle.

These lawsuits dragged on for much of 2014 and 2015, plenty of time for wide media coverage to sow more doubt about what defined and constituted a craft spirit or craft distillery in America. Most of the coverage seemed to suggest that the labels could not be trusted, nor the distilleries themselves, whether relatively old ones such as Maker's Mark or newer ones such as Templeton. The lawsuits merged with the copious coverage of the stealth distilleries and their products—and the rancor among smaller producers because of them. It looked as the 2010s moved along that the American small-batch spirits movement had arrived not quite ready for the spotlight: no parameters for what its spirits or its distilleries were; no single institutional voice speaking for the industry; and, aside from a relative handful of seasoned tasters and critics, no real way to tell the macro from the micro until that moment of tasting truth.

Yet arrive American small-batch spirits did around 2010. While sales of small-batch spirits still accounted for a negligible slice of the overall American spirits marketplace—all estimates put it at below 10 percent, if not below 5 percent—the presence of small-batch distillation through new entrants and new products was growing at an "exponential pace." The number of small-batch distilleries nationwide, including stealth ones, topped 400 by 2011 and then 470 by the following year, according to federal statistics, which defined what it called a craft distillery as an operation paying taxes on fewer than one hundred thousand cases annually (a further clouding of the definitional waters). In 2013 the number tipped above five hundred—more than double the number five years before, never mind leaps and bounds ahead of the total at the start of the century or in 1990. Several states, including California, Colorado, Texas, and New York, could number their craft distilleries in the double digits. Even the Great Recession that struck the national economy in 2008 could not derail the growth, although it did bite into the sales of premium and superpremium spirits. The people likeliest to drop forty dollars or more on a bottle of vodka or whiskey, including financial workers in cities such as New York and San Francisco, were far less likely to for a while. Still, thanks in no small part to historically low interest rates for financing as a result of the recession, the founding of new small-batch distilleries continued largely unabated. One estimate placed the number of distilleries, small-batch or otherwise, at an all-time post-Prohibition high of more than a thousand by 2011, and then more than fifteen hundred two years later. The sky seemed the limit in terms of numerical growth.

The comparisons to fine wine's numerical growth in the 1960s and 1970s, and to craft beer's in particular in the 1980s and 1990s, flew fast and furious. But fine wine sales-wise had long overtaken its generic brethren, with higher-end grape varietals such as Chardonnay and Cabernet Sauvignon accounting for the majority of retail and restaurant sales since at least the early 1970s. And craft beer sales had become such a threat in the 2010s to macrobrewers such as the recently formed Anheuser-Busch InBev that those larger concerns went on a veritable shopping spree, snapping up craft competitors coast-to-coast—AB InBev alone would buy eight craft breweries by the spring of 2016—as well as continuing to co-opt their marketing approaches through phantom crafts. Small-batch spirits, on the other hand, were no threat to the likes of

Diageo, Pernod Ricard, Suntory, and Brown Forman—the world's four biggest distillation firms at the start of 2014, with brands such as Maker's Mark, Jim Beam, Jack Daniel's, and Smirnoff in their portfolios. It was not demand, then, nor the promise of relative riches driving so much media coverage and so many novice small-batch distillers in the 2010s. It was something else at this point. The land rush was on because of the promise the movement held.

The entire small-batch spirits movement in the United States could be traced back to Bill Samuels Sr.'s decision in the early 1950s to make a smoother-tasting bourbon, one that would not "blow your ears off," in his wife's memorable phrasing. For a long while after that, there was nothing in terms of what would come to be called craft or small-batch spirits or micro-distilling—the movement rattled in its barrel, awaiting events. The first truly seismic event was the spectacular bourbon collapse beginning at the end of the 1960s, followed by the rise of clear spirits, vodka in particular, and fine wine. The second event was a key federal legal change at the end of the 1970s that made it much cheaper to open a distillery. Seizing this opportunity were the first small-batch entrants after Maker's Mark, which by then was already beyond the realm it had done so much to create, ownership having passed from the Samuels family and production having spiked after that *Wall Street Journal* rhapsody. The likes of St. George, Germain-Robin, Charbay, and others remained outliers in the wider marketplace, isolated distribution-wise and little understood culturally. Craft beer in America was just toddling forth, really, soon to give consumers a context for understanding small-batch spirits. Along the way came phenomenally popular brands such as Absolut and Grey Goose, the sorts that finally had Americans on a wide scale ordering spirits by label rather than price point. The neo-Prohibitionist crackdown in the late 1980s, beginning after the drugs-related death of basketball star Len Bias, very nearly derailed the momentum that Absolut et al. gave spirits in the United States.

But newer curiosities such as single malt whiskeys from Scotland and single-barrel bourbons from Kentucky, areas that had not seen any major innovations in decades, carried things forward, particularly in bigger metropolitan areas. A wider foodie culture in the 1990s merged comfortably with a resurgence in cocktails, and as the new century dawned, several more small-batch distilleries had emerged to augment the earliest pioneers. They had a context to play in, too, in both these foodie and cocktail cultures, as well as within what craft beer had created: the idea of an alcoholic beverage made in small batches the traditional way that, while perhaps costing a little more, was well worth it. Altogether, these trends, events, and pioneers formed a

popular perception that seemed to be carrying the small-batch spirits movement into and through its echoing boom.

The critic Wayne Curtis attended that first American Craft Spirits Association convention in Denver (when the group called itself the American Craft
Distillers Association). He listened to several attendees complain sotto voce
about newer spirits released before they were "ready for prime time: the liquor
is too rough-edged or funky, pitiably less valuable than its $40-a-bottle price
tag promises." He also noticed that it did not seem to matter in the short
run. "Folks from Nielsen who attended the conference reported that Gen
Xers and Millennials ranked 'local' and 'authentic' higher as qualities they
valued in a spirit than did their Baby Boomer elders, who sought out some
obscure factor called 'taste.'" Simply put, according to another analyst of the
booming young movement, "small, or the image of small, sells; it connotes
authenticity, care, continuity."

American small-batch spirits were more popular than ever and full of
promise for the future—but that popularity was based more on perception
than anything. Nothing illustrated that better than the American small-batch
spirits market overseas. Here the biggest challenge did not seem to be choice,
as export companies had sprung up to fill the demand. It was certainly not
about availability, given the number of small-batch distilleries now. And
demand was a sure thing: "Where the in-crowds of Berlin and Hong Kong
might have previously asked for a Grey Goose vodka or a Macallan single-
malt Scotch," reported the *New York Times* in August 2014, "today more
drinkers are demanding a Balcones whiskey from Waco, Tex., or a Perry's
Tot gin from Williamsburg in Brooklyn." Instead, the biggest challenge in
foreign markets was the same as domestically: that dearth of definition, the
lack of clear lines yet for understanding just what decades of turning points
and epiphanies had spawned. Lance Winters at St. George, one of the pioneers
of American small-batch spirits, noted that even in the United States it might
still be difficult in the mid-2010s to get domestic wholesalers to understand
the products such distilleries wanted them to carry. Overseas, it was even
tougher. "Craft distillers are usually making something not like anything
else on the market," he said, "so someone needs to explain it." Solving that
biggest challenge would be the movement's biggest triumph.

Digestif

"DISTILLED IN INDIANA"

2015–2016 | Lawrenceburg, Indiana

On December 16, 2015, John Hansell's *Whisky Advocate* announced what had become one of the more coveted nods in American spirits, craft or otherwise: its Distiller of the Year. The honoree this time was the spartanly named MGP Ingredients out of the Ohio River town of Lawrenceburg, Indiana.

The decision surprised if not shocked many, especially within the American small-batch spirits movement. MGP Ingredients was best known as a plant that turned out grain-based goods such as pastas and frozen doughs—the MGP stood for Midwest Grain Products—though it had also been supplying Seagram for seventy-plus years with the rye whiskey for its perennially popular blended brands such as Seagram's 7. What really made *Whisky Advocate*'s selection particularly jarring was that MGP Ingredients contained the large-scale distillery behind several stealth "craft" distilleries. That fact had come widely—and harshly—to public light the year before through the Templeton Rye lawsuit. The Iowa distillery had been forced to admit that its signature product was actually distilled in Indiana, a disclosure that lost it money, customers, and prestige. Soon, consumer media began spinning MGP Ingredients as some sort of bogeyman, the impersonal factory behind dodgy labels. Never mind that the company's distillery had been in operation since 1847. Or that critics, and consumers through social media, had lauded the spirits it produced, however they were packaged and marketed. Or that MGP Ingredients' Greg Metze was a bona fide master distiller, with decades of experience and the respect of his peers. Or that MGP Ingredients' spirits work was hardly new at the end of 2015—the critic Fred Minnick had profiled Metze and his operation for *Whisky Advocate* back in 2013.

All that seemed to matter to journalists parachuting into the controversy and to the wider public was that *Whisky Advocate*, a venerable media force within the American spirits industry, had appeared to legitimize the wizard behind a sizable chunk of the small-batch spirits curtain. Whatever Metze's reputation or his distillery's integrity, "MGP has acted as an enabler to allow these companies to thrive," one small-batch distillery owner told a reporter right before the new year, phrasing the MGP-client relationship in terms of drug addiction. *Whisky Advocate* saw it differently, of course. Lew Bryson wrote the magazine's Distiller of the Year announcement, infusing it with a sense of history as well as of the present.

> MGP's story mirrors that of the American whiskey industry. A huge place that was booming in the 1960s, it was quickly forgotten as "white goods" took over the spirits market, but kept on making great whiskey that was sold cheaply. But when things turned around, there it was, just waiting to be discovered. MGP still makes whiskey almost exclusively for other bottlers, and plans to continue that business, but it has had a huge effect on the industry, and on consumer tastes. Look for "Distilled in Indiana" in tiny print on all those whiskey labels; you can count on quality.

Be that as it may, the manufactured maelstrom seemed to only accentuate that gnawing controversy about authenticity in a booming American small-batch spirits movement. And it was booming—that was beyond dispute. About ten months after *Whisky Advocate*'s announcement, the American Craft Spirits Association released the final numbers from a sweeping study the trade group had commissioned to determine just how many independently owned distilleries in America there were making small batches of spirits in more traditional ways. It turns out there were a lot, especially when compared with just a relatively short time before. According to ACSA, there were 1,315 of what the group called craft distillers in the United States by August 2016. That number itself was up from an estimated 1,209 in March. More than 34 percent, too, were located in the West, including Alaska and Hawaii, though sizable percentages could be found in every region of the nation. The group defined craft distillers in large part as those licensed operations making fewer than 750,000 taxable gallons annually, a more elastic benchmark than the federal government or the rival American Distilling Institute. That of course meant that the ACSA did not consider Tito's and other larger, independently owned distilleries craft, whatever their packaging said—never mind the small-batch offerings of macroproducers.

Whichever ways organizations chose to define smaller distillers—and even those making up to 750,000 were comparatively smaller than the likes of Diageo and Bacardí—the trend was unmistakable: the number of small-batch distilleries was marching upward, whatever the challenges, permeating ever deeper into American commerce and culture as the second decade of the twenty-first century rolled along. That same ACSA report concluded that small-batch spirits' market share nationally had reached 2.2 percent in volume in 2015 and 3 percent in value, up from 0.8 percent and 1.1 percent respectively in 2010—tiny in the grand sweep of the nation's long relationship with alcoholic spirits, but bracingly sharp growth nonetheless. As for the people who pioneered this unlikely growth, some were seeing their own changes during the same decade.

Gunnar Broman

The early creative force behind the Absolut vodka brand, particularly its bottle design, retired from advertising in the early 1990s.

Jim Bendis

Bendis still owns and runs his Bendistillery in southern Oregon.

James Busuttil

The distiller of the first small-batch tequila in the United States still runs Saint James, though in late 2015 he was searching for a buyer.

Margaret Chatey

Chatey still runs Connecticut Westford Hill, the oldest stand-alone craft distillery in the northeast, with her husband, Louis Chatey.

Ansley Coale

The cofounder of Germain-Robin still runs Craft Distillers, the company he started in 2003 to market Hangar 1 vodka and that now includes several other brands. In 2014 St. George stopped producing Hangar 1, and Proximo, which had acquired the brand from Craft Distillers in 2010, took over.

Rob Cooper

The creator of St-Germain, which was so vital to the resurgence in popularity of liqueurs, died in April 2016 at age thirty-nine.

Ralph Erenzo

In December 2010 a one-car accident near his Tuthilltown distillery left Erenzo in a coma for weeks and led to several surgeries to heal injuries to his upper body. He returned to work in the summer of 2011.

Sydney Frank

Grey Goose's godfather died in 2006.

Hubert Germain-Robin

The cofounder of Germain-Robin continues to distill through Craft Distillers. He is also a sought-after consultant in the industry.

John Hansell

John Hansell and wife, Amy Westlake, continue to run *Whisky Advocate* and WhiskyFest.

Michael Jackson

The famed whiskey critic died in 2007.

Bruce Joseph

Anchor Distilling's head distiller marked his thirty-fifth year under the Anchor umbrella in late 2015.

Miles Karakasevic

The cofounder of Charbay Distillery & Winery, with wife, Susan Karakasevic, is officially retired, though he continues to work at the family company his children now run.

Jim Koch

Boston Beer Company's cofounder and chairman remains active in the craft beer industry.

Fritz Maytag

Anchor Distilling Company's founder sold it and the Anchor Brewing Company in 2010 to the forces behind the Skyy vodka brand.

Steve McCarthy

The founder of Clear Creek Distillery sold it to fellow Portland, Oregon, firm Hood River Distillers in early 2014.

Greg Metze

MGP Ingredients' master distiller left the company in early 2016 to start his own consultancy.

Chuck Miller

Miller continues to run Belmont Farm in Culpeper County, Virginia, which now bills itself as "the first craft distillery of American whiskey in the United States."

Robert Mondavi

The most influential American winery owner since Prohibition died in 2008, four years after selling the family firm to Constellation Brands of upstate New York.

Tom Mooney

Mooney remains a co-owner of House Spirits and ended his two-year presidency of the American Craft Spirits Association in 2016. House sold its Aviation American Gin brand in November 2016 for an undisclosed price to Davos Brands, the marketing firm that helped popularize it.

Bill Owens

The brewing pioneer–turned–spirits pioneer continues to run the American Distilling Institute, which he founded.

Paul Pacult

The groundbreaking critic continues to publish his quarterly *Spirit Journal* and to write and lecture widely on the industry and its wares.

Dave Pickerell

The former Maker's Mark master distiller remains the most sought-after consultant in the small-batch spirits industry.

Phil Prichard

Prichard continues to run his Kelso, Tennessee–based distillery. The company opened a second distillery in Nashville in 2014. The year before, Prichard won an exemption from a new Tennessee regulation that required any spirit calling itself Tennessee whiskey go through the so-called Lincoln County Process of repeated charcoal filtration—a process developed by Jack Daniel's, which pushed the regulation. Prichard argued not only that he wanted to make whiskey the way his forebears in Tennessee had but also that such filtration had little to no effect on the taste of the spirit. Frustratingly enough for Prichard, the new Nashville distillery was forced to abide by the regulation.

Michel Roux

The man who popularized Absolut and Bombay Sapphire is still involved in the spirits industry.

Bill Samuels Jr.

The guiding hand behind Maker's Mark since the late 1970s retired as president and CEO in early 2011, handing the reins to his son, Rob Samuels. The younger man's job, according to his father, is to make the distillery's signature bourbon a "global icon." Samuels Jr. would have to do so under a new corporate umbrella. Fortune Brands broke up in 2011 and spun off Maker's Mark under a new entity called Beam Inc., which included Jim Beam. In a bit of serendipity, considering American distillers' influence on Japanese whiskey makers, Osaka-based Suntory Holdings bought Beam Inc. in early 2014 for $16 billion.

Marge Samuels

The wife of Bill Samuels Sr., who contributed to the packaging design for Maker's Mark, including its famed red wax seal, died in 1985.

Lance Winters

The former brewer became St. George's master distiller in 2010, the year Jörg Rupf retired. Winters now owns St. George with his wife, Ellie Winters. The pair married at the distillery in 2009.

ACKNOWLEDGMENTS

I am profoundly grateful to many people and organizations for making this book possible. When I started it, I was not sure I could finish it, and the deeper I went, the more grateful I became for the insights and exertions of those who burrowed into small-batch spirits, and spirits in general, before me.

To start, I would like to thank those involved in the American spirits industry for giving of their time and expertise, including Ansley Coale, Hubert Germain-Robin, Dave Pickerell, Jörg Rupf, Lance and Ellie Winters, Ralph Erenzo, Tom Mooney, Phil Prichard, Chuck Miller, Bruce Joseph, Bill Samuels Jr., and Steve McCarthy. Bill Owens and the American Distilling Institute were also a fantastic fount of information, as was the American Craft Spirits Association and its members and staff.

I commenced my research with an excellent white paper on the growth of American small-batch spirits that Michael Kinstlick prepared (and regularly updated). He was kind enough to talk at length about his own findings. And Tom Hogue at the Alcohol and Tobacco Tax and Trade Bureau indulged my various requests for information, as did Susan Ciccone at the Cambridge Public Library. Fellow writers in the spirits field were also particularly helpful, especially Paul Pacult and John Hansell. Other writers whose shoulders I stood upon, and some of whom freely shared their thoughts, include Chuck Cowdery, Clay Risen, Lew Bryson, David Wondrich, Robert Simonson, Philip Green, and the late, great Michael Jackson, whom I first happily encountered researching beer.

My longtime editor now, Yuval Taylor, suggested substantial rewrites of the original manuscript and new ways of thinking about a trend that, as the reader now hopefully knows, is next to impossible to clearly define. The entire crew at Chicago Review Press, especially project editor Ellen Hornor, was once again instrumental in steering this book to print. I would also like to give a nod to Adam Chromy, my exceedingly no-nonsense agent who exhibits the finest in New York values.

Finally, I would like to thank my family, particularly my wife, Elizabeth, who again helped shepherd this idea toward reality. This book is dedicated to her parents, John and Suzanne Rudy. My father-in-law planted the idea originally (and, as with my previous books, provided astute proofreading). I am also grateful to my parents, my siblings, their families, and especially my children, Josephine and Mathieu—even though they're too young to understand what Dad does beyond "type."

TJA
Cambridge, Massachusetts
March 24, 2016

ENDNOTES

Aperitif: And Then There Were Craft Spirits

distillery numbers: white paper from Michael Kinstlick, CEO of Coppersea Distilling.

found that nearly 60 percent: Inaugural Craft Spirits Economic Briefing, American Craft Spirits Association in conjunction with Park Street and IWSR, New York City, October 18, 2016. The complete report can be found here: www.americancraftspirits.org /wp-content/uploads/2016/10/CSDP-10182016FINAL.pdf.

"There is no universally accepted": Ibid.

"That Shit Will Blow Your Ears Off"

Samuels history: Bill Samuels Jr., interview by author, May 19, 2015; Geoff Kleinman, "The Story of Maker's Mark," Drink Spirits, March 15, 2012, www.drinkspirits.com /bourbon/story-makers-mark-whiskey/.

"That shit will blow your ears off": Kleinman, "The Story of Maker's Mark."

had a physical aversion: Samuels interview.

"swill": Ibid.

World War II takeover: "The History of Kentucky Bourbon," Kentucky Distillers Association, accessed May 21, 2015, www.tiki-toki.com/timeline/entry/151454/The-History -of-Kentucky-Bourbon/#vars!panel=1481778.

Block sale, Samuels exit: John F. Lipman, "American Spirits: Kentucky's Shiny Jewel," EllenJaye.com, April 2011, www.ellenjaye.com/makersmark.htm#deatsville; Brian Haara, "Country Distillers vs. Samuels—the Rise of Maker's Mark," Sipp'n Corn (blog), accessed May 21, 2015, http://sippncorn.blogspot.com/2013/09/country-distillers-v -samuels-rise-of.html; Country Distillers Products, Inc. v. Samuels, Inc., 217 S.W.2d 216 (Ky. 1948). Block's entry into the T. W. Samuels tale and the subsequent sale to the New York firm were not unusual features of the Kentucky bourbon industry. It needed the infusions of cash following Prohibition. Large-scale consolidation, however, was still decades off (Dane Huckelbridge, *Bourbon: A History of the American Spirit* [New York: William Morrow, 2014], 207–8).

Star Hill Farm had made an industrial alcohol: Lipman, "American Spirits."

Stitzel-Weller, Van Winkle: Clay Risen, *American Whiskey, Bourbon & Rye: A Guide to the Nation's Favorite Spirit* (New York: Sterling Epicure, 2013), 219–23. The Stitzel-Weller distillery should not be confused with the current cult favorite, Pappy Van Winkle, a brand started in the 1990s by Pappy Van Winkle's grandson using old stocks of Stitzel-Weller (ibid.).

purchase of Star Hill, restoration: Ned McGrath, "A Distillery with Landmark Status," *New York Times,* January 4, 1981.

George Washington's distillery: Huckelbridge, *Bourbon,* 243.

bourbon history: Ibid.; Andrew F. Smith, ed., *The Oxford Companion to American Food and Drink* (Oxford: Oxford University Press, 2007), 61.

The Bottled-in-Bond Act also saved distillers money. Before, the tax was levied irregularly on the volume of whiskey in a barrel; after, it was taxed only after periods of aging, which invariably resulted in some whiskey evaporating.

bourbon production, sales; corn cultivation: Huckelbridge, *Bourbon,* 67, 126, 227–8. Another theory for the origin of bourbon's name is that it was particularly popular along Bourbon Street in New Orleans and saloon-goers would ask for that "bourbon whiskey" (Michael R. Veach, *Kentucky Bourbon Whiskey: An American Heritage* [Lexington: University of Kentucky Press, 2013], 25–6).

There is much debate in the spirits industry and among consumers and critics regarding column versus pot stills. Generally, pot stills will impart more texture and flavor to darker spirits, including all varieties of whiskey, though that does not necessarily mean that pots are better than column stills. The latter can be more efficient and can turn out a more purified spirit, better for clearer spirits such as vodka. Plus, as others have pointed out, a column still is little more than a stack of pot stills. Bourbon makers, including Maker's Mark, use both column and pot stills at different points in the distilling process.

bourbon on US Army bases: Veach, *Kentucky Bourbon Whiskey,* 106–7. In this spread, American bourbon whiskey mimicked Scottish whisky, which found a wider international audience through its shipment to British military bases beginning in the nineteenth century (ibid.).

advertising numbers, approach: Ibid., 226.

to outselling gas-range stovetops: "Microwave Oven," Southwest Museum of Engineering, Communications and Computation website, accessed March 3, 2015, www.smecc .org/microwave_oven.htm.

Gallo sales: Ernest and Julio Gallo, with Bruce Henderson, *Ernest & Julio: Our Story* (New York: Random House, 1994), 167.

Merlot, Alicante Bouschet acreage: Frank Schoonmaker, *Encyclopedia of Wine* (New York: Hastings House, 1965), 358–61.

For details on the post–World War II histories of beer and wine, the reader is directed to the author's previous books, *The Audacity of Hops: The History of America's Craft Beer Revolution* and *American Wine: A Coming-of-Age Story.*

label, wax origins: Joel Whitaker, "How Maker's Mark Got Its Iconic Red Wax Seal," DCGourmet.net, January 18, 2011, www.dcgourmet.net/archives/127; Colleen Graham, "An Interview with Bill Samuels Jr., President of Maker's Mark Bourbon," About Food, September 9, 2015, http://cocktails.about.com/od/history/a/makersmark_invw.htm.

A later *Wall Street Journal* article that would play an outsized role in the success of Maker's Mark reported that an advertising executive visiting the Samuels family's Bardstown home noticed a mark on a pewter mug they had, and the name sprang from that (David P. Garino, "Maker's Mark Goes Against the Grain to Make Its Mark," *Wall Street Journal,* August 1, 1980). The name was also said to have come from an advertising agency's pitch to Bill Samuels Sr. (Lipman, "American Spirits"). The accepted story, of Marge Samuels creating the name and the wax seal, appears to have originated with Bill Samuels Jr.

whose family rescued and resurrected: Janet Patton, "After 80 Years in Business, Heaven Hill to Fill Seven Millionth Barrel of Kentucky Bourbon," *Lexington Herald-Leader,* February 8, 2015.

releases, distribution: Samuels interview. The original Maker's Mark bottles retailed for between seven and eight dollars each.

ceremonial recipe burning: Joel Whitaker, "The Maker's Mark Story: It Began When Mom Told Dad to Get a Job," DCGourmet.net, January 17, 2011, www.dcgourmet.net/archives/125.

Changes Brewing

Kuh-Maytag conversation: Tom Acitelli, *The Audacity of Hops: The History of America's Craft Beer Revolution* (Chicago: Chicago Review Press, 2013), 4.

Maytag, Anchor backgrounds: Ibid., 3–5.

"I saw the pride": Ibid, 11.

"crude and primitive": Ibid., 24.

Anchor growth, innovation: Ibid., 24–28; and throughout *Audacity of Hops.*

Light beer; bestselling style: Ibid., 28–30.

Mondavi family, Charles Krug: Tom Acitelli, *American Wine: A Coming-of-Age Story* (Chicago: Chicago Review Press, 2015), 25–34.

"If that's the case": Ibid., 34.

Robert Mondavi Winery start, early success: Ibid., 39–42; 44–47.

Coffee with Dinner

Rupf background, observations of United States: Jörg Rupf, interview by author, March 11, 2015.

it horrified him: Rupf interview.

"the size of oil refineries": Frank J. Prial, "A Feud and a Book Unplug the Cork on the Gallo Empire," *New York Times,* April 14, 1993.

manufacture its own bottles: Ibid.

"alcoholic soda pop": Jim Koch, interview by author, March 12, 2012.

Miller Lite background: Acitelli, *Audacity of Hops,* 28–30. The background on beer-related material can be found in the author's earlier work. He is also aware that some will argue Belgium has slightly fewer than dozens of beer styles—and some will argue it has many, many more. The author is going by Tim Webb's *Good Beer Guide to Belgium,* 6th ed. (Hertfordshire, UK: Campaign for Real Ale, 2009). Also, the lager style that American macrobrewers were bastardizing in the 1970s was pilsner, first developed in the now-Czech town of Pilsen in the early 1840s.

eau-de-vie background: Ibid.; Paul F. Pacult, *Kindred Spirits: The Spirit Journal Guide to the World's Distilled Spirits and Fortified Wines* (New York: Hyperion, 1997), 117. Eau-de-vie should not be confused with brandy. Both are made from distilled fruit juice, but brandy is aged in wooden barrels.

Napa crop figures: Napa County Department of Agriculture, "Annual Crop Report 1976."

Sonoma crop figures: Sonoma County Department of Agriculture, "Sonoma County Agricultural Crop Report 1976."

"Such beautiful fruit": Rupf interview.

Judgment of Paris: Acitelli, *American Wine,* 75–118. The reader is also directed to George Taber's account of the event and its aftermath, *Judgment of Paris: California vs. France and the Historic 1976 Paris Tasting That Revolutionized Wine* (New York: Scribner, 2005).

Mondavi background and effects: Acitelli, *American Wine,* 25–63, and throughout the book.

Judgment of Paris planning, results: Acitelli, *American Wine*, 101–17; George Taber, "Judgment of Paris," *Time*, June 7, 1976, 58. Taber's *Judgment of Paris* also has information throughout on the event and its fallout. The winning American red wine was a 1973 Stag's Leap Cabernet Sauvignon and the winning white was a 1973 Chateau Montelena Chardonnay.

Media reaction; sales, tourism, media coverage jumps: Acitelli, *American Wine*, 106–18; Taber, *Judgment*, 212–24.

Rupf inspired by Judgment: Rupf interview.

A Clear Favorite

"like a fjord": Carl Hamilton, *Absolut: Biography of a Bottle* (New York: Texere, 2000), 15.

N. W. Ayer meeting, including name ideas: Ibid., 15–48; "Absolut Vodka," *Advertising Age*, September 15, 2003.

spirits consumption figures: National Institute on Alcohol Abuse and Alcoholism, "Surveillance Report #92," August 2011.

collectively over $1 trillion: "Baby Boom," AP US History Notes, accessed February 7, 2014, www.apstudynotes.org/us-history/topics/baby-boom/.

college enrollment record: "Table 187: College Enrollment Rates for High School Graduates, By Sex, 1960–1998," National Center for Education Statistics, accessed March 5, 2015, http://nces.ed.gov/programs/digest/d99/d99t187.asp.

Contrary to popular myth, potatoes are not the only base nor basis for vodka. In fact, the vast majority of vodkas today are *not* made with spuds. Any starchy, sugary grain will do, including rye and corn, as will fruit. Unlike most other spirits, vodka is defined less by its ingredients than by the final result.

"vile-tasting panaceas," vodka uses: Pacult, *Kindred Spirits*, 161.

Russian relationship with vodka: Victorino Mathus, *Vodka: How a Colorless, Odorless, Flavorless Spirit Conquered America* (Guilford, CT: Lyons, 2014), 11–13.

Smirnoff background: Ibid., 11–25; Hamilton, *Absolut*, 151.

Heublein-Smirnoff background: Mathus, *Vodka*, 27–28; Hamilton, *Absolut*, 152–55; Bill Ryan, "'Smirnoff White Whiskey—No Smell, No Taste,'" *New York Times*, February 19, 1995.

vodka history, sales: Mathus, *Vodka*, 27–43.

only 0.5 percent: Hamilton, *Absolut*, 154.

"vodka was Smirnoff": Ibid., 155. Emphasis in the original.

The infinitesimal market share of imports would only start to grow after 1974, when Pepsi-Cola struck a deal to import concentrate for its signature soft drink into the Soviet Union in exchange for exclusive distribution rights for Stolichnaya vodka (John Thor-Dahlburg, "Pepsico to Swap Cola for Soviet Vodka and Ships," *Los Angeles Times*, April 10, 1990).

pitch meeting with N. W. Ayer: Hamilton, *Absolut*, 25–43.

Hamilton's *Absolut* book covers the saga of Absolut in minute detail, including the marginalization of Jerry Siano, Gunnar Broman, and others who worked on the early campaigns.

Front-Page News

Wall Street Journal *article quotations:* Garino, "Maker's Mark."

Maker's Mark production, popularity: Ibid.

bourbon decline: Huckelbridge, *Bourbon*, 239–42; Veach, *Kentucky Bourbon Whiskey*, 110–11; Samuels interview.

Jack Daniel's, the phenomenally popular Tennessee whiskey, is pretty much a bourbon in that it's made to the federally mandated specifications of a bourbon, including its grain bill being primarily corn. It is, however, made differently enough, including via charcoal filtration, that it does not brand itself as bourbon. Tennessee whiskey is a style unto itself, delineated largely by geography and filtration. See Risen, *American Whiskey, Bourbon & Rye*, 9–11.

became America's bestselling spirit: Huckelbridge, *Bourbon*, 240.

sales figures: Ibid., 241.

"a mere shadow": Ibid.

Maker's Mark, Jim Beam capacities: Charles Hillinger, "Sales Keep Getting Better," *Los Angeles Times*, September 12, 1987.

place its wares on commercial airlines: Bill Samuels Jr. representative, e-mail exchange with author, February 2016.

fate of Stitzel-Weller: Veach, *Kentucky Bourbon Whiskey*, 100–101.

ten Kentucky bourbon makers disappeared: There were twenty-four distilleries in 1967 and fourteen in 1987 (Hillinger, "Sales Keep Getting Better").

gradually relegated Four Roses: Risen, *American Whiskey, Bourbon & Rye*, 3.

Van Winkle–Samuels Jr. meeting: Reid Mitenbuler, *Bourbon Empire: The Past and Future of America's Whiskey* (New York: Viking, 2015), 246.

Samuels Jr. education, engineer work: Kleinman, "The Story of Maker's Mark."

"You need to go": Ibid.

Motlow and Samuels family: Ibid.

"Bill, we've got a problem": Ibid.

"Your job . . . is to go out": Ibid.

from a foot infection: Amanda Macias, "This Is the Safe That Killed Whiskey Distiller Jack Daniel," Business Insider, December 12, 2013, www.businessinsider.com/jack -daniel-killed-by-a-safe-2013-12.

unfamiliar role, Samuels's instructions: Samuels interview.

Sanders and Samuels, including exchange: Mitenbuler, *Bourbon Empire*, 245.

Samuels visiting accounts; debt payoff: Garino, "Maker's Mark."

Doe-Anderson hiring, campaign idea: Samuels interview; Tom Eblen, "Maker's Mark Leadership to Change, But It Stays in the Samuels Family," *Lexington Herald-Leader*, April 11, 2011.

Globe and Mail: Beverly Gray, "The Legacy of Elijah Craig Bourbon Runs Neck and Neck with Thoroughbreds in Kentucky," *Globe and Mail*, May 26, 1979. The dollar amounts in the article used Canadian currency; these totals represent a rough conversion into American greenbacks.

Garino-Samuels meeting, planning for it; article fallout: Samuels interview; Joel Whitaker, "A Front-Page Story Puts Tiny Distillery on Map," DCGourmet.com, January 19, 2011, www.dcgourmet.net/archives/131; William D. Bygrave and Andrew Zacharakis, *The Portable MBA in Entrepreneurship* (Hoboken: Wiley, 2010), 101.

"The sales line on bourbon whiskey": Carl Cannon, "Firm to Market 114-Proof Bourbon to Reverse Decade-Long Sales Slide," *Washington Post* (via Los Angeles Times Service), September 2, 1980. The *Milwaukee Journal* also picked up the story.

The Hitchhiker's Guide to Cognac

Ansley Coale had had his doubts; "I can't believe": Frank J. Prial, "A Choice Encounter," *New York Times*, September 4, 1988.

Coale–Germain-Robin conversation: Ansley Coale, interview by author, March 23, 2015; Hubert Germain-Robin, interview by author, March 31, 2015.

Germain-Robin background: Germain-Robin interview; Jim Morris, "Time in a Bottle," *California Bountiful,* January/February 2008, www.californiabountiful.com/features /article.aspx?arID=285; Prial, "A Choice Encounter"; David Driscoll, "California Pioneers—Part III: Hubert Germain-Robin," *Spirits Journal,* December 8, 2014, http:// spiritsjournal.klwines.com/klwinescom-spirits-blog/2014/12/8/california-pioneers -part-iii-hubert-germain-robin.html.

the Big Four of Cognac: Pacult, *Kindred Spirits,* 49. The other three of the Big Four were Hennessy, Rémy Martin, and Courvoisier. Seagram would acquire Martell in 1988 (ibid.).

into the Big Two first: Kyle Jarrard, *Cognac: The Seductive Saga of the World's Most Coveted Spirit* (New York: John Wiley & Sons, 2005), 133.

The Saint Emilion des Charentes has nothing to do with the Saint Emilion winemaking town in Bordeaux (Prial, "A Choice Encounter").

Cognac background, including counterfeits: Pacult, *Kindred Spirits,* 22–23; Jarrard, *Cognac,* 35–64, 107–9.

"could hardly produce": Pacult, *Kindred Spirits,* 23.

legal changes: Jarrard, *Cognac,* 108–9; Nicholas Faith, *Cognac: The Story of the World's Greatest Brandy* (Oxford, UK: Infinite Ideas, 2013), 95. Around this time Cognac producers began creating their own designations denoting how long certain Cognac blends had aged. This gave rise to the VS (Very Special), VSOP (Very Special Old Pale), etc., designations still found on many labels (Jarrard, *Cognac,* 107).

Cognac during the world wars: Jarrard, *Cognac,* 111–25.

Gustav Klaebisch was much more benevolent toward Cognac than his brother Otto was toward Champagne, the famed wine region he ruled during the occupation. Readers are directed to Don and Petie Kladstrup's 2001 book, *Wine & War: The French, the Nazis, and the Battle for France's Greatest Treasure,* for more on the Germans' rapacious thirst for French wines.

Cognac production, acreage: Jarrard, *Cognac,* 127–30.

"cognac, already a globally known": Ibid., 134.

consolidations: Ibid., 132–34.

Ugni Blanc had gradually supplanted fellow white wine grape Folle Blanche as the preferred grape for Cognac production. Some saw the usurper as popular only because it was physically hardier and less prone to frost damage; others saw it becoming popular because it was less aromatic and therefore gave distillers more room to play (Jarrard, *Cognac,* 109).

that bothered Germain-Robin: Germain-Robin interview.

Ansley Coale Sr. background: Wolfgang Saxon, "Ansley Johnson Coale, 84, Expert on Population Trends," *New York Times,* November 17, 2002.

Ansley Coale Jr. background, ranch purchase: Coale interview; Prial, "A Choice Encounter."

accessible only via: Corby Kummer, "Don't Call It Cognac," *Atlantic,* December 1995, www.theatlantic.com/magazine/archive/1995/12/dont-call-it-cognac/376505/; R. W. Apple Jr., "Cognac, Made in America," *New York Times,* January 27, 1999.

conversation in the car: Germain-Robin interview; Coale interview.

"This will be six times": Coale interview.

Fresh Fruit in the "Rottenest City"

"rottenest city," Emeryville boundaries: Findery, "Rottenest City on the Pacific Coast," Huffington Post, January 13, 2015, www.huffingtonpost.com/findery/rottenest-city -on-the-pac_b_6153880.html.

St. George start-up: Rupf interview. This would be the same St. George of the St. George and the dragon legend. In fact, he was a Roman soldier who converted to and later died for the Christian faith. He never lived in present-day Germany, but he has long been a popular saint throughout the West, venerated as a protector.

beer, wine distribution: Acitelli, *Audacity of Hops*, 222; Acitelli, *American Wine*, 53–54.

to provide lodging: Details of the 1979–1980 legal change taken from the United States Code, 2000, Title 26; Dave Pickerell, interview by author, April 1, 2015.

sales figures, production numbers: Rupf interview.

"I am from Europe and": Ibid.

sales peak, changing drinking habits: National Institute on Alcohol Abuse and Alcoholism, "Surveillance Report #92," August 2011; Pamela G. Hollie, "Seagram Revamping in U.S.," *New York Times*, January 17, 1985. Estimates for average spirits intake vary, though all show a sharp drop in the mid-1970s and into much of the 1980s.

Great Chardonnay Showdown: Craig Goldwyn, interview by author, December 18, 2013; Craig Goldwyn, "The Great Chardonnay Shootout," *Chicago Tribune Magazine*, November 9, 1980. It was held at what was then Solomon's wine warehouse. The *Tribune* called it the shootout; most subsequent coverage called it a showdown or the Great Chicago Chardonnay Showdown (Goldwyn interview).

"Everyone's buying white table wine": Sandra Salmans, "A Year of Slumping Spirits," *New York Times*, December 31, 1980.

Some analysts were saying: Ibid.

Chardonnay growth: Susan Arrhenius and Leo McCloskey, "End of History of New California Grape Varietals: Winning Is Winning Forty Years After the 1976 Paris Tasting," Enologix newsletter, September 29, 2014.

for 10 percent of wine consumption: Kristin N. Curry, "Tasting Separates the Aaaahhh from the Awful of Wine Coolers," *Los Angeles Times*, August 29, 1985. Details of the rise of Sutter Home and White Zinfandel, as well as more on wine coolers, can be found in *American Wine: A Coming-of-Age Story*.

he might have reconsidered: Rupf interview.

Falcon Crest success: Jerry Buck, "Vintage Years," Associated Press, July 19, 1981.

vodka-infused version of the orange blossom special: Mark Will-Weber, "A Complete List of Every President's Favorite Drink," *New York Post*, October 18, 2014.

a chance to acquire for cheap : Rupf interview.

American Cognac

could not have been happier: Germain-Robin interview.

set about building a distillery: Ibid.; Coale interview; Apple, "Cognac, Made in America."

Pinot Noir cultivation, descriptions: John Winthrop Haeger, *North American Pinot Noir* (Berkeley: University of California Press, 2004), 49.

spent $85,000: Apple, "Cognac, Made in America."

blew Germain-Robin's mind: Germain-Robin interview.

"itinerant German barber": Frank J. Prial, "Jack Davies, 74, an Innovator in the Sparkling Wine Industry," *New York Times*, March 13, 1998.

Their Schramsberg Vineyards: Ibid.; "History," Schramsberg website, accessed November 9, 2016, www.schramsberg.com/about/history/.

Baccala's operation was: Gerald Asher, *The Pleasures of Wine* (San Francisco: Chronicle Books, 2002), 264–65; "Baccala Estate Winery," Gold Medal Wine Club, accessed November 9, 2016, www.goldmedalwineclub.com/winery/baccala-estate-winery -mendocino-ava; Paul Franson, "Charbay's Marko Karakasevic Releases His First Spirit," *St. Helena Star*, January 13, 2011.

Rémy Martin Schramsberg distillery was: Terry Robards, Wine Talk, *New York Times*, September 29, 1982; Kristine M. Curry, "First California Distillery Since Prohibition Ready to Offer a Unique Brandy," *Chicago Tribune*, January 23, 1986; Daniel P. Puzo, "Remy to Carry on Brandy Venture Sans Schramsberg," *Los Angeles Times*, January 1, 1987.

Seagram could record: "Corporate Reports Financial Statements," Seagram, *Globe and Mail*, September 20, 1979; David M. Fahey and Jon S. Miller, eds., *Alcohol and Drugs in North America: A Historical Encyclopedia* (Santa Barbara: ABC-CLIO, 2013), 101.

Cognac sales growth: "The Lure of Cognac," *New York Times*, November 22, 1981, www .nytimes.com/1981/11/22/business/business-conditions-the-lure-of-cognac.html.

Glitter and Gekko

Pacult: Paul Pacult, interview by author, May 21, 2015.

Strong: Eric Asimov, "Rodney Strong, 78, Dancer Turned Pioneering California Vintner, Is Dead," *New York Times*, March 9, 2006. Strong eventually renamed the winery after himself.

"seemed a permanent curse": Editorial board, "Still Bad, Still Getting Worse," *New York Times*, December 24, 1982.

"Acquisitiveness, or, if you will, greed"; marathon tastings: Frank J. Prial, Wine Talk, *New York Times*, August 3, 1988. Details of the marathon tastings were taken from Prial's article and from the books *The Billionaire's Vinegar: The Mystery of the World's Most Expensive Bottle of Wine* by Benjamin Wallace and *The Emperor of Wine: The Rise of Robert M. Parker Jr. and the Reign of American Taste* by Elin McCoy. Further details on the hoopla that arose around fine wine in the early 1980s can be found in the author's previous book, *American Wine: A Coming-of-Age Story*.

"What is a wine bar?": Jo Hawkins, "Wine Alone Doth Not a Wine Bar Make," *Washington Post*, May 24, 1981.

"the wine trade's most glittering": Frank J. Prial, Wine Talk, *New York Times*, May 27, 1985.

Four Seasons California Barrel Tasting: Acitelli, *American Wine*, 131–32.

"to the center of public relations": William Rice, "California's New York Showcase," *Washington Post*, March 27, 1977.

it was usually about the pricing: Pacult interview.

Eckhardt: Acitelli, *Audacity of Hops*, 124–25.

Karakasevic and Charbay start-up: Kip Davis, "The Master Distillers of Domaine Charbay," *Napa Valley Register*, April 25, 2013; Lou Bustamante, "Karakasevic Family Keeps Spirits Alive in Napa," *San Francisco Chronicle*, October 11, 2013; Pete Wells, "Reinventing Vodka," *Food & Wine*, April 2000.

"brought equality": Wells, "Reinventing Vodka."

"No fruit is safe from Miles": R. W. Apple Jr., "A New Gauntlet: Cognac, Made in America," *New York Times*, January 27, 1999.

Maker's Mark sale: Hillinger, "Sales Keep Getting Better."

could not keep pace: Chuck Cowdery, "How Maker's Mark Was Made," *The Chuck Cowdery Blog*, October 7, 2011, http://chuckcowdery.blogspot.com/2011/10/how-makers-mark -was-made.html.

A Singular Idea

accounted for nearly 99 percent: Joshua Mills, "The Single-Malt Whisky of the Highlands," *New York Times*, December 17, 1980.

"a more unusual spirit": Ibid.

Scottish distillers shipped: Ibid.

116 distilleries: Ibid. The number is as of December 1980.

Scots' love of single malt, "cooking whisky": Ibid.

UK unemployment: James Denman and Paul McDonald, "Unemployment Statistics from 1881 to the Present Day," Government Statistical Service.

UK unrest, outages: "Your 1970s: Strikes and Blackouts," BBC News online, June 7, 2007, http://news.bbc.co.uk/2/hi/uk_news/magazine/6729683.stm.

dropped a full 10 percent; nearly 90 percent: "No Longer Whisky Galore," *Guardian Weekly*, January 2, 1983.

rum history: Bacardí website, accessed July 2, 2015, www.bacardilimited.com/our-heritage; Tom Gjelten, *Bacardi and the Long Fight for Cuba* (New York: Penguin, 2009), 17–21.

"Rum is vodka": Terry Robards, "Bacardi Is Most Popular Drink," *New York Times*, February 21, 1981.

Slavery's role in rum's rise: Gjelten, *Bacardi*, 17; "The Triangular Trade," the Abolition Project, accessed July 2, 2015, http://abolition.e2bn.org/slavery_43.html.

Bacardí history: Bacardí website; Gjelten, *Bacardi*.

rum, Bacardí sales: Robards, "Bacardi Is Most Popular Drink"; Harry Hurt III, "Bacardi, the Puerto Rican Rum That Will Be Forever Cuban," *New York Times*, September 20, 2008.

Bacardí market share: "Walker's Bacardi Stock Purchase Deemed Astute Move," *Globe and Mail*, January 27, 1978.

nearly five times: Florence Fabricant, "Sales Soaring for Tongue-Twisting Single-Malt Scotches," *New York Times*, December 18, 1985.

"single-malts seem to appeal": Ibid.

"Not only can you": Ibid.

"are usually sipped neat": Ibid.

"They should be drunk": Jo Hawkins, "Leading Us by the Nose," *Washington Post*, May 8, 1983.

number of brands, US market share: Fabricant, "Sales Soaring."

Lightning in a Barrel

Elmer T. Lee looked and sounded; Lee-Baranaskas conversation: Elmer T. Lee, interview by Thomas Troland, October 30, 2008, transcript, Louie B. Nunn Center for Oral History, University of Kentucky Libraries, https://nyx.uky.edu/oh/render. php?cachefile=2009OH023_BIK004_Lee_acc.xml.; Paul Vitello, "Elmer T. Lee, Whose Premium Bourbon Revived an Industry, Dies at 93," *New York Times*, July 21, 2013.

Age International, its plans: Chuck Cowdery, "It Was the Best of Times, It Was the Worst of Times," *The Chuck Cowdery Blog*, December 9, 2013, http://chuckcowdery.blogspot. com/2013/12/it-was-best-of-times-it-was-worst-of.html.

Japanese demand: "Bourbon Boom Gives Japanese Taste of U.S. 'Bluegrass' Roots," *Japan Economic Journal,* November 26, 1988.

Warehouse H, Blanton: Blanton's Bourbon website, accessed July 4, 2015, www.blantons bourbon.com/.

debuted first: Ibid.; Lee interview.

"It didn't do much": Lee interview.

felt compelled: Ibid.

blind tasting; "but not before": Veach, *Kentucky Bourbon Whiskey,* 113–14.

equivalent of one hundred dollars: Ibid., 116.

Booker Noe: Florence Fabricant, "Boutique Bourbons Win Prestige at Home and Sales Abroad," *New York Times,* December 16, 1992.

"General Motors Corp. coming out": Cannon, "Firm to Market 114-Proof Bourbon."

would in 1991 slide: Fabricant, "Boutique Bourbons."

"the best bourbons ever"; "These are bourbons for connoisseurs": Ibid.

"Yuppie Beer"

Reich, New Amsterdam: Acitelli, *Audacity of Hops,* 93–95, 108–11; Matthew Reich, interview by author, January 20, 2012.

"This is yuppie beer": Sandra Salmans, "A Local Beer Not for Everyone," *New York Times,* February 19, 1995.

Great American Beer Festival: Acitelli, *Audacity of Hops,* 89–92; Charlie Papazian, interview by author, July 2010 (via e-mailed recordings that Papazian provided of answers to the author's questions).

"a workingman's drink": Mike Leary, "New Brand of Beer Is 'Fresher'," *Boca Raton News,* September 18, 1983.

Koch, Samuel Adams: Acitelli, *Audacity of Hops,* 104–7. Koch and Reich used the same consultant for their brewing—Joseph Owades, a biochemist most famous for devising the formula for light beer. Reich also contract-brewed for a number of years before launching a physical brewpub in West Chelsea, Manhattan.

sometimes ruthless: Koch regularly sued competitors, particularly those he thought were encroaching on his brand and company names. He also often sought to undercut the same competitors by offering his beer cheaper or in larger quantities. Finally, and perhaps most annoyingly to smaller craft brewers, he tried—and failed—to trademark the phrase "the Best Beer in America" after Samuel Adams Boston Lager won a string of consumer preference polls at the Great American Beer Festival.

Geary: David Geary, interview by author, February 29, 2012.

The New White Wine

For the description of Absolut's taste and texture, the author consulted Paul Pacult's review on page 162 of *Kindred Spirits.* Other critics could not seem to *not* describe the vodka as some variation of smooth.

Ekelund himself spent: Hamilton, *Absolut,* 213–18.

a newly built plant: Ibid, 214.

$750,000: "Absolut Vodka," *Advertising Age.*

Turner, Hayes, "Absolut Perfection": Ibid.

more than one in five: Florence Fabricant, "Vodka Is a Matter of Taste," *New York Times,* December 26, 1984.

might run to four dollars: Bryan Miller, "Diner's Journal," *New York Times,* May 4, 1984.

Andy Warhol first saw: Rebecca Greenfield, "The Evolution of Absolut Vodka's Advertising Strategy," Fast Company, accessed July 13, 2015, www.fastcompany.com/3032598 /most-creative-people/the-evolution-of-absolut-vodkas-advertising-strategy.

for $65,000: Joan Gibbons, *Art and Advertising* (London: I.B. Tauris, 2005), 139. Warhol had already painted one of Carillon's other products, La Grand Passion (ibid.).

was one of the world's most famous artists; "Being good in business": Douglas C. McGill, "Andy Warhol, Pop Artist, Dies," *New York Times,* February 23, 1987.

"People treated [Roux]": Hamilton, *Absolut,* 284.

Absolut sales, market share: Stuart Elliott, "Absolut Marketing," *USA Today,* November 22, 1989.

"ran out of booze"; twenty-four-hour gear: Hamilton, *Absolut,* 276.

was very likely the first spirit: The author talked to various people who said much the same thing about Absolut. Also, the media by the late 1980s reported that consumers were apt to order the brand by name.

vying to take career-making credit: Carl Hamilton's *Absolut: Biography of a Bottle* provides an excellent in-depth look at the machinations behind the development of the Absolut advertising campaign—and the reaping of its rewards.

"A lot of yuppies": Michael Freitag, "Vodka Import Boom: New Entries Rush In," *New York Times,* June 6, 1989.

"white wine of the 1990s": Ibid.

Of Pears and Bears

McCarthy, Rupf meeting: Rupf interview.

McCarthy: Steve McCarthy, interviews and e-mails with author, summer 2016; Frank J. Prial, "Oregon Original," *New York Times,* February 5, 1989; Eric Asimov, "An Orchard in a Bottle, at 80 Proof," The Pour, *New York Times,* August 15, 2007.

"It's just so logical"; "greatest way": Prial, "Oregon Original."

Portland craft beer: Acitelli, *Audacity of Hops,* 100.

Oregon fine wine: Acitelli, *American Wine,* 61.

"Producing wonderful eau de vie": Asimov, "Orchard in a Bottle."

Distribution; twenty-two dollars a pop: Prial, "Oregon Original."

production did not creep: McCarthy interview.

declined five straight years: N. R. Kleinfield, "Decline in Drinking Changes Liquor Industry," *New York Times,* September 17, 1984.

retail sales three: Nicholas E. Lefferts, "What's New in the Liquor Business," *New York Times,* December 29, 1985.

new products: Kleinfield, "Decline in Drinking"; Kim Foltz, Mary Hager, Patricia King, and Nadine Joseph, "Alcohol on the Rocks," *Newsweek,* December 31, 1984, 52.

Guinness also partnered: "The Liquor Consolidations," *New York Times,* October 1, 1987.

Seagram set about: Hollie, "Seagram Revamping."

"The industry has been": Ibid. Shanken also edited an oft-cited alcohol-industry newsletter called *Impact.*

"An After-School Special Brought to Life"

Bias death; dispatcher-Tribble dialogue: Michael Weinreb, "The Day Innocence Died," ESPN.com, June 2008, http://sports.espn.go.com/espn/eticket/story?page=bias.

college career, praise, draft reaction: Sally Jenkins, "'A Dream Within a Dream,'" *Washington Post,* June 17, 1986.

"This was a moralistic passion play": Weinreb, "The Day Innocence Died."

"Bias, a student leader": Peter McFarlane, "U.S. Basketball's No. 1 Dies," The Advertiser, June 21, 1986, from an AP wire report. The born-again Christian aspect of Bias and his mother appeared frequently in media reports. The author relied on Weinreb's "The Day Innocence Died" for the recounting of the formation of the false narrative of Bias's life and death. The author himself, however, remembers being told as a grade-school student that Bias did, in fact, die from trying cocaine only once.

"He had passed every random drug test": Editorial board, "Len Bias," Washington Post, June 21, 1986.

dismissed as "innuendo"; taken cocaine accidentally: Michael Goodwin, "Bias's Parents Seek to Fight 'Innuendo,'" New York Times, July 25, 1986.

"He made a bad decision": Weinreb, "The Day Innocence Died."

news soon emerged: Ibid.

"the most socially influential moment": Ibid.

"Drug abuse is no longer": Bernard Weinraub, "White House Says Reagan Plans New Campaign Against Drug Use," New York Times, July 29, 1986; Reginald Stuart, "O'Neill Proposes Congress Mount Attack on Drugs," New York Times, July 24, 1986.

political, legislative moves: Stuart, "O'Neill Proposes"; Weinreb, "The Day Innocence Died."

"the Archduke Ferdinand": Weinreb, "The Day Innocence Died."

Crusade

Reagan address: "Address to the Nation on the Campaign Against Drug Abuse," University of Texas's Reagan speech archives, September 14, 1986, www.reagan.utexas.edu/archives/speeches/1986/091486a.htm.

"perpetual stream": Michael E. Hill, "Dr. Tim Johnson: Diet Books," Washington Post, November 13, 1983.

whether it was beer or Chinese takeout: William Langewiesche, "The Million-Dollar Nose," Atlantic, December 2000.

more than two dozen countries: Virginia Corner, "Staying Slim a Way of Life, Head Weight Watcher Says," Toronto Star, February 18, 1988.

"There is a fundamental attitude change": Kleinfield, "Decline in Drinking."

Lightner, MADD background: John J. O'Connor, "'MADD,' Drama Fights Drunken Driving," New York Times, March 14, 1983.

a 43 percent drop: Jay Mathews, "Deaths Drop After California Stiffens Drunken Driving Laws," Washington Post, January 5, 1982.

bought a bottle of Hennessy Cognac: Sue Anne Pressley, "Questions Surround Bias's Final Hours," Washington Post, June 29, 1986.

"It's almost stylish not to": Kleinfield, "Decline in Drinking."

"Now we order at least a case": Michael Kernan, "The Whiskey Rebellion," Washington Post, October 21, 1984.

"alcohol is a gateway drug": Richard Mendelson, From Demon to Darling: A Legal History of Wine in America (Berkeley: University of California Press, 2010), 164. The full quotation contains further dread: "While alcohol is a gateway drug that can lead to other, stronger chemical dependencies, it has its own addiction: alcoholism."

"Americans came closest": Ibid., 163.

"The industry feels intimidated": Kleinfield, "Decline in Drinking."

distributor, producer changes: Ibid.; Hollie, "Seagram Revamping in U.S."

Bush address: "Presidential Address on National Drug Policy," C-SPAN archive, September 5, 1989, www.c-span.org/video/?8921-1/presidential-address-national-drug-policy.

counter-commercials: Kleinfield, "Decline in Drinking."

"increasingly vocal anti-alcohol": Lawrence M. Fisher, "Smaller Wineries Gain in Power," *New York Times,* June 12, 1990.

Cigarette Machines

sales pitch; "God, this is fabulous"; "What am I": Coale interview.

Coale likened it all: Ibid.

about fourteen thousand cases; around $1 million: Ibid.

could produce twenty thousand cases; $10-million: Curry, "First California Distillery."

Alambic is the French spelling of *alembic.*

A bottle of Germain-Robin retailed for twenty-eight dollars, the same price as Rémy Martin VSOP (Coale e-mail exchange with author, July 2015).

knew the people behind: Coale interview.

David Berkley; Reagan wine selections: Nancy Faber, "Choosing the Reagans' Wine Makes David Berkley the Toast of the White House," *People,* December 13, 1982.

served Germain-Robin privately: W. Blake Gray, "Germain-Robin Makes Superb Brandies, Yet They're Hard to Sell," *San Francisco Chronicle,* January 27, 2005. The Ronald Reagan Presidential Foundation and Library confirmed to the author in a July 2015 e-mail exchange that the brandy was not served during the Gorbachev state dinner in December 1987—in fact, it was not on the menu—and would likely have been served privately.

Prial column: Prial, "A Choice Encounter."

Coale himself pretty much held: Coale interview.

The Write Time

Pacult-Colandrea dialogue; Pacult reaction, decision: Pacult, *Kindred Spirits,* 2–3; Neil Wilson and Ian Buxton, eds., *Beer Hunter, Whisky Chaser: New Writing on Beer and Whisky in Honour of Michael Jackson* (Castle Douglas, UK: Neil Wilson, 2013), chapter 9; Pacult interview.

The only spirits publication of any real consequence in the United States by 1988 was the trade newsletter *Impact,* which Marvin Shanken started. Shanken was much better known as the publisher of *Wine Spectator; Impact* covered other alcoholic beverages.

with some three million readers: Based upon 1990 subscriber total of 1.1 million and the old newspaper shorthand that one subscriber equals three readers.

"Let me just say": Wilson and Buxton, eds., *Beer Hunter, Whisky Chaser,* chapter 9.

For more on wine writers and their impact, the reader is directed to "The Year of the Wine Writer" chapter in the author's previous book, *American Wine: A Coming of Age Story.* Robert Parker's *Wine Advocate* belted Robert Finigan's *Private Guide to Wines* from its top spot among wine newsletters following their divergent coverage of the 1982 Bordeaux—Finigan dismissed the vintage; Parker raved about it.

was born in Yorkshire; beer discovery, influence: Acitelli, *Audacity of Hops,* 45–49; Roger Protz, "Michael Jackson," *(UK) Guardian,* September 3, 2007, www.theguardian.com /news/2007/sep/04/guardianobituaries.lifeandhealth. Jackson's father, Isaac Jackowitz, anglicized the family name and named his son Michael—thereby setting up years of jokes by the critic about the identically named pop star.

Jackson whiskey discovery, influence: Protz, "Michael Jackson"; Tony Aspler, "This Michael Jackson Known as 'Guru of Grain,'" *Toronto Star*, June 30, 1990.

"Because none of us"; "the first to take": Aspler, "This Michael Jackson."

Pacult workload, Spirit Journal *launch:* Wilson and Buxton, eds., *Beer Hunter, Whisky Chaser,* chapter 49.

bourbon revival: Fabricant, "Boutique Bourbons."

Virginia Lightning

Miller background; distillery start-up: Chuck Miller, interview by author, July 31, 2015; Bill Sautter, "Still Life," *Washington Post Magazine*, December 12, 1993; Kyle Peterson, "Shine On, Chuck," *The American Spectator*, May 2014; Donnie Johnston, "Pilot Takes Time to 'Shine for Government," *Fredericksburg Free Lance-Star*, February 27, 2000. Some vineyardists and winemakers had better luck than Miller. In the early 1970s in Fauquier County, north of Culpeper, Elizabeth Furness started Virginia's first winery since Prohibition dedicated to higher-end grapes (Acitelli, *American Wine*, 64).

Although they are corn based, Miller's whiskeys are not bourbons. Among the major differences are that his whiskeys are not aged like bourbon, nor are their recipes reliant on other grain, but on sugar instead.

grandfather stories: Peterson, "Shine On, Chuck."

"my grandfather made corn": "Culpeper Moonshiner—Tim Trudell Reports," February 20, 2010, YouTube, www.youtube.com/watch?v=qXJ7C5-CNvA.

rules and regulations: Linda Lipman and John Lipman, "American Whiskey: Belmont Farms of Virginia," EllenJaye.com, June 2005, www.ellenjaye.com/wh_belmontfarms. htm; Peterson, "Shine On, Chuck."

initial production run, profit: Peterson, "Shine On, Chuck"; Donnie Johnston, "Corn Liquor Operation One of Few Run Legally," *Fredericksburg Free Lance-Star*, February 27, 2000; Sautter, "Still Life"; Rusty Dennen, "Taking a Shine to Corn Whiskey," *Fredericksburg Free Lance-Star*, December 22, 1990.

were soon coming in: Miller interview.

Dennen article: Dennen, "Taking a Shine to Corn Whiskey."

sought out Miller's autograph: Peterson, "Shine On, Chuck."

Young Blood from an Old Brewery

"Old Potrero represents a wholehearted": Michael Jackson, "Still Crazy," *(UK) Independent*, November 9, 1996.

"survived only vestigially": Ibid.

Born in eastern Pennsylvania: David Wondrich, "How Pennsylvania Rye Whiskey Lost Its Way," Daily Beast, September 12, 2016, http://www.thedailybeast.com/articles /2016/09/12/how-pennsylvania-rye-whiskey-lost-its-way.html.

Anchor Distilling background, experimentation: Bruce Joseph, interview by author, August 21, 2015; Susannah Skiver Barton, "Anchor Distilling Co.: Anchored in Authenticity," *Market Watch Magazine*, June 2015.

Joseph background: Joseph interview.

"It was a category waiting": Jerry Shriver, "Here's to the Spirited Return of Rye Whiskey," *USA Today*, December 8, 2000.

Blue Moon: Acitelli, *Audacity of Hops*, 206–8. Most of the new craft breweries were brewpubs.

Maytag and wine: Acitelli, *American Wine*, 195.

distribution, reaction: Joseph interview.

"We sell our whiskey": Rick Lyke, "Small Stills, Big Spirits," *All About Beer,* January 1, 2001.

GABF statistics: Dick Kreck, "Brew Fest's Mug Runneth Over in 15th Year of Sampling Suds," *Denver Post,* September 18, 1996.

Jackson whiskey tasting; Joseph's thought: Joseph interview.

Making Marks

Pickerell: Pickerell interview.

"I will do you one": Ibid.

Pickerell-Samuels conversation: Ibid. Bill Samuels Sr. died in 1992.

Pickerell cost-cutting, Maker's Mark work: Ibid.; Clay Risen, "Meet Mr. Whiskey," *Garden & Gun,* February/March 2014.

"You have to give people": Pickerell interview.

Goosing Sales

Frank upbringing, early businesses; Schenley work: Douglas Martin, "Sidney Frank, 86, Dies," *New York Times,* January 12, 2006; Seth Stevenson, "The Cocktail Creationist," *New York,* January 10, 2005, http://nymag.com/nymetro/news/bizfinance/biz/features/10816/.

"I figured out the name"; "Go to France": Stevenson, "The Cocktail Creationist."

Jägermeister discovery, success: Ibid.; Martin, "Sidney Frank, 86, Dies."

consumption increase: National Institute on Alcohol Abuse and Alcoholism, "Surveillance Report #92," August 2011.

"It's a liquor with an unpronounceable name": Stevenson, "The Cocktail Creationist."

"the hottest clubs": Ibid.

Smirnoff Black; "In bars and restaurants"; "tired of being told": Melanie Wells, "Liquor Firms Enjoy Happy Hour," *USA Today,* July 14, 1995.

Swingers budget, gross: "Swingers," Box Office Mojo, accessed August 20, 2015, www .boxofficemojo.com/movies/?id=swingers.htm.

Sasha Petraske: Robert Simonson, "Sasha Petraske, 42, Dies," *New York Times,* August 21, 2015. Petraske's Milk & Honey kicked off the contemporary boom in cocktail bars.

"the same wine the French": Joe Pollack, "French Paradox Spurs Sales of Red Wine," *St. Louis Post-Dispatch,* August 6, 1992. More details on fine wine and craft beer sales in the 1990s can be found in the author's previous books, *The Audacity of Hops* and *American Wine.*

Little Bert and the Big Idea

Beveridge background, quotations: Meghan Casserly, "The Troubling Success of Tito's Handmade Vodka," *Forbes,* June 26, 2013. In the mid-1990s Texas was on its way to surpassing New York as the second-largest state.

Saint Arnold: Acitelli, *Audacity of Hops,* 302–3. There are at least a few Catholic saints and other venerated figures often associated with brewing and attendant industries such as hop harvesting. See Steve Frank and Arnold Meltzer, "Saints of Suds," BeerHistory.com, accessed August 26, 2015, www.beerhistory.com/library/holdings/patron_saints.shtml.

"Well, here's a home-grown": Michael Lonsford, "Spirit of the Week," *Houston Chronicle,* May 7, 1997. Interestingly—and certainly not accidentally—later Tito's marketing material would drop the colon from Lonsford's symphonic sentence and add an exclamation point instead.

flavored vodka popularity: William Grimes, "Flavored Vodka: A Revolution the Romanovs Missed," *New York Times*, January 21, 1998; Stuart Elliott, "Absolut, the Top-Selling Imported Vodka in the Country, Extends Its Brand for a Fourth Time," *New York Times*, July 12, 1999.

"a fruit-filled tidal wave"; "Banana vodka": Grimes, "Flavored Vodka."

Karakasevic noticing, Domaine Charbay vodka: Franson, "Charbay's Marko Karakasevic"; Wells, "Reinventing Vodka."

Absolut Citron production: Elliott, "Absolut, the Top-Selling."

vodka sales: Matthew Miller, "Absolut Chaos," *Forbes*, December 13, 2004.

Craft vs. Crafty

Dateline *segment, effects*: Acitelli, *Audacity of Hops*, 245–54. The only real exception to the lackluster sales of faux crafts was Coors's Blue Moon line, beginning with a wheat beer that carried no mention of its macro origins on its powder-blue packaging.

Getting a Taste for It

Hansell background, early start: John Hansell, interview by author, August 24, 2015.

beer, wine media: Acitelli, *Audacity of Hops*, 187–93, 281–88 Acitelli, *American Wine*, 83–86.

"put a serious dent in it"; "This is pretty good": Hansell interview.

"What's up with everybody?": Ibid.

WhiskyFest organization, success: Ibid.; Fred Minnick, *Whiskey Women: The Untold Story of How Women Saved Bourbon, Scotch and Irish Whiskey* (Lincoln: University of Nebraska Press, 2013), 145–46; "Calendar," *New York Times*, November 11, 1998; Ron Givens, "Side Dish Dram Majors," *New York Daily News*, November 8, 1998.

"No way it will work": Minnick, *Whiskey Women*, 145.

"the Holy Grail"; "no respectable": Ibid., 146.

Walsh, Whiskeys of the World: Fritz Allhoff and Marcus P. Adams, eds., *Whiskey & Philosophy: A Small Batch of Spirited Ideas* (Hoboken: John Wiley & Sons, 2010), 86.

Rise of the Foodies

Slow Food background, manifesto: Acitelli, *Audacity of Hops*, 149–50; 165–68.

"I am not a foodie": "The Busboy," June 26, 1991, Seinfeld Scripts, www.seinfeldscripts.com/TheBusboy.htm.

The rise of the word *foodie* in the lexicon is based on a LexisNexis search for the word back to the 1970s in newspapers and magazines. The *Oxford English Dictionary*'s first citation for *foodie* apparently came from a *New York* magazine article in 1980 (Steve Poole, "Let's Start the Foodie Backlash," *[UK] Guardian*, September 28, 2012).

Cook's Illustrated was relaunched in 1993 by founder Christopher Kimball, after the previous owner shuttered it.

AOL Cooking Club: Patricia Montemurri, "Food Lovers Are Finding Everything from Recipes to Friends Online," *Philadelphia Inquirer*, July 19, 1995.

Divining the first food blogs is difficult as the term *blog* was not in wide use. The initial prototypes undoubtedly arose in the late 1990s. See Bruce Kraig and Andrew Smith, eds., "Blogs," in *The Oxford Encyclopedia of Food and Drink in America*, vol. 1, 173.

Starbucks numbers: Stanley Holmes, "Planet Starbucks," *Bloomberg Businessweek*, September 9, 2002, 100–110.

"the next food craze": Jack Hayes, "On the Rise: Café-Bakeries," *Nation's Restaurant News*, November 7, 1994, 57.

made veritable rock stars; Child quotation: Kim Severson, "The New Pop Icons Are in the Kitchen," *(Montreal) Gazette*, October 18, 2000. Courteney Cox's Monica was the chef on *Friends*. John Ventimiglia's Artie was the chef on *The Sopranos*.

Matthew Weiner began honing: Marlow Stern, "'Mad Men' Creator Matthew Weiner on Don Draper vs. Tony Soprano and No Spin-Offs," Daily Beast, April 2, 2015, www .thedailybeast.com/articles/2015/04/02/mad-men-creator-matthew-weiner-on-don -draper-vs-tony-soprano-and-no-spin-offs.html. Weiner did not start writing for *The Sopranos* until its later seasons after the turn of the century. He, however, started conceiving *Mad Men* in the late 1990s and used the spec script to land the writing job with *The Sopranos*.

population growth: Marc J. Perry and Paul J. Mackun, "Population Change and Distribution," Census Brief 2000.

More about the rise of urban-based craft breweries can be found throughout the author's *The Audacity of Hops: The History of America's Craft Beer Revolution*.

Multiple Singles

Winters background: Lance Winters, interview by author, March 9, 2015.

"the nation's first and only": John M. Leighty, "Californian Distills the 'Water of Life,'" *Chicago Tribune*, October 22, 1987.

Fabricant article: Florence Fabricant, "European-Inspired After-Dinner Drinks, Made in the U.S.A.," *New York Times*, December 12, 1990.

Artisan Distillers of California: Ibid.; Lawrence M. Fisher, "California Cognac—More Than Just a Curio? A Rival with French Roots," *New York Times*, May 5, 1991.

Winters-Rupf exchange, Winters job acceptance: Winters interview.

St. George Single-Malt: Ibid.; Andrew Strenio, "Single Malt, American Style: A Delicious New World of Whiskey," Serious Eats, October 1, 2014, www.seriouseats.com/2014/10 /best-american-single-malt-whiskey-scotch-style-st-george-mccarthys-lost -spirits-cut-spike.html; Florence Fabricant, "Made in America, But Will It Lift a Kilt?," *New York Times*, September 27, 2000.

"This single-malt is": Fabricant, "Made in America."

McCarthy's Oregon Single-Malt; "Let's make": Lew Bryson, "Why in the World?," *Chicago Tribune*, October 16, 2002; Gary Regan and Mardee Haidin Regan, "A New Breed of American Whiskeys," *Malt Advocate*, March 2000, 24; McCarthy interview.

Malt Advocate review: Regan and Regan, "A New Breed."

"tinkering obsessively": Apple, "A New Gauntlet."

took a particular liking: Clay Risen, "American Single-Malt Whiskeys Serve Notice," *New York Times*, January 15, 2013.

about 80 percent: Winters interview.

"We are on the verge of": Jerry Shriver, "Distillers Lift Spirits to New Levels," *USA Today*, May 4, 2001.

Tequila from a Brandy Snifter

St. James, Busuttil background: Peter Y. Hong, "Teacher's Spirited Quest Pays Off," *Los Angeles Times*, November 27, 1998.

Peregrine Rock: Ibid.; Lucy Howard and Paul O'Donnell, "Have a Wee Dram, Dude," *Newsweek*, October 19, 1998. The *Newsweek* quotation is taken from this brief item as well.

tequila history: Chantal Martineau, *How the Gringos Stole Tequila: The Modern Age of Mexico's Most Traditional Spirit* (Chicago: Chicago Review Press, 2015), 1–75.

"Tequila in America": Ibid., x.

Tequila's name did not necessarily come from the city of Tequila, though that is the most popular etymological theory. The spirit's name—and the town's—may, in fact, have come from the name of a local tribe or even a nearby volcano (Martineau, *Gringos,* xi). Also, tequila should not be confused with mescal or mezcal, the more rustic Mexican spirit made from a different kind of agave than blue.

"Before 1970 . . . liquor stores": "Modern Living: Aztec," *Time,* January 26, 1976.

then quadruple: "Brands of Tequila—How Many Are There?," Tequila.net, accessed September 23, 2015, www.tequila.net/faqs/tequila/brands-of-tequila-how-many-are-there .html.

for cranking out frozen versions fast: Martineau, *Gringos,* 175. Previously, frozen margaritas had been made with blended ice, a much more time-consuming process.

"one unknown genius"; "which had the dual benefits": Simon Houpt, "A Hangover That's Lasted 50 Years," *Globe and Mail,* December 17, 2010.

Denton, Smith: Martineau, *Gringos,* 83; "Tequila in the USA," IanChadwick.com, accessed September 23, 2015, www.ianchadwick.com/tequila/usa.htm.

"They didn't mind"; "The finest tequilas": Florence Fabricant, "A Long Way from Margaritaville," *New York Times,* September 9, 1998.

sales share: Ibid.

Riedel glass: Martineau, *Gringos,* 87.

California Agave Gold distribution: Hong, "Teacher's Spirited Quest."

Mixing in Gin

perhaps the world's largest; a thought struck him: Emily Hutto, "Bendistillery: Pure, Oregon -Inspired Spirits," TheHoochLife.com, June 13, 2012, http://thehoochlife.com /distilleries/bendistillery-pure-oregon-inspired-spirits/ (domain no longer in use).

gin history: "18th Century Gin Craze," History Channel UK, accessed October 2, 2015, www.history.co.uk/study-topics/history-of-london/18th-century-gin-craze; Kal Raustiala, "The Imperial Cocktail," Slate, August 28, 2013, www.slate.com/articles /health_and_science/foreigners/2013/08/gin_and_tonic_kept_the_british_empire _healthy_the_drink_s_quinine_powder.html; "From the Crack Cocaine of Its Day to Craft Gin," *Economist,* April 19, 2015.

"the crack cocaine of its day": "From the Crack Cocaine," *Economist.*

tonic water, medicinal purposes: Ibid.; Raustiala, "The Imperial Cocktail."

with its genesis either: April Fulton, "The Martini: This American Cocktail May Have an International Twist," NPR's *The Salt* (blog), June 19, 2013, www.npr.org/sections/thesalt /2013/06/18/193198710/martini-s-muddled-history-may-have-international-ties.

gin production, taste: "About Gin and Genever," Tastings, accessed November 13, 2016, www.tastings.com/Spirits-Categories/About-Gin-And-Genever.aspx.

peaking in 1975: Terry Robards, "Liquor Sales Register Decline," *New York Times,* October 9, 1982.

per-capita consumption: J.S. and G.D., "High Spirits," *Economist* online, June 17, 2013, www.economist.com/blogs/graphicdetail/2013/06/daily-chart-9.

Bombay Sapphire production, packaging: "Bombay Sapphire," Gin Foundry, December 21, 2014, www.ginfoundry.com/gin/bombay-sapphire-gin/; "Champions of Design," *Marketing Magazine (UK),* January 8, 2013, www.campaignlive.co.uk/article/1165917

/champions-design-bombay-sapphire; Richard Barnett, *The Book of Gin: A Spirited World History From Alchemists' Stills and Colonial Outposts to Gin Palaces, Bathtub Gin and Artisanal Cocktails* (New York: Grove Press, 2012), 181–82.

the difference between: "Champions of Design."

"the first new premium gin"; "provided the model": Barnett, *Book of Gin,* 181–82.

"The first crack in the ice": Paul F. Pacult, "The Gin Game," *Wine Enthusiast,* June 2001.

Cascade Mountain Gin rollout: Mike Freeman, "Micro-Distilled Vodka, Gin Blossom in Oregon," Associated Press, March 14, 1997.

"It seems like the next": Ibid.

The respective histories of Oregon fine wine and craft beer can be found in the author's previous books, *The Audacity of Hops: The History of America's Craft Beer Revolution* and *American Wine: A Coming-of-Age Story.*

"Southern distillation of craft spirits": John T. Edge, "High-Class Hooch," *Atlanta Journal-Constitution,* February 1, 2007.

"During the last two decades": Shriver, "Distillers Lift Spirits."

retailed for slightly less: Ibid. The cost per bottle in 2001 was ninety dollars.

Jackson anecdote; "It was big in body": Michael Jackson, "The Spirit World," *(London) Observer,* May 9, 1999.

Asimov touting: Eric Asimov, "Gin Fights Back," *New York Times,* April 26, 2000.

No Need for a Smuggler's Tree

Westford Hill history: Richard W. Langer, "In Connecticut, 'Waters of Life' Flow Mightily," *New York Times,* March 19, 2003; Tyler Magrid, "Westford Hill: Pioneers of a Distilling Renaissance," Ashford Business Association publication, September/October 2016; Eric D. Lehman and Amy Nowricki, *A History of Connecticut Wine: A Vineyard in Your Backyard* (Mt. Pleasant, SC: History Press, 2011), 103–5; Elin McCoy, "An Entrepreneurial Spirit: America's Small Distilleries Are Crafting Sophisticated Eau de Vie," Bloomberg Markets, October 26, 2004.

"We lived in the oldest": McCoy, "An Entrepreneurial Spirit."

per-capita wine consumption: "Wine Consumption in the U.S.," Wine Institute website, July 8, 2016, www.wineinstitute.org/resources/statistics/article86.

Westford production, distribution: Langer, "In Connecticut"; Magrid, "Westford Hill."

"a cross between": McCoy, "An Entrepreneurial Spirit."

"opening up a whole new": Langer, "In Connecticut."

"a burgeoning, loose-knit": Shriver, "Distillers Lift Spirits."

Aloha Spirits: Les Griffith, "Bean Sip: Kona Gold Coffee Liqueur," *Honolulu Magazine,* August 25, 2011.

Vermont Spirits: Rick Nichols, "A Maple Vodka with Its Own Spirit," *Philadelphia Inquirer,* October 16, 2003; Marian Burros, "Around the World and Back," Edible Network (blog network), February 19, 2014.

number of distilleries: Kinstlick white paper.

Local Color vodka: Shriver, "Distillers Lift Spirits."

Knapp distillery: "Knapp Vineyards," Snooth, accessed October 1, 2015, www.snooth.com /winery/knapp-vineyards-romulus/.

James Michalopoulos, Celebration Distillation; quotations: Glen Abbot, "Take a Tour of Old New Orleans Rum, a Hidden Gem in Gentilly," *New Orleans Times-Picayune,* February 1, 2012, www.nola.com/nolavie/index.ssf/2012/02/old_new_orleans

rum--_touring.html; John Michalopoulos website, accessed October 9, 2015, www
.michalopoulos.com/southern-living-sits-down-with-michalopoulos/.

sugarcane yield: Kenneth Gravois, "History of Sugarcane in Louisiana," LSU Ag Center, February 25, 2005, www.lsuagcenter.com/en/crops_livestock/crops/sugarcane
/Cultural+Practices/History+of+Sugarcane+in+Louisiana.htm.

Phil Prichard, Prichard's Distillery, dialogue with Robilio: Phil Prichard, interview by author,
March 2, 2016, and follow-up e-mails that month; Edge, "High-Class Hooch"; John
F. Lipman, "American Whiskey: Prichard's Distillery Kelso, Tennessee," EllenJaye.
com, April 29, 2011, www.ellenjaye.com/prichard.htm. Prichard originally called his
distillery Prichards' but switched to Prichard's Distillery because of confusion among
the public regarding plural possessives.

Robilio and fine wine: Ted Evanoff, "Memphis-Based Victor L. Robilio Is Acquired by
Glazer's Inc., a Leading Wine and Spirits Distributor," *Memphis Commercial Appeal,*
November 4, 2011.

Outterson background, Woodstone Creek: "About Us," Woodstone Creek website, accessed
October 1, 2015, http://woodstonecreek.com/aboutus.html; Rob Willey, "Craft Brewers Turn to Whiskey Chasers," *New York Times,* February 28, 2007; David Holthaus,
"Couple Ventures into Microdistilleries," Cincinnati.com, July 16, 2011, http://
myemail.constantcontact.com/DISTILLER-eNewsletter--August-1--2011.html?soid
=1011324010003&aid=MleXhzyryEg.

well under one million cases: Based on a Distilled Spirits Council of the United States
report on the wider industry in 2014, which noted that "small distillers" produced
seven hundred thousand cases in 2010. Full report: www.discus.org/assets/1/7
/Distilled_Spirits_Industry_Briefing_Feb_3_2015_Final2.pdf.

entrants' spirits focus: Kinstlick white paper.

home-distillers had been targeted: Jacob Sullum, "Feds Take a Sudden Interest in Bust-
ing Home Distillers," Reason.com, July 15, 2014, http://reason.com/blog/2014/07/15
/feds-take-a-sudden-interest-in-busting-h.

taxes: Author's attendance and interviews at the American Craft Spirits Association conference in March 2016—a large part of the conference's focus was on reducing the
federal excise tax. More information on the tax and the efforts to reduce it can be
found on the association's website, www.americancraftspirits.org/, and through the
TTB, www.ttb.gov/applications/pdf/tax_and_fee_rate.pdf.

"We wanted to make": Edge, "High-Class Hooch."

Breakout Stars

Coale-Rupf sit-down: Coale interview.

Hangar 1 start-up, financing, rationale: Ibid.; Elizabeth Browne, "Hangar One Charts New
Course," *San Francisco Business Journal,* November 4, 2007.

were about to spike: Browne, "Hangar One Charts New Course."

Grey Goose sales: Frank J. Prial, "The Seller of the Goose That Laid a Golden Egg," *New
York Times,* January 1, 2005.

St. George, Germain-Robin sales: Based on media reports from the 1990s.

was eating into the distribution channels: Coale interview.

number of California wineries: Wine Institute website, "Number of Californian Wineries,"
July 20, 2015, www.wineinstitute.org/resources/statistics/article124.

St. George accolades: Apple, "A New Gauntlet."

Berger quotations, Germain-Robin praise: Dan Berger, "Is the World's Best Cognac Made in Ukiah?," *Los Angeles Times*, February 18, 1993.

"Extraordinary": "Hangar 1 Vodka," Reserve Bar, accessed October 15, 2015, www.reserve bar.com/t/type/spirits/vodka/hangar-1-vodka.

Fabricant descriptions: Florence Fabricant, "You've Heard of Garage Bands? Now There's Hangar Vodka, But Don't Jump to Conclusions," *New York Times*, August 14, 2002.

"Where are the girls"; "quality, taste": Browne, "Hangar One Charts New Course."

made with bulk railroad deliveries: David L. Beck, "Booze Bottler Combines Agrarian History With Technology," *San Jose Mercury News*, May 15, 2005.

Yahoo! Finance video from BNET can be found here www.youtube.com/watch?v=EwLrZTk _vRc.

sales figures, reach; vast majority: Browne, "Hangar One Charts New Course."

Tito's growth, awards: Wes Marshall, "Beveridge Man," *Austin Chronicle*, April 19, 2002; David McLemore, "Texan a Big Shot in Vodka," *Dallas Morning News*, April 2, 2005.

The San Francisco World Spirits Competition results come from the competition's website: http://sfspiritscomp.com/results/archives.

even though the critic had awarded: Paul Pacult, e-mail exchange with author, October 19, 2015.

Pacult awarded five: Frank J. Prial, "A Favorite Wherever Glasses Are Lifted," *New York Times*, February 7, 2001.

"beat . . . every other vodka entered": Marshall, "Beveridge Man."

"I'm tempted to describe Tito": Ibid.

"I had plans to do": Michael Barnes, "Tito's Pours Into Restaurants and Bars," *Austin American-Statesman*, February 17, 2005.

Beveridge also tended to change the specifics of his pre–Fifth Generation business experience and what it taught him. The author by no means intends to suggest that Beveridge lied about his background or his plans for Fifth Generation and Tito's—only that the backstory of the distillery and its brand tended to vary from interview to interview and article to article.

The details about Jim Koch's rise can be found in *The Audacity of Hops*, pages 105–8, 185, and 239–41.

Buffalo Bill and the Legal Stampede

Owens background, Buffalo Bill's start-up: Bill Owens, interview by author, May 2012; Acitelli, *Audacity of Hops*, 98, 192; Paul Kilduff, "'Suburbia' Photographer Unveils New Book," *San Jose Mercury News*, June 23, 2015; Bill Owens and Alan Dikty, eds., *The Art of Distilling Whiskey and Other Spirits* (London: Quarry Books, 2009), 10–11.

"kid who liked to drink beer": Jane Ryan, "Bill Owens," Difford's Guide, accessed October 22, 2015, www.diffordsguide.com/people/18863/distiller/bill-owens.

"White out 'almond farm'": Acitelli, *Audacity of Hops*, 98.

"For one hundred, thirty dollars'": Ibid. Owens was talking to William Least Heat Moon, who was writing a lengthy profile of American craft brewing in the mid-1980s for the *Atlantic* magazine.

"like a grandfather": Ruth Reichl, "The Yeasty World of Brewpubs," *Los Angeles Times*, August 31, 1986.

road trip: Owens interview.

"All the guys I know": Ryan, "Bill Owens."

ADI start-up, initial conference: Owens interview.

Hurdles Fall

Torgersen: John Torgersen, interview by author, November 28, 2016; David Haskell and Colin Spoelman, *The Kings County Distillery Guide to Urban Moonshining: How to Drink and Make Whiskey* (New York: Henry N. Abrams, 2013), 90–91; Victoria R. Spagnoli, "Renewed Spirits," *Schenectady Daily Gazette*, August 25, 2002.

Havens, Flip: Torgersen interview.

Storm King plans: Ibid.; Spagnoli, "Renewed Spirits."

upstate New York conditions: "The Regional Economy of Upstate New York," Federal Reserve Bank of New York, winter 2005.

"dead": Spagnoli, "Renewed Spirits."

Torgersen lobbying efforts, success: Ibid.; Torgersen interview; Haskell and Spoelman, *Kings County Distillery Guide*, 90–91.

New York distilleries producing fruit-based eau-de-vie or brandies did not have to pay the three-year licensing fee.

Farm Winery Act, influence: Tom Acitelli, "Small Wineries Laid Groundwork for Similar Industry," *Albany Times-Union*, September 20, 2015.

excise-tax cut: Acitelli, *Audacity of Hops*, 62–63.

rankled Torgersen: Torgersen interview.

"Prior to Prohibition": Spagnoli, "Renewed Spirits."

proved too much: Torgersen interview.

The Golden Age Begins

Erenzo background, climbing-wall business: Ralph Erenzo, interview by author, March 3, 2016; Ralph Erenzo, e-mail exchange with author, January 2016; Matt Logan, "Interview: Ralph Erenzo—Gunks Climber and Distiller at Tuthilltown Spirits," Gunks Climbers' Coalition, September 22, 2105, http://gunksclimbers.org/interview-ralph-erenzo-tuthilltown/; Corey Kilgannon, "Rock Wall Has an Unwanted Alpine Climate," *New York Times*, February 13, 2000; Ingrid Abramovitch, "Radical! New York Is Adventure-Sport City," *New York Times*, June 28, 1998.

"thrilled to find": Logan, "Interview: Ralph Erenzo."

greatest rock climbing area: Cliff Ransom, "Climbing in the Gunks, New York," National Geographic Online, accessed October 28, 2015, www.nationalgeographic.com/adventure /trips/americas-best-adventures/climb-new-york-gunks/.

exchanges with neighbor, zoning official: Logan, "Interview: Ralph Erenzo."

Erenzo-Lee meeting; Lee: Erenzo interview; Erenzo e-mail exchange; Ned Smith, "Startup Distills a Partnership Down to Success," Business News Daily, August 18, 2010; "The History of Tuthilltown," Tuthilltown Spirits website, accessed October 28, 2015, www .tuthilltown.com/history/.

"It's not a career change"; "OK, let's build"; "less than amateurs": Erenzo interview; Erenzo e-mail exchange.

Tuthilltown spirits rollout: Paul Adams, "Whiskey's Hudson Valley Revival," *New York Times*, June 21, 2006.

New York growth: "Governor Cuomo Highlights Savings to Craft Distilleries Across New York State," Gov. Andrew Cuomo's press office, August 3, 2015, www.governor .ny.gov/news/governor-cuomo-highlights-savings-craft-distilleries-across-new-york -state.

Great Lakes Distillery: Nancy A. Herrick, "Hobbyist Turns Craft Distiller," *Milwaukee Journal Sentinel*, May 15, 2012; Erin Toner, "Milwaukee Distillery Wins Award, Plans

Move Across Town," WUWM News, April 18, 2008, http://preview.wuwm.com/news /wuwm_news.php?articleid=1835 (page no longer active).

"just about every decent beer": Toner, "Milwaukee Distillery."

Jess Graber responded to a call: "How It All Began," Stranahan's website, accessed October 29, 2015, www.stranahans.com/about/. More on George Stranahan and Flying Dog can be found in the author's craft beer history, *The Audacity of Hops.*

Dry Fly Distilling: Bert Caldwell, "Local Distillers in High Spirits," *Spokane Spokesman Review*, March 15, 2008; Parker Howell, "Would-Be Distillers Aim for Top Shelf," *Spokane Spokesman Review*, April 17, 2007.

Growth statistics are based upon incorporation records and the Kinstlick white paper, as well as media searches over LexisNexis. State incorporation filings were used as often as possible to determine the foundational dates of different distilleries.

Don Draper Orders an Old Fashioned

1.2 million: Kimberly Nordyke, "Viewers Salute Debut of AMC 'Mad Men,'" *Hollywood Reporter*, July 23, 2007.

"I'm trying to tell a story": Carly Severn, "Drinking with 'Mad Men': Cocktail Culture and the Myth of Don Draper," NPR's *The Salt* (blog), April 5, 2015, www.npr.org /sections/thesalt/2015/04/05/397352082/drinking-with-mad-men-cocktail-culture -and-the-myth-of-don-draper.

"Mad Men effect": Ibid.; Dan Freed, "Mad Men Still Driving Liquor Sales?," The Street, December 27, 2013, www.thestreet.com/story/12181697/1/mad-men-still-driving -liquor-sales.html.

"The show not only": Severn, "Drinking with 'Mad Men.'"

whiskey sales; vodka and gin fears: Freed, "Mad Men Still Driving Liquor Sales?"; Matt Clinch, "Vodka Reigns Supreme as Whiskey's 'Mad Men' Effect Fades," CNBC.com, June 28, 2013, www.cnbc.com/id/100851957.

"The 'Mad Men effect' is widely talked about": Freed, "Mad Men Still Driving Liquor Sales?" It should be noted that there were critical and commercial *Mad Men* effects on furniture and fashion, too.

"alcoholic candy"; "The first half"; "Surrendering": Jonathan Miles, "A Good Decade to Have a Drink," *New York Times*, January 5, 2010.

was never as high: Brian Ashcraft, "The Mystery of the Green Menace," *Wired*, November 5, 2005, www.wired.com/2005/11/absinthe/.

absinthe fall, rise: Ibid.; Cindy Skrzycki, "A Notorious Spirit Finds Its Way Back to Bars," *Washington Post*, October 16, 2007.

"What difference is there": Brendan I. Koerner, "Absinthe: The American Remix," *New York Times*, April 29, 2007.

Viridian sales, who had long realized: Lindsay Blakely, "The Perfect Market Opportu- nity—If Only It Was Legal," CBS Moneywatch, May 9, 2011, www.cbsnews.com /news/the-perfect-market-opportunity-if-only-it-was-legal/.

bitters rise: Rob Willey, "A Bit of History, Reborn in a Glass," *New York Times*, June 27, 2007; Mary Orlin, "Artisanal Craft Bitters Shaking Up Cocktail World," *San Jose Mercury News*, December 22, 2014.

bitters popularity, ordering by brand name: Orlin, "Artisanal Craft Bitters."

hundreds of brands of bitters; there were two; "a cottage industry"; "bitters-starved": Robert Simonson, *A Proper Drink* (Berkeley: Ten Speed Press, 2016), 243.

Cooper; success of St. Germain; "bartender's ketchup": Ibid., 242.

was likely the first; Clear Creek: Steve McCarthy, interview by author, September 2016.

not necessarily integral: David Wondrich, interview by author, September 26, 2016.

"What had once": Miles, "A Good Decade."

Pouring Out Words

Robert Burr background, first rum festivals: Robert Steward, "Interview with Rum Expert Robert Burr: Part 1," *Total Wine* (blog), April 5, 2013, http://blog.totalwine .com/2013/04/05/interview-with-rum-expert-robert-burr-part-1/.

"a central stage"; "It's not a college-beach bacchanal": Tim Padgett, "Rum Renaissance Revives the Spirit's Rough Reputation," NPR's *The Salt* (blog), April 25, 2014, www .npr.org/sections/thesalt/2014/04/25/306826984/rum-renaissance-revives-the-spirits -rough-reputation. Also broadcast on *All Things Considered*.

"That's a great idea, Charlie": Acitelli, *Audacity of Hops*, 90.

"If your knowledge of Scotch begins": Seth Kugel, "Lift a Wee Dram All Over Town," *New York Times*, January 28, 2007.

Cowdery: "Charles K. Cowdery," Amazon author's profile, accessed November 4, 2015, www.amazon.com/Charles-K.-Cowdery/e/B000APGWH0.

Minnick: "About," Fred Minnick website, accessed November 4, 2015, www.fredminnick .com/contact/.

Gillespie; "the NPR of whisky": Fred Minnick, "Why This Podcast Is the NPR of Whisky," *Parade*, September 19, 2014.

Curtis: Wayne Curtis's LinkedIn profile, accessed November 4, 2015, www.linkedin.com /in/waynecurtis.

Risen: Clay Risen, interview by author, December 10, 2015.

Bryson: Lew Bryson, *Tasting Whiskey: An Insider's Guide to the Unique Pleasures of the World's Finest Spirits* (North Adams, MA: Storey, 2014), 55.

e-mails from Asimov article: McCarthy interview.

Sales from Jim Murray, worries: Ibid.

Malt Advocate changes: Hansell interview; "Malt Advocate Inc. Joins M. Shanken Communications," June 15, 2010, Whisky Advocate, http://whiskyadvocate.com/2010/06/15 /breaking-news-malt-advocate-inc-joins-m-shanken-communications-inc/.

grew to 225,000: "Whisky Advocate Media Kit 2015," accessed November 4, 2015, www .mshanken.com/images/wa/2015WhiskyAdvocateMediaKit.pdf.

Craft Before There Was Craft

Pickerell-Samuels-Roedemeier exchanges: Nino Marchetti, "Master Whiskey Wizard Dave Pickerel Interview: Part 1," The Whiskey Wash, September 17, 2015, http:// thewhiskeywash.com/2015/09/17/master-whiskey-wizard-dave-pickerell-interview -part-1/.

Maker's Mark production figures: Andi Esposito, "Bourbon Maker Shows How to Sell a Product," *Worcester (MA) Sunday Telegram*, February 2, 2003; Clay Risen, "Meet Mr. Whiskey."

thirty straight years of sales: Esposito, "Bourbon Maker."

production expansion; "We're not trying to be": Douglas MacMillan, "Making a Market for Maker's Mark," *Bloomberg*, October 26, 2006.

Jim Beam was selling more than three million cases annually of its signature bourbon by 2000 (Fortune Brands press release, October 3, 2011).

"not screwing up Dad's company"; Samuels's marketing approach; "Our number one marketing goal": Kleinman, "The Story of Maker's Mark"; Samuels interview.

premium, superpremium growth; other brands' decline: MacMillan, "Making a Market."

Maker's 46 recipe, production: Bruce Scheiner, "Maker's Mark 46 Bourbon: Distillery's First New Product in Five Decades," Huffington Post, June 8, 2010, www .huffingtonpost.com/2010/06/08/makers-mark-46-bourbon-di_n_604108.html (page no longer active).

"a drop in the bucket": Ibid.

Samuels's marketing approach, lack thereof: Samuels interview.

The presence of other wheated bourbons on the market in the early 1950s rarely made it into Bill Samuels Jr.'s sales and marketing pitches. Though, admittedly, few up until Maker's Mark had featured wheat so prominently in place of rye.

The Movement's Defining Moment

Phone call, Erenzo reaction, negotiations: Erenzo interview.

Stolichnaya's Russian producers pulled the vodka from W. Grant & Son's distribution portfolio in 2012.

Hudson deal: Ibid.; Kevin Kane, "The Samuel Adams of Whiskey," CNBC, June 16, 2015, www.cnbc.com/2015/06/16/adams-of-whiskey.html.

rippled through: Erenzo interview.

Craft Distillers, Proximo deal: "Farewell to Hangar One," St. George Spirits website, April 2014, www.stgeorgespirits.com/news/announcements/page/2/; "News Briefs for July 6, 2011," Shanken News Daily, www.shankennewsdaily.com/index.php/2011/07/06/1071 /californias-2009-pinot-noirs-might-be-best-ever-wine-spectator-says/. Proximo required the distribution rights for Jose Cuervo from Diageo in early 2013.

Mooney background, Koch conversation: Tom Mooney, interview by author, March 2, 2016; Wendy Culverwell, "Q&A with House Spirits Founder Cristian Krogstad," *Portland Business Journal*, February 28, 2013.

Great American Distillers Festival: Fred Eckhardt, "Third Great American Distillers Festival," *Celebrator News* (beer publication), December 2007/January 2008; Hannah C. Feldman, "Over a Barrel," *Willamette Week*, October 20, 2009.

proved remunerative: Mooney interview; Mooney's comments at media luncheon at the 2016 American Craft Spirits Association conference, Chicago, March 2016.

federal excise taxes, concerns: As of 2016 small-batch distillers pay $2.14 in excise tax per 750-milliliter, eighty-proof bottle. That is comparatively far less than what smaller brewers and most makers of fine wine pay per bottle or can. More information on the federal excise tax can be found at the American Craft Spirits Association's website: www.americancraftspirits.org/wp-content/uploads/2014/10/background -federal_excise_tax_parity.pdf.

formation of ACDA: Erenzo interview; Mooney interview; Chuck Cowdery, "New Group, the American Craft Distillers Association, Is Announced," *The Chuck Cowdery Blog*, April 11, 2013, http://chuckcowdery.blogspot.com/2013/04/new-group-american -craft-distillers.html.

The American Craft Distillers Association's incorporation actually dates from January 2013.

declined to seriously entertain: According to Erenzo, Bill Owens would not disclose the financials of the ADI.

visited a new distillery; Curtis excerpt, quotations: Wayne Curtis, "When That 'Local,' 'Craft' Liquor You Pay Big Bucks for Is Neither," *Atlantic*, June 2013.

Brooklyn distilleries: Sumathi Reddy, "Brooklyn Whiskey Rum," *Wall Street Journal*, June 25, 2010.

WhistlePig background, praise: Larry Olmsted, "World-Class Whiskey—From Vermont?," *Forbes*, March 25, 2012; Davin De Kergommeaux, "A Revealing Chat with WhistlePig's Raj Bhakta," *Whisky Advocate*, March 19, 2014, http://whiskyadvocate. com/2014/03/19/a-revealing-chat-with-whistlepigs-raj-bhatka/.

"Look, I'm a salesman": De Kergommeaux, "Revealing Chat."

"like an English country gentleman": Dan D'Ambrosio, "Vermont's WhistlePig Whiskey Fires Up Distillery," *Burlington Free Press*, November 13, 2015.

"Although there's no across-the-board": Katy Steinmetz, "A Booze of One's Own: The Micro-Distillery Boom," *Time*, April 6, 2012.

trade group definitions: Through their respective websites: www.discus.org/; www .americancraftspirits.org/; http://distilling.com/.

DISCUS craft membership affiliation: "Distilled Spirits Council Launches Craft Distiller Membership," Distilled Spirits Council of the United States, February 23, 2010, www .discus.org/distilled-spirits-council-launches-craft-distiller-membership/. DISCUS was formed in 1973, when the Bourbon Institute, the Distilled Spirits Institute, and the Licensed Beverage Industries merged.

"Every producer wants": Wayne Curtis, "What Exactly Defines a 'Craft' Spirit?," *Punch*, April 21, 2014, http://punchdrink.com/articles/what-exactly-defines-a-craft-spirit/.

"Potemkin distilleries": Eric Felten, "Your 'Craft' Rye Whiskey Is Probably from a Factory Distillery in Indiana," *Daily Beast*, July 28, 2014, www.thedailybeast.com /articles/2014/07/28/your-craft-whiskey-is-probably-from-a-factory-distillery-in-indiana .html.

Craft Distillers–ACDA dispute; Coale quotations; Craft Distillers would end up challenging: "ACDA Challenges Ownership of 'Craft Distilllers' Trademark," *Wine & Spirits Daily*, March 17, 2014, www.winespiritsdaily.com/publications_daily.php?id=2232.

top inertia category: Mooney interview; Tom Mooney, e-mail exchange with author, March 2016. The inertia-category ranking applied to sales only at off-premise locations such as stores, bars, and clubs.

One in five members: Danny Brager, "Generations on Tap: Beverage Alcohol Purchases Vary by Age Group," Nielsen, August 11, 2014.

"Those people are just top-notch salesmen": Bill Atkinson, "Has Spuds Met His Match?," *Business Journal San Jose*, May 11, 1987.

thirty bestselling; "Those bottles may look beautiful": Keith Wallace, "How Wine Became Like Fast Food," *Daily Beast*, November 3, 2009, www.thedailybeast.com/articles /2009/11/03/how-wine-became-like-fast-food.html.

"moonshiney": Wayne Curtis, "Has Craft Distilling Lost Its Spirit?," *Atlantic*, June 2014. Curtis, like other critics, wrote repeatedly about the trend of stealth craft distilleries and their practices and effects. Other journalists also quoted these critics' takes on the trend.

kept cranking out; "All that they do is hire": Felten, "Your 'Craft' Rye Whiskey."

found themselves offered: Curtis, "Has Craft Distilling Lost Its Spirit?"

"There's no reason to think": Felten, "Your 'Craft' Rye Whiskey."

"The stuff made by the guy": Jeffrey Morgenthaler, "To Order Craft Spirits or Not to Order Craft Spirits? That Is the Question," *Food Republic*, November 10, 2015, www .foodrepublic.com/2015/11/10/to-order-craft-spirits-or-not-to-order-craft-spirits-that -is-the-question/.

"Hell, I could call myself": Fred Minnick, "Master Distillers: A History, the Truth & Fake Bourbon," Fred Minnick website, September 29, 2014, www.fredminnick. com/2014/09/29/master-distillers-history-truth-fake-bourbon/.

"This individual should have": Nancy Fraley, "What Is a Master Distiller?," White Mule Press, posted online December 3, 2014, excerpted from the Winter 2014 issue of *Distiller*, http://whitemulepress.com/?p=816.

The Challenge Ahead

reporter visit; Tito's production; "Shit": Casserly, "The Troubling Success."

Tito's, Maker's Mark lawsuits: Melita Kiely, "Judge Dismisses Most Tito's 'Handmade' Lawsuits," *Spirits Business*, September 25, 2015; "Tito's Handmade Vodka Maker Pushes for Dismissal of Class Action," Law Offices of Wolf & Pravato, October 7, 2015; Paula Mejia, "Maker's Mark Wins 'Handmade' Claim Lawsuit," *Newsweek*, July 30, 2015.

"the fear of God": Author's conversation with critic at ACSA conference, March 2, 2016.

Templeton lawsuit: Josh Noel, "Templeton Rye Reaches Lawsuit Settlement, Will Pay Refunds," *Chicago Tribune*, July 14, 2015. Refunds depended on how many bottles bought and whether a customer still had proofs of purchase.

"no consumer would reasonably": Kiely, "Judge Dismisses."

"exponential pace": Kinstlick white paper.

numerical growth: Provided by the TTB in an e-mail from Tom Hogue to the author, May 8, 2015.

did bite into the sales: Keith Greggor, interviewed by author, March 21, 2012. Greggor's firm would buy Anchor Distilling (and Brewing Co.) in 2010. Greggor previously worked in the macrospirits world, helping promote Skyy vodka in particular.

Curtis ACSA visit, observations: Curtis, "Has Craft Distilling Lost Its Spirit?"

"small, or the image of small": "Prohibition Hangover," *Economist*, September 8, 2012.

"Where the in-crowds of Berlin": Clay Risen, "Raising a Glass to American Upstart Distillers," *New York Times*, August 24, 2013.

"Craft distillers are usually": Ibid.

Digestif: "Distilled in Indiana"

Distiller of the Year, including excerpt: Lew Bryson, "Distiller of the Year—MGP Ingredients," *Whisky Advocate* online, December 16, 2015, http://whiskyadvocate.com/2015/12/16/whisky-advocates-22nd-annual-distillery-of-the-year-award/.

Metze, respect of peers: Chris Chamberlain, "Who Really Made Your Favorite Small Batch Rye Whiskey," Food Republic, December 22, 2015, www.foodrepublic.com/2015/12/22/who-really-made-your-favorite-small-batch-rye-whiskey/; Aaron Goldfarb, "Greg Metze, Unsung Hero of Whiskey, Takes the Spotlight," *Esquire*, October 4, 2015, www.esquire.com/food-drink/drinks/a38465/unsung-hero-of-whiskey/.

1,385 craft distillers; other ACSA report details: American Craft Spirits Association in conjunction with Park Street and IWSR, Inaugural Craft Spirits Economic Briefing.

SELECTED BIBLIOGRAPHY

The following is not intended to be a complete bibliography. It instead contains books related to craft spirits that might be of interest to the reader, and ones that the author consulted for this book.

Acitelli, Tom. *American Wine: A Coming-of-Age Story*. Chicago: Chicago Review Press, 2013.
———. *The Audacity of Hops: The History of America's Craft Beer Revolution*. Chicago: Chicago Review Press, 2013.
Allhoff, Fritz, and Marcus P. Adams, eds. *Whiskey & Philosophy: A Small Batch of Spirited Ideas*. Hoboken: John Wiley & Sons, 2010.
Broom, Dave. *The World Atlas of Whiskey*. London: Mitchell Beazley, 2010.
Bryson, Lew. *Tasting Whiskey: An Insider's Guide to the Unique Pleasures of the World's Finest Spirits*. North Adams, MA: Storey, 2014.
Curtis, Wayne. *And a Bottle of Rum: A History of the New World in Ten Cocktails*. New York: Broadway Books, 2007.
Gjelten, Tom. *Bacardi and the Long Fight for Cuba: The Biography of a Cause*. New York: Penguin Books, 2009.
Greene, Heather. *Whiskey Distilled: A Populist Guide to the Water of Life*. New York: Viking Studio, 2014.
Greene, Philip. *To Have and Have Another: A Hemingway Cocktail Companion*. New York: Perigree, 2012.
Hamilton, Carl. *Absolut: Biography of a Bottle*. Abington, MD: Texere, 2002.
Haskell, David, and Colin Spoelman. *The Kings County Distillery Guide to Urban Moonshining: How to Drink and Make Whiskey*. New York: Henry N. Abrams, 2013.
Himelstein, Linda. *The King of Vodka: The Story of Pyotr Smirnov and the Upheaval of an Empire*. New York: Harper Perennial, 2010.
Huckelbridge, Dane. *Bourbon: A History of the American Spirit*. New York: William Morrow, 2014.
Jackson, Michael. *Whiskey: The Definitive World Guide*. London: DK, 2005.
Pacult, F. Paul. *A Double Scotch: How Chivas Regal and the Glenlivet Became Global Icons*. Hoboken: John Wiley & Sons, 2005.
———. *Kindred Spirits: The Spirit Journal Guide to the World's Distilled Spirits and Fortified Wines*. New York: Hyperion, 1997.
Matus, Viktorino. *Vodka: How a Colorless, Odorless, Flavorless Spirit Conquered America*. New York: Lyons, 2014.

Minnick, Fred. *Whiskey Women: The Untold Story of How Women Saved Bourbon, Scotch and Irish Whiskey.* Lincoln: University of Nebraska Press, 2013.

Risen, Clay. *American Whiskey, Bourbon & Rye: A Guide to the Nation's Favorite Spirit.* New York: Sterling, 2015.

Smith, Andrew F., ed. *The Oxford Companion to American Food and Drink.* Oxford: Oxford University Press, 2007.

Teacher, Matt. *The Spirit of Gin: A Stirring Miscellany of the New Gin Revival.* Kennebunkport, ME: Cider Mill, 2014.

Veach, Michael. *Kentucky Bourbon Whiskey: An American Heritage.* Louisville: University Press of Kentucky, 2013.

Wilson, Neil, and Ian Buxton, eds. *Beer Hunter, Whisky Chaser: New Writing on Beer and Whisky in Honour of Michael Jackson.* Castle Douglas, UK: Neil Wilson, 2013.

Wondrich, David. *Imbibe!: From Absinthe Cocktail to Whiskey Smash, a Salute in Stories and Drinks to "Professor" Jerry Thomas, Pioneer of the American Bar Featuring the Original Formulae.* New York: Tarcher Perigree, 2007.

INDEX